ALL GLORY TO ŚRĪ GURU AND GAURĀṄGA

ŚRĪMAD BHĀGAVATAM

of

KṚṢṆA-DVAIPĀYANA VYĀSA

श्रीराजोवाच

येन येनावतारेण भगवान् हरिरीश्वरः ।
करोति कर्णरम्याणि मनोज्ञानि च नः प्रभो ॥
यच्छृण्वतोऽपैत्यरतिर्वितृष्णा
सत्त्वं च शुद्ध्यत्यचिरेण पुंसः ।
भक्तिर्हरौ तत्पुरुषे च सख्यं
तदेव हारं वद मन्यसे चेत् ॥

śrī-rājovāca
yena yenāvatāreṇa
bhagavān harir īśvaraḥ
karoti karṇa-ramyāṇi
mano-jñāni ca naḥ prabho

yac-chṛṇvato 'paity aratir vitṛṣṇā
sattvaṁ ca śuddhyaty acireṇa puṁsaḥ
bhaktir harau tat-puruṣe ca sakhyaṁ
tad eva hāraṁ vada manyase cet (p. 40)

BOOKS by
His Divine Grace
A. C. Bhaktivedanta Swami Prabhupāda

Bhagavad-gītā As It Is
Śrīmad-Bhāgavatam, Cantos 1–10 (50 Vols.)
Śrī Caitanya-caritāmṛta (17 Vols.)
Teachings of Lord Caitanya
The Nectar of Devotion
The Nectar of Instruction
Śrī Īśopaniṣad
Easy Journey to Other Planets
Kṛṣṇa Consciousness: The Topmost Yoga System
Kṛṣṇa, the Supreme Personality of Godhead (3 Vols.)
Perfect Questions, Perfect Answers
Dialectical Spiritualism—A Vedic View of Western Philosophy
Teachings of Lord Kapila, the Son of Devahūti
Transcendental Teachings of Prahlad Mahārāja
Kṛṣṇa, the Reservoir of Pleasure
Life Comes From Life
The Perfection of Yoga
Beyond Birth and Death
On the Way to Kṛṣṇa
Geetār-gan (Bengali)
Rāja-vidyā: The King of Knowledge
Elevation to Kṛṣṇa Consciousness
Kṛṣṇa Consciousness: The Matchless Gift
Back to Godhead Magazine (Founder)

A complete catalog is available upon request

Bhaktivedanta Book Trust
3764 Watseka Avenue
Los Angeles, California 90034

Endpapers: Śukadeva Gosvāmī speaking *Śrīmad-Bhāgavatam* to Mahārāja Parīkṣit in the presence of exalted sages.

Puranas. Bhāgavatapurāna.

ŚRĪMAD-BHĀGAVATAM

Tenth Canto
"The Summum Bonum"

(Part Two—Chapters 6–12)

With the Original Sanskrit Text,
Its Roman Transliteration, Synonyms,
Translation and Elaborate Purports

by

His Divine Grace
A.C. Bhaktivedanta Swami Prabhupāda
Founder-*Ācārya* of the International Society for Krishna Consciousness

THE BHAKTIVEDANTA BOOK TRUST
New York · Los Angeles · London · Bombay

Readers interested in the subject matter of this book are invited by the International Society for Krishna Consciousness to correspond with its Secretary.

International Society for Krishna Consciousness
3764 Watseka Avenue
Los Angeles, California 90034

First Printing, 1977: 50,000 copies

Printed in the United States of America

Library of Congress Cataloging in Publication Data (Revised)

Puranas. Bhāgavatapurāna.
Śrīmad-Bhāgavatam.

Includes bibliographical references and indexes.
CONTENTS: Canto 1. Creation. 3 v.—Canto 2. The cosmic manifestation. 2 v.—Canto 3. The status quo. 4 v.—Canto 4. The creation of the Fourth Order. 4 v.—Canto 5. The creative impetus. 2 v.
1. Chaitanya, 1486-1534. I. Bhaktivedanta Swami, A. C., 1896- II. Title.
BL1135.P7A22 1972 73-169353
ISBN 0-912776-98-6

CHAPTER NINE

Mother Yaśodā Binds Lord Kṛṣṇa

CHAPTER TEN

Deliverance of the Yamala-arjuna Trees

Table of Contents

CHAPTER ELEVEN

The Childhood Pastimes of Kṛṣṇa

CHAPTER TWELVE

The Killing of the Demon Aghāsura

Appendixes

Preface

We must know the present need of human society. And what is that need? Human society is no longer bounded by geographical limits to particular countries or communities. Human society is broader than in the Middle Ages, and the world tendency is toward one state or one human society. The ideals of spiritual communism, according to *Śrīmad-Bhāgavatam*, are based more or less on the oneness of the entire human society, nay, of the entire energy of living beings. The need is felt by great thinkers to make this a successful ideology. *Śrīmad-Bhāgavatam* will fill this need in human society. It begins, therefore, with the aphorism of Vedānta philosophy *janmādy asya yataḥ* to establish the ideal of a common cause.

Human society, at the present moment, is not in the darkness of oblivion. It has made rapid progress in the field of material comforts, education and economic development throughout the entire world. But there is a pinprick somewhere in the social body at large, and therefore there are large-scale quarrels, even over less important issues. There is need of a clue as to how humanity can become one in peace, friendship and prosperity with a common cause. *Śrīmad-Bhāgavatam* will fill this need, for it is a cultural presentation for the re-spiritualization of the entire human society.

Śrīmad-Bhāgavatam should be introduced also in the schools and colleges, for it is recommended by the great student-devotee Prahlāda Mahārāja in order to change the demoniac face of society.

kaumāra ācaret prājño
dharmān bhāgavatān iha
durlabhaṁ mānuṣaṁ janma
tad apy adhruvam arthadam
(*Bhāg.* 7.6.1)

Disparity in human society is due to lack of principles in a godless civilization. There is God, or the Almighty One, from whom everything emanates, by whom everything is maintained and in whom everything is merged to rest. Material science has tried to find the ultimate source of creation very insufficiently, but it is a fact that there is one ultimate source of everything that be. This ultimate source is explained rationally and authoritatively in the beautiful *Bhāgavatam* or *Śrīmad-Bhāgavatam.*

Śrīmad-Bhāgavatam is the transcendental science not only for knowing the ultimate source of everything but also for knowing our relation with Him and our duty towards perfection of the human society on the basis of this perfect knowledge. It is powerful reading matter in the Sanskrit language, and it is now rendered into English elaborately so that simply by a careful reading one will know God perfectly well, so much so that the reader will be sufficiently educated to defend himself from the onslaught of atheists. Over and above this, the reader will be able to convert others to accepting God as a concrete principle.

Śrīmad-Bhāgavatam begins with the definition of the ultimate source. It is a bona fide commentary on the *Vedānta-sūtra* by the same author, Śrīla Vyāsadeva, and gradually it develops into nine cantos up to the highest state of God realization. The only qualification one needs to study this great book of transcendental knowledge is to proceed step by step cautiously and not jump forward haphazardly like with an ordinary book. It should be gone through chapter by chapter, one after another. The reading matter is so arranged with its original Sanskrit text, its English transliteration, synonyms, translation and purports so that one is sure to become a God-realized soul at the end of finishing the first nine cantos.

The Tenth Canto is distinct from the first nine cantos because it deals directly with the transcendental activities of the Personality of Godhead Śrī Kṛṣṇa. One will be unable to capture the effects of the Tenth Canto without going through the first nine cantos. The book is complete in twelve cantos, each independent, but it is good for all to read them in small installments one after another.

I must admit my frailties in presenting *Śrīmad-Bhāgavatam*, but still I am hopeful of its good reception by the thinkers and leaders of society on the strength of the following statement of *Śrīmad-Bhāgavatam* (1.5.11):

tad-vāg-visargo janatāgha-viplavo
yasmin prati-ślokam abaddhavaty api

nāmāny anantasya yaśo 'ṅkitāni yac
chṛṇvanti gāyanti gṛṇanti sādhavaḥ

"On the other hand, that literature which is full with descriptions of the transcendental glories of the name, fame, form and pastimes of the unlimited Supreme Lord is a transcendental creation meant to bring about a revolution in the impious life of a misdirected civilization. Such transcendental literatures, even though irregularly composed, are heard, sung and accepted by purified men who are thoroughly honest."

Oṁ tat sat

A. C. Bhaktivedanta Swami

Introduction

"This *Bhāgavata Purāṇa* is as brilliant as the sun, and it has arisen just after the departure of Lord Kṛṣṇa to His own abode, accompanied by religion, knowledge, etc. Persons who have lost their vision due to the dense darkness of ignorance in the age of Kali shall get light from this *Purāṇa.*" (*Śrīmad-Bhāgavatam* 1.3.43)

The timeless wisdom of India is expressed in the *Vedas,* ancient Sanskrit texts that touch upon all fields of human knowledge. Originally preserved through oral tradition, the *Vedas* were first put into writing five thousand years ago by Śrīla Vyāsadeva, the "literary incarnation of God." After compiling the *Vedas,* Vyāsadeva set forth their essence in the aphorisms known as *Vedānta-sūtras. Śrīmad-Bhāgavatam* is Vyāsadeva's commentary on his own *Vedānta-sūtras.* It was written in the maturity of his spiritual life under the direction of Nārada Muni, his spiritual master. Referred to as "the ripened fruit of the tree of Vedic literature," *Śrīmad-Bhāgavatam* is the most complete and authoritative exposition of Vedic knowledge.

After compiling the *Bhāgavatam,* Vyāsa impressed the synopsis of it upon his son, the sage Śukadeva Gosvāmī. Śukadeva Gosvāmī subsequently recited the entire *Bhāgavatam* to Mahārāja Parīkṣit in an assembly of learned saints on the bank of the Ganges at Hastināpura (now Delhi). Mahārāja Parīkṣit was the emperor of the world and was a great *rājarṣi* (saintly king). Having received a warning that he would die within a week, he renounced his entire kingdom and retired to the bank of the Ganges to fast until death and receive spiritual enlightenment. The *Bhāgavatam* begins with Emperor Parīkṣit's sober inquiry to Śukadeva Gosvāmī: "You are the spiritual master of great saints and devotees. I am therefore begging you to show the way of perfection for all persons, and especially for one who is about to die. Please let me know what a man should hear, chant, remember and worship, and also what he should not do. Please explain all this to me."

Śukadeva Gosvāmī's answer to this question, and numerous other questions posed by Mahārāja Parīkṣit, concerning everything from the nature of the self to the origin of the universe, held the assembled sages in rapt attention continuously for the seven days leading to the King's death. The sage Sūta Gosvāmī, who was present on the bank of the Ganges when Śukadeva Gosvāmī first recited *Śrīmad-Bhāgavatam*, later repeated the *Bhāgavatam* before a gathering of sages in the forest of Naimiṣāraṇya. Those sages, concerned about the spiritual welfare of the people in general, had gathered to perform a long, continuous chain of sacrifices to counteract the degrading influence of the incipient age of Kali. In response to the sages' request that he speak the essence of Vedic wisdom, Sūta Gosvāmī repeated from memory the entire eighteen thousand verses of *Śrīmad-Bhāgavatam*, as spoken by Śukadeva Gosvāmī to Mahārāja Parīkṣit.

The reader of *Śrīmad-Bhāgavatam* hears Sūta Gosvāmī relate the questions of Mahārāja Parīkṣit and the answers of Śukadeva Gosvāmī. Also, Sūta Gosvāmī sometimes responds directly to questions put by Śaunaka Ṛṣi, the spokesman for the sages gathered at Naimiṣāraṇya. One therefore simultaneously hears two dialogues: one between Mahārāja Parīkṣit and Śukadeva Gosvāmī on the bank of the Ganges, and another at Naimiṣāraṇya between Sūta Gosvāmī and the sages at Naimiṣāraṇya Forest, headed by Śaunaka Ṛṣi. Furthermore, while instructing King Parīkṣit, Śukadeva Gosvāmī often relates historical episodes and gives accounts of lengthy philosophical discussions between such great souls as the saint Maitreya and his disciple Vidura. With this understanding of the history of the *Bhāgavatam*, the reader will easily be able to follow its intermingling of dialogues and events from various sources. Since philosophical wisdom, not chronological order, is most important in the text, one need only be attentive to the subject matter of *Śrīmad-Bhāgavatam* to appreciate fully its profound message.

The translator of this edition compares the *Bhāgavatam* to sugar candy—wherever you taste it, you will find it equally sweet and relishable. Therefore, to taste the sweetness of the *Bhāgavatam*, one may begin by reading any of its volumes. After such an introductory taste, however, the serious reader is best advised to go back to Volume One of the First Canto and then proceed through the *Bhāgavatam*, volume after volume, in its natural order.

This edition of the *Bhāgavatam* is the first complete English translation of this important text with an elaborate commentary, and it is the first widely available to the English-speaking public. It is the product of the scholarly and devotional effort of His Divine Grace A. C. Bhaktivedanta Swami Prabhupāda, the world's most distinguished teacher of Indian religious and philosophical thought. His consummate Sanskrit scholarship and intimate familiarity with Vedic culture and thought as well as the modern way of life combine to reveal to the West a magnificent exposition of this important classic.

Readers will find this work of value for many reasons. For those interested in the classical roots of Indian civilization, it serves as a vast reservoir of detailed information on virtually every one of its aspects. For students of comparative philosophy and religion, the *Bhāgavatam* offers a penetrating view into the meaning of India's profound spiritual heritage. To sociologists and anthropologists, the *Bhāgavatam* reveals the practical workings of a peaceful and scientifically organized Vedic culture, whose institutions were integrated on the basis of a highly developed spiritual world view. Students of literature will discover the *Bhāgavatam* to be a masterpiece of majestic poetry. For students of psychology, the text provides important perspectives on the nature of consciousness, human behavior and the philosophical study of identity. Finally, to those seeking spiritual insight, the *Bhāgavatam* offers simple and practical guidance for attainment of the highest self-knowledge and realization of the Absolute Truth. The entire multivolume text, presented by the Bhaktivedanta Book Trust, promises to occupy a significant place in the intellectual, cultural and spiritual life of modern man for a long time to come.

—The Publishers

His Divine Grace
A. C. Bhaktivedanta Swami Prabhupāda
Founder-Ācārya of the International Society for Krishna Consciousness

PLATE ONE

One day the demoness Pūtanā came down from outer space into Gokula, the home of Nanda Mahārāja. Having been sent by the cruel King Kaṁsa to kill all the babies in the Vṛndāvana area, Pūtanā displayed her mystic power and assumed the disguise of a very beautiful woman. Taking courage, she immediately entered Kṛṣṇa's bedroom without permission, but everyone was so overwhelmed by her beauty that they did not protest. The baby Kṛṣṇa, who resembled a fire covered by ashes, looked upon Pūtanā and thought that He would have to kill her. Pūtanā could understand the great potency of Kṛṣṇa, but, enchanted by the influence of Kṛṣṇa's internal energy, she took Kṛṣṇa upon her lap anyway and offered Him her poison-smeared breast to suck. Suddenly, baby Kṛṣṇa became very angry at Pūtanā, and taking hold of her breast, He squeezed it very hard with both hands and began to suck out both the poison and her life. In unbearable agony, Pūtanā perspired heavily, flailed her arms and legs wildly, and cried out, "Please leave me, leave me! Suck my breast no longer!" But Kṛṣṇa persisted, and as the demoness lost her life she assumed her original, huge form. Then, before the amazed *gopīs*, Kṛṣṇa began fearlessly playing on the breast of Pūtanā's twelve-mile-long corpse. (*pp. 1–16*)

PLATE TWO

Just after baby Kṛṣṇa turned three months old, mother Yaśodā saw that He was slanting His body in an attempt to rise and turn around. To celebrate this auspicious occasion, she arranged to observe the Vedic ceremony called *utthāna*, a bathing ceremony performed when a child is due to leave the house for the first time. So mother Yaśodā called together the other women of the neighborhood to assist her, and the *brāhmaṇas* joined by chanting Vedic hymns while professional musicians played their instruments and sang. (*pp. 44–45*)

PLATE THREE

During baby Kṛṣṇa's *utthāna* ceremony, mother Yaśodā saw that He was falling asleep, and she placed the child in a cradle underneath a household cart. While the child slept, mother Yaśodā became absorbed in receiving guests. When Kṛṣṇa awoke, He began crying for His mother, wanting to drink the milk from her breast. But mother Yaśodā could not hear Him. All of a sudden Kṛṣṇa threw His legs upward and struck the cart, and although His legs were as soft as newly-grown leaves, the cart turned over violently and collapsed. The wheels separated from the axle, the hubs and spokes fell apart, and the pole of the handcart broke. On the cart there were many little utensils made of various metals, and all of them scattered hither and thither. When mother Yaśodā, Nanda Mahārāja and their guests saw the situation, they began to wonder aloud: "Is it the work of some demon or evil planet?" Then the small children present said, "As soon as baby Kṛṣṇa kicked the cart's wheel, the cart collapsed. There is no doubt about it." But the adults could not believe that baby Kṛṣṇa had such inconceivable power. (*pp. 46–52*)

PLATE FOUR

One day, when mother Yaśodā was sitting with Kṛṣṇa on her lap, she suddenly observed that He had assumed the weight of the entire universe. Astonished, she had to put the child down. Then she left Kṛṣṇa sitting in the courtyard and she engaged in her household duties. All at once a demon named Tṛṇāvarta, who was a servant of King Kaṁsa's, came there in the form of a whirlwind and very easily carried the child up into the air. Covering the whole land of Gokula with particles of dust, Tṛṇāvarta began vibrating everywhere with a greatly fearful sound. For a moment, the whole pasturing ground became overcast with dense darkness from the dust storm, and mother Yaśodā, unable to find her son where she had placed Him, began to lament pitifully. Meanwhile, the whirlwind demon took Kṛṣṇa very high into the sky, but Kṛṣṇa suddenly became heavier than the demon and stopped him from going any farther. To Tṛṇāvarta, Kṛṣṇa felt as heavy as a mountain or a huge hunk of iron. But because Kṛṣṇa was tightly holding on to the demon's neck, the demon was unable to throw Him off. (*pp. 60–68*)

PLATE FIVE

One day Vasudeva inspired Gargamuni, the family priest of the Yadu dynasty, to go to Nanda Mahārāja's house in Vṛndāvana and perform the name-giving ceremony for Kṛṣṇa and Balarāma. To keep the ceremony hidden from King Kaṁsa, Nanda Mahārāja requested Gargamuni to perform it in Nanda's very secluded cowshed. As Gargamuni cradled baby Kṛṣṇa in his hands, he said to Nanda Mahārāja, "To increase the transcendental bliss of the cowherd men of Gokula, this child Kṛṣṇa will always act auspiciously for you. And by His grace only, you will surpass all difficulties. Demons cannot harm the demigods, who always have Lord Viṣṇu on their side. Similarly, any person or group attached to Kṛṣṇa is extremely fortunate. Because such persons are very much affectionate toward Kṛṣṇa, they cannot be defeated by demons like the associates of Kaṁsa. O Nanda Mahārāja, in His transcendental qualities, opulence, name, fame and influence, this child of yours is exactly like Nārāyaṇa. You should therefore raise Him very carefully and cautiously." (*pp. 82–103*)

PLATE SIX

Kṛṣṇa would sometimes enter the house of a neighbor and steal curd, butter and milk from the pots in the storeroom. Then the cowherd men would find Him and angrily say, "Here is the butter thief! Better capture Him!" But Kṛṣṇa would simply go on eating the curd and butter, and when He smiled at the cowherd men they would forget everything. (*pp. 113–14*)

PLATE SEVEN

One day, while Kṛṣṇa was playing with His brother, Balarāma, and His other small playmates, all Kṛṣṇa's friends came together and complained to mother Yaśodā. "Mother," they submitted, "Kṛṣṇa has eaten some earth." Upon hearing this from Kṛṣṇa's playmates, mother Yaśodā picked Kṛṣṇa up and said, "Dear Kṛṣṇa, why are You so restless that You have eaten dirt in a solitary place? How is this?" Kṛṣṇa replied, "My dear mother, I have never eaten dirt. All my friends complaining against Me are liars. If you think they are being truthful, you can directly look into My mouth and examine it." When Kṛṣṇa opened His mouth wide, mother Yaśodā saw within His mouth all moving and nonmoving entities, outer space and all directions, along with mountains, islands, oceans, the surface of the earth, the blowing wind, fire, the moon and the stars. She saw the planetary systems, water, light, air, sky, and creation by transformation of false ego. She also saw the senses, the mind, sense perception, and the three qualities goodness, passion and ignorance. She saw the time allotted for the living entities, she saw natural instinct and the reactions of *karma*, and she saw the varieties of bodies produced by different desires. Seeing all these aspects of the cosmic manifestation, along with herself and Vṛndāvana-dhāma, she became doubtful and fearful of her son's nature. (*pp. 117–23*)

PLATE EIGHT

Sometimes Kṛṣṇa and Balarāma would secretly enter the storeroom, steal yogurt and butter, and feed it to the monkeys. On one such occasion mother Yaśodā caught Kṛṣṇa and Balarāma in the act. Kṛṣṇa was standing on an upside-down wooden grinding mortar, distributing the yogurt and butter to the monkeys as He liked, and Balarāma was hiding behind a pillar. When the two boys saw the stick in mother Yaśodā's hand, They began to look at her with great anxiety, as if They were afraid she would chastise Them. (*pp. 152–53*)

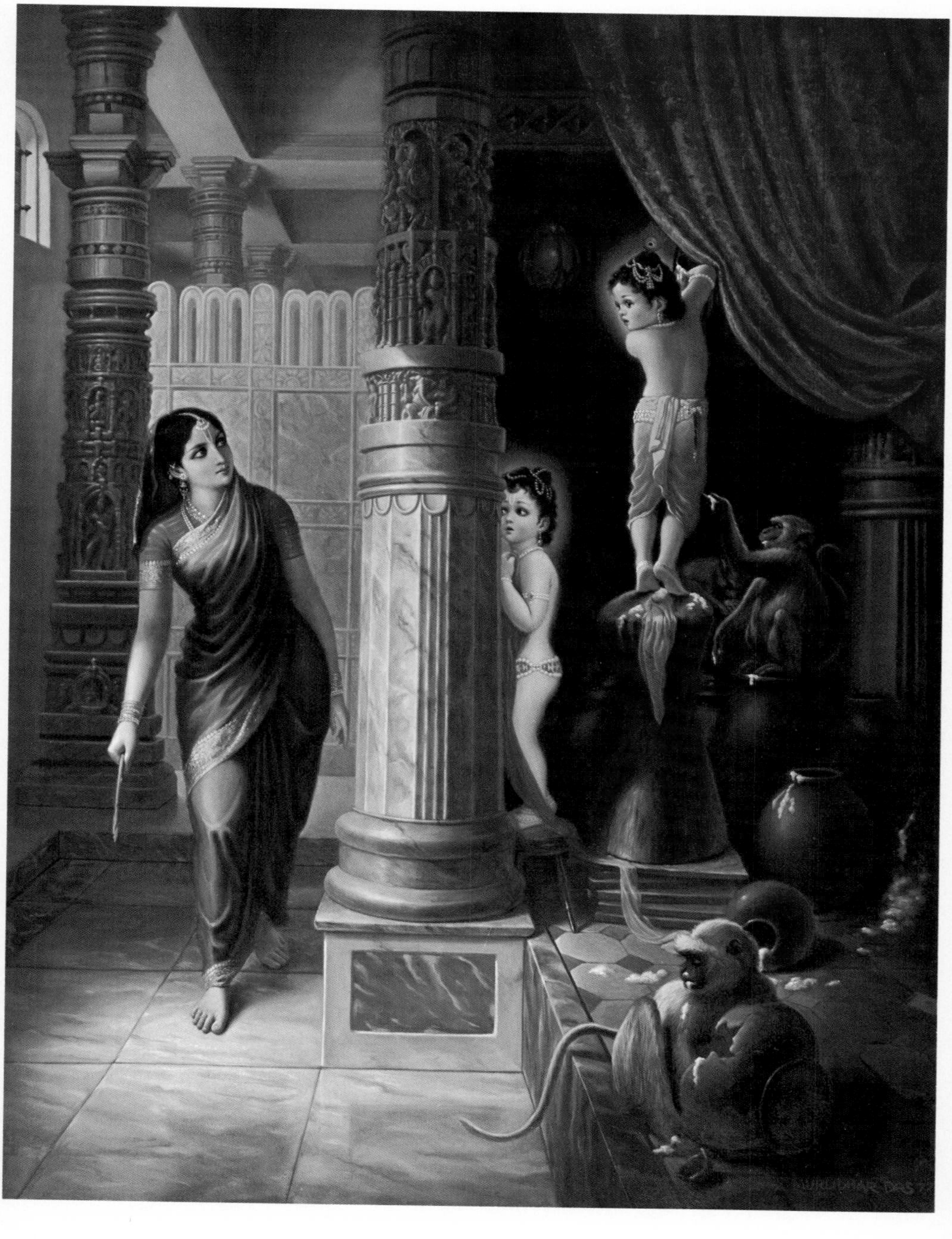

PLATE NINE

One day Kṛṣṇa stole some butter and went to a secluded place to eat it. As He ate He looked all around with great anxiety, suspecting He might be chastised by His mother. Finally, mother Yaśodā found Him by tracing His butter-smeared footprints, but as she very cautiously approached Kṛṣṇa from behind, He suddenly noticed her and quickly began to flee as if very much afraid. While following Kṛṣṇa, mother Yaśodā, her thin waist overburdened by her heavy breasts, naturally had to reduce her speed. Because of following Kṛṣṇa very swiftly, her hair became loose, and the flowers in her hair were falling after her. Finally, because of her great love and devotion, Kṛṣṇa allowed mother Yaśodā to capture Him. (*pp. 150–54*)

PLATE TEN

The two brothers Nalakūvara and Maṇigrīva were great devotees of Lord Śiva, but because of material opulence they became so extravagant and senseless that one day they were enjoying with naked girls in a lake and shamelessly walking here and there. Suddenly the great saint Nārada Muni passed by, but the two brothers were so maddened by their wealth and false prestige that even though they saw Nārada, they remained naked and were not even ashamed. Just to show them mercy, Nārada Muni cursed them as follows: "These two young men, Nalakūvara and Maṇigrīva, are by fortune the sons of the great demigod Kuvera, but because of false prestige and madness after drinking liquor, they are so fallen that they are naked but cannot understand that they are. Therefore, because they are living like trees (for trees are naked but are not conscious), these two young men should receive the bodies of trees. This will be proper punishment. Nonetheless, after they become trees and until they are released, by my mercy they will have remembrance of their past sinful activities. Moreover, by my special favor, after the expiry of one hundred years by the measurement of the demigods, they will be able to see the Supreme Personality of Godhead, Kṛṣṇa, face to face, and thus revive their real position as devotees." (*p. 195*)

PLATE ELEVEN

After stealing butter one day, Kṛṣṇa had allowed mother Yaśodā to catch Him and bind Him to a grinding mortar. Thus, by His own arrangement, Kṛṣṇa was now ready to fulfill the words of His great devotee Nārada Muni. Nārada Muni had cursed the two brothers Nalakūvara and Maṇigrīva to become twin *arjuna* trees in Nanda Mahārāja's courtyard, but Nārada had also promised that one day they would see the Supreme Personality of Godhead, Kṛṣṇa, face to face. Seeing the two *arjuna* trees in front of Him, Kṛṣṇa thought, "These two trees were formerly Nalakūvara and Maṇigrīva. But although these two young men are the sons of the very rich Kuvera, I actually have nothing to do with them. Yet Nārada Muni is My very dear and affectionate devotee, and therefore, because he wanted Me to come face to face with them, I must do so for their deliverance." Having thus decided to deliver the two brothers, Kṛṣṇa dragged the big mortar between the two *arjuna* trees and caused it to become stuck between them. Then, with great force, Kṛṣṇa uprooted the two trees, which trembled severely and fell to the ground with a great crash. Thereafter, in that very place where the two *arjuna* trees had fallen, two great, perfect personalities appeared, their effulgent beauty illuminating all directions. (*pp. 198–202*)

PLATE TWELVE

In any situation, Kṛṣṇa is always the infinitely powerful Supreme Personality of Godhead. But just to increase the ecstatic emotion of His intimate, loving devotees like mother Yaśodā and Nanda Mahārāja, Kṛṣṇa agrees to come under their control. Sometimes Nanda Mahārāja would ask Kṛṣṇa to bring him his wooden slippers, and Kṛṣṇa, with great difficulty, would put the slippers on His head and take them to His father. At such times Nanda Mahārāja would exclaim, "My dear Yaśodā, just look at your offspring, Kṛṣṇa! See His blackish bodily luster, His eyes tinged with red color, His broad chest and His beautiful pearl ornaments. How wonderful He looks, and how He is increasing my transcendental bliss more and more!" (*p. 226*)

PLATE THIRTEEN

Once an aborigine woman, a fruit vendor, came into Vṛndāvana. "O inhabitants of Vrajabhūmi," she called out, "if you want to purchase some fruits, come here!" Upon hearing this, Kṛṣṇa immediately took some grains in the palms of His hands and went to barter for some fruits. While Kṛṣṇa very hastily approached the fruit vendor, most of the grains He was holding fell out of His hands. Nonetheless, the fruit vendor filled Kṛṣṇa's hands with fruits, and her fruit basket was immediately filled with jewels and gold. (*pp. 227–28*)

PLATE FOURTEEN

One day all the boys, including Kṛṣṇa and Balarāma, brought their respective groups of calves to a reservoir of water to drink. First the animals drank, and then the boys drank also. Right by the reservoir the boys saw a gigantic body resembling a mountain peak broken and struck down by a thunderbolt. The boys were afraid even to see such a huge living being. The great creature was actually a demon in the form of a duck with a very sharp beak. His name was Bakāsura, and having come to the reservoir, he immediately swallowed Kṛṣṇa. When Balarāma and the other boys saw that Kṛṣṇa had been devoured by the gigantic duck, they became almost unconscious, like senses without life. (*pp. 254–56*)

PLATE FIFTEEN

One day a great demon named Aghāsura appeared in Vṛndāvana. Having been sent by King Kaṁsa to kill Kṛṣṇa, Aghāsura assumed the form of a huge python, as thick as a big mountain and as long as eight miles. He spread his mouth like a big mountain cave and laid down on the road, expecting to swallow Kṛṣṇa and His cowherd boy friends. Upon seeing this wonderful demon, the cowherd boys were unafraid. On the contrary, at first they thought that it was a statue made in the shape of a great python for their enjoyment. Then they began to discuss the demon among themselves. "Dear friends," said one boy, "is this creature dead, or is it actually a living python with its mouth spread wide just to swallow us all? Kindly clear up this doubt." At last they decided that the creature was indeed a huge python who intended to swallow them up. Then one boy began to point out the unusual features of the creature: "Dear friends, just see, this creature's upper lip resembles a cloud reddened by the sunshine, and its lower lip resembles the reddish shadows of the cloud. On the left and right, the two depressions resembling mountain caves are the corners of its mouth, and the high mountain peaks are its teeth." Then all the boys said, "If this creature tries to swallow us, Kṛṣṇa will immediately kill him, just as He killed Bakāsura." Thus, looking at the beautiful face of Kṛṣṇa and laughing loudly and clapping their hands, the boys entered the mouth of Aghāsura. (*pp. 278–86*)

CHAPTER SIX

The Killing of the Demon Pūtanā

A summary of the Sixth Chapter is as follows: when Nanda Mahārāja, following the instructions of Vasudeva, was returning home, he saw a great demoniac woman lying on the road, and then he heard about her death.

While Nanda Mahārāja, the King of Vraja, was thinking about Vasudeva's words concerning disturbances in Gokula, he was a little afraid and sought shelter at the lotus feet of Śrī Hari. Meanwhile, Kaṁsa sent to the village of Gokula a Rākṣasī named Pūtanā, who was wandering here and there killing small babies. Of course, wherever there is no Kṛṣṇa consciousness, there is the danger of such Rākṣasīs, but since the Supreme Personality of Godhead Himself was in Gokula, Pūtanā could accept nothing there but her own death.

One day, Pūtanā arrived from outer space in Gokula, the home of Nanda Mahārāja, and by displaying her mystic power, she assumed the disguise of a very beautiful woman. Taking courage, she immediately entered Kṛṣṇa's bedroom without anyone's permission; by the grace of Kṛṣṇa, no one forbade her to enter the house or the room, because that was Kṛṣṇa's desire. The baby Kṛṣṇa, who resembled a fire covered by ashes, looked upon Pūtanā and thought that He would have to kill this demon, the beautiful woman. Enchanted by the influence of *yogamāyā* and the Personality of Godhead, Pūtanā took Kṛṣṇa upon her lap, and neither Rohiṇī nor Yaśodā objected. The demon Pūtanā offered her breast for Kṛṣṇa to suck, but her breast was smeared with poison. The child Kṛṣṇa, therefore, squeezed Pūtanā's breast so severely that in unbearable pain she had to assume her original body and fell to the ground. Then Kṛṣṇa began playing on her breast just like a small child. When Kṛṣṇa was playing, the *gopīs* were pacified and took the child away to their own laps. After this incident, the *gopīs* took precautions because of the attack of the Rākṣasī. Mother Yaśodā gave the child her breast to suck and then laid Him in bed.

Meanwhile, Nanda and his associates the cowherd men returned from Mathurā, and when they saw the great dead body of Pūtanā, they were struck with wonder. Everyone was astonished that Vasudeva had foretold this mishap, and they praised Vasudeva for his power of foresight. The inhabitants of Vraja cut the gigantic body of Pūtanā into pieces, but because Kṛṣṇa had sucked her breast, she had been freed from all sins, and therefore when the cowherd men burned the pieces of her body in a fire, the smoke filled the air with a very pleasing fragrance. Ultimately, although Pūtaña had desired to kill Kṛṣṇa, she attained the Lord's abode. From this incident we gain the instruction that if one is attached to Kṛṣṇa somehow or other, even as an enemy, one ultimately attains success. What then is to be said of devotees who are naturally attached to Kṛṣṇa in love? When the inhabitants of Vraja heard about the killing of Pūtanā and the welfare of the child, they were very much satisfied. Nanda Mahārāja took the baby Kṛṣṇa on his lap and was filled with satisfaction.

TEXT 1

श्रीशुक उवाच
नन्दः पथि वचः शौरेर्न मृषेति विचिन्तयन् ।
हरिं जगाम शरणमुत्पातागमशङ्कितः ॥ १ ॥

śrī-śuka uvāca
nandaḥ pathi vacaḥ śaurer
na mṛṣeti vicintayan
hariṁ jagāma śaraṇam
utpātāgama-śaṅkitaḥ

śrī-śukaḥ uvāca—Śrī Śukadeva Gosvāmī said; *nandaḥ*—Nanda Mahārāja; *pathi*—on his way back home; *vacaḥ*—the words; *śaureḥ*—of Vasudeva; *na*—not; *mṛṣā*—without purpose or cause; *iti*—thus; *vicintayan*—while thinking about inauspiciousness for his little son, Kṛṣṇa; *harim*—unto the Supreme Lord, the controller; *jagāma*—took; *śaraṇam*—shelter; *utpāta*—of disturbances; *āgama*—with the expectation; *śaṅkitaḥ*—thus being afraid.

TRANSLATION

Śukadeva Gosvāmī continued: My dear King, while Nanda Mahārāja was on the way home, he considered that what Vasudeva had said could not be false or useless. There must have been some danger of disturbances in Gokula. As Nanda Mahārāja thought about the danger for his beautiful son, Kṛṣṇa, he was afraid, and he took shelter at the lotus feet of the supreme controller.

PURPORT

Whenever there is danger, the pure devotee thinks of the protection and shelter of the Supreme Personality of Godhead. This is also advised in *Bhagavad-gītā* (9.33): *anityam asukhaṁ lokam imaṁ prāpya bhajasva mām.* In this material world there is danger at every step (*padaṁ padaṁ yad vipadām*). Therefore a devotee has no other course than to take shelter of the Lord at every step.

TEXT 2

कंसेन प्रहिता घोरा पूतना बालघातिनी ।
शिशूंश्चचार निघ्नन्ती पुरग्रामव्रजादिषु ॥ २ ॥

kaṁsena prahitā ghorā
pūtanā bāla-ghātinī
śiśūṁś cacāra nighnantī
pura-grāma-vrajādiṣu

kaṁsena—by King Kaṁsa; *prahitā*—engaged previously; *ghorā*—very fierce; *pūtanā*—by the name Pūtanā; *bāla-ghātinī*—a Rākṣasī who killed; *śiśūn*—small babies; *cacāra*—wandered; *nighnantī*—killing; *pura-grāma-vraja-ādiṣu*—in towns, cities and villages here and there.

TRANSLATION

While Nanda Mahārāja was returning to Gokula, the same fierce Pūtanā whom Kaṁsa had previously engaged to kill babies was wandering about in the towns, cities and villages, doing her nefarious duty.

TEXT 3

न यत्र श्रवणादीनि रक्षोघ्नानि स्वकर्मसु ।
कुर्वन्ति सात्वतां भर्तुर्यातुधान्यश्च तत्र हि ॥ ३ ॥

na yatra śravaṇādīni
rakṣo-ghnāni sva-karmasu
kurvanti sātvatāṁ bhartur
yātudhānyaś ca tatra hi

na—not; *yatra*—wherever; *śravaṇa-ādīni*—the activities of *bhakti-yoga*, beginning with hearing and chanting; *rakṣaḥ-ghnāni*—the sound vibration to kill all danger and bad elements; *sva-karmasu*—if one is engaged in his own occupational duty; *kurvanti*—such things are done; *sātvatām bhartuḥ*—of the protector of the devotees; *yātudhānyaḥ*—disturbing elements, bad elements; *ca*—also; *tatra hi*—there must be.

TRANSLATION

My dear King, wherever people in any position perform their occupational duties of devotional service by chanting and hearing [śravaṇaṁ kīrtanaṁ viṣṇoḥ], there cannot be any danger from bad elements. Therefore there was no need for anxiety about Gokula while the Supreme Personality of Godhead was personally present.

PURPORT

Śukadeva Gosvāmī spoke this verse to mitigate the anxiety of Mahārāja Parīkṣit. Mahārāja Parīkṣit was a devotee of Kṛṣṇa, and therefore when he understood that Pūtanā was causing disturbances in Gokula, he was somewhat perturbed. Śukadeva Gosvāmī therefore assured him that there was no danger in Gokula. Śrīla Bhaktivinoda Ṭhākura has sung: *nāmāśraya kari' yatane tumi, thākaha āpana kāje.* Everyone is thus advised to seek shelter in the chanting of the Hare Kṛṣṇa *mahā-mantra* and remain engaged in his own occupational duty. There is no loss in this, and the gain is tremendous. Even from a material point of view, everyone should take to chanting the Hare Kṛṣṇa *mantra* to be saved from all kinds of danger. This world is full of danger (*padaṁ padaṁ yad vipadām*). Therefore we should be encouraged to chant the

Hare Kṛṣṇa *mahā-mantra* so that in our family, society, neighborhood and nation, everything will be smooth and free from danger.

TEXT 4

सा खेचर्येकदोत्पत्य पूतना नन्दगोकुलम् ।
योषित्वा माययात्मानं प्राविशत् कामचारिणी ॥४॥

sā khe-cary ekadotpatya
pūtanā nanda-gokulam
yoṣitvā māyayātmānaṁ
prāviśat kāma-cāriṇī

sā—that (Pūtanā); *khe-carī*—who traveled in outer space; *ekadā*—once upon a time; *utpatya*—was flying; *pūtanā*—the demon Pūtanā; *nanda-gokulam*—at the place of Nanda Mahārāja, Gokula; *yoṣitvā*—converting into a very beautiful woman; *māyayā*—by mystic power; *ātmānam*—herself; *prāviśat*—entered; *kāma-cāriṇī*—one who could move according to her own desire.

TRANSLATION

Once upon a time, Pūtanā Rākṣasī, who could move according to her desire and was wandering in outer space, converted herself by mystic power into a very beautiful woman and thus entered Gokula, the abode of Nanda Mahārāja.

PURPORT

Rākṣasīs learn mystic powers by which they can travel in outer space without machines. In some parts of India there are still such mystical witches, who can sit on a stick and use it to fly from one place to another in a very short time. This art was known to Pūtanā. Assuming the feature of a very beautiful woman, she entered Nanda Mahārāja's abode, Gokula.

TEXTS 5–6

तां केशबन्धव्यतिषक्तमल्लिकां
बृहन्नितम्बस्तनकृच्छ्रमध्यमाम् ।

सुवाससं कल्पितकर्णभूषण-
त्विषोल्लसत्कुन्तलमण्डिताननाम् ॥ ५ ॥
वल्गुस्मितापाङ्गविसर्गवीक्षितै-
र्मनो हरन्तीं वनितां व्रजौकसाम् ।
अमंसताम्भोजकरेण रूपिणीं
गोप्यः श्रियं द्रष्टुमिवागतां पतिम् ॥ ६ ॥

tāṁ keśa-bandha-vyatiṣakta-mallikāṁ
bṛhan-nitamba-stana-kṛcchra-madhyamām
suvāsasaṁ kalpita-karṇa-bhūṣaṇa-
tviṣollasat-kuntala-maṇḍitānanām

valgu-smitāpāṅga-visarga-vīkṣitair
mano harantīṁ vanitāṁ vrajaukasām
amaṁsatāmbhoja-kareṇa rūpiṇīṁ
gopyaḥ śriyaṁ draṣṭum ivāgatāṁ patim

tām—her; *keśa-bandha-vyatiṣakta-mallikām*—whose arrangement of hair was decorated with a garland of *mallikā* flowers; *bṛhat*—very, very big; *nitamba-stana*—by her hips and firm breasts; *kṛcchra-madhyamām*—whose slim waist was overburdened; *su-vāsasam*—nicely painted or very attractively dressed; *kalpita-karṇa-bhūṣaṇa*—of the earrings arranged on her ears; *tviṣā*—by the brilliance; *ullasat*—very attractive; *kuntala-maṇḍita-ānanām*—whose beautiful face was surrounded by black hair; *valgu-smita-apāṅga-visarga-vīkṣitaiḥ*—by her casting her smiling glance on everyone very attractively; *manaḥ harantīm*—everyone's attention was attracted (by her); *vanitām*—an especially attractive woman; *vraja-okasām*—of the inhabitants of Gokula; *amaṁsata*—thought; *ambhoja*—holding a lotus flower; *kareṇa*—with her hand; *rūpiṇīm*—very beautiful; *gopyaḥ*—the *gopī* inhabitants of Gokula; *śriyam*—the goddess of fortune; *draṣṭum*—to see; *iva*—as if; *āgatām*—had come; *patim*—her husband.

TRANSLATION

Her hips were full, her breasts were large and firm, seeming to overburden her slim waist, and she was dressed very nicely. Her

hair, adorned with a garland of mallikā flowers, was scattered about her beautiful face. Her earrings were brilliant, and as she smiled very attractively, glancing upon everyone, her beauty drew the attention of all the inhabitants of Vraja, especially the men. When the gopīs saw her, they thought that the beautiful goddess of fortune, holding a lotus flower in her hand, had come to see her husband, Kṛṣṇa.

TEXT 7

बालग्रहस्तत्र विचिन्वती शिशून्
यदृच्छया नन्दगृहेऽसदन्तकम् ।
बालं प्रतिच्छन्ननिजोरुतेजसं
ददर्श तल्पेऽग्निमिवाहितं भसि ॥ ७ ॥

bāla-grahas tatra vicinvatī śiśūn
yadṛcchayā nanda-gṛhe 'sad-antakam
bālaṁ praticchanna-nijoru-tejasaṁ
dadarśa talpe 'gnim ivāhitaṁ bhasi

bāla-grahaḥ—the witch, whose business was to kill small babies; *tatra*—standing there; *vicinvatī*—thinking of, searching for; *śiśūn*—children; *yadṛcchayā*—independently; *nanda-gṛhe*—in the house of Nanda Mahārāja; *asat-antakam*—who could kill all demons; *bālam*—the child; *praticchanna*—covered; *nija-uru-tejasam*—whose unlimited power; *dadarśa*—she saw; *talpe*—(lying) on the bed; *agnim*—fire; *iva*—just like; *āhitam*—covered; *bhasi*—within ashes.

TRANSLATION

While searching for small children, Pūtanā, whose business was to kill them, entered the house of Nanda Mahārāja unobstructed, having been sent by the superior potency of the Lord. Without asking anyone's permission, she entered Nanda Mahārāja's room, where she saw the child sleeping in bed, His unlimited power covered like a powerful fire covered by ashes. She could understand that this child was not ordinary, but was meant to kill all demons.

PURPORT

Demons are always busy creating disturbances and killing. But the child lying on the bed in the house of Nanda Mahārāja was meant to kill many demons.

TEXT 8

विबुध्य तां बालकमारिकाग्रहं
चराचरात्मा स निमीलितेक्षणः ।
अनन्तमारोपयदङ्कमन्तकं
यथोरगं सुप्तमबुद्धिरज्जुधीः ॥ ८ ॥

vibudhya tāṁ bālaka-mārikā-grahaṁ
carācarātmā sa nimīlitekṣaṇaḥ
anantam āropayad aṅkam antakaṁ
yathoragaṁ suptam abuddhi-rajju-dhīḥ

vibudhya—understanding; *tām*—her (Pūtanā); *bālaka-mārikā-graham*—a witch very expert in killing small babies; *cara-acara-ātmā*—Kṛṣṇa, the all-pervading Supersoul; *saḥ*—He; *nimīlita-īkṣaṇaḥ*—closed His eyes; *anantam*—the Unlimited; *āropayat*—she placed; *aṅkam*—on her lap; *antakam*—for her own annihilation; *yathā*—as; *uragam*—a snake; *suptam*—while sleeping; *abuddhi*—a person who has no intelligence; *rajju-dhīḥ*—one who thinks a snake to be a rope.

TRANSLATION

Lord Śrī Kṛṣṇa, the all-pervading Supersoul, lying on the bed, understood that Pūtanā, a witch who was expert in killing small children, had come to kill Him. Therefore, as if afraid of her, Kṛṣṇa closed His eyes. Thus Pūtanā took upon her lap Him who was to be her own annihilation, just as an unintelligent person places a sleeping snake on his lap, thinking the snake to be a rope.

PURPORT

In this verse there are two perplexities. When Kṛṣṇa saw that Pūtanā had come to kill Him, He thought that since this woman was present with motherly affection, although artificial, He had to offer her a benediction. Therefore He looked at her with a little perplexity and then closed His eyes again. Pūtanā Rākṣasī also was perplexed. She was not intelligent enough to understand that she was taking a sleeping snake on her lap; she thought the snake to be an ordinary rope. The two words *antakam* and *anantam* are contradictory. Because of not being intelligent, Pūtanā thought that she could kill her *antakam*, the source of her annihilation; but because He is *ananta*, unlimited, no one can kill Him.

TEXT 9

तां तीक्ष्णचित्तामतिवामचेष्टितां
वीक्ष्यान्तरा कोषपरिच्छदासिवत् ।
वरस्त्रियं तत्प्रभया च धर्षिते
निरीक्ष्यमाणे जननी ह्यतिष्ठताम् ॥ ९ ॥

tāṁ tīkṣṇa-cittām ativāma-ceṣṭitāṁ
vīkṣyāntarā koṣa-paricchadāsivat
vara-striyaṁ tat-prabhayā ca dharṣite
nirīkṣyamāṇe jananī hy atiṣṭhatām

tām—that (Pūtanā Rākṣasī); *tīkṣṇa-cittām*—having a very fierce heart for killing the child; *ati-vāma-ceṣṭitām*—although she was trying to treat the child better than a mother; *vīkṣya antarā*—seeing her within the room; *koṣa-paricchada-asi-vat*—like a sharp sword within a soft sheath; *vara-striyam*—the very beautiful woman; *tat-prabhayā*—by her influence; *ca*—also; *dharṣite*—being overwhelmed; *nirīkṣyamāṇe*—were seeing; *jananī*—the two mothers; *hi*—indeed; *atiṣṭhatām*—they remained silent, without prohibiting.

TRANSLATION

Pūtanā Rākṣasī's heart was fierce and cruel, but she looked like a very affectionate mother. Thus she resembled a sharp sword in a soft sheath. Although seeing her within the room, Yaśodā and Rohiṇī, overwhelmed by her beauty, did not stop her, but remained silent because she treated the child like a mother.

PURPORT

Although Pūtanā was an outsider and although she personified fierce death because the determination within her heart was to kill the child, when she directly came and placed the child on her lap to offer the child her breast to suck, the mothers were so captivated by her beauty that they did not prohibit her. Sometimes a beautiful woman is dangerous because everyone, being captivated by external beauty (*māyā-mohita*), is unable to understand what is in her mind. Those who are captivated by the beauty of the external energy are called *māyā-mohita. Mohitaṁ nābhijānāti mām ebhyaḥ param avyayam* (Bg. 7.13). *Na te viduḥ svārtha-gatiṁ hi viṣṇuṁ durāśayā ye bahir-artha-māninaḥ* (*Bhāg.* 7.5.31). Here, of course, the two mothers Rohiṇī and Yaśodā were not *māyā-mohita*, deluded by the external energy, but to develop the pastimes of the Lord, they were captivated by *yogamāyā.* Such *māyā-moha* is the action of *yogamāyā.*

TEXT 10

तस्मिन् स्तनं दुर्जरवीर्यमुल्बणं
घोराङ्कमादाय शिशोर्ददावथ ।
गाढं कराभ्यां भगवान् प्रपीड्य तत्-
प्राणैः समं रोषसमन्वितोऽपिबत् ॥१०॥

tasmin stanaṁ durjara-vīryam ulbaṇaṁ
ghorāṅkam ādāya śiśor dadāv atha
gāḍhaṁ karābhyāṁ bhagavān prapīḍya tat-
prāṇaiḥ samaṁ roṣa-samanvito 'pibat

tasmin—in that very spot; *stanam*—the breast; *durjara-vīryam*—a very powerful weapon mixed with poison; *ulbaṇam*—which was fierce; *ghorā*—the most ferocious Pūtanā; *aṅkam*—on her lap; *ādāya*—placing; *śiśoḥ*—in the mouth of the child; *dadau*—pushed; *atha*—thereupon; *gāḍham*—very hard; *karābhyām*—with both hands; *bhagavān*—the Supreme Personality of Godhead; *prapīḍya*—giving her great pain; *tat-prāṇaiḥ*—her life; *samam*—along with; *roṣa-samanvitaḥ*—being very angry at her; *apibat*—sucked the breast.

TRANSLATION

On that very spot, the fiercely dangerous Rākṣasī took Kṛṣṇa on her lap and pushed her breast into His mouth. The nipple of her breast was smeared with a dangerous, immediately effective poison, but the Supreme Personality of Godhead, Kṛṣṇa, becoming very angry at her, took hold of her breast, squeezed it very hard with both hands, and sucked out both the poison and her life.

PURPORT

Lord Kṛṣṇa was not angry at Pūtanā for His own sake. Rather, He was angry because the Rākṣasī had killed so many small children in Vrajabhūmi. Therefore He decided that she should be punished by having to forfeit her life.

TEXT 11

सा मुञ्च मुञ्चालमिति प्रभाषिणी
निष्पीड्यमानाखिलजीवमर्मणि ।
विवृत्य नेत्रे चरणौ भुजौ मुहुः
प्रस्विन्नगात्रा क्षिपती रुरोद ह ॥११॥

sā muñca muñcālam iti prabhāṣiṇī
niṣpīḍyamānākhila-jīva-marmaṇi
vivṛtya netre caraṇau bhujau muhuḥ
prasvinna-gātrā kṣipatī ruroda ha

sā—she (Pūtanā Rākṣasī); *muñca*—give up; *muñca*—give up; *alam*—suck my breast no longer; *iti*—thus; *prabhāṣiṇī*—crying; *niṣpīḍyamānā*—being pressed severely; *akhila-jīva-marmaṇi*—in every center of her vitality; *vivṛtya*—opening wide; *netre*—her two eyes; *caraṇau*—two legs; *bhujau*—two hands; *muhuḥ*—again and again; *prasvinna-gātrā*—with her body perspiring; *kṣipatī*—throwing; *ruroda*—cried severely; *ha*—indeed.

TRANSLATION

Unbearably pressed in every vital point, the demon Pūtanā began to cry, "Please leave me, leave me! Suck my breast no

longer!" Perspiring, her eyes wide open and her arms and legs flailing, she cried very loudly again and again.

PURPORT

The Rākṣasī was severely punished by Kṛṣṇa. She threw her arms and legs about, and Kṛṣṇa also began to kick her with His legs to punish her properly for her mischievous activities.

TEXT 12

तस्याः स्वनेनातिगभीररंहसा
साद्रिर्मही द्यौश्च चचाल सग्रहा ।
रसा दिशश्च प्रतिनेदिरे जनाः
पेतुः क्षितौ वज्रनिपातशङ्कया ॥१२॥

tasyāḥ svanenātigabhīra-raṁhasā
sādrir mahī dyauś ca cacāla sa-grahā
rasā diśaś ca pratinedire janāḥ
petuḥ kṣitau vajra-nipāta-śaṅkayā

tasyāḥ—of the great Rākṣasī Pūtanā; *svanena*—by the vibration of the sound; *ati*—very; *gabhīra*—deep; *raṁhasā*—forceful; *sa-adriḥ*—with the mountains; *mahī*—the surface of the world; *dyauḥ ca*—and outer space; *cacāla*—trembled; *sa-grahā*—with the stars; *rasā*—below the planet earth; *diśaḥ ca*—and all directions; *pratinedire*—vibrated; *janāḥ*—people in general; *petuḥ*—fell down; *kṣitau*—on the surface of the world; *vajra-nipāta-śaṅkayā*—by suspecting that thunderbolts were falling.

TRANSLATION

As Pūtanā screamed loudly and forcefully, the earth with its mountains, and outer space with its planets, trembled. The lower planets and all directions vibrated, and people fell down, fearing that thunderbolts were falling upon them.

PURPORT

Śrīla Viśvanātha Cakravartī Ṭhākura remarks that in this verse the word *rasā* refers to the planetary systems below the earth, such as Rasātala, Atala, Vitala, Sutala and Talātala.

TEXT 13

निशाचरीत्थं व्यथितस्तना व्यसु-
व्यादाय केशांश्चरणौ भुजावपि ।
प्रसार्य गोष्ठे निजरूपमास्थिता
वज्राहतो वृत्र इवापतन्नृप ॥१३॥

niśā-carītthaṁ vyathita-stanā vyasur
vyādāya keśāṁś caraṇau bhujāv api
prasārya goṣṭhe nija-rūpam āsthitā
vajrāhato vṛtra ivāpatan nṛpa

niśā-carī—the Rākṣasī; *ittham*—in this way; *vyathita-stanā*—being severely aggrieved because of pressure on her breast; *vyasuḥ*—lost her life; *vyādāya*—opening her mouth wide; *keśān*—bunch of hairs; *caraṇau*—her two legs; *bhujau*—her two hands; *api*—also; *prasārya*—expanding; *goṣṭhe*—in the pasturing ground; *nija-rūpam āsthitā*—remained in her original demoniac form; *vajra-āhataḥ*—killed by the thunderbolt of Indra; *vṛtraḥ*—Vṛtrāsura; *iva*—as if; *apatat*—fell down; *nṛpa*—O King.

TRANSLATION

In this way the demon Pūtanā, very much aggrieved because her breast was being attacked by Kṛṣṇa, lost her life. O King Parīkṣit, opening her mouth wide and spreading her arms, legs and hair, she fell down in the pasturing ground in her original form as a Rākṣasī, as Vṛtrāsura had fallen when killed by the thunderbolt of Indra.

PURPORT

Pūtanā was a great Rākṣasī who knew the art of covering her original form by mystic power, but when she was killed her mystic power could not hide her, and she appeared in her original form.

TEXT 14

पतमानोऽपि तद्देहस्त्रिगव्यूत्यन्तरद्रुमान् ।
चूर्णयामास राजेन्द्र महदासीत्तदद्भुतम् ॥१४॥

patamāno 'pi tad-dehas
tri-gavyūty-antara-drumān
cūrṇayām āsa rājendra
mahad āsīt tad adbhutam

patamānaḥ api—even while falling down; *tat-dehaḥ*—her gigantic body; *tri-gavyūti-antara*—within a limit of twelve miles; *drumān*—all kinds of trees; *cūrṇayām āsa*—smashed; *rājendra*—O King Parīkṣit; *mahat āsīt*—was quite gigantic; *tat*—that body; *adbhutam*—and very, very wonderful.

TRANSLATION

O King Parīkṣit, when the gigantic body of Pūtanā fell to the ground, it smashed all the trees within a limit of twelve miles. Appearing in a gigantic body, she was certainly extraordinary.

PURPORT

Because of the grievous hurt imposed upon her by Kṛṣṇa's sucking her breast, Pūtanā, while dying, not only left the room but abandoned the village and fell down in the pasturing ground in her gigantic body.

TEXTS 15–17

ईषामात्रोग्रदंष्ट्रास्यं गिरिकन्दरनासिकम् ।
गण्डशैलस्तनं रौद्रं प्रकीर्णारुणमूर्धजम् ॥१५॥
अन्धकूपगभीराक्षं पुलिनारोहभीषणम् ।
बद्धसेतुभुजोर्वङ्घ्रि शून्यतोयह्रदोदरम् ॥१६॥
सन्तत्रसुः स्म तद् वीक्ष्य गोपा गोप्यः कलेवरम् ।
पूर्वं तु तन्निःस्वनितभिन्नहृत्कर्णमस्तकाः ॥१७॥

īṣā-mātrogra-daṁṣṭrāsyaṁ
giri-kandara-nāsikam
gaṇḍa-śaila-stanaṁ raudraṁ
prakīrṇāruṇa-mūrdhajam

andha-kūpa-gabhīrākṣaṁ
pulināroha-bhīṣaṇam
baddha-setu-bhujorv-aṅghri
śūnya-toya-hradodaram

santatrasuḥ sma tad vīkṣya
gopā gopyaḥ kalevaram
pūrvaṁ tu tan-niḥsvanita-
bhinna-hṛt-karṇa-mastakāḥ

īṣā-mātra—like the front of a plow; *ugra*—fierce; *daṁṣṭra*—the teeth; *āsyam*—having a mouth in which; *giri-kandara*—like mountain caves; *nāsikam*—the nostrils of whom; *gaṇḍa-śaila*—like big slabs of stone; *stanam*—the breasts of whom; *raudram*—very fierce; *prakīrṇa*—scattered; *aruṇa-mūrdha-jam*—whose hair was the color of copper; *andha-kūpa*—like blind wells; *gabhīra*—deep; *akṣam*—eye sockets; *pulina-āroha-bhīṣaṇam*—whose thighs were fearful like the banks of a river; *baddha-setu-bhuja-uru-aṅghri*—whose arms, thighs and feet were strongly built bridges; *śūnya-toya-hrada-udaram*—whose abdomen was like a lake without water; *santatrasuḥ sma*—became frightened; *tat*—that; *vīkṣya*—seeing; *gopāḥ*—the cowherd men; *gopyaḥ*—and the cowherd women; *kalevaram*—such a gigantic body; *pūrvam tu*—before that; *tat-niḥsvanita*—because of her loud vibration; *bhinna*—were shocked; *hṛt*—whose hearts; *karṇa*—ears; *mastakāḥ*—and heads.

TRANSLATION

The Rākṣasī's mouth was full of teeth, each resembling the front of a plow, her nostrils were deep like mountain caves, and her breasts resembled big slabs of stone fallen from a hill. Her scattered hair was the color of copper. The sockets of her eyes

appeared like deep blind wells, her fearful thighs resembled the banks of a river, her arms, legs and feet seemed like big bridges, and her abdomen appeared like a dried-up lake. The hearts, ears and heads of the cowherd men and women were already shocked by the Rākṣasī's screaming, and when they saw the fierce wonder of her body, they were even more frightened.

TEXT 18

बालं च तस्या उरसि क्रीडन्तमकुतोभयम् ।
गोप्यस्तूर्णं समभ्येत्य जगृहुर्जातसम्भ्रमाः ॥१८॥

bālaṁ ca tasyā urasi
krīḍantam akutobhayam
gopyas tūrṇaṁ samabhyetya
jagṛhur jāta-sambhramāḥ

bālam ca—the child also; *tasyāḥ*—of that (Rākṣasī Pūtanā); *urasi*—on the upper portion of the breast; *krīḍantam*—engaged in playing; *akutobhayam*—without fear; *gopyaḥ*—all the cowherd women; *tūrṇam*—immediately; *samabhyetya*—coming near; *jagṛhuḥ*—picked up; *jāta-sambhramāḥ*—with the same affection and respect they always maintained.

TRANSLATION

Without fear, the child Kṛṣṇa was playing on the upper portion of Pūtanā Rākṣasī's breast, and when the gopīs saw the child's wonderful activities, they immediately came forward with great jubilation and picked Him up.

PURPORT

Here is the Supreme Personality of Godhead—Kṛṣṇa. Although the Rākṣasī Pūtanā could increase or decrease her bodily size by her mystic abilities and thus gain proportionate power, the Supreme Personality of Godhead is equally powerful in any transcendental form. Kṛṣṇa is the real Personality of Godhead because whether as a child or as a grown-up young man, He is the same person. He does not need to become powerful by meditation or any other external endeavor. Therefore when the greatly powerful Pūtanā expanded her body, Kṛṣṇa remained the same small child and fearlessly played on the upper portion of her breast. *Ṣaḍ-aiśvarya-pūrṇa.* Bhagavān, the Supreme Personality of Godhead, is always full in all potencies, regardless of whether He is present in this form or that. His potencies are always full. *Parāsya śaktir vividhaiva śrūyate.* He can display all potencies under any circumstances.

TEXT 19

यशोदारोहिणीभ्यां ताः समं बालस्य सर्वतः ।
रक्षां विदधिरे सम्यग्गोपुच्छभ्रमणादिभिः ॥१९॥

yaśodā-rohiṇībhyāṁ tāḥ
samaṁ bālasya sarvataḥ
rakṣāṁ vidadhire samyag
go-puccha-bhramaṇādibhiḥ

yaśodā-rohiṇībhyām—with mother Yaśodā and mother Rohiṇī, who principally took charge of the child; *tāḥ*—the other *gopīs; samam*—equally as important as Yaśodā and Rohiṇī; *bālasya*—of the child; *sarvataḥ*—from all dangers; *rakṣām*—protection; *vidadhire*—executed; *samyak*—completely; *go-puccha-bhramaṇa-ādibhiḥ*—by waving around the switch of a cow.

TRANSLATION

Thereafter, mother Yaśodā and Rohiṇī, along with the other elderly gopīs, waved about the switch of a cow to give full protection to the child Śrī Kṛṣṇa.

PURPORT

When Kṛṣṇa was saved from such a great danger, mother Yaśodā and Rohiṇī were principally concerned, and the other elderly *gopīs*, who were almost equally concerned, followed the activities of mother Yaśodā and Rohiṇī. Here we find that in household affairs, ladies could take charge of protecting a child simply by taking help from the cow. As described here, they knew how to wave about the switch of a cow so as to protect the child from all types of danger. There are so many facilities afforded by cow protection, but people have forgotten these arts. The importance of protecting cows is therefore stressed by Kṛṣṇa in *Bhagavad-gītā* (*kṛṣi-go-rakṣya-vāṇijyaṁ vaiśya-karma svabhāvajam*). Even now in the Indian villages surrounding Vṛndāvana, the villagers live happily simply by giving protection to the cow. They keep cow dung very carefully and dry it to use as fuel. They keep a sufficient stock of grains, and because of giving protection to the cows, they have sufficient milk and milk products to solve all economic problems. Simply by giving protection to the cow, the villagers live so peacefully. Even the urine and stool of cows have medicinal value.

TEXT 20

गोमूत्रेण स्नापयित्वा पुनर्गोरजसार्भकम् ।
रक्षां चक्रुश्च शकृता द्वादशाङ्गेषु नामभिः ॥२०॥

go-mūtreṇa snāpayitvā
punar go-rajasārbhakam
rakṣāṁ cakruś ca śakṛtā
dvādaśāṅgeṣu nāmabhiḥ

go-mūtreṇa—with the urine of the cows; *snāpayitvā*—after thoroughly washing; *punaḥ*—again; *go-rajasā*—with the dust floating because of the movements of the cows; *arbhakam*—unto the child; *rakṣām*—protection; *cakruḥ*—executed; *ca*—also; *śakṛtā*—with the cow dung; *dvādaśa-aṅgeṣu*—in twelve places (*dvādaśa-tilaka*); *nāmabhiḥ*—by imprinting the holy names of the Lord.

TRANSLATION

The child was thoroughly washed with cow urine and then smeared with the dust raised by the movements of the cows. Then different names of the Lord were applied with cow dung on twelve different parts of His body, beginning with the forehead, as done in applying tilaka. In this way, the child was given protection.

TEXT 21

गोप्यः संस्पृष्टसलिला अङ्गेषु करयोः पृथक् ।
न्यस्यात्मन्यथ बालस्य बीजन्यासमकुर्वत ॥२१॥

gopyaḥ saṁspṛṣṭa-salilā
aṅgeṣu karayoḥ pṛthak
nyasyātmany atha bālasya
bīja-nyāsam akurvata

gopyaḥ—the *gopīs; saṁspṛṣṭa-salilāḥ*—touching a cup of water and drinking; *aṅgeṣu*—on their bodies; *karayoḥ*—on their two hands; *pṛthak*—separately; *nyasya*—after placing the letters of the *mantra; ātmani*—on their own; *atha*—then; *bālasya*—of the child; *bīja-nyāsam*—the process of *mantra-nyāsa; akurvata*—executed.

TRANSLATION

The gopīs first executed the process of ācamana, drinking a sip of water from the right hand. They purified their bodies and hands with the nyāsa-mantra and then applied the same mantra upon the body of the child.

PURPORT

Nyāsa-mantra includes *ācamana,* or first drinking a sip of water kept in the right hand. There are different *viṣṇu-mantras* to purify the body. The *gopīs,* and in fact any householders, knew the process for being purified by chanting Vedic hymns. The *gopīs* executed this process first to purify themselves and then to purify the child Kṛṣṇa. One executes the process of *aṅga-nyāsa* and *kara-nyāsa* simply by drinking a little sip of water and chanting the *mantra.* The *mantra* is preceded with the first letter of the name, followed by *anusvāra* and the word *namaḥ: aṁ namo 'jas tavāṅghrī avyāt, maṁ mano maṇimāṁs tava jānunī avyāt,* and so on. By losing Indian culture, Indian householders have forgotten how to execute the *aṅga-nyāsa* and are simply busy in sense gratification, without any advanced knowledge of human civilization.

TEXTS 22–23

अव्याद्जोऽङ्घ्रि मणिमांस्तव जान्वथोरू
यज्ञोऽच्युतः कटितटं जठरं हयास्यः ।
हृत् केशवस्त्वदुर ईश इनस्तु कण्ठं
विष्णुर्भुजं मुखमुरुक्रम ईश्वरः कम् ॥२२॥
चक्रयग्रतः सहगदो हरिरस्तु पश्चात्
त्वत्पार्श्वयोर्धनुरसी मधुहाजनश्च ।
कोणेषु शङ्ख उरुगाय उपर्युपेन्द्र-
स्तार्क्ष्यः क्षितौ हलधरः पुरुषः समन्तात् ॥२३॥

avyād ajo 'ṅghri maṇimāṁs tava jānv athorū
yajño 'cyutaḥ kaṭi-taṭaṁ jaṭharaṁ hayāsyaḥ
hṛt keśavas tvad-ura īśa inas tu kaṇṭhaṁ
viṣṇur bhujaṁ mukham urukrama īśvaraḥ kam

cakry agrataḥ saha-gado harir astu paścāt
tvat-pārśvayor dhanur-asī madhu-hājanaś ca
koṇeṣu śaṅkha urugāya upary upendras
tārkṣyaḥ kṣitau haladharaḥ puruṣaḥ samantāt

avyāt—may protect; *ajaḥ*—Lord Aja; *aṅghri*—legs; *maṇimān*—Lord Maṇimān; *tava*—Your; *jānu*—knees; *atha*—thereafter; *urū*—thighs; *yajñaḥ*—Lord Yajña; *acyutaḥ*—Lord Acyuta; *kaṭi-taṭam*—the upper part of the waist; *jaṭharam*—abdomen; *hayāsyaḥ*—Lord Hayagrīva; *hṛt*—the heart; *keśavaḥ*—Lord Keśava; *tvat*—Your; *uraḥ*—chest; *īśaḥ*—the supreme controller, Lord Īśa; *inaḥ*—Sūrya, the sun-god; *tu*—but; *kaṇṭham*—neck; *viṣṇuḥ*—Lord Viṣṇu; *bhujam*—arms; *mukham*—the mouth; *urukramaḥ*—Lord Urukrama; *īśvaraḥ*—Lord Īśvara; *kam*—head; *cakrī*—the carrier of the disc; *agrataḥ*—in front; *saha-gadaḥ*—the carrier of the club; *hariḥ*—Lord Hari; *astu*—may He remain; *paścāt*—on the back; *tvat-pārśvayoḥ*—on both sides; *dhanuḥ-asī*—the carrier of the bow and the sword; *madhu-hā*—the killer of the demon Madhu; *ajanaḥ*—Lord Viṣṇu; *ca*—and; *koṇeṣu*—in the corners;

śaṅkhaḥ—the carrier of the conchshell; *urugāyaḥ*—who is well worshiped; *upari*—above; *upendraḥ*—Lord Upendra; *tārkṣyaḥ*—Garuḍa; *kṣitau*—on the surface; *haladharaḥ*—Lord Haladhara; *puruṣaḥ*—the Supreme Person; *samantāt*—on all sides.

TRANSLATION

[Śukadeva Gosvāmī informed Mahārāja Parīkṣit that the gopīs, following the proper system, protected Kṛṣṇa, their child, with this mantra.] May Aja protect Your legs, may Maṇimān protect Your knees, Yajña Your thighs, Acyuta the upper part of Your waist, and Hayagrīva Your abdomen. May Keśava protect Your heart, Īśa Your chest, the sun-god Your neck, Viṣṇu Your arms, Urukrama Your face, and Īśvara Your head. May Cakrī protect You from the front; may Śrī Hari, Gadādharī, the carrier of the club, protect You from the back; and may the carrier of the bow, who is known as the enemy of Madhu, and Lord Ajana, the carrier of the sword, protect Your two sides. May Lord Urugāya, the carrier of the conchshell, protect You from all corners; may Upendra protect You from above; may Garuḍa protect You on the ground; and may Lord Haladhara, the Supreme Person, protect You on all sides.

PURPORT

Even in the houses of the cultivators, who were not very advanced in the modern ways of civilization, the ladies used to know how to chant *mantras* to give protection to children with the help of cow dung and cow urine. This was a simple and practical way to give the greatest protection from the greatest dangers. People should know how to do this, for this is a part of Vedic civilization.

TEXT 24

इन्द्रियाणि हृषीकेशः प्राणान् नारायणोऽवतु ।
श्वेतद्वीपपतिश्चित्तं मनो योगेश्वरोऽवतु ॥२४॥

indriyāṇi hṛṣīkeśaḥ
prāṇān nārāyaṇo 'vatu

śvetadvīpa-patiś cittaṁ
mano yogeśvaro 'vatu

indriyāṇi—all the senses; *hṛṣīkeśaḥ*—Lord Hṛṣīkeśa, the proprietor of all the senses; *prāṇān*—all kinds of life air; *nārāyaṇaḥ*—Lord Nārāyaṇa; *avatu*—may He give protection; *śvetadvīpa-patiḥ*—the master of Śvetadvīpa, Viṣṇu; *cittam*—the core of the heart; *manaḥ*—the mind; *yogeśvaraḥ*—Lord Yogeśvara; *avatu*—may He give protection.

TRANSLATION

May Hṛṣīkeśa protect Your senses, and Nārāyaṇa Your life air. May the master of Śvetadvīpa protect the core of Your heart, and may Lord Yogeśvara protect Your mind.

TEXTS 25–26

पृश्निगर्भस्तु ते बुद्धिमात्मानं भगवान् परः ।
क्रीडन्तं पातु गोविन्दः शयानं पातु माधवः ॥२५॥
व्रजन्तमव्याद् वैकुण्ठ आसीनं त्वां श्रियः पतिः।
भुञ्जानं यज्ञभुक् पातु सर्वग्रहभयङ्करः ॥२६॥

pṛśnigarbhas tu te buddhim
ātmānaṁ bhagavān paraḥ
krīḍantaṁ pātu govindaḥ
śayānaṁ pātu mādhavaḥ

vrajantam avyād vaikuṇṭha
āsīnaṁ tvāṁ śriyaḥ patiḥ
bhuñjānaṁ yajñabhuk pātu
sarva-graha-bhayaṅkaraḥ

pṛśnigarbhaḥ—Lord Pṛśnigarbha; *tu*—indeed; *te*—Your; *buddhim*—intelligence; *ātmānam*—Your soul; *bhagavān*—the Supreme Personality of Godhead; *paraḥ*—transcendental; *krīḍantam*—while playing; *pātu*—may He protect; *govindaḥ*—Lord Govinda; *śayānam*—while sleeping; *pātu*—may He protect; *mādhavaḥ*—Lord Mādhava;

vrajantam—while walking; *avyāt*—may He protect; *vaikuṇṭhaḥ*—Lord Vaikuṇṭha; *āsīnam*—while sitting down; *tvām*—unto You; *śriyaḥ patiḥ*—Nārāyaṇa, the husband of the goddess of fortune (may protect); *bhuñjānam*—while enjoying life; *yajñabhuk*—Yajñabhuk; *pātu*—may He protect; *sarva-graha-bhayam-karaḥ*—who is fearful to all evil planets.

TRANSLATION

May Lord Pṛśnigarbha protect Your intelligence, and the Supreme Personality of Godhead Your soul. While You are playing, may Govinda protect You, and while You are sleeping may Mādhava protect You. May Lord Vaikuṇṭha protect You while You are walking, and may Lord Nārāyaṇa, the husband of the goddess of fortune, protect You while You are sitting. Similarly, may Lord Yajñabhuk, the fearful enemy of all evil planets, always protect You while You enjoy life.

TEXTS 27–29

डाकिन्यो यातुधान्यश्च कुष्माण्डा येऽर्भकग्रहाः ।
भूतप्रेतपिशाचाश्च यक्षरक्षोविनायकाः ॥२७॥
कोटरा रेवती ज्येष्ठा पूतना मातृकादयः ।
उन्मादा ये ह्यपस्मारा देहप्राणेन्द्रियद्रुहः ॥२८॥
स्वप्नदृष्टा महोत्पाता वृद्धा बालग्रहाश्च ये ।
सर्वे नश्यन्तु ते विष्णोर्नामग्रहणभीरवः ॥२९॥

ḍākinyo yātudhānyaś ca
kuṣmāṇḍā ye 'rbhaka-grahāḥ
bhūta-preta-piśācāś ca
yakṣa-rakṣo-vināyakāḥ

koṭarā revatī jyeṣṭhā
pūtanā mātṛkādayaḥ
unmādā ye hy apasmārā
deha-prāṇendriya-druhaḥ

svapna-dṛṣṭā mahotpātā
vṛddhā bāla-grahāś ca ye
sarve naśyantu te viṣṇor
nāma-grahaṇa-bhīravaḥ

ḍākinyaḥ yātudhānyaḥ ca kuṣmāṇḍāḥ—witches and devils, enemies of children; *ye*—those who are; *arbhaka-grahāḥ*—like evil stars for children; *bhūta*—evil spirits; *preta*—evil hobgoblins; *piśācāḥ*—similar bad spirits; *ca*—also; *yakṣa*—the living entities known as Yakṣas; *rakṣaḥ*—those known as Rākṣasas; *vināyakāḥ*—those by the name Vināyaka; *koṭarā*—by the name Koṭarā; *revatī*—by the name Revatī; *jyeṣṭhā*—by the name Jyeṣṭhā; *pūtanā*—by the name Pūtanā; *mātṛkā-ādayaḥ*—and evil women like Mātṛkā; *unmādāḥ*—those who cause madness; *ye*—which others; *hi*—indeed; *apasmārāḥ*—causing loss of memory; *deha-prāṇa-indriya*—to the body, life air and senses; *druhaḥ*—give trouble; *svapna-dṛṣṭāḥ*—the evil spirits that cause bad dreams; *mahā-utpātāḥ*—those causing great disturbances; *vṛddhāḥ*—the most experienced; *bāla-grahāḥ ca*—and those attacking children; *ye*—who; *sarve*—all of them; *naśyantu*—let be vanquished; *te*—those; *viṣṇoḥ*—of Lord Viṣṇu; *nāma-grahaṇa*—by the chanting of the name; *bhīravaḥ*—become afraid.

TRANSLATION

The evil witches known as Ḍākinīs, Yātudhānīs and Kuṣmāṇḍas are the greatest enemies of children, and the evil spirits like Bhūtas, Pretas, Piśācas, Yakṣas, Rākṣasas and Vināyakas, as well as witches like Koṭarā, Revatī, Jyeṣṭhā, Pūtanā and Mātṛkā, are always ready to give trouble to the body, the life air and the senses, causing loss of memory, madness and bad dreams. Like the most experienced evil stars, they all create great disturbances, especially for children, but one can vanquish them simply by uttering Lord Viṣṇu's name, for when Lord Viṣṇu's name resounds, all of them become afraid and go away.

PURPORT

As stated in the *Brahma-saṁhitā* (5.33):

advaitam acyutam anādim ananta-rūpam
ādyaṁ purāṇa-puruṣaṁ nava-yauvanaṁ ca

vedeṣu durlabham adurlabham ātma-bhaktau
govindam ādi-puruṣaṁ tam ahaṁ bhajāmi

"I worship the Supreme Personality of Godhead, Govinda, who is the original person—nondual, infallible, and without beginning. Although He expands into unlimited forms, He is still the original, and although He is the oldest person, He always appears as a fresh youth. Such eternal, blissful and all-knowing forms of the Lord cannot be understood by the academic wisdom of the *Vedas*, but they are always manifest to pure, unalloyed devotees."

While decorating the body with *tilaka*, we give protection to the body by chanting twelve names of Viṣṇu. Although Govinda, or Lord Viṣṇu, is one, He has different names and forms with which to act differently. But if one cannot remember all the names at one time, one may simply chant, "Lord Viṣṇu, Lord Viṣṇu, Lord Viṣṇu," and always think of Lord Viṣṇu. *Viṣṇor ārādhanaṁ param:* this is the highest form of worship. If one remembers Viṣṇu always, even though one is disturbed by many bad elements, one can be protected without a doubt. The *Āyurveda-śāstra* recommends, *auṣadhi cintayet viṣṇum:* even while taking medicine, one should remember Viṣṇu, because the medicine is not all and all and Lord Viṣṇu is the real protector. The material world is full of danger (*padaṁ padaṁ yad vipadām*). Therefore one must become a Vaiṣṇava and think of Viṣṇu constantly. This is made easier by the chanting of the Hare Kṛṣṇa *mahā-mantra.* Therefore Śrī Caitanya Mahāprabhu has recommended, *kīrtanīyaḥ sadā hariḥ, paraṁ vijayate śrī-kṛṣṇa-saṅkīrtanam,* and *kīrtanād eva kṛṣṇasya mukta-saṅgaḥ paraṁ vrajet.*

TEXT 30

श्रीशुक उवाच
इति प्रणयबद्धाभिर्गोपीभिः कृतरक्षणम् ।
पाययित्वा स्तनं माता संन्यवेशयदात्मजम् ॥३०॥

śrī-śuka uvāca
iti praṇaya-baddhābhir
gopībhiḥ kṛta-rakṣaṇam
pāyayitvā stanaṁ mātā
sannyaveśayad ātmajam

śrī-śukaḥ uvāca—Śrī Śukadeva Gosvāmī said; *iti*—in this way; *praṇaya-baddhābhiḥ*—who were bound with maternal affection; *gopībhiḥ*—by the elderly *gopīs,* headed by mother Yaśodā; *kṛta-rakṣaṇam*—all measures were taken to protect the child; *pāyayitvā*—and after that, feeding the child; *stanam*—the nipple; *mātā*—mother Yaśodā; *sannyaveśayat*—made to lie down on the bed; *ātmajam*—her son.

TRANSLATION

Śrīla Śukadeva Gosvāmī continued: All the gopīs, headed by mother Yaśodā, were bound by maternal affection. After they thus chanted mantras to protect the child, mother Yaśodā gave the child the nipple of her breast to suck and then got Him to lie down on His bed.

PURPORT

When a baby drinks milk from the breast of his mother, this is a good sign of health. So the elderly *gopīs* were not satisfied with chanting *mantras* to give protection to Kṛṣṇa; they also tested whether their child's health was in order. When the child sucked the breast, this confirmed that He was healthy, and when the *gopīs* were fully satisfied, they had the child lie down on His bed.

TEXT 31

तावन्नन्दादयो गोपा मथुराया व्रजं गताः ।
विलोक्य पूतनादेहं बभूवुरतिविस्मिताः ॥३१॥

tāvan nandādayo gopā
mathurāyā vrajaṁ gatāḥ
vilokya pūtanā-dehaṁ
babhūvur ativismitāḥ

tāvat—in the meantime; *nanda-ādayaḥ*—headed by Nanda Mahārāja; *gopāḥ*—all the cowherd men; *mathurāyāḥ*—from Mathurā; *vrajam*—to Vṛndāvana; *gatāḥ*—came back; *vilokya*—when they saw; *pūtanā-deham*—the gigantic body of Pūtanā lying dead; *babhūvuḥ*—became; *ati*—very much; *vismitāḥ*—struck with wonder.

TRANSLATION

Meanwhile, all the cowherd men, headed by Nanda Mahārāja, returned from Mathurā, and when they saw on the way the gigantic body of Pūtanā lying dead, they were struck with great wonder.

PURPORT

Nanda Mahārāja's wonder may be understood in various ways. First of all, the cowherd men had never before seen such a gigantic body in Vṛndāvana, and therefore they were struck with wonder. Then they began to consider where such a body had come from, whether it had dropped from the sky, or whether, by some mistake or by the power of some mystic *yoginī,* they had come to some place other than Vṛndāvana. They could not actually guess what had happened, and therefore they were struck with wonder.

TEXT 32

नूनं बतर्षिः संजातो योगेशो वा समास सः ।
स एव दृष्टो ह्युत्पातो यदाहानकदुन्दुभिः ॥३२॥

nūnaṁ batarṣiḥ sañjāto
yogeśo vā samāsa saḥ
sa eva dṛṣṭo hy utpāto
yad āhānakadundubhiḥ

nūnam—certainly; *bata*—O my friends; *ṛṣiḥ*—a great saintly person; *sañjātaḥ*—has become; *yoga-īśaḥ*—a master of mystic power; *vā*—or; *samāsa*—has become; *saḥ*—he (Vasudeva); *saḥ*—that; *eva*—indeed; *dṛṣṭaḥ*—has been seen (by us); *hi*—because; *utpātaḥ*—kind of disturbance; *yat*—that which; *āha*—predicted; *ānakadundubhiḥ*—Ānakadundubhi (another name of Vasudeva).

TRANSLATION

Nanda Mahārāja and the other gopas exclaimed: My dear friends, you must know that Ānakadundubhi, Vasudeva, has become a great saint or a master of mystic power. Otherwise how could he have foreseen this calamity and predicted it to us?

PURPORT

This verse illustrates the difference between *kṣatriyas* and innocent *vaiśyas.* By studying the political situation, Vasudeva could see what would happen, whereas Nanda Mahārāja, the king of the agriculturalists, could only guess that Vasudeva was a great saintly person and had developed mystic powers. Vasudeva actually had all mystic powers under his control; otherwise he could not have become the father of Kṛṣṇa. But in fact he foresaw the calamities in Vraja by studying Kaṁsa's political activities and thus warned Nanda Mahārāja to take precautions, although Nanda Mahārāja thought that Vasudeva had predicted this incident through wonderful mystic powers. By mystic powers gained through the practice of *haṭha-yoga,* one can study and understand the future.

TEXT 33

कलेवरं परशुभिश्छित्त्वा तत्ते व्रजौकसः ।
दूरे क्षिप्त्वावयवशो न्यदहन् काष्ठवेष्टितम् ॥३३॥

kalevaraṁ paraśubhiś
chittvā tat te vrajaukasaḥ
dūre kṣiptvāvayavaśo
nyadahan kāṣṭha-veṣṭitam

kalevaram—the gigantic body of Pūtanā; *paraśubhiḥ*—with the aid of axes; *chittvā*—after cutting to pieces; *tat*—that (body); *te*—all of those; *vraja-okasaḥ*—inhabitants of Vraja; *dūre*—far, far away; *kṣiptvā*—after throwing; *avayavaśaḥ*—different parts of the body, piece by piece; *nyadahan*—burned to ashes; *kāṣṭha-veṣṭitam*—covered by wood.

TRANSLATION

The inhabitants of Vraja cut the gigantic body of Pūtanā into pieces with the help of axes. Then they threw the pieces far away, covered them with wood and burned them to ashes.

PURPORT

It is the practice that after a snake has been killed, its body is cut into various pieces for fear that it may come to life again simply by interacting with air. Merely killing a serpent is not sufficient; after it is killed, it must be cut to pieces and burned, and then the danger will be over. Pūtanā resembled a great serpent, and therefore the cowherd men took the same precautions by burning her body to ashes.

TEXT 34

दह्यमानस्य देहस्य धूमश्चागुरुसौरभः ।
उत्थितः कृष्णनिर्भुक्तसपद्याहतपाप्मनः ॥३४॥

dahyamānasya dehasya
dhūmaś cāguru-saurabhaḥ
utthitaḥ kṛṣṇa-nirbhukta-
sapady āhata-pāpmanaḥ

dahyamānasya—while being burnt to ashes; *dehasya*—of the body of Pūtanā; *dhūmaḥ*—the smoke; *ca*—and; *aguru-saurabhaḥ*—turned into saintly scented smoke of the *aguru* herb; *utthitaḥ*—emanating from her body; *kṛṣṇa-nirbhukta*—because of Kṛṣṇa's having sucked her breast; *sapadi*—immediately; *āhata-pāpmanaḥ*—her material body became spiritualized or relieved of all material conditions.

TRANSLATION

Because of Kṛṣṇa's having sucked the breast of the Rākṣasī Pūtanā, when Kṛṣṇa killed her she was immediately freed of all material contamination. Her sinful reactions automatically vanished, and therefore when her gigantic body was being burnt, the smoke emanating from her body was fragrant like aguru incense.

PURPORT

Such are the effects of Kṛṣṇa consciousness. If one somehow or other becomes Kṛṣṇa conscious by applying his senses in the service of the Lord, one is immediately freed from material contamination. *Śṛṇvatāṁ sva-kathāḥ kṛṣṇaḥ puṇya-śravaṇa-kīrtanaḥ* (*Bhāg.* 1.2.17). Hearing about the activities of Kṛṣṇa is the beginning of purified life. *Puṇya-śravaṇa-kīrtanaḥ:* simply by hearing and chanting, one becomes purified. Therefore, in discharging devotional service, *śravaṇa-kīrtana* (hearing and chanting) is most important. Then, with purified senses, one begins to render service to the Lord (*hṛṣīkeṇa hṛṣīkeśa-sevanam*). *Bhaktir ucyate:* this is called *bhakti.* When Pūtanā was somehow or other, directly or indirectly, induced to render some service to the Lord by feeding Him with her breast, she was immediately purified, so much so that when her nasty material body was burnt to ashes, it gave off the fragrance of *aguru*, the most agreeably scented herb.

TEXTS 35–36

पूतना लोकबालघ्नी राक्षसी रुधिराशना ।
जिघांसयापि हरये स्तनं दत्त्वाप सद्गतिम् ॥३५॥
किं पुनः श्रद्धया भक्त्या कृष्णाय परमात्मने ।
यच्छन् प्रियतमं किं नु रक्तास्तन्मातरो यथा ॥३६॥

pūtanā loka-bāla-ghnī
rākṣasī rudhirāśanā
jighāṁsayāpi haraye
stanaṁ dattvāpa sad-gatim

kiṁ punaḥ śraddhayā bhaktyā
kṛṣṇāya paramātmane
yacchan priyatamaṁ kiṁ nu
raktās tan-mātaro yathā

pūtanā—Pūtanā, the professional Rākṣasī; *loka-bāla-ghnī*—who used to kill human children; *rākṣasī*—the she-demon; *rudhira-aśanā*—simply hankering for blood; *jighāṁsayā*—with the desire to kill Kṛṣṇa (being envious of Kṛṣṇa and having been instructed by Kaṁsa); *api*—still; *haraye*—unto the Supreme Personality of Godhead; *stanam*—her breast; *dattvā*—after offering; *āpa*—obtained; *sat-gatim*—the most elevated position of spiritual existence; *kim*—what to speak of; *punaḥ*—again; *śraddhayā*—with faith; *bhaktyā*—by devotion; *kṛṣṇāya*—unto Lord Kṛṣṇa; *paramātmane*—who is the Supreme Person; *yacchan*—offering; *priya-tamam*—the dearmost; *kim*—something; *nu*—indeed;

raktāḥ—those who have an affinity; *tat-mātaraḥ*—Kṛṣṇa's affectionate mothers (offering the beloved child their breasts); *yathā*—exactly like.

TRANSLATION

Pūtanā was always hankering for the blood of human children, and with that desire she came to kill Kṛṣṇa; but because she offered her breast to the Lord, she attained the greatest achievement. What then is to be said of those who had natural devotion and affection for Kṛṣṇa as mothers and who offered Him their breasts to suck or offered something very dear, as a mother offers something to a child?

PURPORT

Pūtanā had no affection for Kṛṣṇa; rather, she was envious and wanted to kill Him. Nonetheless, because with or without knowledge she offered her breast, she attained the highest achievement in life. But the offerings of devotees attracted to Kṛṣṇa in parental love are always sincere. A mother likes to offer something to her child with affection and love; there is no question of envy. So here we can make a comparative study. If Pūtanā could attain such an exalted position in spiritual life by neglectfully, enviously making an offering to Kṛṣṇa, what is to be said of mother Yaśodā and the other *gopīs*, who served Kṛṣṇa with such great affection and love, offering everything for Kṛṣṇa's satisfaction? The *gopīs* automatically achieved the highest perfection. Therefore Śrī Caitanya Mahāprabhu recommended the affection of the *gopīs*, either in maternal affection or in conjugal love, as the highest perfection in life (*ramyā kācid upāsanā vrajavadhū-vargeṇa yā kalpitā*).

TEXTS 37–38

पद्भ्यां भक्तहृदिस्थाभ्यां वन्द्याभ्यां लोकवन्दितैः ।
अङ्गं यस्याः समाक्रम्य भगवानपिबत् स्तनम् ॥३७॥
यातुधान्यपि सा स्वर्गमवाप जननीगतिम् ।
कृष्णभुक्तस्तनक्षीराः किमु गावोऽनुमातरः ॥३८॥

padbhyāṁ bhakta-hṛdi-sthābhyāṁ
vandyābhyāṁ loka-vanditaiḥ
aṅgaṁ yasyāḥ samākramya
bhagavān api tat-stanam

yātudhāny api sā svargam
avāpa jananī-gatim
kṛṣṇa-bhukta-stana-kṣīrāḥ
kim u gāvo 'numātaraḥ

padbhyām—by the two lotus feet; *bhakta-hṛdi-sthābhyām*—which are always thought of by pure devotees, in whose heart the Lord is therefore situated constantly; *vandyābhyām*—which are always to be praised; *loka-vanditaiḥ*—by Lord Brahmā and Lord Śiva, who are praised by all the inhabitants of the three worlds; *aṅgam*—the body; *yasyāḥ*—of whom (Pūtanā); *samākramya*—embracing; *bhagavān*—the Supreme Personality of Godhead; *api*—also; *tat-stanam*—that breast; *yātudhānī api*—although she was a witch (whose only business was to kill small children and who had tried to kill Kṛṣṇa also); *sā*—she; *svargam*—the transcendental abode; *avāpa*—achieved; *jananī-gatim*—the position of a mother; *kṛṣṇa-bhukta-stana-kṣīrāḥ*—therefore, because their breasts were sucked by Kṛṣṇa, who drank the milk flowing from their bodies; *kim u*—what to speak of; *gāvaḥ*—the cows; *anumātaraḥ*—exactly like mothers (who allowed their nipples to be sucked by Kṛṣṇa).

TRANSLATION

The Supreme Personality of Godhead, Kṛṣṇa, is always situated within the core of the heart of the pure devotee, and He is always offered prayers by such worshipable personalities as Lord Brahmā and Lord Śiva. Because Kṛṣṇa embraced Pūtanā's body with great pleasure and sucked her breast, although she was a great witch, she attained the position of a mother in the transcendental world and thus achieved the highest perfection. What then is to be said of the cows whose nipples Kṛṣṇa sucked with great pleasure and who offered their milk very jubilantly with affection exactly like that of a mother?

PURPORT

These verses explain how devotional service rendered to the Supreme Personality of Godhead, whether directly or indirectly, knowingly or unknowingly, becomes successful. Pūtanā was neither a devotee nor a nondevotee; she was actually a demoniac witch instructed by Kaṁsa to kill Kṛṣṇa. Nonetheless, in the beginning she assumed the form of a very beautiful woman and approached Kṛṣṇa exactly like an affectionate mother, so that mother Yaśodā and Rohiṇī did not doubt her sincerity. The Lord took all this into consideration, and thus she was automatically promoted to a position like that of mother Yaśodā. As explained by Viśvanātha Cakravartī Ṭhākura, there are various roles one may play in such a position. Pūtanā was immediately promoted to Vaikuṇṭhaloka, which is also sometimes described as Svarga. The Svarga mentioned in this verse is not the material heavenly planet, but the transcendental world. In Vaikuṇṭhaloka, Pūtanā attained the position of a nurse (*dhātry-ucitām*), as described by Uddhava. Pūtanā was elevated to the position of a nurse and maidservant in Goloka Vṛndāvana to assist mother Yaśodā.

TEXTS 39–40

पयांसि यासामपिबत् पुत्रस्नेहस्नुतान्यलम् ।
भगवान् देवकीपुत्रः कैवल्याद्यखिलप्रदः ॥३९॥
तासामविरतं कृष्णे कुर्वतीनां सुतेक्षणम् ।
न पुनः कल्पते राजन् संसारोऽज्ञानसम्भवः ॥४०॥

payāṁsi yāsām apibat
putra-sneha-snutāny alam
bhagavān devakī-putraḥ
kaivalyādy-akhila-pradaḥ

tāsām aviratam kṛṣṇe
kurvatīnāṁ sutekṣaṇam
na punaḥ kalpate rājan
saṁsāro 'jñāna-sambhavaḥ

payāṁsi—milk (coming from the body); *yāsām*—of all of whom; *apibat*—Lord Kṛṣṇa drank; *putra-sneha-snutāni*—that milk coming from the bodies of the *gopīs*, not artificially but because of maternal affection; *alam*—sufficiently; *bhagavān*—the Supreme Personality of Godhead; *devakī-putraḥ*—who appeared as the son of Devakī; *kaivalya-ādi*—like liberation or merging into the Brahman effulgence; *akhila-pradaḥ*—the bestower of all similar blessings; *tāsām*—of all of them (of all the *gopīs*); *aviratam*—constantly; *kṛṣṇe*—unto Lord Kṛṣṇa; *kurvatīnām*—making; *suta-īkṣaṇam*—as a mother looks upon her child; *na*—never; *punaḥ*—again; *kalpate*—can be imagined; *rājan*—O King Parīkṣit; *saṁsāraḥ*—the material bondage of birth and death; *ajñāna-sambhavaḥ*—which is to be accepted by foolish persons ignorantly trying to become happy.

TRANSLATION

The Supreme Personality of Godhead, Kṛṣṇa, is the bestower of many benedictions, including liberation [kaivalya], or oneness with the Brahman effulgence. For that Personality of Godhead, the gopīs always felt maternal love, and Kṛṣṇa sucked their breasts with full satisfaction. Therefore, because of their relationship as mother and son, although the gopīs were engaged in various family activities, one should never think that they returned to this material world after leaving their bodies.

PURPORT

The advantage of Kṛṣṇa consciousness is described herein. Kṛṣṇa consciousness gradually develops on the transcendental platform. One may think of Kṛṣṇa as the supreme personality, one may think of Kṛṣṇa as the supreme master, one may think of Kṛṣṇa as the supreme friend, one may think of Kṛṣṇa as the supreme son, or one may think of Kṛṣṇa as the supreme conjugal lover. If one is connected with Kṛṣṇa in any of these transcendental relationships, the course of one's material life is understood to have already ended. As confirmed in *Bhagavad-gītā* (4.9), *tyaktvā dehaṁ punar janma naiti mām eti:* for such devotees, going back home, back to Godhead, is guaranteed. *Na punaḥ kalpate rājan saṁsāro 'jñāna-sambhavaḥ.* This verse also guarantees that devotees who constantly think of Kṛṣṇa in a particular relationship will never return to this material world. In this material world of *saṁsāra,* there are the same relationships. One thinks, "Here is my son," "Here is my wife," "Here is my lover," or "Here is my friend." But these relationships are temporary illusions. *Ajñāna-sambhavaḥ:* such a consciousness awakens in ignorance. But when the same relationships awaken in Kṛṣṇa consciousness, one's spiritual life is revived, and one is guaranteed to return home, back to Godhead. Even though the *gopīs* who were friends of Rohiṇī and mother Yaśodā and who allowed their breasts to be sucked by Kṛṣṇa were not directly Kṛṣṇa's mothers, they all had the same chance as Rohiṇī and Yaśodā to go back to Godhead and act as Kṛṣṇa's mothers-in-law, servants and so on. The word *saṁsāra* refers to attachment for one's body, home, husband or wife, and children, but although the *gopīs* and all the other inhabitants of Vṛndāvana had the same affection and attachment for husband and home, their central affection was for Kṛṣṇa in some transcendental relationship, and therefore they were guaranteed to be promoted to Goloka Vṛndāvana in the next life, to live with Kṛṣṇa eternally in spiritual happiness. The easiest way to attain spiritual elevation, to be liberated from this material world, and to go back home, back to Godhead, is recommended by Bhaktivinoda Ṭhākura: *kṛṣṇera saṁsāra kara chāḍi' anācāra.* One should give up all sinful activities and remain in the family of Kṛṣṇa. Then one's liberation is guaranteed.

TEXT 41

कटधूमस्य सौरभ्यमवघ्राय व्रजौकसः ।
किमिदं कुत एवेति वदन्तो व्रजमाययुः ॥४१॥

kaṭa-dhūmasya saurabhyam
avaghrāya vrajaukasaḥ
kim idaṁ kuta eveti
vadanto vrajam āyayuḥ

kaṭa-dhūmasya—of the smoke emanating from the fire burning the different parts of Pūtanā's body; *saurabhyam*—the fragrance; *avaghrāya*—when they smelled through their nostrils; *vraja-okasaḥ*—the inhabitants of Vrajabhūmi in distant places; *kim idam*—what is this fragrance; *kutaḥ*—where does it come from; *eva*—indeed; *iti*—in this way; *vadantaḥ*—speaking; *vrajam*—the place of Nanda Mahārāja, Vrajabhūmi; *āyayuḥ*—reached.

TRANSLATION

Upon smelling the fragrance of the smoke emanating from Pūtanā's burning body, many inhabitants of Vrajabhūmi in distant places were astonished. "Where is this fragrance coming from?" they asked. Thus they went to the spot where Pūtanā's body was being burnt.

PURPORT

The aroma of the smoke emanating from a burning fire is not always very favorable. Therefore upon smelling such a wonderful fragrance, the inhabitants of Vraja were astonished.

TEXT 42

ते तत्र वर्णितं गोपैः पूतनागमनादिकम् ।
श्रुत्वा तन्निधनं स्वस्ति शिशोश्चासन् सुविस्मिताः ॥४२॥

te tatra varṇitaṁ gopaiḥ
pūtanāgamanādikam
śrutvā tan-nidhanaṁ svasti
śiśoś cāsan suvismitāḥ

te—all those persons who arrived; *tatra*—there (in the vicinity of Nanda Mahārāja's estate); *varṇitam*—described; *gopaiḥ*—by the cowherd men; *pūtanā-āgamana-ādikam*—everything about how Pūtanā the witch had come there and played havoc; *śrutvā*—after hearing; *tat-nidhanam*—and about how Pūtanā had died; *svasti*—all auspiciousness; *śiśoḥ*—for the baby; *ca*—and; *āsan*—offered; *su-vismitāḥ*—being struck with great wonder because of what had happened.

TRANSLATION

When the inhabitants of Vraja who had come from distant places heard the whole story of how Pūtanā had come and then been

killed by Kṛṣṇa, they were certainly astonished, and they offered their blessings to the child for His wonderful deed of killing Pūtanā. Nanda Mahārāja, of course, was very much obliged to Vasudeva, who had foreseen the incident, and simply thanked him, thinking how wonderful Vasudeva was.

TEXT 43

नन्दः स्वपुत्रमादाय प्रेत्यागतमुदारधीः ।
मूर्ध्न्युपाघ्राय परमां मुदं लेभे कुरूद्वह ॥४३॥

nandaḥ sva-putram ādāya
pretyāgatam udāra-dhīḥ
mūrdhny upāghrāya paramāṁ
mudaṁ lebhe kurūdvaha

nandaḥ—Mahārāja Nanda; *sva-putram ādāya*—taking his son Kṛṣṇa on his lap; *pretya-āgatam*—as if Kṛṣṇa had returned from death (no one could even imagine that from such danger a child could be saved); *udāra-dhīḥ*—because he was always liberal and simple; *mūrdhni*—on the head of Kṛṣṇa; *upāghrāya*—formally smelling; *paramām*—highest; *mudam*—peace; *lebhe*—achieved; *kuru-udvaha*—O Mahārāja Parīkṣit.

TRANSLATION

O Mahārāja Parīkṣit, best of the Kurus, Nanda Mahārāja was very liberal and simple. He immediately took his son Kṛṣṇa on his lap as if Kṛṣṇa had returned from death, and by formally smelling his son's head, Nanda Mahārāja undoubtedly enjoyed transcendental bliss.

PURPORT

Nanda Mahārāja could not understand how the inhabitants of his house had allowed Pūtanā to enter the house, nor could he imagine the gravity of the situation. He did not understand that Kṛṣṇa had wanted to kill Pūtanā and that His pastimes were performed by *yogamāyā*. Nanda Mahārāja simply thought that someone had entered his house and created havoc. This was Nanda Mahārāja's simplicity.

TEXT 44

य एतत् पूतनामोक्षं कृष्णस्यार्भकमद्भुतम् ।
शृणुयाच्छ्रद्धया मर्त्यो गोविन्दे लभते रतिम् ॥४४॥

ya etat pūtanā-mokṣaṁ
kṛṣṇasyārbhakam adbhutam
śṛṇuyāc chraddhayā martyo
govinde labhate ratim

yaḥ—anyone who; *etat*—this; *pūtanā-mokṣam*—salvation of Pūtanā; *kṛṣṇasya*—of Kṛṣṇa; *ārbhakam*—the childhood pastimes; *adbhutam*—wonderful; *śṛṇuyāt*—should hear; *śraddhayā*—with faith and devotion; *martyaḥ*—any person within this material world; *govinde*—for the Supreme Person, Govinda, Ādi-puruṣa; *labhate*—gains; *ratim*—attachment.

TRANSLATION

Any person who hears with faith and devotion about how Kṛṣṇa, the Supreme Personality of Godhead, killed Pūtanā, and who thus invests his hearing in such childhood pastimes of Kṛṣṇa, certainly attains attachment for Govinda, the supreme, original person.

PURPORT

The incident in which the great witch attempted to kill the child but was killed herself is certainly wonderful. Therefore this verse uses the word *adbhutam*, meaning "specifically wonderful." Kṛṣṇa has left us many wonderful narrations about Him. Simply by reading these narrations, as they are described in *Kṛṣṇa, the Supreme Personality of Godhead*, one gains salvation from this material world and gradually develops attachment to and devotion for Govinda, Ādi-puruṣa.

Thus end the Bhaktivedanta purports of the Tenth Canto, Sixth Chapter, of the Śrīmad-Bhāgavatam, *entitled "The Killing of the Demon Pūtanā."*

CHAPTER SEVEN

The Killing of the Demon Tṛṇāvarta

In this chapter, Śrī Kṛṣṇa's pastimes of breaking the cart (*śakaṭa-bhañjana*), killing the *asura* known as Tṛṇāvarta, and demonstrating the entire universe within His mouth are especially described.

When Śukadeva Gosvāmī saw that Mahārāja Parīkṣit was eagerly waiting to hear about Lord Kṛṣṇa's pastimes as a child, he was very much pleased, and he continued to speak. When Śrī Kṛṣṇa was only three months old and was just trying to turn backside up, before He even attempted to crawl, mother Yaśodā wanted to observe a ritualistic ceremony with her friends for the good fortune of the child. Such a ritualistic ceremony is generally performed with ladies who also have small children. When mother Yaśodā saw that Kṛṣṇa was falling asleep, because of other engagements she put the child underneath a household cart, called *śakaṭa*, and while the child was sleeping, she engaged herself in other business pertaining to the auspicious ritualistic ceremony. Underneath the cart was a cradle, and mother Yaśodā placed the child in that cradle. The child was sleeping, but suddenly He awakened and, as usual for a child, began to kick His small legs. This kicking shook the cart, which collapsed with a great sound, breaking completely and spilling all its contents. Children who were playing nearby immediately informed mother Yaśodā that the cart had broken, and therefore she hastily arrived there in great anxiety with the other *gopīs*. Mother Yaśodā immediately took the child on her lap and allowed Him to suck her breast. Then various types of Vedic ritualistic ceremonies were performed with the help of the *brāhmaṇas*. Not knowing the real identity of the child, the *brāhmaṇas* showered the child with blessings.

Another day, when mother Yaśodā was sitting with her child on her lap, she suddenly observed that he had assumed the weight of the entire universe. She was so astonished that she had to put the child down, and in the meantime Tṛṇāvarta, one of the servants of Kaṁsa, appeared there as a whirlwind and took the child away. The whole tract of land known as Gokula became surcharged with dust, no one could see where the child had been taken, and all the *gopīs* were overwhelmed because He had been taken away in the dust storm. But up in the sky, the *asura*, being overburdened by the child, could not carry the child far away, although he also could not drop the child because the child had caught him so tightly that it was difficult for him to separate the child from his body. Thus Tṛṇāvarta himself fell down from a very great height, the child grasping him tightly by the shoulder, and immediately died. The demon having fallen, the *gopīs* picked the child up and delivered Him to the lap of mother Yaśodā. Thus mother Yaśodā was struck with wonder, but because of *yogamāyā's* influence, no one could understand who Kṛṣṇa was and what had actually happened. Rather, everyone began to praise fortune for the child's having been saved from such a calamity. Nanda Mahārāja, of course, was thinking of the wonderful foretelling of Vasudeva and began to praise him as a great *yogī*. Later, when the child was on the lap of mother Yaśodā, the child yawned, and mother Yaśodā could see within His mouth the entire universal manifestation.

TEXTS 1–2

श्रीराजोवाच

येन येनावतारेण भगवान् हरिरीश्वरः ।
करोति कर्णरम्याणि मनोज्ञानि च नः प्रभो ॥ १ ॥
यच्छृण्वतोऽपैत्यरतिर्वितृष्णा
सत्त्वं च शुद्ध्यत्यचिरेण पुंसः ।
भक्तिर्हरौ तत्पुरुषे च सख्यं
तदेव हारं वद मन्यसे चेत् ॥ २ ॥

śrī-rājovāca
yena yenāvatāreṇa
bhagavān harir īśvaraḥ
karoti karṇa-ramyāṇi
mano-jñāni ca naḥ prabho

yac-chṛṇvato 'paity aratir vitṛṣṇā
sattvaṁ ca śuddhyaty acireṇa puṁsaḥ

bhaktir harau tat-puruṣe ca sakhyaṁ
tad eva hāraṁ vada manyase cet

śrī-rājā uvāca—the King inquired (from Śukadeva Gosvāmī); *yena yena avatāreṇa*—the pastimes exhibited by different varieties of incarnations; *bhagavān*—the Supreme Personality of Godhead; *hariḥ*—the Lord; *īśvaraḥ*—the controller; *karoti*—presents; *karṇa-ramyāṇi*—were all very pleasing to the ear; *manaḥ-jñāni*—very attractive to the mind; *ca*—also; *naḥ*—of us; *prabho*—my lord, Śukadeva Gosvāmī; *yat-śṛṇvataḥ*—of anyone who simply hears these narrations; *apaiti*—vanishes; *aratiḥ*—unattractiveness; *vitṛṣṇā*—dirty things within the mind that make us uninterested in Kṛṣṇa consciousness; *sattvam ca*—the existential position in the core of the heart; *śuddhyati*—becomes purified; *acireṇa*—very soon; *puṁsaḥ*—of any person; *bhaktiḥ harau*—devotional attachment and service to the Lord; *tat-puruṣe*—with Vaiṣṇavas; *ca*—also; *sakhyam*—attraction to association; *tat eva*—that only; *hāram*—the activities of the Lord, which should be heard and kept on the neck as a garland; *vada*—kindly speak; *manyase*—you think it fit; *cet*—if.

TRANSLATION

King Parīkṣit said: My lord, Śukadeva Gosvāmī, all the various activities exhibited by the incarnations of the Supreme Personality of Godhead are certainly pleasing to the ear and to the mind. Simply by one's hearing of these activities, the dirty things in one's mind immediately vanish. Generally we are reluctant to hear about the activities of the Lord, but Kṛṣṇa's childhood activities are so attractive that they are automatically pleasing to the mind and ear. Thus one's attachment for hearing about material things, which is the root cause of material existence, vanishes, and one gradually develops devotional service to the Supreme Lord, attachment for Him, and friendship with devotees who give us the contribution of Kṛṣṇa consciousness. If you think it fit, kindly speak about those activities of the Lord.

PURPORT

As stated in the *Prema-vivarta:*

kṛṣṇa-bahirmukha haiyā bhoga-vāñchā kare
nikaṭa-stha māyā tāre jāpaṭiyā dhare

Our material existence is *māyā*, or illusion, in which we desire different varieties of material enjoyment and therefore change to different varieties of bodies (*bhrāmayan sarva-bhūtāni yantrārūḍhāni māyayā*). *Asann api kleśada āsa dehaḥ:* as long as we have these temporary bodies, they give us many varieties of tribulation—*ādhyātmika*, *ādhibhautika* and *ādhidaivika*. This is the root cause of all suffering, but this root cause of suffering can be removed by revival of our Kṛṣṇa consciousness. All the Vedic literatures presented by Vyāsadeva and other great sages are therefore intended to revive our Kṛṣṇa consciousness, which begins to revive with *śravaṇa-kīrtanam. Śṛṇvatāṁ sva-kathāḥ kṛṣṇaḥ* (*Bhāg.* 1.2.17). *Śrīmad-Bhāgavatam* and other Vedic literatures exist simply to give us a chance to hear about Kṛṣṇa. Kṛṣṇa has different *avatāras*, or incarnations, all of which are wonderful and which arouse one's inquisitiveness, but generally such *avatāras* as Matsya, Kūrma and Varāha are not as attractive as Kṛṣṇa. First of all, however, we have no attraction for hearing about Kṛṣṇa, and this is the root cause of our suffering.

But Parīkṣit Mahārāja specifically mentions that the wonderful activities of baby Kṛṣṇa, which amazed mother Yaśodā and the other inhabitants of Vraja, are especially attractive. From the very beginning of His childhood, Kṛṣṇa killed Pūtanā, Tṛṇāvarta and Śakaṭāsura and showed the entire universe within His mouth. Thus the pastimes of Kṛṣṇa, one after another, kept mother Yaśodā and all the inhabitants of Vraja in great astonishment. The process to revive one's Kṛṣṇa consciousness is *ādau śraddhā tataḥ sādhu-saṅgaḥ* (*Bhakti-rasāmṛta-sindhu* 1.4.15). The pastimes of Kṛṣṇa can be properly received from devotees. If one has developed a little bit of Kṛṣṇa consciousness by hearing from Vaiṣṇavas about the activities of Kṛṣṇa, one becomes attached to Vaiṣṇavas who are interested only in Kṛṣṇa consciousness. Therefore Parīkṣit Mahārāja recommends that one hear about Kṛṣṇa's childhood activities, which are more attractive than the activities of other incarnations, such as Matsya, Kūrma and Varāha. Wanting to hear more and more from Śukadeva Gosvāmī, Mahārāja Parīkṣit requested him to continue describing Kṛṣṇa's childhood activities, which are especially easy to hear and which create more and more inquisitiveness.

TEXT 3

अथान्यदपि कृष्णस्य तोकाचरितमद्भुतम् ।
मानुषं लोकमासाद्य तज्जातिमनुरुन्धतः ॥ ३ ॥

athānyad api kṛṣṇasya
tokācaritam adbhutam
mānuṣaṁ lokam āsādya
taj-jātim anurundhataḥ

atha—also; *anyat api*—other pastimes also; *kṛṣṇasya*—of child Kṛṣṇa; *toka-ācaritam adbhutam*—they are also wonderful childhood pastimes; *mānuṣam*—as if playing as a human child; *lokam āsādya*—appearing on this planet earth in human society; *tat-jātim*—exactly like a human child; *anurundhataḥ*—who was imitating.

TRANSLATION

Please describe other pastimes of Kṛṣṇa, the Supreme Personality, who appeared on this planet earth, imitating a human child and performing wonderful activities like killing Pūtanā.

PURPORT

Mahārāja Parīkṣit requested Śukadeva Gosvāmī to narrate other childhood pastimes exhibited by Kṛṣṇa while playing as a human child. The Supreme Personality of Godhead incarnates at different times in different planets and universes, and according to the nature of those places, He exhibits His unlimited potency. That a child sitting on the lap of his mother was able to kill the gigantic Pūtanā is extremely wonderful for the inhabitants of this planet, but on other planets the inhabitants are more advanced, and therefore the pastimes the Lord performs there are still more wonderful. Kṛṣṇa's appearance on this planet like a human being makes us more fortunate than the demigods in the higher planets, and therefore Mahārāja Parīkṣit was very much interested in hearing about Him.

TEXT 4

श्रीशुक उवाच

कदाचिदौत्थानिककौतुकाप्लवे
जन्मर्क्षयोगे समवेतयोषिताम् ।
वादित्रगीतद्विजमन्त्रवाचकै-
श्चकार सूनोरभिषेचनं सती ॥ ४ ॥

śrī-śuka uvāca
kadācid autthānika-kautukāplave
janmarkṣa-yoge samaveta-yoṣitām
vāditra-gīta-dvija-mantra-vācakaiś
cakāra sūnor abhiṣecanaṁ satī

śrī-śukaḥ uvāca—Śrī Śukadeva Gosvāmī continued to speak (at the request of Mahārāja Parīkṣit); *kadācit*—at that time (when Kṛṣṇa was three months old); *autthānika-kautuka-āplave*—when Kṛṣṇa was three or four months old and His body was developing, He attempted to turn around, and this pleasing occasion was observed with a festival and bathing ceremony; *janma-ṛkṣa-yoge*—at that time, there was also a conjunction of the moon with the auspicious constellation Rohiṇī; *samaveta-yoṣitām*—(the ceremony was observed) among the assembled women, a ceremony of mothers; *vāditra-gīta*—different varieties of music and singing; *dvija-mantra-vācakaiḥ*—with chanting of Vedic hymns by qualified *brāhmaṇas; cakāra*—executed; *sūnoḥ*—of her son; *abhiṣecanam*—the bathing ceremony; *satī*—mother Yaśodā.

TRANSLATION

Śukadeva Gosvāmī said: When mother Yaśodā's baby was slanting His body to attempt to rise and turn around, this attempt was observed by a Vedic ceremony. In such a ceremony, called utthāna, which is performed when a child is due to leave the house for the first time, the child is properly bathed. Just after Kṛṣṇa turned three months old, mother Yaśodā celebrated this ceremony with

other women of the neighborhood. On that day, there was a conjunction of the moon with the constellation Rohiṇī. As the brāhmaṇas joined by chanting Vedic hymns and professional musicians also took part, this great ceremony was observed by mother Yaśodā.

PURPORT

There is no question of overpopulation or of children's being a burden for their parents in a Vedic society. Such a society is so well organized and people are so advanced in spiritual consciousness that childbirth is never regarded as a burden or a botheration. The more a child grows, the more his parents become jubilant, and the child's attempts to turn over are also a source of jubilation. Even before the child is born, when the mother is pregnant, many recommended ritualistic ceremonies are performed. For example, when the child has been within the womb for three months and for seven months, there is a ceremony the mother observes by eating with neighboring children. This ceremony is called *svāda-bhakṣaṇa.* Similarly, before the birth of the child there is the *garbhādhāna* ceremony. In Vedic civilization, childbirth or pregnancy is never regarded as a burden; rather, it is a cause for jubilation. In contrast, people in modern civilization do not like pregnancy or childbirth, and when there is a child, they sometimes kill it. We can just consider how human society has fallen since the inauguration of Kali-yuga. Although people still claim to be civilized, at the present moment there is actually no human civilization, but only an assembly of two-legged animals.

TEXT 5

नन्दस्य पत्नी कृतमज्जनादिकं
विप्रैः कृतस्वस्त्ययनं सुपूजितैः ।
अन्नाद्यवासःस्रगभीष्टधेनुभिः
संजातनिद्राक्षमशीशयच्छनैः ॥ ५ ॥

nandasya patnī kṛta-majjanādikaṁ
vipraiḥ kṛta-svastyayanaṁ supūjitaiḥ
annādya-vāsaḥ-srag-abhīṣṭa-dhenubhiḥ
sañjāta-nidrākṣam aśīśayac chanaiḥ

nandasya—of Mahārāja Nanda; *patnī*—the wife (mother Yaśodā); *kṛta-majjana-ādikam*—after she and the other members of the house had bathed and the child had been bathed also; *expraiḥ*—by the *brāhmaṇas; kṛta-svastyayanam*—engaging them in chanting auspicious Vedic hymns; *su-pūjitaiḥ*—who were all received and worshiped with proper respect; *anna-ādya*—by offering them sufficient grains and other eatables; *vāsaḥ*—garments; *srak-abhīṣṭa-dhenubhiḥ*—by offering flower garlands and very desirable cows; *sañjāta-nidrā*—had become sleepy; *akṣam*—whose eyes; *aśīśayat*—laid the child down; *śanaiḥ*—for the time being.

TRANSLATION

After completing the bathing ceremony for the child, mother Yaśodā received the brāhmaṇas by worshiping them with proper respect and giving them ample food grains and other eatables, clothing, desirable cows, and garlands. The brāhmaṇas properly chanted Vedic hymns to observe the auspicious ceremony, and when they finished and mother Yaśodā saw that the child felt sleepy, she lay down on the bed with the child until He was peacefully asleep.

PURPORT

An affectionate mother takes great care of her child and is always anxious to see that the child is not disturbed even for a moment. As long as the child wants to remain with the mother, the mother stays with the child, and the child feels very comfortable. Mother Yaśodā saw that her child felt sleepy, and to give Him all facilities for sleep, she lay down with the child, and when He was peaceful, she got up to attend to her other household affairs.

TEXT 6

औत्थानिकौत्सुक्यमना मनस्विनी
समागतान् पूजयती व्रजौकसः ।
नैवाश्रृणोद् वै रुदितं सुतस्य सा
रुदन् स्तनार्थी चरणावुदक्षिपत् ॥ ६ ॥

autthānikautsukya-manā manasvinī
samāgatān pūjayatī vrajaukasaḥ
naivāśṛṇod vai ruditaṁ sutasya sā
rudan stanārthī caraṇāv udakṣipat

autthānika-autsukya-manāḥ—mother Yaśodā was very busy celebrating the *utthāna* ceremony of her child; *manasvinī*—very liberal in distributing food, clothing, ornaments and cows, according to necessity; *samāgatān*—to the assembled guests; *pūjayatī*—just to satisfy them; *vraja-okasaḥ*—to the inhabitants of Vraja; *na*—not; *eva*—certainly; *aśṛṇot*—did hear; *vai*—indeed; *ruditam*—the crying; *sutasya*—of her child; *sā*—mother Yaśodā; *rudan*—crying; *stana-arthī*—Kṛṣṇa, who was hankering to drink His mother's milk by sucking her breast; *caraṇau udakṣipat*—out of anger, threw His two legs hither and thither.

TRANSLATION

The liberal mother Yaśodā, absorbed in celebrating the utthāna ceremony, was busy receiving guests, worshiping them with all respect and offering them clothing, cows, garlands and grains. Thus she could not hear the child crying for His mother. At that time, the child Kṛṣṇa, demanding to drink the milk of His mother's breast, angrily threw His legs upward.

PURPORT

Kṛṣṇa had been placed underneath a household handcart, but this handcart was actually another form of the Śakaṭāsura, a demon who had come there to kill the child. Now, on the plea of demanding to suck His mother's breast, Kṛṣṇa took this opportunity to kill the demon. Thus He kicked Śakaṭāsura just to expose him. Although Kṛṣṇa's mother was engaged in receiving guests, Lord Kṛṣṇa wanted to draw her attention by killing the Śakaṭāsura, and therefore he kicked that cart-shaped demon. Such are the pastimes of Kṛṣṇa. Kṛṣṇa wanted to draw the attention of His mother, but while doing so He created a great havoc not understandable by ordinary persons. These narrations are wonderfully enjoyable, and those who are fortunate are struck with wonder upon hearing of these extraordinary activities of the Lord. Although the less intelligent regard them as mythological because a dull brain cannot understand them, they are real facts. These narrations are actually so enjoyable and enlightening that Mahārāja Parīkṣit and Śukadeva Gosvāmī took pleasure in them, and other liberated persons, following in their footsteps, become fully jubilant by hearing about the wonderful activities of the Lord.

TEXT 7

अधःशयानस्य शिशोरनोऽल्पक-
प्रवालमृद्वङ्घ्रिहतं व्यवर्तत ।
विध्वस्तनानारसकुप्यभाजनं
व्यत्यस्तचक्राक्षविभिन्नकूबरम् ॥ ७ ॥

adhaḥ-śayānasya śiśor ano 'lpaka-
pravāla-mṛdv-aṅghri-hataṁ vyavartata
vidhvasta-nānā-rasa-kupya-bhājanaṁ
vyatyasta-cakrākṣa-vibhinna-kūbaram

adhaḥ-śayānasya—who was put underneath the handcart; *śiśoḥ*—of the child; *anaḥ*—the cart; *alpaka*—not very much grown; *pravāla*—just like a new leaf; *mṛdu-aṅghri-hatam*—struck by His beautiful, delicate legs; *vyavartata*—turned over and fell down; *vidhvasta*—scattered; *nānā-rasa-kupya-bhājanam*—utensils made of various metals; *vyatyasta*—dislocated; *cakra-akṣa*—the two wheels and the axle; *vibhinna*—broken; *kūbaram*—the pole of the handcart.

TRANSLATION

Lord Śrī Kṛṣṇa was lying down underneath the handcart in one corner of the courtyard, and although His little legs were as soft as leaves, when He struck the cart with His legs, it turned over violently and collapsed. The wheels separated from the axle, the hubs and spokes fell apart, and the pole of the handcart broke. On the cart there were many little utensils made of various metals, and all of them scattered hither and thither.

PURPORT

Śrīla Viśvanātha Cakravartī Ṭhākura has commented on this verse as follows. When Lord Kṛṣṇa was of a very tender age, His hands and legs resembled soft new leaves, yet simply by touching the handcart with His legs, He made the cart fall to pieces. It was quite possible for Him to act in this way and yet not exert Himself very much. The Lord in His Vāmana *avatāra* had to extend His foot to the greatest height to penetrate the covering of the universe, and when the Lord killed the gigantic demon Hiraṇyakaśipu, He had to assume the special bodily feature of Nṛsiṁhadeva. But in His Kṛṣṇa *avatāra*, the Lord did not need to exert such energy. Therefore, *kṛṣṇas tu bhagavān svayam:* Kṛṣṇa is the Supreme Personality of Godhead Himself. In other incarnations, the Lord had to exert some energy according to the time and circumstances, but in this form He exhibited unlimited potency. Thus the handcart collapsed, its joints broken, and all the metal pots and utensils scattered.

The *Vaiṣṇava-toṣaṇī* remarks that although the handcart was higher than the child, the child could easily touch the wheel of the cart, and this was sufficient to send the demon down to the earth. The Lord simultaneously pushed the demon to the earth and superficially broke the handcart.

TEXT 8

दृष्ट्वा यशोदाप्रमुखा व्रजस्त्रिय
औत्थानिके कर्मणि याः समागताः ।
नन्दादयश्चाद्भुतदर्शनाकुलाः
कथं स्वयं वै शकटं विपर्यगात् ॥ ८ ॥

dṛṣṭvā yaśodā-pramukhā vraja-striya
autthānike karmaṇi yāḥ samāgatāḥ
nandādayaś cādbhuta-darśanākulāḥ
kathaṁ svayaṁ vai śakaṭaṁ viparyagāt

dṛṣṭvā—after seeing; *yaśodā-pramukhāḥ*—headed by mother Yaśodā; *vraja-striyaḥ*—all the ladies of Vraja; *autthānike karmaṇi*—in the celebration of the *utthāna* ceremony; *yāḥ*—those who; *samāgatāḥ*—

assembled there; *nanda-ādayaḥ ca*—and the men, headed by Nanda Mahārāja; *adbhuta-darśana*—by seeing the wonderful calamity (that the heavily loaded cart had broken upon the small baby, who still lay there unhurt); *ākulāḥ*—and thus they were very much perturbed as to how it had happened; *katham*—how; *svayam*—by itself; *vai*—indeed; *śakaṭam*—the handcart; *viparyagāt*—became so heavily damaged, dismantled.

TRANSLATION

When mother Yaśodā and the other ladies who had assembled for the utthāna festival, and all the men, headed by Nanda Mahārāja, saw the wonderful situation, they began to wonder how the handcart had collapsed by itself. They began to wander here and there, trying to find the cause, but were unable to do so.

TEXT 9

ऊचुरव्यवसितमतीन् गोपान् गोपीश्च बालकाः ।
रुदतानेन पादेन क्षिप्तमेतन्न संशयः ॥ ९ ॥

ūcur avyavasita-matīn
gopān gopīś ca bālakāḥ
rudatānena pādena
kṣiptam etan na saṁśayaḥ

ūcuḥ—said; *avyavasita-matīn*—who had lost all intelligence in the present situation; *gopān*—to the cowherd men; *gopīḥ ca*—and to the ladies; *bālakāḥ*—the children; *rudatā anena*—as soon as the child cried; *pādena*—with one leg; *kṣiptam etat*—this cart was dashed apart and immediately fell dismantled; *na saṁśayaḥ*—there is no doubt about it.

TRANSLATION

The assembled cowherd men and ladies began to contemplate how this thing had happened. "Is it the work of some demon or evil planet?" they asked. At that time, the small children present asserted that the cart had been kicked apart by the baby Kṛṣṇa. As

soon as the crying baby had kicked the cart's wheel, the cart had collapsed. There was no doubt about it.

PURPORT

We have heard of people's being haunted by ghosts. Having no gross material body, a ghost seeks shelter of a gross body to stay in and haunt. The Śakaṭāsura was a ghost who had taken shelter of the handcart and was looking for the opportunity to do mischief to Kṛṣṇa. When Kṛṣṇa kicked the cart with His small and very delicate legs, the ghost was immediately pushed down to the earth and his shelter dismantled, as already described. This was possible for Kṛṣṇa because He has full potency, as confirmed in the *Brahma-saṁhitā* (5.32):

aṅgāni yasya sakalendriya-vṛttimanti
paśyanti pānti kalayanti ciraṁ jaganti
ānanda-cinmaya-sad-ujjvala-vigrahasya
govindam ādi-puruṣaṁ tam ahaṁ bhajāmi

Kṛṣṇa's body is *sac-cid-ānanda-vigraha*, or *ānanda-cinmaya-rasa-vigraha*. That is, any of the parts of His *ānanda-cinmaya* body can act for any other part. Such are the inconceivable potencies of the Supreme Personality of Godhead. The Supreme Lord does not need to acquire these potencies; He already has them. Thus Kṛṣṇa kicked His little legs, and His whole purpose was fulfilled. Also, when the handcart broke, an ordinary child could have been injured in many ways, but because Kṛṣṇa is the Supreme Personality of Godhead, He enjoyed the dismantling of the cart, and nothing injured Him. Everything done by Him is *ānanda-cinmaya-rasa*, full transcendental bliss. Thus Kṛṣṇa factually enjoyed.

The nearby children saw that actually Kṛṣṇa had kicked the wheel of the cart and this was how the accident happened. By the arrangement of *yogamāyā*, all the *gopīs* and *gopas* thought that the accident had taken place because of some bad planet or some ghost, but in fact everything was done by Kṛṣṇa and enjoyed by Him. Those who enjoy the activities of Kṛṣṇa are also on the platform of *ānanda-cinmaya-rasa;* they are liberated from the material platform. When one develops the practice of hearing *kṛṣṇa-kathā*, he is certainly transcendental to material existence, as confirmed in *Bhagavad-gītā* (*sa guṇān samatītyaitān brahma-bhūyāya kalpate*). Unless one is on the spiritual platform, one cannot enjoy the transcendental activities of Kṛṣṇa; or in other words, whoever engages in hearing the transcendental activities of Kṛṣṇa is not on the material platform, but on the transcendental, spiritual platform.

TEXT 10

न ते श्रद्दधिरे गोपा बालभाषितमित्युत ।
अप्रमेयं बलं तस्य बालकस्य न ते विदुः ॥१०॥

na te śraddadhire gopā
bāla-bhāṣitam ity uta
aprameyaṁ balaṁ tasya
bālakasya na te viduḥ

na—not; *te*—the cowherd men and ladies; *śraddadhire*—put their faith (in such statements); *gopāḥ*—the cowherd men and women; *bāla-bhāṣitam*—childish talk from the assembled children; *iti uta*—thus spoken; *aprameyam*—unlimited, inconceivable; *balam*—the power; *tasya bālakasya*—of the small baby Kṛṣṇa; *na*—not; *te*—the *gopīs* and *gopas*; *viduḥ*—were aware of.

TRANSLATION

The assembled gopīs and gopas, unaware that Kṛṣṇa is always unlimited, could not believe that baby Kṛṣṇa had such inconceivable power. They could not believe the statements of the children, and therefore they neglected these statements as being childish talk.

TEXT 11

रुदन्तं सुतमादाय यशोदा ग्रहशङ्किता ।
कृतस्वस्त्ययनं विप्रैः सूक्तैः स्तनमपाययत् ॥११॥

rudantaṁ sutam ādāya
yaśodā graha-śaṅkitā
kṛta-svastyayanaṁ vipraiḥ
sūktaiḥ stanam apāyayat

rudantam—crying; *sutam*—son; *ādāya*—picking up; *yaśodā*—mother Yaśodā; *graha-śaṅkitā*—fearing some bad planet; *kṛta-svastyayanam*—immediately performed a ritualistic ceremony for good fortune; *vipraiḥ*—by calling all the *brāhmaṇas; sūktaiḥ*—by Vedic hymns; *stanam*—her breast; *apāyayat*—made the child suck.

TRANSLATION

Thinking that some bad planet had attacked Kṛṣṇa, mother Yaśodā picked up the crying child and allowed Him to suck her breast. Then she called for experienced brāhmaṇas to chant Vedic hymns and perform an auspicious ritualistic ceremony.

PURPORT

Whenever there is some danger or some inauspicious occurrence, it is the custom of Vedic civilization to have qualified *brāhmaṇas* immediately chant Vedic hymns to counteract it. Mother Yaśodā did this properly and allowed the baby to suck her breast.

TEXT 12

पूर्ववत् स्थापितं गोपैर्बलिभिः सपरिच्छदम् ।
विप्रा हुत्वार्चयाञ्चक्रुर्दध्यक्षतकुशाम्बुभिः ॥१२॥

pūrvavat sthāpitaṁ gopair
balibhiḥ sa-paricchadam
viprā hutvārcayāṁ cakrur
dadhy-akṣata-kuśāmbubhiḥ

pūrva-vat—as the handcart had been situated before; *sthāpitam*—again assembled with the pots situated properly; *gopaiḥ*—by the cowherd men; *balibhiḥ*—all of whom were very strong and stout and who could therefore assemble the parts without difficulty; *sa-paricchadam*—with all the paraphernalia kept on it; *viprāḥ*—the *brāhmaṇas; hutvā*—after performing a fire ceremony; *arcayām cakruḥ*—performed ritualistic ceremonies; *dadhi*—with curd; *akṣata*—grains of rice; *kuśa*—and *kuśa* grass; *ambubhiḥ*—with water.

TRANSLATION

After the strong, stout cowherd men assembled the pots and paraphernalia on the handcart and set it up as before, the brāhmaṇas performed a ritualistic ceremony with a fire sacrifice to appease the bad planet, and then, with rice grains, kuśa, water and curd, they worshiped the Supreme Lord.

PURPORT

The handcart was loaded with heavy utensils and other paraphernalia. To set the cart back in its original position required much strength, but this was easily done by the cowherd men. Then, according to the system of the *gopa-jāti,* various Vedic ceremonies were performed to appease the calamitous situation.

TEXTS 13–15

येऽसूयानृतदम्भेर्षाहिंसामानविवर्जिताः ।
न तेषां सत्यशीलानामाशिषो विफलाः कृताः ॥१३॥
इति बालकमादाय सामर्ग्यजुरुपाकृतैः ।
जलैः पवित्रौषधिभिरभिषिच्य द्विजोत्तमैः ॥१४॥
वाचयित्वा स्वस्त्ययनं नन्दगोपः समाहितः ।
हुत्वा चाग्निं द्विजातिभ्यः प्रादादन्नं महागुणम् ॥१५॥

ye 'sūyānṛta-dambherṣā-
hiṁsā-māna-vivarjitāḥ
na teṣāṁ satya-śīlānām
āśiṣo viphalāḥ kṛtāḥ

iti bālakam ādāya
sāmarg-yajur-upākṛtaiḥ
jalaiḥ pavitrauṣadhibhir
abhiṣicya dvijottamaiḥ

vāciyitvā svastyayanaṁ
nanda-gopaḥ samāhitaḥ

hutvā cāgniṁ dvijātibhyaḥ
prādād annaṁ mahā-guṇam

ye—those *brāhmaṇas* who; *asūya*—envy; *anṛta*—untruthfulness; *dambha*—false pride; *īrṣā*—grudges; *hiṁsā*—being disturbed by the opulence of others; *māna*—false prestige; *vivarjitāḥ*—completely devoid of; *na*—not; *teṣām*—of such *brāhmaṇas; satya-śīlānām*—who are endowed with perfect brahminical qualifications (*satya, śama, dama,* etc.); *āśiṣaḥ*—the blessings; *viphalāḥ*—useless; *kṛtāḥ*—have become; *iti*—considering all these things; *bālakam*—the child; *ādāya*—taking care of; *sāma*—according to the *Sāma Veda; ṛk*—according to the *Ṛg Veda; yajuḥ*—and according to the *Yajur Veda; upākṛtaiḥ*—purified by such means; *jalaiḥ*—with water; *pavitra-auṣadhibhiḥ*—mixed with pure herbs; *abhiṣicya*—after bathing (the child); *dvija-uttamaiḥ*—with ceremonies performed by first-class *brāhmaṇas* with the above qualifications; *vācayitvā*—requested to be chanted; *svasti-ayanam*—auspicious hymns; *nanda-gopaḥ*—Mahārāja Nanda, the head of the cowherd men; *samāhitaḥ*—liberal and good; *hutvā*—after offering oblations; *ca*—also; *agnim*—unto the sacred fire; *dvijātibhyaḥ*—unto those first-class *brāhmaṇas; prādāt*—gave in charity; *annam*—food grains; *mahā-guṇam*—excellent.

TRANSLATION

When brāhmaṇas are free from envy, untruthfulness, unnecessary pride, grudges, disturbance by the opulence of others, and false prestige, their blessings never go in vain. Considering this, Nanda Mahārāja soberly took Kṛṣṇa on his lap and invited such truthful brāhmaṇas to perform a ritualistic ceremony according to the holy hymns of the Sāma Veda, Ṛg Veda and Yajur Veda. Then, while the hymns were being chanted, he bathed the child with water mixed with pure herbs, and after performing a fire ceremony, he sumptuously fed all the brāhmaṇas with first-class grains and other food.

PURPORT

Nanda Mahārāja was very confident about the qualifications of the *brāhmaṇas* and their blessings. He was fully confident that simply if the good *brāhmaṇas* showered their blessings, the child Kṛṣṇa would be happy. The blessings of qualified *brāhmaṇas* can bring happiness not only to Kṛṣṇa, the Supreme Personality of Godhead, but to everyone. Because Kṛṣṇa is self-sufficient, He does not require anyone's blessings, yet Nanda Mahārāja thought that Kṛṣṇa required the blessings of the *brāhmaṇas*. What then is to be said of others? In human society, therefore, there must be an ideal class of men, *brāhmaṇas*, who can bestow blessings upon others, namely, upon the *kṣatriyas*, *vaiśyas* and *śūdras*, so that everyone will be happy. Kṛṣṇa therefore says in *Bhagavad-gītā* (4.13) that human society must have four social orders (*cātur-varṇyaṁ mayā sṛṣṭaṁ guṇa-karma-vibhāgaśaḥ*); it is not that everyone should become a *śūdra* or a *vaiśya* and human society will prosper. As enunciated in *Bhagavad-gītā*, there must be a class of *brāhmaṇas* with qualities like *satya* (truthfulness), *śama* (peacefulness), *dama* (self-control) and *titikṣā* (tolerance).

Here also, in the *Bhāgavatam*, Nanda Mahārāja invites qualified *brāhmaṇas*. There may be caste *brāhmaṇas*, and we have all respect for them, but their birth in *brāhmaṇa* families does not mean that they are qualified to bestow blessings upon the other members of human society. This is the verdict of the *śāstras*. In Kali-yuga, caste *brāhmaṇas* are accepted as *brāhmaṇas*. *Vipratve sūtram eva hi* (*Bhāg*. 12.2.3): in Kali-yuga, simply by putting on a thread worth two paise, one becomes a *brāhmaṇa*. Such *brāhmaṇas* were not called for by Nanda Mahārāja. As stated by Nārada Muni (*Bhāg*. 7.11.35), *yasya yal lakṣaṇaṁ proktam*. The symptoms of a *brāhmaṇa* are stated in *śāstra*, and one must be qualified with these symptoms.

The blessings of *brāhmaṇas* who are not envious, disturbed or puffed up with pride and false prestige and who are fully qualified with truthfulness will be useful. Therefore a class of men must be trained as *brāhmaṇas* from the very beginning. *Brahmacārī guru-kule vasan dānto guror hitam* (*Bhāg*. 7.12.1). The word *dāntaḥ* is very important. *Dāntaḥ* refers to one who is not envious, disturbing or puffed up with false prestige. With the Kṛṣṇa consciousness movement, we are trying to introduce such *brāhmaṇas* in society. *Brāhmaṇas* must ultimately be Vaiṣṇavas, and if one is a Vaiṣṇava, he has already acquired the qualifications of a *brāhmaṇa*. *Brahma-bhūtaḥ prasannātmā* (Bg. 18.54). The word *brahma-bhūta* refers to becoming a *brāhmaṇa*, or understanding what is Brahman (*brahma jānātīti brāhmaṇaḥ*). One who is *brahma-bhūta* is always happy (*prasannātmā*). *Na śocati na kāṅkṣati:* he is never disturbed about material necessities. *Samaḥ sarveṣu bhūteṣu:* he is ready to bestow blessings upon everyone equally. *Mad-bhaktiṁ labhate parām:* then he becomes a Vaiṣṇava. In this age, Śrīla Bhaktisiddhānta Sarasvatī Ṭhākura introduced the sacred thread ceremony for his Vaiṣṇava disciples, with the idea that people should understand that when one becomes a Vaiṣṇava he has already acquired the qualifications of a *brāhmaṇa.* Therefore in the International Society for Krishna Consciousness, those who are twice initiated so as to become *brāhmaṇas* must bear in mind their great responsibility to be truthful, control the mind and senses, be tolerant, and so on. Then their life will be successful. It was such *brāhmaṇas* that Nanda Mahārāja invited to chant the Vedic hymns, not ordinary *brāhmaṇas.* Verse thirteen distinctly mentions *hiṁsā-māna.* The word *māna* refers to false prestige or false pride. Those who were falsely proud, thinking that they were *brāhmaṇas* because they were born in *brāhmaṇa* families, were never invited by Nanda Mahārāja on such occasions.

Verse fourteen mentions *pavitrauṣadhi.* In any ritualistic ceremony, many herbs and leaves were required. These were known as *pavitra-patra.* Sometimes there were *nimba* leaves, sometimes bael leaves, mango leaves, *aśvattha* leaves or *āmalakī* leaves. Similarly, there were *pañca-gavya, pañca-śasya* and *pañca-ratna.* Although Nanda Mahārāja belonged to the *vaiśya* community, everything was known to him.

The most important word in these verses is *mahā-guṇam,* indicating that the *brāhmaṇas* were offered very palatable food of exalted quality. Such palatable dishes were generally prepared with two things, namely food grains and milk products. *Bhagavad-gītā* (18.44) therefore enjoins that human society must give protection to the cows and encourage agriculture (*kṛṣi-go-rakṣya-vāṇijyaṁ vaiśya-karma svabhāvajam*). Simply by expert cooking, hundreds and thousands of palatable dishes can be prepared from agricultural produce and milk products. This is indicated here by the words *annaṁ mahā-guṇam.* Still today in India, from these two things, namely food grains and milk, hundreds and thousands of varieties of food are prepared, and then they are offered to the Supreme Personality of Godhead. (*Catur-vidha-śrī-bhagavat-prasāda. Patraṁ puṣpaṁ phalaṁ toyaṁ yo me bhaktyā prayacchati.*) Then the *prasāda* is distributed. Even today in Jagannātha-kṣetra and other big temples, very palatable dishes are offered to the Deity, and *prasāda* is distributed profusely. Cooked by first-class *brāhmaṇas* with expert knowledge and then distributed to the public, this *prasāda* is also a blessing from the *brāhmaṇas* or Vaiṣṇavas. There are four kinds of *prasāda* (*catur-vidha*). Salty, sweet, sour and pungent tastes are made with different types of spices, and the food is prepared in four divisions, called *carvya, cūṣya, lehya* and *pehya*—*prasāda* that is chewed, *prasāda* that is licked, *prasāda* tasted with the tongue, and *prasāda* that is drunk. Thus there are many varieties of *prasāda*, prepared very nicely with grains and ghee, offered to the Deity and distributed to the *brāhmaṇas* and Vaiṣṇavas and then to the general public. This is the way of human society. Killing the cows and spoiling the land will not solve the problem of food. This is not civilization. Uncivilized men living in the jungle and being unqualified to produce food by agriculture and cow protection may eat animals, but a perfect human society advanced in knowledge must learn how to produce first-class food simply by agriculture and protection of cows.

TEXT 16

गावः सर्वगुणोपेता वासःस्रग्रुक्ममालिनीः ।
आत्मजाभ्युदयार्थाय प्रादात्ते चान्वयुञ्जत ॥१६॥

gāvaḥ sarva-guṇopetā
vāsaḥ-srag-rukma-mālinīḥ
ātmajābhyudayārthāya
prādāt te cānvayuñjata

gāvaḥ—cows; *sarva-guṇa-upetāḥ*—being fully qualified by giving sufficient milk, etc.; *vāsaḥ*—well dressed; *srak*—with flower garlands; *rukma-mālinīḥ*—and with garlands of gold; *ātmaja-abhyudaya-arthāya*—for the purpose of his son's affluence; *prādāt*—gave in charity; *te*—those *brāhmaṇas; ca*—also; *anvayuñjata*—accepted them.

TRANSLATION

Nanda Mahārāja, for the sake of the affluence of his own son Kṛṣṇa, gave the brāhmaṇas cows fully decorated with garments,

flower garlands and gold necklaces. These cows, fully qualified to give ample milk, were given to the brāhmaṇas in charity, and the brāhmaṇas accepted them and bestowed blessings upon the whole family, and especially upon Kṛṣṇa.

PURPORT

Nanda Mahārāja first fed the *brāhmaṇas* sumptuously and then gave them in charity first-class cows fully decorated with golden necklaces, garments and flower garlands.

TEXT 17

विप्रा मन्त्रविदो युक्तास्तैर्याः प्रोक्तास्तथाशिषः ।
ता निष्फला भविष्यन्ति न कदाचिदपि स्फुटम् ॥१७॥

viprā mantra-vido yuktās
tair yāḥ proktās tathāśiṣaḥ
tā niṣphalā bhaviṣyanti
na kadācid api sphuṭam

viprāḥ—the *brāhmaṇas; mantra-vidaḥ*—completely expert in chanting the Vedic hymns; *yuktāḥ*—perfect mystic *yogīs; taiḥ*—by them; *yāḥ*—whatsoever; *proktāḥ*—was spoken; *tathā*—becomes just so; *āśiṣaḥ*—all blessings; *tāḥ*—such words; *niṣphalāḥ*—useless, without fruit; *bhaviṣyanti na*—never will become; *kadācit*—at any time; *api*—indeed; *sphuṭam*—always factual, as it is.

TRANSLATION

The brāhmaṇas, who were completely expert in chanting the Vedic hymns, were all yogīs fully equipped with mystic powers. Whatever blessings they spoke were certainly never fruitless.

PURPORT

Brāhmaṇas fully equipped with the brahminical qualifications are always *yogīs* fully powerful in mystic *yoga*. Their words never fail. In every transaction with other members of society, *brāhmaṇas* are certainly dependable. In this age, however, one must take into account that the *brāhmaṇas* are uncertain in their qualifications. Because there are no yajñic *brāhmaṇas,* all *yajñas* are forbidden. The only *yajña* recommended in this age is *saṅkīrtana-yajña. Yajñaiḥ saṅkīrtana-prāyair yajanti hi sumedhasaḥ* (*Bhāg.* 11.5.32). *Yajña* is meant to satisfy Viṣṇu (*yajñārthāt karmaṇo 'nyatra loko 'yaṁ karma-bandhanaḥ*). Because in this age there are no qualified *brāhmaṇas,* people should perform *yajña* by chanting the Hare Kṛṣṇa *mantra* (*yajñaiḥ saṅkīrtana-prāyair yajanti hi sumedhasaḥ*). Life is meant for *yajña,* and *yajña* is performed by the chanting of Hare Kṛṣṇa, Hare Kṛṣṇa, Kṛṣṇa Kṛṣṇa, Hare Hare/ Hare Rāma, Hare Rāma, Rāma Rāma, Hare Hare.

TEXT 18

एकदारोहमारूढं लालयन्ती सुतं सती ।
गरिमाणं शिशोर्वोढुं न सेहे गिरिकूटवत् ॥१८॥

ekadāroham ārūḍhaṁ
lālayantī sutaṁ satī
garimāṇaṁ śiśor voḍhuṁ
na sehe giri-kūṭavat

ekadā—one time (estimated to have been when Kṛṣṇa was one year old); *āroham*—on His mother's lap; *ārūḍham*—who was sitting; *lālayantī*—was patting; *sutam*—her son; *satī*—mother Yaśodā; *garimāṇam*—because of an increase in heaviness; *śiśoḥ*—of the child; *voḍhum*—to bear Him; *na*—not; *sehe*—was able; *giri-kūṭa-vat*—appearing like the weight of a mountain peak.

TRANSLATION

One day, a year after Kṛṣṇa's appearance, mother Yaśodā was patting her son on her lap. But suddenly she felt the child to be heavier than a mountain peak, and she could no longer bear His weight.

PURPORT

Lālayantī. Sometimes a mother lifts her child, and when the child falls in her hands, the child laughs, and the mother also enjoys pleasure. Yaśodā used to do this, but this time Kṛṣṇa became very heavy, and she could not bear His weight. Under the circumstances, it is to be understood that Kṛṣṇa was aware of the coming of Tṛṇāvartāsura, who would take Him far away from His mother. Kṛṣṇa knew that when Tṛṇāvarta came and took Him away from His mother's lap, mother Yaśodā would be greatly bereaved. He did not want His mother to suffer any difficulty from the demon. Therefore, because He is the source of everything (*janmādy asya yataḥ*), He assumed the heaviness of the entire universe. The child was on the lap of Yaśodā, who was therefore in possession of everything in the world, but when the child assumed such heaviness, she had to put Him down in order to give Tṛṇāvartāsura an opportunity to take Him away and play with Him for some time before the child returned to the lap of His mother.

TEXT 19

भूमौ निधाय तं गोपी विस्मिता भारपीडिता ।
महापुरुषमादध्यौ जगतामास कर्मसु ॥१९॥

bhūmau nidhāya taṁ gopī
vismitā bhāra-pīḍitā
mahā-puruṣam ādadhyau
jagatām āsa karmasu

bhūmau—on the ground; *nidhāya*—placing; *tam*—the child; *gopī*—mother Yaśodā; *vismitā*—being astonished; *bhāra-pīḍitā*—being aggrieved by the weight of the child; *mahā-puruṣam*—Lord Viṣṇu, Nārāyaṇa; *ādadhyau*—took shelter of; *jagatām*—as if the weight of the whole world; *āsa*—engaged herself; *karmasu*—in other household affairs.

TRANSLATION

Feeling the child to be as heavy as the entire universe and therefore being anxious, thinking that perhaps the child was being attacked by some other ghost or demon, the astonished mother Yaśodā put the child down on the ground and began to think of Nārāyaṇa. Foreseeing disturbances, she called for the brāhmaṇas to counteract this heaviness, and then she engaged in her other household affairs. She had no alternative than to remember the lotus feet of Nārāyaṇa, for she could not understand that Kṛṣṇa was the original source of everything.

PURPORT

Mother Yaśodā did not understand that Kṛṣṇa is the heaviest of all heavy things and that Kṛṣṇa rests within everything (*mat-sthāni sarva-bhūtāni*). As confirmed in *Bhagavad-gītā* (9.4), *mayā tatam idaṁ sarvaṁ jagad avyakta-mūrtinā:* Kṛṣṇa is everywhere in His impersonal form, and everything rests upon Him. Nonetheless, *na cāhaṁ teṣv avasthitaḥ:* Kṛṣṇa is not everywhere. Mother Yaśodā was unable to understand this philosophy because she was dealing with Kṛṣṇa as His real mother by the arrangement of *yogamāyā.* Not understanding the importance of Kṛṣṇa, she could only seek shelter of Nārāyaṇa for Kṛṣṇa's safety and call the *brāhmaṇas* to counteract the situation.

TEXT 20

दैत्यो नाम्ना तृणावर्तः कंसभृत्यः प्रणोदितः ।
चक्रवातस्वरूपेण जहारासीनमर्भकम् ॥२०॥

daityo nāmnā tṛṇāvartaḥ
kaṁsa-bhṛtyaḥ praṇoditaḥ
cakravāta-svarūpeṇa
jahārāsīnam arbhakam

daityaḥ—another demon; *nāmnā*—by the name; *tṛṇāvartaḥ*—Tṛṇāvartāsura; *kaṁsa-bhṛtyaḥ*—a servant of Kaṁsa; *praṇoditaḥ*—having been induced by him; *cakravāta-svarūpeṇa*—in the form of a whirlwind; *jahāra*—swept away; *āsīnam*—the sitting; *arbhakam*—child.

TRANSLATION

While the child was sitting on the ground, a demon named Tṛṇāvarta, who was a servant of Kaṁsa's, came there as a whirlwind, at Kaṁsa's instigation, and very easily carried the child away into the air.

PURPORT

Kṛṣṇa's heaviness was unbearable for the child's mother, but when Tṛṇāvartāsura came, he immediately carried the child away. This was another demonstration of Kṛṣṇa's inconceivable energy. When the Tṛṇāvarta demon came, Kṛṣṇa became lighter than the grass so that the demon could carry Him away. This was *ānanda-cinmaya-rasa*, Kṛṣṇa's blissful, transcendental pleasure.

TEXT 21

गोकुलं सर्वमावृण्वन् मुष्णंश्चक्षूंषि रेणुभिः ।
ईरयन् सुमहाघोरशब्देन प्रदिशो दिशः ॥२१॥

gokulaṁ sarvam āvṛṇvan
muṣṇaṁś cakṣūṁṣi reṇubhiḥ
īrayan sumahā-ghora-
śabdena pradiśo diśaḥ

gokulam—the whole tract of land known as Gokula; *sarvam*—everywhere; *āvṛṇvan*—covering; *muṣṇan*—taking away; *cakṣūṁṣi*—the power of vision; *reṇubhiḥ*—by particles of dust; *īrayan*—was vibrating; *su-mahā-ghora*—very fierce and heavy; *śabdena*—with a sound; *pradiśaḥ diśaḥ*—entered everywhere, in all directions.

TRANSLATION

Covering the whole land of Gokula with particles of dust, that demon, acting as a strong whirlwind, covered everyone's vision and began vibrating everywhere with a greatly fearful sound.

PURPORT

Tṛṇāvartāsura assumed the form of a whirlwind and covered with a dust storm the whole tract of land known as Gokula, so that no one could see even the nearest thing.

TEXT 22

मुहूर्तमभवद् गोष्ठं रजसा तमसावृतम् ।
सुतं यशोदा नापश्यत्तस्मिन् न्यस्तवती यतः ॥२२॥

muhūrtam abhavad goṣṭhaṁ
rajasā tamasāvṛtam
sutaṁ yaśodā nāpaśyat
tasmin nyastavatī yataḥ

muhūrtam—for a moment; *abhavat*—there was; *goṣṭham*—throughout the whole pasturing ground; *rajasā*—by big particles of dust; *tamasā āvṛtam*—covered with darkness; *sutam*—her son; *yaśodā*—mother Yaśodā; *na apaśyat*—could not find; *tasmin*—in that very spot; *nyastavatī*—she had placed Him; *yataḥ*—where.

TRANSLATION

For a moment, the whole pasturing ground was overcast with dense darkness from the dust storm, and mother Yaśodā was unable to find her son where she had placed Him.

TEXT 23

नापश्यत् कश्चनात्मानं परं चापि विमोहितः ।
तृणावर्तनिसृष्टाभिः शर्कराभिरुपद्रुतः ॥२३॥

nāpaśyat kaścanātmānaṁ
paraṁ cāpi vimohitaḥ
tṛṇāvarta-nisṛṣṭābhiḥ
śarkarābhir upadrutaḥ

na—not; *apaśyat*—saw; *kaścana*—anyone; *ātmānam*—himself; *param ca api*—or another; *vimohitaḥ*—being illusioned; *tṛṇāvarta-nisṛṣṭābhiḥ*—thrown by Tṛṇāvartāsura; *śarkarābhiḥ*—by the sands; *upadrutaḥ*—and thus being disturbed.

TRANSLATION

Because of the bits of sand thrown about by Tṛṇāvarta, people could not see themselves or anyone else, and thus they were illusioned and disturbed.

TEXT 24

इति खरपवनचक्रपांशुवर्षे
सुतपदवीमबलाविलक्ष्य माता ।
अतिकरुणमनुस्मरन्त्यशोचद्
भुवि पतिता मृतवत्सका यथा गौः ॥२४॥

iti khara-pavana-cakra-pāṁśu-varṣe
suta-padavīm abalāvilakṣya mātā
atikaruṇam anusmaranty aśocad
bhuvi patitā mṛta-vatsakā yathā gauḥ

iti—thus; *khara*—very strong; *pavana-cakra*—by a whirlwind; *pāṁśu-varṣe*—when there were showers of dust and small dust particles; *suta-padavīm*—the place of her son; *abalā*—the innocent woman; *avilakṣya*—not seeing; *mātā*—because of being His mother; *ati-karuṇam*—very pitifully; *anusmarantī*—she was thinking of her son; *aśocat*—lamented extraordinarily; *bhuvi*—on the ground; *patitā*—fell down; *mṛta-vatsakā*—who has lost her calf; *yathā*—like; *gauḥ*—a cow.

TRANSLATION

Because of the dust storm stirred up by the strong whirlwind, mother Yaśodā could find no trace of her son, nor could she understand why. Thus she fell down on the ground like a cow who has lost her calf and began to lament very pitifully.

TEXT 25

रुदितमनुनिशम्य तत्र गोप्यो
भृशमनुतप्तधियोऽश्रुपूर्णमुख्यः ।
रुरुदुरनुपलभ्य नन्दसूनुं
पवन उपारतपांशुवर्षवेगे ॥२५॥

ruditam anuniśamya tatra gopyo
bhṛśam anutapta-dhiyo 'śru-pūrṇa-mukhyaḥ

rurudur anupalabhya nanda-sūnuṁ
pavana upārata-pāṁśu-varṣa-vege

ruditam—mother Yaśodā, crying pitifully; *anuniśamya*—after hearing; *tatra*—there; *gopyaḥ*—the other ladies, the *gopīs; bhṛśam*—highly; *anutapta*—lamenting sympathetically after mother Yaśodā; *dhiyaḥ*—with such feelings; *aśru-pūrṇa-mukhyaḥ*—and the other *gopīs*, their faces full of tears; *ruruduḥ*—they were crying; *anupalabhya*—without finding; *nanda-sūnum*—the son of Nanda Mahārāja, Kṛṣṇa; *pavane*—when the whirlwind; *upārata*—had ceased; *pāṁśu-varṣa-vege*—its force of showering dust.

TRANSLATION

When the force of the dust storm and the winds subsided, Yaśodā's friends, the other gopīs, approached mother Yaśodā, hearing her pitiful crying. Not seeing Kṛṣṇa present, they too felt very much aggrieved and joined mother Yaśodā in crying, their eyes full of tears.

PURPORT

This attachment of the *gopīs* to Kṛṣṇa is wonderful and transcendental. The center of all the activities of the *gopīs* was Kṛṣṇa. When Kṛṣṇa was there they were happy, and when Kṛṣṇa was not there, they were unhappy. Thus when mother Yaśodā was lamenting Kṛṣṇa's absence, the other ladies also began to cry.

TEXT 26

तृणावर्तः शान्तरयो वात्यारूपधरो हरन् ।
कृष्णं नभोगतो गन्तुं नाशक्नोद् भूरिभारभृत् ॥२६॥

tṛṇāvartaḥ śānta-rayo
vātyā-rūpa-dharo haran
kṛṣṇaṁ nabho-gato gantuṁ
nāśaknod bhūri-bhāra-bhṛt

tṛṇāvartaḥ—the demon Tṛṇāvarta; *śānta-rayaḥ*—the force of the blast reduced; *vātyā-rūpa-dharaḥ*—who had assumed the form of a forceful whirlwind; *haran*—and had thus taken away; *kṛṣṇam*—Kṛṣṇa, the Supreme Personality of Godhead; *nabhaḥ-gataḥ*—went up to the top of the sky; *gantum*—to go further; *na aśaknot*—was not able; *bhūri-bhāra-bhṛt*—because Kṛṣṇa then became more powerful and heavy than the demon.

TRANSLATION

Having assumed the form of a forceful whirlwind, the demon Tṛṇāvarta took Kṛṣṇa very high in the sky, but when Kṛṣṇa became heavier than the demon, the demon had to stop his force and could go no further.

PURPORT

Here is a competition in yogic power between Kṛṣṇa and Tṛṇāvartāsura. By practicing mystic *yoga, asuras* generally attain some perfection in the eight *siddhis*, or perfections, namely *aṇimā, laghimā, mahimā, prāpti, prākāmya, īśitva, vaśitva* and *kāmāvasāyitā*. But although a demon may acquire such powers to a very limited extent, he cannot compete with the mystic power of Kṛṣṇa, for Kṛṣṇa is Yogeśvara, the source of all mystic power (*yatra yogeśvaro hariḥ*). No one can compete with Kṛṣṇa. Sometimes, of course, having acquired a fragmental portion of Kṛṣṇa's mystic power, *asuras* demonstrate their power to the foolish public and assert themselves to be God, not knowing that God is the supreme Yogeśvara. Here also we see that Tṛṇāvarta assumed the *mahimā-siddhi* and took Kṛṣṇa away as if Kṛṣṇa were an ordinary child. But Kṛṣṇa also became a mystic *mahimā-siddha*. When mother Yaśodā was carrying Him, He became so heavy that His mother, who was usually accustomed to carrying Him, could not bear Him and had to place Him down on the ground. Thus Tṛṇāvarta had been able to take Kṛṣṇa away in the presence of mother Yaśodā. But when Kṛṣṇa, high in the sky, assumed the *mahimā-siddhi*, the demon, unable to go further, was obliged to stop his force and come down according to Kṛṣṇa's desire. One should not, therefore, compete with Kṛṣṇa's mystic power.

Devotees automatically have all mystic power, but they do not like to compete with Kṛṣṇa. Instead, they fully surrender to Kṛṣṇa, and their yogic power is demonstrated by Kṛṣṇa's mercy. Devotees can show mystic *yoga* so powerful that a demon could not even dream of it, but they never try to demonstrate it for their personal sense gratification.

Whatever they do is for the service of the Lord, and therefore they are always in a position superior to that of the demons. There are many *karmīs*, *yogīs* and *jñānīs* who artificially try to compete with Kṛṣṇa, and thus ordinary, foolish people who do not care to hear *Śrīmad-Bhāgavatam* from authorities consider some rascal *yogī* to be Bhagavān, the Supreme Personality of Godhead. At the present moment there are many so-called *bābās* who present themselves as incarnations of God by showing some insignificant mystic wonder, and foolish people regard them as God because of lacking knowledge of Kṛṣṇa.

TEXT 27

तमश्मानं मन्यमान आत्मनो गुरुमत्तया ।
गले गृहीत उत्स्रष्टुं नाशक्नोदद्भुतार्भकम् ॥२७॥

tam aśmānaṁ manyamāna
ātmano guru-mattayā
gale gṛhīta utsraṣṭuṁ
nāśaknod adbhutārbhakam

tam—Kṛṣṇa; *aśmānam*—very heavy stone like a lump of iron; *manyamānaḥ*—thinking like that; *ātmanaḥ guru-mattayā*—because of being heavier than he could personally perceive; *gale*—his neck; *gṛhīte*—being embraced or encircled by His arms; *utsraṣṭum*—to give up; *na aśaknot*—was not able; *adbhuta-arbhakam*—this wonderful child who was different from an ordinary child.

TRANSLATION

Because of Kṛṣṇa's weight, Tṛṇāvarta considered Him to be like a great mountain or a hunk of iron. But because Kṛṣṇa had caught the demon's neck, the demon was unable to throw Him off. He therefore thought of the child as wonderful, since he could neither bear the child nor cast aside the burden.

PURPORT

Tṛṇāvarta intended to take Kṛṣṇa up in the sky and kill Him, but Kṛṣṇa enjoyed the pastime of riding on Tṛṇāvarta's body and traveling for a while in the sky. Thus Tṛṇāvarta's attempt to kill Kṛṣṇa failed, while Kṛṣṇa, *ānanda-cinmaya-rasa-vigraha,* enjoyed this pastime. Now, since Tṛṇāvarta was falling because of Kṛṣṇa's heaviness, he wanted to save himself by throwing Kṛṣṇa off from his neck, but was unable to do so because Kṛṣṇa held him very tightly. Consequently, this would be the last time for Tṛṇāvarta's yogic power. Now he was going to die by the arrangement of Kṛṣṇa.

TEXT 28

गलग्रहणनिश्चेष्टो दैत्यो निर्गतलोचनः ।
अव्यक्तरावो न्यपतत् सहबालो व्यसुर्व्रजे ॥२८॥

gala-grahaṇa-niśceṣṭo
daityo nirgata-locanaḥ
avyakta-rāvo nyapatat
saha-bālo vyasur vraje

gala-grahaṇa-niśceṣṭaḥ—because of Kṛṣṇa's grasping the neck of the demon Tṛṇāvarta, the demon choked and could not do anything; *daityaḥ*—the demon; *nirgata-locanaḥ*—his eyes popped out because of pressure; *avyakta-rāvaḥ*—because of choking, he could not even make a sound; *nyapatat*—fell down; *saha-bālaḥ*—with the child; *vyasuḥ vraje*—lifeless on the ground of Vraja.

TRANSLATION

With Kṛṣṇa grasping him by the throat, Tṛṇāvarta choked, unable to make even a sound or even to move his hands and legs. His eyes popping out, the demon lost his life and fell, along with the little boy, down to the ground of Vraja.

TEXT 29

तमन्तरिक्षात् पतितं शिलायां
विशीर्णसर्वावयवं करालम् ।
पुरं यथा रुद्रशरेण विद्धं
स्त्रियो रुदत्यो ददृशुः समेताः ॥२९॥

tam antarikṣāt patitaṁ śilāyāṁ
viśīrṇa-sarvāvayavaṁ karālam
puraṁ yathā rudra-śareṇa viddhaṁ
striyo rudatyo dadṛśuḥ sametāḥ

tam—unto the demon Tṛṇāvarta; *antarikṣāt*—from outer space; *patitam*—fallen; *śilāyām*—on a slab of stone; *viśīrṇa*—scattered, separated; *sarva-avayavam*—all the parts of his body; *karālam*—very fierce hands and legs; *puram*—the place of Tripurāsura; *yathā*—as; *rudra-śareṇa*—by the arrow of Lord Śiva; *viddham*—pierced; *striyaḥ*—all the women, the *gopīs; rudatyaḥ*—although crying because Kṛṣṇa was separated from them; *dadṛśuḥ*—they saw in front of them; *sametāḥ*—all together.

TRANSLATION

While the gopīs who had gathered were crying for Kṛṣṇa, the demon fell from the sky onto a big slab of stone, his limbs dislocated, as if he had been pierced by the arrow of Lord Śiva like Tripurāsura.

PURPORT

In transcendental life, as soon as devotees of the Lord merge in lamentation, they immediately experience the Lord's transcendental activities and merge in transcendental bliss. Actually such devotees are always in transcendental bliss, and such apparent calamities provide a further impetus for that bliss.

TEXT 30

प्रादाय मात्रे प्रतिहृत्य विस्मिताः
कृष्णं च तस्योरसि लम्बमानम् ।
तं स्वस्तिमन्तं पुरुषादनीतं
विहायसा मृत्युमुखात् प्रमुक्तम् ।
गोप्यश्च गोपाः किल नन्दमुख्या
लब्ध्वा पुनः प्रापुरतीव मोदम् ॥३०॥

prādāya mātre pratihṛtya vismitāḥ
kṛṣṇaṁ ca tasyorasi lambamānam
taṁ svastimantaṁ puruṣāda-nītaṁ
vihāyasā mṛtyu-mukhāt pramuktam
gopyaś ca gopāḥ kila nanda-mukhyā
labdhvā punaḥ prāpur atīva modam

prādāya—after picking up; *mātre*—unto His mother (Yaśodā); *pratihṛtya*—delivered; *vismitāḥ*—all surprised; *kṛṣṇam ca*—and Kṛṣṇa; *tasya*—of the demon; *urasi*—on the chest; *lambamānam*—situated; *tam*—Kṛṣṇa; *svastimantam*—endowed with all auspiciousness; *puruṣa-ada-nītam*—who was taken by the man-eating demon; *vihāyasā*—into the sky; *mṛtyu-mukhāt*—from the mouth of death; *pramuktam*—now liberated; *gopyaḥ*—the *gopīs; ca*—and; *gopāḥ*—the cowherd men; *kila*—indeed; *nanda-mukhyāḥ*—headed by Nanda Mahārāja; *labdhvā*—after getting; *punaḥ*—again (their son); *prāpuḥ*—enjoyed; *atīva*—very much; *modam*—bliss.

TRANSLATION

The gopīs immediately picked Kṛṣṇa up from the chest of the demon and delivered Him, free from all inauspiciousness, to mother Yaśodā. Because the child, although taken into the sky by the demon, was unhurt and now free from all danger and misfortune, the gopīs and cowherd men, headed by Nanda Mahārāja, were extremely happy.

PURPORT

The demon fell flat from the sky, and Kṛṣṇa was playing on his chest very happily, uninjured and free from misfortune. Not at all disturbed because of being taken high in the sky by the demon, Kṛṣṇa was playing and enjoying. This is *ānanda-cinmaya-rasa-vigraha.* In any condition, Kṛṣṇa is *sac-cid-ānanda-vigraha.* He has no unhappiness. Others might have thought that He was in difficulty, but because the demon's chest was sufficiently broad to play on, the baby was happy in all respects. It was most astonishing that although the demon went so high in the sky, the child did not fall down. Therefore, the child had been saved virtually from the mouth of death. Now that He was saved, all the inhabitants of Vṛndāvana were happy.

TEXT 31

अहो बतात्यद्भुतमेष रक्षसा
बालो निवृत्तिं गमितोऽभ्यगात् पुनः ।
हिंस्रः स्वपापेन विहिंसितः खलः
साधुः समत्वेन भयाद् विमुच्यते ॥३१॥

aho batāty-adbhutam eṣa rakṣasā
bālo nivṛttiṁ gamito 'bhyagāt punaḥ
hiṁsraḥ sva-pāpena vihiṁsitaḥ khalaḥ
sādhuḥ samatvena bhayād vimucyate

aho—alas; *bata*—indeed; *ati*—very much; *adbhutam*—this incident is wonderfully astonishing; *eṣaḥ*—this (child); *rakṣasā*—by the man-eating demon; *bālaḥ*—the innocent child Kṛṣṇa; *nivṛttim*—taken away just to be killed and eaten; *gamitaḥ*—went away; *abhyagāt punaḥ*—but He has come back again unhurt; *hiṁsraḥ*—one who is envious; *sva-pāpena*—because of his own sinful activities; *vihiṁsitaḥ*—now (that demon) has been killed; *khalaḥ*—because he was envious and polluted; *sādhuḥ*—any person who is innocent and free from sinful life; *samatvena*—being equal to everyone; *bhayāt*—from all kinds of fear; *vimucyate*—becomes relieved.

TRANSLATION

It is most astonishing that although this innocent child was taken away by the Rākṣasa to be eaten, He has returned without having been killed or even injured. Because this demon was envious, cruel and sinful, he has been killed for his own sinful activities. This is the law of nature. An innocent devotee is always protected by the Supreme Personality of Godhead, and a sinful person is always vanquished for his sinful life.

PURPORT

Kṛṣṇa conscious life means innocent devotional life, and a *sādhu* is one who is fully devoted to Kṛṣṇa. As confirmed by Kṛṣṇa in *Bhagavad-gītā*

(9.30), *bhajate māṁ ananya-bhāk sādhur eva sa mantavyaḥ:* anyone fully attached to Kṛṣṇa is a *sādhu.* Nanda Mahārāja and the *gopīs* and other cowherd men could not understand that Kṛṣṇa was the Supreme Personality of Godhead playing as a human child and that His life was not in danger under any circumstances. Rather, because of their intense parental love for Kṛṣṇa, they thought that Kṛṣṇa was an innocent child and had been saved by the Supreme Lord.

In the material world, because of intense lust and desire for enjoyment, one becomes implicated in sinful life more and more (*kāma eṣa krodha eṣa rajo-guṇa-samudbhavaḥ*). Therefore the quality of fear is one of the aspects of material life (*āhāra-nidrā-bhaya-maithunaṁ ca*). But if one becomes Kṛṣṇa conscious, the process of devotional service, *śravaṇaṁ kīrtanam,* diminishes one's polluted life of material existence, and one is purified and protected by the Supreme Personality of Godhead. *Śṛṇvatāṁ sva-kathāḥ kṛṣṇaḥ puṇya-śravaṇa-kīrtanaḥ.* In devotional life, one has faith in this process. Such faith is one of the six kinds of surrender. *Rakṣiṣyatīti viśvāsaḥ* (*Hari-bhakti-vilāsa* 11.676). One of the processes of surrender is that one should simply depend on Kṛṣṇa, convinced that He will give one all protection. That Kṛṣṇa will protect His devotee is a fact, and Nanda Mahārāja and the other inhabitants of Vṛndāvana accepted this very simply, although they did not know that the Supreme Lord Himself was present before them. There have been many instances in which a devotee like Prahlāda Mahārāja or Dhruva Mahārāja has been put in difficulty even by his father but has been saved under all circumstances. Therefore our only business is to become Kṛṣṇa conscious and depend fully on Kṛṣṇa for all protection.

TEXT 32

किं नस्तपश्चीर्णमधोक्षजार्चनं
पूर्तेष्टदत्तमुत भूतसौहृदम् ।
यत्संपरेतः पुनरेव बालको
दिष्ट्या स्वबन्धून् प्रणयन्नुपस्थितः ॥३२॥

kiṁ nas tapaś cīrṇam adhokṣajārcanaṁ
pūrteṣṭa-dattam uta bhūta-sauhṛdam

yat samparetaḥ punar eva bālako
diṣṭyā sva-bandhūn praṇayann upasthitaḥ

kim—what kind of; *naḥ*—by us; *tapaḥ*—austerity; *cīrṇam*—has been done for a very long time; *adhokṣaja*—of the Supreme Personality of Godhead; *arcanam*—worshiping; *pūrta*—constructing public roads, etc.; *iṣṭa*—activities for public benefit; *dattam*—giving charity; *uta*—or else; *bhūta-sauhṛdam*—because of love for the general public; *yat*—by the result of which; *samparetaḥ*—even though the child was practically lost in death; *punaḥ eva*—even again because of pious activities; *bālakaḥ*—the child; *diṣṭyā*—by fortune; *sva-bandhūn*—all His relatives; *praṇayan*—to please; *upasthitaḥ*—is present here.

TRANSLATION

Nanda Mahārāja and the others said: We must previously have performed austerities for a very long time, worshiped the Supreme Personality of Godhead, performed pious activities for public life, constructing public roads and wells, and also given charity, as a result of which this boy, although faced with death, has returned to give happiness to His relatives.

PURPORT

Nanda Mahārāja confirmed that by pious activities one can become a *sādhu* so that one will be happy at home and one's children will be protected. In *śāstra* there are many injunctions for *karmīs* and *jñānīs*, especially for *karmīs*, by which they can become pious and happy even in material life. According to Vedic civilization, one should perform activities for the benefit of the public, such as constructing public roads, planting trees on both sides of the road so that people can walk in the shade, and constructing public wells so that everyone can take water without difficulty. One should perform austerity to control one's desires, and one must simultaneously worship the Supreme Personality of Godhead. Thus one becomes pious, and as a result one is happy even in material conditions of life.

TEXT 33

दृष्ट्वाद्भुतानि बहुशो नन्दगोपो बृहद्वने ।
वसुदेववचो भूयो मानयामास विस्मितः ॥३३॥

dṛṣṭvādbhutāni bahuśo
nanda-gopo bṛhadvane
vasudeva-vaco bhūyo
mānayām āsa vismitaḥ

dṛṣṭvā—after seeing; *adbhutāni*—the very wonderful and astonishing incidents; *bahuśaḥ*—many times; *nanda-gopaḥ*—Nanda Mahārāja, the head of the cowherd men; *bṛhadvane*—in Bṛhadvana; *vasudeva-vacaḥ*—the words spoken by Vasudeva when Nanda Mahārāja was in Mathurā; *bhūyaḥ*—again and again; *mānayām āsa*—accepted how true they were; *vismitaḥ*—in great astonishment.

TRANSLATION

Having seen all these incidents in Bṛhadvana, Nanda Mahārāja became more and more astonished, and he remembered the words spoken to him by Vasudeva in Mathurā.

TEXT 34

एकदार्भकमादाय स्वाङ्कमारोप्य भामिनी ।
प्रस्नुतं पाययामास स्तनं स्नेहपरिप्लुता ॥३४॥

ekadārbhakam ādāya
svāṅkam āropya bhāminī
prasnutaṁ pāyayām āsa
stanaṁ sneha-pariplutā

ekadā—once upon a time; *arbhakam*—the child; *ādāya*—taking; *sva-aṅkam*—on her own lap; *āropya*—and placing Him; *bhāminī*—mother Yaśodā; *prasnutam*—breast milk oozing out; *pāyayām āsa*—fed the child; *stanam*—her breast; *sneha-pariplutā*—with great affection and love.

TRANSLATION

One day mother Yaśodā, having taken Kṛṣṇa up and placed Him on her lap, was feeding Him milk from her breast with maternal affection. The milk was flowing from her breast, and the child was drinking it.

TEXTS 35–36

पीतप्रायस्य जननी सुतस्य रुचिरस्मितम् ।
मुखं लालयती राजञ्जृम्भतो ददृशे इदम् ॥३५॥
खं रोदसी ज्योतिरनीकमाशाः
सूर्येन्दुवह्निश्वसनाम्बुधींश्च ।
द्वीपान् नगांस्तद्दुहितॄर्वनानि
भूतानि यानि स्थिरजङ्गमानि ॥३६॥

pīta-prāyasya jananī
sutasya rucira-smitam
mukhaṁ lālayatī rājañ
jṛmbhato dadṛśe idam

khaṁ rodasī jyotir-anīkam āśāḥ
sūryendu-vahni-śvasanāmbudhīṁś ca
dvīpān nagāṁs tad-duhitṝr vanāni
bhūtāni yāni sthira-jaṅgamāni

pīta-prāyasya—of child Kṛṣṇa, who was being offered breast milk and was almost satisfied; *jananī*—mother Yaśodā; *sutasya*—of her son; *rucira-smitam*—seeing the child fully satisfied and smiling; *mukham*—the face; *lālayatī*—patting and softly rubbing with her hand; *rājan*—O King; *jṛmbhataḥ*—while the child was yawning; *dadṛśe*—she saw; *idam*—the following; *kham*—the sky; *rodasī*—both the higher planetary system and the earth; *jyotiḥ-anīkam*—the luminaries; *āśāḥ*—the directions; *sūrya*—the sun; *indu*—the moon; *vahni*—fire; *śvasana*—the air; *ambudhīn*—the seas; *ca*—and; *dvīpān*—the islands; *nagān*—the mountains; *tat-duhitṝḥ*—the daughters of the mountains (the rivers); *vanāni*—forests; *bhūtāni*—all kinds of living entities; *yāni*—which are; *sthira-jaṅgamāni*—nonmoving and moving.

TRANSLATION

O King Parīkṣit, when the child Kṛṣṇa was almost finished drinking His mother's milk and mother Yaśodā was touching Him and looking at His beautiful, brilliantly smiling face, the baby yawned, and mother Yaśodā saw in His mouth the whole sky, the higher planetary system and the earth, the luminaries in all directions, the sun, the moon, fire, air, the seas, islands, mountains, rivers, forests, and all kinds of living entities, moving and nonmoving.

PURPORT

By the arrangement of *yogamāyā*, Kṛṣṇa's pastimes with mother Yaśodā were all regarded as ordinary. So here was an opportunity for Kṛṣṇa to show His mother that the whole universe is situated within Him. In His small form, Kṛṣṇa was kind enough to show His mother the *virāṭ-rūpa*, the universal form, so that she could enjoy seeing what kind of child she had on her lap. The rivers have been mentioned here as the daughters of the mountains (*nagāṁs tad-duhitṝḥ*). It is the flowing of the rivers that makes big forests possible. There are living entities everywhere, some of them moving and some of them not moving. No place is vacant. This is a special feature of God's creation.

TEXT 37

सा वीक्ष्य विश्वं सहसा राजन् सञ्जातवेपथुः ।
सम्मील्य मृगशावाक्षी नेत्रे आसीत् सुविस्मिता ॥३७॥

sā vīkṣya viśvaṁ sahasā
rājan sañjāta-vepathuḥ
sammīlya mṛgaśāvākṣī
netre āsīt suvismitā

sā—mother Yaśodā; *vīkṣya*—by seeing; *viśvam*—the whole universe; *sahasā*—suddenly within the mouth of her son; *rājan*—O King

(Mahārāja Parīkṣit); *sañjāta-vepathuḥ*—whose heart was beating; *sammīlya*—opening; *mṛgaśāva-akṣī*—like the eyes of a deer cub; *netre*—her two eyes; *āsīt*—became; *su-vismitā*—astonished.

TRANSLATION

When mother Yaśodā saw the whole universe within the mouth of her child, her heart began to throb, and in astonishment she wanted to close her restless eyes.

PURPORT

Because of her pure maternal love, mother Yaśodā thought that this wonderful child playing so many tricks must have had some disease. She did not appreciate the wonders shown by her child; rather, she wanted to close her eyes. She was expecting another danger, and therefore her eyes became restless like those of a deer cub. This was all the arrangement of *yogamāyā.* The relationship between mother Yaśodā and Kṛṣṇa is one of pure maternal love. In that love, mother Yaśodā did not very much appreciate the display of the Supreme Personality of Godhead's opulences.

At the beginning of this chapter, two extra verses sometimes appear:

evaṁ bahūni karmāṇi
gopānāṁ śaṁ sa-yoṣitām
nandasya gehe vavṛdhe
kurvan viṣṇu-janārdanaḥ

"In this way, to chastise and kill the demons, the child Kṛṣṇa demonstrated many activities in the house of Nanda Mahārāja, and the inhabitants of Vraja enjoyed these incidents."

evaṁ sa vavṛdhe viṣṇur
nanda-gehe janārdanaḥ
kurvann aniśam ānandaṁ
gopālānāṁ sa-yoṣitām

"To increase the transcendental pleasure of the *gopas* and the *gopīs*, Kṛṣṇa, the killer of all demons, was thus raised by His father and mother, Nanda and Yaśodā."

Śrīpāda Vijayadhvaja Tīrtha also adds another verse after the third verse in this chapter:

vistareṇeha kāruṇyāt
sarva-pāpa-praṇāśanam
vaktum arhasi dharma-jña
dayālus tvam iti prabho

"Parīkṣit Mahārāja then requested Śukadeva Gosvāmī to continue speaking such narrations about the pastimes of Kṛṣṇa, so that the King could enjoy from them transcendental bliss."

Thus end the Bhaktivedanta purports of the Tenth Canto, Seventh Chapter, of the Śrīmad-Bhāgavatam, *entitled "The Killing of the Demon Tṛṇāvarta."*

CHAPTER EIGHT

Lord Kṛṣṇa Shows the Universal Form Within His Mouth

The summary of the Eighth Chapter is as follows. This chapter describes the ceremony of giving a name to Kṛṣṇa. It also describes His crawling, His playing with the cows, and His eating earth and again showing the universal form to His mother.

One day, Vasudeva sent for Gargamuni, the family priest of the *yadu-vaṁśa,* and thus Gargamuni went to the house of Nanda Mahārāja, who received him very well and requested him to give names to Kṛṣṇa and Balarāma. Gargamuni, of course, reminded Nanda Mahārāja that Kaṁsa was looking for the son of Devakī and said that if he performed the ceremony very gorgeously, the ceremony would come to the notice of Kaṁsa, who would then suspect that Kṛṣṇa was the son of Devakī. Nanda Mahārāja therefore requested Gargamuni to perform this ceremony without anyone's knowledge, and Gargamuni did so. Because Balarāma, the son of Rohiṇī, increases the transcendental bliss of others, His name is Rāma, and because of His extraordinary strength, He is called Baladeva. He attracts the Yadus to follow His instructions, and therefore His name is Saṅkarṣaṇa. Kṛṣṇa, the son of Yaśodā, previously appeared in many other colors, such as white, red and yellow, and He had now assumed the color black. Because He was sometimes the son of Vasudeva, His name is Vāsudeva. According to His various activities and qualities, He has many other names. After thus informing Nanda Mahārāja and completing the name-giving ceremony, Gargamuni advised Nanda Mahārāja to protect his son very carefully and then departed.

Śukadeva Gosvāmī next described how the two children crawled, walked on Their small legs, played with the cows and calves, stole butter and other milk products and broke the butter pots. In this way, he described many naughty activities of Kṛṣṇa and Balarāma. The most wonderful of these occurred when Kṛṣṇa's playmates complained to mother Yaśodā that Kṛṣṇa was eating earth. Mother Yaśodā wanted to open

Kṛṣṇa's mouth to see the evidence so that she could chastise Him. Sometimes she assumed the position of a chastising mother, and at the next moment she was overwhelmed with maternal love. After describing all this to Mahārāja Parīkṣit, Śukadeva Gosvāmī, at Mahārāja Parīkṣit's request, praised the fortune of mother Yaśodā and Nanda. Nanda and Yaśodā were formerly Droṇa and Dharā, and by the order of Brahmā they came to this earth and had the Supreme Personality of Godhead as their son.

TEXT 1

श्रीशुक उवाच
गर्गः पुरोहितो राजन् यदूनां सुमहातपाः ।
व्रजं जगाम नन्दस्य वसुदेवप्रचोदितः ॥ १ ॥

śrī-śuka uvāca
gargaḥ purohito rājan
yadūnāṁ sumahā-tapāḥ
vrajaṁ jagāma nandasya
vasudeva-pracoditaḥ

śrī-śukaḥ uvāca—Śrī Śukadeva Gosvāmī said; *gargaḥ*—Gargamuni; *purohitaḥ*—the priest; *rājan*—O King Parīkṣit; *yadūnām*—of the Yadu dynasty; *su-mahā-tapāḥ*—highly elevated in austerity and penance; *vrajam*—to the village known as Vrajabhūmi; *jagāma*—went; *nandasya*—of Mahārāja Nanda; *vasudeva-pracoditaḥ*—being inspired by Vasudeva.

TRANSLATION

Śukadeva Gosvāmī said: O Mahārāja Parīkṣit, the priest of the Yadu dynasty, namely Gargamuni, who was highly elevated in austerity and penance, was then inspired by Vasudeva to go see Nanda Mahārāja at his home.

TEXT 2

तं दृष्ट्वा परमप्रीतः प्रत्युत्थाय कृताञ्जलिः ।
आनर्चाधोक्षजधिया प्रणिपातपुरःसरम् ॥ २ ॥

taṁ dṛṣṭvā parama-prītaḥ
pratyutthāya kṛtāñjaliḥ
ānarcādhokṣaja-dhiyā
praṇipāta-puraḥsaram

tam—him (Gargamuni); *dṛṣṭvā*—after seeing; *parama-prītaḥ*—Nanda Mahārāja was very much pleased; *pratyutthāya*—standing up to receive him; *kṛta-añjaliḥ*—with folded hands; *ānarca*—worshiped; *adhokṣaja-dhiyā*—although Gargamuni was visible to the senses, Nanda Mahārāja maintained a very high respect for him; *praṇipāta-puraḥsaram*—Nanda Mahārāja fell down before him and offered obeisances.

TRANSLATION

When Nanda Mahārāja saw Gargamuni present at his home, Nanda was so pleased that he stood up to receive him with folded hands. Although seeing Gargamuni with his eyes, Nanda Mahārāja could appreciate that Gargamuni was adhokṣaja; that is, he was not an ordinary person seen by material senses.

TEXT 3

सूपविष्टं कृतातिथ्यं गिरा सूनृतया मुनिम् ।
नन्दयित्वाब्रवीद् ब्रह्मन् पूर्णस्य करवाम किम् ॥ ३ ॥

sūpaviṣṭaṁ kṛtātithyaṁ
girā sūnṛtayā munim
nandayitvābravīd brahman
pūrṇasya karavāma kim

su-upaviṣṭam—when Gargamuni was seated very comfortably; *kṛta-ātithyam*—and he had been properly received as a guest; *girā*—by words; *sūnṛtayā*—very sweet; *munim*—Gargamuni; *nandayitvā*—pleasing him in this way; *abravīt*—said; *brahman*—O brāhmaṇa; *pūrṇasya*—of one who is full in everything; *karavāma kim*—what can I do for you (kindly order me).

TRANSLATION

When Gargamuni had been properly received as a guest and was very comfortably seated, Nanda Mahārāja submitted with gentle and submissive words: Dear sir, because you are a devotee, you are full in everything. Yet my duty is to serve you. Kindly order me. What can I do for you?

TEXT 4

महद्विचलनं नृणां गृहिणां दीनचेतसाम् ।
निःश्रेयसाय भगवन् कल्पते नान्यथा क्वचित् ॥ ४ ॥

mahad-vicalanaṁ nṝṇāṁ
gṛhiṇāṁ dīna-cetasām
niḥśreyasāya bhagavan
kalpate nānyathā kvacit

mahat-vicalanam—the movement of great personalities; *nṝṇām*—in the houses of ordinary persons; *gṛhiṇām*—especially householders; *dīna-cetasām*—who are very simple-minded, being engaged in family maintenance and nothing more; *niḥśreyasāya*—a great personality has no reason to go to the *gṛhastha* but to benefit him; *bhagavan*—O most powerful devotee; *kalpate*—is to be taken that way; *na anyathā*—not for any other purpose; *kvacit*—at any time.

TRANSLATION

O my lord, O great devotee, persons like you move from one place to another not for their own interests but for the sake of poor-hearted gṛhasthas [householders]. Otherwise they have no interest in going from one place to another.

PURPORT

As factually stated by Nanda Mahārāja, Gargamuni, being a devotee, had no needs. Similarly, when Kṛṣṇa comes He has no needs, for He is *pūrṇa, ātmārāma.* Nonetheless, He descends to this material world to protect the devotees and vanquish miscreants (*paritrāṇāya sādhūnāṁ vināśāya ca duṣkṛtām*). This is the mission of the Supreme Personality of Godhead, and devotees also have the same mission. One who executes this mission of *para-upakāra*, performing welfare activities for people in general, is recognized by Kṛṣṇa, the Supreme Personality of Godhead, as being very, very dear to Him (*na ca tasmān manuṣyeṣu kaścin me priya-kṛttamaḥ*). Similarly, Caitanya Mahāprabhu has advised this *para-upakāra*, and He has especially advised the inhabitants of India:

bhārata-bhūmite haila manuṣya-janma yāra
janma sārthaka kari' kara para-upakāra

"One who has taken his birth as a human being in the land of India [Bhāratavarṣa] should make his life successful and work for the benefit of all other people." (Cc. *Ādi.* 9.41) On the whole, the duty of a pure Vaiṣṇava devotee is to act for the welfare of others.

Nanda Mahārāja could understand that Gargamuni had come for this purpose and that his own duty now was to act according to Gargamuni's advice. Thus he said, "Please tell me what is my duty." This should be the attitude of everyone, especially the householder. The *varṇāśrama* society is organized into eight divisions: *brāhmaṇa, kṣatriya, vaiśya, śūdra, brahmacarya, gṛhastha, vānaprastha* and *sannyāsa.* Nanda Mahārāja represented himself as *gṛhiṇām*, a householder. A *brahmacārī* factually has no needs, but *gṛhī*, householders, are engaged in sense gratification. As stated in *Bhagavad-gītā* (2.44), *bhogaiśvarya-prasaktānāṁ tayāpahṛta-cetasām.* Everyone has come to this material world for sense gratification, and the position of those who are too attached to sense gratification and who therefore accept the *gṛhastha-āśrama* is very precarious. Since everyone in this material world is searching for sense gratification, *gṛhasthas* are required to be trained as *mahat*, great *mahātmās.* Therefore Nanda Mahārāja specifically used the word *mahad-vicalanam.* Gargamuni had no interest to serve by going to Nanda Mahārāja, but Nanda Mahārāja, as a *gṛhastha*, was always perfectly ready to receive instructions from a *mahātmā* to gain the real benefit in life. Thus he was ready to execute Gargamuni's order.

TEXT 5

ज्योतिषामयनं साक्षाद् यत्तज्ज्ञानमतीन्द्रियम् ।
प्रणीतं भवता येन पुमान् वेद परावरम् ॥ ५ ॥

jyotiṣām ayanaṁ sākṣād
yat taj jñānam atīndriyam
praṇītaṁ bhavatā yena
pumān veda parāvaram

jyotiṣām—knowledge of astrology (along with other aspects of culture in human society, and specifically in civilized society, there must be knowledge of astrology); *ayanam*—the movements of the stars and planets in relationship to human society; *sākṣāt*—directly; *yat tat jñānam*—such knowledge; *ati-indriyam*—which an ordinary person cannot understand because it is beyond his vision; *praṇītam bhavatā*—you have prepared a perfect book of knowledge; *yena*—by which; *pumān*—any person; *veda*—can understand; *para-avaram*—the cause and effect of destiny.

TRANSLATION

O great saintly person, you have compiled the astrological knowledge by which one can understand past and present unseen things. By the strength of this knowledge, any human being can understand what he has done in his past life and how it affects his present life. This is known to you.

PURPORT

The word "destiny" is now defined. Unintelligent persons who do not understand the meaning of life are just like animals. Animals do not know the past, present and future of life, nor are they able to understand it. But a human being can understand this, if he is sober. Therefore, as stated in *Bhagavad-gītā* (2.13), *dhīras tatra na muhyati:* a sober person is not bewildered. The simple truth is that although life is eternal, in this material world one changes from one body to another. Foolish people, especially in this age, do not understand this simple truth. Kṛṣṇa says:

dehino 'smin yathā dehe
kaumāraṁ yauvanaṁ jarā
tathā dehāntara-prāptir
dhīras tatra na muhyati

"As the embodied soul continually passes, in this body, from boyhood to youth to old age, the soul similarly passes into another body at death. The self-realized soul is not bewildered by such a change." (Bg. 2.13) Kṛṣṇa, the greatest authority, says that the body will change. And as soon as the body changes, one's whole program of work changes also. Today I am a human being or a great personality, but with a little deviation from nature's law, I shall have to accept a different type of body. Today I am a human being, but tomorrow I may become a dog, and then whatever activities I have performed in this life will be a failure. This simple truth is now rarely understood, but one who is a *dhīra* can understand this. Those in this material world for material enjoyment should know that because their present position will cease to exist, they must be careful in how they act. This is also stated by Ṛṣabhadeva. *Na sādhu manye yata ātmano 'yam asann api kleśada āsa dehaḥ* (*Bhāg.* 5.5.4). Although this body is temporary, as long as we have to live in this body we must suffer. Whether one has a short life or a long life, one must suffer the threefold miseries of material life. Therefore any gentleman, *dhīra*, must be interested in *jyotiṣa*, astrology.

Nanda Mahārāja was trying to take advantage of the opportunity afforded by Gargamuni's presence, for Gargamuni was a great authority in this knowledge of astrology, by which one can see the unseen events of past, present and future. It is the duty of a father to understand the astrological position of his children and do what is needed for their happiness. Now, taking advantage of the opportunity afforded by the presence of Gargamuni, Nanda Mahārāja suggested that Gargamuni prepare a horoscope for Nanda's two sons, Kṛṣṇa and Balarāma.

TEXT 6

त्वं हि ब्रह्मविदां श्रेष्ठः संस्कारान् कर्तुमर्हसि ।
बालयोरनयोर्नृणां जन्मना ब्राह्मणो गुरुः ॥ ६ ॥

tvaṁ hi brahma-vidāṁ śreṣṭhaḥ
saṁskārān kartum arhasi
bālayor anayor nṝṇāṁ
janmanā brāhmaṇo guruḥ

tvam—Your Holiness; *hi*—indeed; *brahma-vidām*—of all *brāhmaṇas*, or persons who understand what is Brahman (*brahma jānātīti brāhmaṇaḥ*); *śreṣṭhaḥ*—you are the best; *saṁskārān*—ceremonies performed for reformation (because by these reformatory activities one takes one's second birth: *saṁskārād bhaved dvijaḥ*); *kartum arhasi*—because you have kindly come here, kindly execute; *bālayoḥ*—of these two sons (Kṛṣṇa and Balarāma); *anayoḥ*—of both of Them; *nṝṇām*—not only of Them, but of all human society; *janmanā*—as soon as he takes birth; *brāhmaṇaḥ*—immediately the *brāhmaṇa* becomes; *guruḥ*—the guide.*

TRANSLATION

My lord, you are the best of the brāhmaṇas, especially because you are fully aware of the jyotiḥ-śāstra, the astrological science. Therefore you are naturally the spiritual master of every human being. This being so, since you have kindly come to my house, kindly execute the reformatory activities for my two sons.

PURPORT

The Supreme Personality of Godhead, Kṛṣṇa, says in *Bhagavad-gītā* (4.13), *cātur-varṇyaṁ mayā sṛṣṭaṁ guṇa-karma-vibhāgaśaḥ:* the four *varṇas*—*brāhmaṇa, kṣatriya, vaiśya* and *śūdra*—must be present in society. The *brāhmaṇas* are required for the guidance of the whole society. If there is no such institution as *varṇāśrama-dharma* and if human society has no such guide as the *brāhmaṇa*, human society will be hellish. In Kali-yuga, especially at the present moment, there is no such thing as a real *brāhmaṇa*, and therefore society is in a chaotic condition. Formerly there were qualified *brāhmaṇas*, but at present, although there are certainly persons who think themselves *brāhmaṇas*, they actually have no ability to guide society. The Kṛṣṇa consciousness movement is therefore very much eager to reintroduce the *varṇāśrama* system into human society so that those who are bewildered or less intelligent will be able to take guidance from qualified *brāhmaṇas*.

Brāhmaṇa means Vaiṣṇava. After one becomes a *brāhmaṇa*, the next stage of development in human society is to become a Vaiṣṇava. People

---

*The *śāstras* enjoin, *tad-vijñānārthaṁ sa gurum evābhigacchet* (*Muṇḍaka Upaniṣad* 1.2.12). It is the duty of everyone to approach a *brāhmaṇa* as the *guru.*

in general must be guided to the destination or goal of life, and therefore they must understand Viṣṇu, the Supreme Personality of Godhead. The whole system of Vedic knowledge is based on this principle, but people have lost the clue (*na te viduḥ svārtha-gatiṁ hi viṣṇum*), and they are simply pursuing sense gratification, with the risk of gliding down to a lower grade of life (*mṛtyu-saṁsāra-vartmani*). It doesn't matter whether one is born a *brāhmaṇa* or not. No one is born a *brāhmaṇa;* everyone is born a *śūdra.* But by the guidance of a *brāhmaṇa* and by *saṁskāra,* one can become *dvija,* twice-born, and then gradually become a *brāhmaṇa.* Brahmanism is not a system meant to create a monopoly for a particular class of men. Everyone should be educated so as to become a *brāhmaṇa.* At least there must be an opportunity to allow everyone to attain the destination of life. Regardless of whether one is born in a *brāhmaṇa* family, a *kṣatriya* family or a *śūdra* family, one may be guided by a proper *brāhmaṇa* and be promoted to the highest platform of being a Vaiṣṇava. Thus the Kṛṣṇa consciousness movement affords an opportunity to develop the right destiny for human society. Nanda Mahārāja took advantage of the opportunity of Gargamuni's presence by requesting him to perform the necessary reformatory activities for his sons to guide Them toward the destination of life.

TEXT 7

श्रीगर्ग उवाच

यदूनामहमाचार्यः ख्यातश्च भुवि सर्वदा ।
सुतं मया संस्कृतं ते मन्यते देवकीसुतम् ॥ ७ ॥

śrī-garga uvāca
yadūnām aham ācāryaḥ
khyātaś ca bhuvi sarvadā
sutaṁ mayā saṁskṛtaṁ te
manyate devakī-sutam

śrī-gargaḥ uvāca—Gargamuni said; *yadūnām*—of the Yadu dynasty; *aham*—I am; *ācāryaḥ*—the priestly guide, or *purohita; khyātaḥ ca*—this is already known; *bhuvi*—everywhere; *sarvadā*—always; *sutam*—the son; *mayā*—by me; *saṁskṛtam*—having undergone the purificatory process; *te*—of you; *manyate*—would be considered; *devakī-sutam*—the son of Devakī.

TRANSLATION

Gargamuni said: My dear Nanda Mahārāja, I am the priestly guide of the Yadu dynasty. This is known everywhere. Therefore, if I perform the purificatory process for your sons, Kaṁsa will consider Them the sons of Devakī.

PURPORT

Gargamuni indirectly disclosed that Kṛṣṇa was the son of Devakī, not of Yaśodā. Since Kaṁsa was already searching for Kṛṣṇa, if the purificatory process were undertaken by Gargamuni, Kaṁsa might be informed, and that would create a catastrophe. It may be argued that although Gargamuni was the priest of the Yadu dynasty, Nanda Mahārāja also belonged to that dynasty. Nanda Mahārāja, however, was not acting as a *kṣatriya*. Therefore Gargamuni said, "If I act as your priest, this will confirm that Kṛṣṇa is the son of Devakī."

TEXTS 8–9

कंसः पापमतिः सख्यं तव चानकदुन्दुभेः ।
देवक्या अष्टमो गर्भो न स्त्री भवितुमर्हति ॥ ८ ॥
इति सञ्चिन्तयञ्छ्रुत्वा देवक्या दारिकावचः ।
अपि हन्ता गताशङ्कस्तर्हि तन्नोऽनयो भवेत् ॥ ९ ॥

kaṁsaḥ pāpa-matiḥ sakhyaṁ
tava cānakadundubheḥ
devakyā aṣṭamo garbho
na strī bhavitum arhati

iti sañcintayañ chrutvā
devakyā dārikā-vacaḥ
api hantā gatāśaṅkas
tarhi tan no 'nayo bhavet

kaṁsaḥ—King Kaṁsa; *pāpa-matiḥ*—very, very sinful, having a polluted mind; *sakhyam*—friendship; *tava*—your; *ca*—also; *ānaka-dundubheḥ*—of Vasudeva; *devakyāḥ*—of Devakī; *aṣṭamaḥ garbhaḥ*—the eighth pregnancy; *na*—not; *strī*—a woman; *bhavitum arhati*—is possible to be; *iti*—in this way; *sañcintayan*—considering; *śrutvā*—and hearing (this news); *devakyāḥ*—of Devakī; *dārikā-vacaḥ*—the message from the daughter; *api*—although there was; *hantā gata-āśaṅkaḥ*—there is a possibility that Kaṁsa would take steps to kill this child; *tarhi*—therefore; *tat*—that incident; *naḥ*—for us; *anayaḥ bhavet*—may not be very good.

TRANSLATION

Kaṁsa is both a great diplomat and a very sinful man. Therefore, having heard from Yogamāyā, the daughter of Devakī, that the child who will kill him has already been born somewhere else, having heard that the eighth pregnancy of Devakī could not bring forth a female child, and having understood your friendship with Vasudeva, Kaṁsa, upon hearing that the purificatory process has been performed by me, the priest of the Yadu dynasty, may certainly consider all these points and suspect that Kṛṣṇa is the son of Devakī and Vasudeva. Then he might take steps to kill Kṛṣṇa. That would be a catastrophe.

PURPORT

Kaṁsa knew very well that Yogamāyā was, after all, the maidservant of Kṛṣṇa and Viṣṇu and that although Yogamāyā had appeared as the daughter of Devakī, she might have been forbidden to disclose this fact. Actually this was what had happened. Gargamuni argued very soberly that his taking part in performing the reformatory process for Kṛṣṇa would give rise to many doubts, so that Kaṁsa might take very severe steps to kill the child. Kaṁsa had already sent many demons to attempt to kill this child, but none of them had survived. If Gargamuni were to perform the purificatory process, Kaṁsa's suspicions would be fully confirmed, and he would take very severe steps. Gargamuni gave this warning to Nanda Mahārāja.

TEXT 10

श्रीनन्द उवाच
अलक्षितोऽस्मिन् रहसि मामकैरपि गोव्रजे ।
कुरु द्विजातिसंस्कारं स्वस्तिवाचनपूर्वकम् ॥१०॥

śrī-nanda uvāca
alakṣito 'smin rahasi
māmakair api go-vraje
kuru dvijāti-saṁskāraṁ
svasti-vācana-pūrvakam

śrī-nandaḥ uvāca—Nanda Mahārāja said (to Gargamuni); *alakṣitaḥ*—without Kaṁsa's knowledge; *asmin*—in this cow shed; *rahasi*—in a very solitary place; *māmakaiḥ*—even by my relatives; *api*—a still more secluded place; *go-vraje*—in the cow shed; *kuru*—just execute; *dvijāti-saṁskāram*—the purificatory process of second birth (*saṁskārād bhaved dvijaḥ*); *svasti-vācana-pūrvakam*—by chanting the Vedic hymns to perform the purificatory process.

TRANSLATION

Nanda Mahārāja said: My dear great sage, if you think that your performing this process of purification will make Kaṁsa suspicious, then secretly chant the Vedic hymns and perform the purifying process of second birth here in the cow shed of my house, without the knowledge of anyone else, even my relatives, for this process of purification is essential.

PURPORT

Nanda Mahārāja did not like the idea of avoiding the purificatory process. Despite the many obstacles, he wanted to take advantage of Gargamuni's presence and do what was needed. The purificatory process is essential specifically for *brāhmaṇas*, *kṣatriyas* and *vaiśyas*. Therefore, since Nanda Mahārāja presented himself as a *vaiśya*, this process of purification was essential. Formerly, such institutional activities were compulsory. *Cātur-varṇyaṁ mayā sṛṣṭaṁ guṇa-karma-vibhāgaśaḥ*

(Bg. 4.13). Without these activities of purification, the society would be considered a society of animals. To take advantage of Gargamuni's presence, Nanda Mahārāja wanted to perform the *nāma-karaṇa* ceremonies, even secretly, without any gorgeous arrangements. Therefore, the opportunity for purification should be regarded as the essential duty of human society. In Kali-yuga, however, people have forgotten the essence. *Mandāḥ sumanda-matayo manda-bhāgyā hy upadrutāḥ* (*Bhāg.* 1.1.10). In this age, people are all bad and unfortunate, and they do not accept Vedic instructions to make their life successful. Nanda Mahārāja, however, did not want to neglect anything. To keep intact a happy society advanced in spiritual knowledge, he took full advantage of Gargamuni's presence to do what was necessary. How degraded society has become within five thousand years. *Mandāḥ sumanda-matayo manda-bhāgyāḥ.* The human life is obtained after many, many millions of births, and it is intended for purification. Previously, a father was eager to give all kinds of help to elevate his children, but at present, because of being misguided, people are prepared even to kill to avoid the responsibility of raising children.

TEXT 11

श्रीशुक उवाच

एवं सम्प्रार्थितो विप्रः स्वचिकीर्षितमेव तत् ।
चकार नामकरणं गूढो रहसि बालयोः ॥११॥

śrī-śuka uvāca
evaṁ samprārthito vipraḥ
sva-cikīrṣitam eva tat
cakāra nāma-karaṇaṁ
gūḍho rahasi bālayoḥ

śrī-śukaḥ uvāca—Śrī Śukadeva Gosvāmī said; *evam*—in this way; *samprārthitaḥ*—being eagerly requested; *vipraḥ*—the *brāhmaṇa* Gargamuni; *sva-cikīrṣitam eva*—which he already desired to do and for which he had gone there; *tat*—that; *cakāra*—performed; *nāma-karaṇam*—the name-giving ceremony; *gūḍhaḥ*—confidentially; *rahasi*—in a secluded place; *bālayoḥ*—of the two boys (Kṛṣṇa and Balarāma).

TRANSLATION

Śukadeva Gosvāmī continued: Having thus been especially requested by Nanda Mahārāja to do that which he already desired to do, Gargamuni performed the name-giving ceremony for Kṛṣṇa and Balarāma in a solitary place.

TEXT 12

श्रीगर्ग उवाच

अयं हि रोहिणीपुत्रो रमयन् सुहृदो गुणैः ।
आख्यास्यते राम इति बलाधिक्याद् बलं विदुः ।
यदूनामपृथग्भावात् सङ्कर्षणमुशन्त्यपि ॥१२॥

śrī-garga uvāca
ayaṁ hi rohiṇī-putro
ramayan suhṛdo guṇaiḥ
ākhyāsyate rāma iti
balādhikyād balaṁ viduḥ
yadūnām apṛthag-bhāvāt
saṅkarṣaṇam uśanty api

śrī-gargaḥ uvāca—Gargamuni said; *ayam*—this; *hi*—indeed; *rohiṇī-putraḥ*—the son of Rohiṇī; *ramayan*—pleasing; *suhṛdaḥ*—all His friends and relatives; *guṇaiḥ*—by transcendental qualities; *ākhyāsyate*—will be called; *rāmaḥ*—by the name Rāma, the supreme enjoyer; *iti*—in this way; *bala-ādhikyāt*—because of extraordinary strength; *balam viduḥ*—will be known as Balarāma; *yadūnām*—of the Yadu dynasty; *apṛthak-bhāvāt*—because of not being separated from you; *saṅkarṣaṇam*—by the name Saṅkarṣaṇa, or uniting two families; *uśanti*—attracts; *api*—also.

TRANSLATION

Gargamuni said: This child, the son of Rohiṇī, will give all happiness to His relatives and friends by His transcendental qualities. Therefore He will be known as Rāma. And because He will manifest extraordinary bodily strength, He will also be known as

Bala. Moreover, because He unites two families—Vasudeva's family and the family of Nanda Mahārāja—He will be known as Saṅkarṣaṇa.

PURPORT

Baladeva was actually the son of Devakī, but He was transferred from Devakī's womb to that of Rohiṇī. This fact was not disclosed. According to a statement in the *Hari-vaṁśa:*

pratyuvāca tato rāmaḥ
sarvāṁs tān abhitaḥ sthitān
yādaveṣv api sarveṣu
bhavanto mama vallabhāḥ

Gargamuni did disclose to Nanda Mahārāja that Balarāma would be known as Saṅkarṣaṇa because of uniting two families—the *yadu-vaṁśa* and the *vaṁśa* of Nanda Mahārāja—one of which was known as *kṣatriya* and the other as *vaiśya.* Both families had the same original forefather, the only difference being that Nanda Mahārāja was born of a *vaiśya* wife whereas Vasudeva was born of a *kṣatriya* wife. Later, Nanda Mahārāja married a *vaiśya* wife, and Vasudeva married a *kṣatriya* wife. So although the families of Nanda Mahārāja and Vasudeva both came from the same father, they were divided as *kṣatriya* and *vaiśya.* Now Baladeva united them, and therefore He was known as Saṅkarṣaṇa.

TEXT 13

आसन् वर्णास्त्रयो ह्यस्य गृह्णतोऽनुयुगं तनूः ।
शुक्लो रक्तस्तथा पीत इदानीं कृष्णतां गतः ॥१३॥

āsan varṇās trayo hy asya
gṛhṇato 'nuyugaṁ tanūḥ
śuklo raktas tathā pīta
idānīṁ kṛṣṇatāṁ gataḥ

āsan—were assumed; *varṇāḥ trayaḥ*—three colors; *hi*—indeed; *asya*—of your son Kṛṣṇa; *gṛhṇataḥ*—accepting; *anuyugam tanūḥ*—

transcendental bodies according to the different *yugas; śuklaḥ*—sometimes white; *raktaḥ*—sometimes red; *tathā*—as well as; *pītaḥ*—sometimes yellow; *idānīm kṛṣṇatām gataḥ*—at the present moment He has assumed a blackish color.

TRANSLATION

Your son Kṛṣṇa appears as an incarnation in every millennium. In the past, He assumed three different colors—white, red and yellow—and now He has appeared in a blackish color. [In another Dvāpara-yuga, He appeared (as Lord Rāmacandra) in the color of śuka, a parrot. All such incarnations have now assembled in Kṛṣṇa.]

PURPORT

Partially explaining the position of Lord Kṛṣṇa and partially covering the facts, Gargamuni indicated, "Your son is a great personality, and He can change the color of His body in different ages." The word *gṛhṇataḥ* indicates that Kṛṣṇa is free to make His choice. In other words, He is the Supreme Personality of Godhead and may therefore do whatever He desires. In Vedic literature the different colors assumed by the Personality of Godhead in different millenniums are stated, and therefore when Gargamuni said, "Your son has assumed these colors," he indirectly said, "He is the Supreme Personality of Godhead." Because of Kaṁsa's atrocities, Gargamuni tried to avoid disclosing this fact, but he indirectly informed Nanda Mahārāja that Kṛṣṇa, his son, was the Supreme Personality of Godhead.

It may be noted that Śrīla Jīva Gosvāmī, in his book *Krama-sandarbha*, has enunciated the purport of this verse. In every millennium, Kṛṣṇa appears in a different form, either as white, red or yellow, but this time He personally appeared in His original, blackish form and, as predicted by Gargamuni, exhibited the power of Nārāyaṇa. Because in this form the Supreme Personality of Godhead exhibits Himself fully, His name is Śrī Kṛṣṇa, the all-attractive.

Factually, Kṛṣṇa is the source of all *avatāras*, and therefore all the different features of the different *avatāras* are present in Kṛṣṇa. When Kṛṣṇa incarnates, all the features of other incarnations are already present within Him. Other incarnations are partial representations of Kṛṣṇa, who is the full-fledged incarnation of the Supreme Being. It is to be understood that the Supreme Being, whether appearing as *śukla*, *rakta* or *pīta* (white, red or yellow), is the same person. When He appears in different incarnations, He appears in different colors, just like the sunshine, which contains seven colors. Sometimes the colors of sunshine are represented separately; otherwise the sunshine is observed mainly as bright light. The different *avatāras*, such as the *manvantara-avatāras*, *līlā-avatāras* and *daśa-avatāras*, are all included in the *kṛṣṇa-avatāra*. When Kṛṣṇa appears, all the *avatāras* appear with Him. As described in *Śrīmad-Bhāgavatam* (1.3.26):

avatārā hy asaṅkhyeyā
hareḥ sattva-nidher dvijāḥ
yathāvidāsinaḥ kulyāḥ
sarasaḥ syuḥ sahasraśaḥ

The *avatāras* incessantly appear, like incessantly flowing water. No one can count how many waves there are in flowing water, and similarly there is no limitation of the *avatāras*. And Kṛṣṇa is the full representation of all *avatāras* because He is the source of all *avatāras*. Kṛṣṇa is *aṁśī*, whereas others are *aṁśa*, part of Kṛṣṇa. All living entities, including us, are *aṁśas* (*mamaivāṁśo jīva-loke jīva-bhūtaḥ sanātanaḥ*). These *aṁśas* are of different magnitude. Human beings (who are minute *aṁśas*) and the demigods, *viṣṇu-tattva* and all other living beings are all part of the Supreme. *Nityo nityānāṁ cetanaś cetanānām* (*Kaṭha Upaniṣad* 2.2.13). Kṛṣṇa is the full representation of all living entities, and when Kṛṣṇa is present, all *avatāras* are included in Him.

The Eleventh Canto of *Śrīmad-Bhāgavatam* describes the incarnations for each *yuga* in chronological order. The *Bhāgavatam* says, *kṛte śuklaś catur-bāhuḥ, tretāyāṁ rakta-varṇo 'sau, dvāpare bhagavān śyāmaḥ* and *kṛṣṇa-varṇaṁ tviṣākṛṣṇam*. We actually see that in Kali-yuga, Bhagavān has appeared in *pīta-varṇa*, or a yellow color, as Gaurasundara, although the *Bhāgavatam* speaks of *kṛṣṇa-varṇam*. To adjust all these statements, one should understand that although in some *yugas* some of the colors are prominent, in every *yuga*, whenever Kṛṣṇa appears, all the colors are present. *Kṛṣṇa-varṇaṁ tviṣākṛṣṇam:* although Caitanya Mahāprabhu appears without *kṛṣṇa,* or a blackish color, He is understood to be Kṛṣṇa Himself. *Idānīṁ kṛṣṇatāṁ gataḥ.* The same original Kṛṣṇa who appears in different *varṇas* has now appeared. The word *āsan* indicates that He is always present. Whenever the Supreme Personality of Godhead appears in His full feature, He is understood to be *kṛṣṇa-varṇam,* although He appears in different colors. Prahlāda Mahārāja states that Caitanya Mahāprabhu is *channa;* that is, although He is Kṛṣṇa, He is covered by a yellow color. Thus the Gauḍīya Vaiṣṇavas accept the conclusion that although Caitanya Mahāprabhu appeared in *pīta* color, He is Kṛṣṇa.

kṛṣṇa-varṇaṁ tviṣākṛṣṇaṁ
sāṅgopāṅgāstra-pārṣadam
yajñaiḥ saṅkīrtana-prāyair
yajanti hi sumedhasaḥ
(*Bhāg.* 11.5.32)

TEXT 14

प्रागयं वसुदेवस्य क्वचिज्जातस्तवात्मजः ।
वासुदेव इति श्रीमानभिज्ञाः सम्प्रचक्षते ॥१४॥

prāg ayaṁ vasudevasya
kvacij jātas tavātmajaḥ
vāsudeva iti śrīmān
abhijñāḥ sampracakṣate

prāk—before; *ayam*—this child; *vasudevasya*—of Vasudeva; *kvacit*—sometimes; *jātaḥ*—was born; *tava*—your; *ātmajaḥ*—Kṛṣṇa, who has taken birth as your child; *vāsudevaḥ*—therefore He may be given the name Vāsudeva; *iti*—thus; *śrīmān*—very beautiful; *abhijñāḥ*—those who are learned; *sampracakṣate*—also say that Kṛṣṇa is Vāsudeva.

TRANSLATION

For many reasons, this beautiful son of yours sometimes appeared previously as the son of Vasudeva. Therefore, those who are learned sometimes call this child Vāsudeva.

PURPORT

Gargamuni indirectly disclosed, "This child was originally born as the son of Vasudeva, although He is acting as your child. Generally He is your child, but sometimes He is the son of Vasudeva."

TEXT 15

बहूनि सन्ति नामानि रूपाणि च सुतस्य ते ।
गुणकर्मानुरूपाणि तान्यहं वेद नो जनाः ॥१५॥

bahūni santi nāmāni
rūpāṇi ca sutasya te
guṇa-karmānurūpāṇi
tāny ahaṁ veda no janāḥ

bahūni—various; *santi*—there are; *nāmāni*—names; *rūpāṇi*—forms; *ca*—also; *sutasya*—of the son; *te*—your; *guṇa-karma-anu-rūpāṇi*—according to His attributes and activities; *tāni*—them; *aham*—I; *veda*—know; *no janāḥ*—not ordinary persons.

TRANSLATION

For this son of yours there are many forms and names according to His transcendental qualities and activities. These are known to me, but people in general do not understand them.

PURPORT

Bahūni: the Lord has many names. *Advaitam acyutam anādim ananta-rūpam ādyaṁ purāṇa-puruṣaṁ nava-yauvanaṁ ca.* As stated in the *Brahma-saṁhitā* (5.33), the Lord is one, but He has many forms and many names. It was not that because Gargamuni gave the child the name Kṛṣṇa, that was His only name. He has other names, such as Bhakta-vatsala, Giridhārī, Govinda and Gopāla. If we analyze the *nirukti*, or semantic derivation, of the word "Kṛṣṇa," we find that *na* signifies that He stops the repetition of birth and death, and *kṛṣ* means *sattārtha*, or "existence." (Kṛṣṇa is the whole of existence.) Also, *kṛṣ* means "attraction," and *na* means *ānanda*, or "bliss." Kṛṣṇa is known as Mukunda because He wants to give everyone spiritual, eternal, blissful life. Unfortunately, because of the living entity's little independence, the living entity wants to "deprogram" the program of Kṛṣṇa. This is the material disease. Nonetheless, because Kṛṣṇa wants to give transcendental bliss to the living entities, He appears in various forms. Therefore He is called Kṛṣṇa. Because Gargamuni was an astrologer, he knew what others did not know. Yet Kṛṣṇa has so many names that even Gargamuni did not know them all. It is to be concluded that Kṛṣṇa, according to His transcendental activities, has many names and many forms.

TEXT 16

एष वः श्रेय आधास्यद् गोपगोकुलनन्दनः ।
अनेन सर्वदुर्गाणि यूयमञ्जस्तरिष्यथ ॥१६॥

eṣa vaḥ śreya ādhāsyad
gopa-gokula-nandanaḥ
anena sarva-durgāṇi
yūyam añjas tariṣyatha

eṣaḥ—this child; *vaḥ*—for all of you people; *śreyaḥ*—the most auspicious; *ādhāsyat*—will act all-auspiciously; *gopa-gokula-nandanaḥ*—just like a cowherd boy, born in a family of cowherd men as the son of the estate of Gokula; *anena*—by Him; *sarva-durgāṇi*—all kinds of miserable conditions; *yūyam*—all of you; *añjaḥ*—easily; *tariṣyatha*—will overcome.

TRANSLATION

To increase the transcendental bliss of the cowherd men of Gokula, this child will always act auspiciously for you. And by His grace only, you will surpass all difficulties.

PURPORT

For the cowherd men and the cows, Kṛṣṇa is the supreme friend. Therefore He is worshiped by the prayer *namo brahmaṇya-devāya go-brāhmaṇa-hitāya ca.* His pastimes in Gokula, His *dhāma*, are always favorable to the *brāhmaṇas* and the cows. His first business is to give all comfort to the cows and the *brāhmaṇas.* In fact, comfort for the *brāhmaṇas* is secondary, and comfort for the cows is His first concern. Because of His presence, all people would overcome all difficulties and always be situated in transcendental bliss.

TEXT 17

पुरानेन व्रजपते साधवो दस्युपीडिताः ।
अराजके रक्ष्यमाणा जिग्युर्दस्यून् समेधिताः ॥१७॥

purānena vraja-pate
sādhavo dasyu-pīḍitāḥ
arājake rakṣyamāṇā
jigyur dasyūn samedhitāḥ

purā—formerly; *anena*—by Kṛṣṇa; *vraja-pate*—O King of Vraja; *sādhavaḥ*—those who were honest; *dasyu-pīḍitāḥ*—being disturbed by rogues and thieves; *arājake*—when there was an irregular government; *rakṣyamāṇāḥ*—were protected; *jigyuḥ*—conquered; *dasyūn*—the rogues and thieves; *samedhitāḥ*—flourished.

TRANSLATION

O Nanda Mahārāja, as recorded in history, when there was an irregular, incapable government, Indra having been dethroned, and people were being harassed and disturbed by thieves, this child appeared in order to protect the people and enable them to flourish, and He curbed the rogues and thieves.

PURPORT

Indra is the king of the universe. Demons, thieves and rogues always disturb Indra (*indrāri-vyākulaṁ lokam*), but when *indrāris*, the enemies of Indra, become prominent, Kṛṣṇa appears. *Kṛṣṇas tu bhagavān svayaṁ/ indrāri-vyākulaṁ lokaṁ mṛḍayanti yuge yuge* (*Bhāg.* 1.3.28).

TEXT 18

य एतस्मिन् महाभागाः प्रीतिं कुर्वन्ति मानवाः ।
नारयोऽभिभवन्त्येतान् विष्णुपक्षानिवासुराः ॥१८॥

ya etasmin mahā-bhāgāḥ
prītiṁ kurvanti mānavāḥ
nārayo 'bhibhavanty etān
viṣṇu-pakṣān ivāsurāḥ

ye—those persons who; *etasmin*—unto this child; *mahā-bhāgāḥ*—very fortunate; *prītim*—affection; *kurvanti*—execute; *mānavāḥ*—such persons; *na*—not; *arayaḥ*—the enemies; *abhibhavanti*—do overcome; *etān*—those who are attached to Kṛṣṇa; *viṣṇu-pakṣān*—the demigods, who always have Lord Viṣṇu on their side; *iva*—like; *asurāḥ*—the demons.

TRANSLATION

Demons [asuras] cannot harm the demigods, who always have Lord Viṣṇu on their side. Similarly, any person or group attached to Kṛṣṇa is extremely fortunate. Because such persons are very much affectionate toward Kṛṣṇa, they cannot be defeated by demons like the associates of Kaṁsa [or by the internal enemies, the senses].

TEXT 19

तस्मान्नन्दात्मजोऽयं ते नारायणसमो गुणैः ।
श्रिया कीर्त्यानुभावेन गोपायस्व समाहितः ॥१९॥

tasmān nandātmajo 'yaṁ te
nārāyaṇa-samo guṇaiḥ
śriyā kīrtyānubhāvena
gopāyasva samāhitaḥ

tasmāt—therefore; *nanda*—O Nanda Mahārāja; *ātmajaḥ*—your son; *ayam*—this; *te*—of you; *nārāyaṇa-samaḥ*—is as good as Nārāyaṇa (Nārāyaṇa Himself showing transcendental qualities); *guṇaiḥ*—by qualities; *śriyā*—by opulence; *kīrtyā*—especially by His name and fame; *anubhāvena*—and by His influence; *gopāyasva*—just raise this child; *samāhitaḥ*—with great attention and precaution.

TRANSLATION

In conclusion, therefore, O Nanda Mahārāja, this child of yours is as good as Nārāyaṇa. In His transcendental qualities, opulence,

name, fame and influence, He is exactly like Nārāyaṇa. You should all raise this child very carefully and cautiously.

PURPORT

In this verse, the word *nārāyaṇa-samaḥ* is significant. Nārāyaṇa has no equal. He is *asamaurdhva:* no one is equal to Him, and no one is greater than He is. As stated in *śāstra:*

yas tu nārāyaṇaṁ devaṁ
brahma-rudrādi-daivataiḥ
samatvenaiva vīkṣeta
sa pāṣaṇḍī bhaved dhruvam

One who equates Nārāyaṇa even with great exalted demigods like Lord Śiva or Lord Brahmā is a *pāṣaṇḍī,* an agnostic. No one can equal Nārāyaṇa. Nonetheless, Gargamuni used the word *sama,* meaning "equal," because he wanted to treat Kṛṣṇa as the Supreme Personality of Godhead who had become Nanda Mahārāja's son. Gargamuni wanted to impress upon the mind of Nanda Mahārāja, "Your worshipable Deity, Nārāyaṇa, is so pleased with you that He has sent you a son almost equal to Him in qualifications. Therefore you may designate your son with a similar name, such as Mukunda or Madhusūdana. But you must always remember that whenever you want to do something very good, there will be many hindrances. Therefore you should raise and protect this child with great care. If you can protect this child very cautiously, as Nārāyaṇa always protects you, the child will be as good as Nārāyaṇa." Gargamuni also indicated that although the child was exaltedly qualified like Nārāyaṇa, He would enjoy more than Nārāyaṇa as *rāsa-vihārī,* the central enjoyer of the *rāsa* dance. As stated in the *Brahma-saṁhitā,* *lakṣmī-sahasra-śata-sambhrama-sevyamānam:* He would be served by many *gopīs,* who would all be as good as the goddess of fortune.

TEXT 20

श्रीशुक उवाच

इत्यात्मानं समादिश्य गर्गे च स्वगृहं गते ।
नन्दः प्रमुदितो मेने आत्मानं पूर्णमाशिषाम् ॥२०॥

śrī-śuka uvāca
ity ātmānaṁ samādiśya
garge ca sva-gṛhaṁ gate
nandaḥ pramudito mene
ātmānaṁ pūrṇam āśiṣām

śrī-śukaḥ uvāca—Śrī Śukadeva Gosvāmī said; *iti*—thus; *ātmānam*—about the Absolute Truth, the Supreme Soul; *samādiśya*—after fully instructing; *garge*—when Gargamuni; *ca*—also; *sva-gṛham*—to his own abode; *gate*—had departed; *nandaḥ*—Mahārāja Nanda; *pramuditaḥ*—became extremely pleased; *mene*—considered; *ātmānam*—his own self; *pūrṇam āśiṣām*—full of all good fortune.

TRANSLATION

Śrīla Śukadeva Gosvāmī continued: After Gargamuni, having instructed Nanda Mahārāja about Kṛṣṇa, departed for his own home, Nanda Mahārāja was very pleased and considered himself full of all good fortune.

PURPORT

Kṛṣṇa is the Supersoul, and Nanda Mahārāja is the individual soul. By the instructions of Gargamuni, both of them were blessed. Nanda Mahārāja was thinking of Kṛṣṇa's safety from the hands of demons like Pūtanā and Śakaṭāsura, and because he possessed such a son, he thought of himself as most fortunate.

TEXT 21

कालेन व्रजताल्पेन गोकुले रामकेशवौ ।
जानुभ्यां सह पाणिभ्यां रिङ्गमाणौ विजह्रतुः ॥२१॥

kālena vrajatālpena
gokule rāma-keśavau
jānubhyāṁ saha pāṇibhyāṁ
riṅgamāṇau vijahratuḥ

kālena—of time; *vrajatā*—passing; *alpena*—a very small duration; *gokule*—in Gokula, Vraja-dhāma; *rāma-keśavau*—both Balarāma and

Kṛṣṇa; *jānubhyām*—by the strength of Their knees; *saha pāṇibhyām*—resting on Their hands; *riṅgamāṇau*—crawling; *vijahratuḥ*—enjoyed childhood play.

TRANSLATION

After a short time passed, both brothers, Rāma and Kṛṣṇa, began to crawl on the ground of Vraja with the strength of Their hands and knees and thus enjoy Their childhood play.

PURPORT

One *brāhmaṇa* devotee says:

śrutim apare smṛtim itare bhāratam anye bhajantu bhava-bhītāḥ
aham iha nandaṁ vande yasyālinde paraṁ brahma

"Let others, fearing material existence, worship the *Vedas*, the Vedic supplementary *Purāṇas* and the *Mahābhārata*, but I shall worship Nanda Mahārāja, in whose courtyard the Supreme Brahman is crawling." For a highly exalted devotee, *kaivalya*, merging into the existence of the Supreme, appears no better than hell (*narakāyate*). But here one can simply think of the crawling of Kṛṣṇa and Balarāma in the courtyard of Nanda Mahārāja and always merge in transcendental happiness. As long as one is absorbed in thoughts of *kṛṣṇa-līlā*, especially Kṛṣṇa's childhood pastimes, as Parīkṣit Mahārāja desired to be, one is always merged in actual *kaivalya.* Therefore Vyāsadeva compiled *Śrīmad-Bhāgavatam. Lokasyājānato vidvāṁś cakre sātvata-saṁhitām* (*Bhāg.* 1.7.6). Vyāsadeva compiled *Śrīmad-Bhāgavatam*, under the instruction of Nārada, so that anyone can take advantage of this literature, think of Kṛṣṇa's pastimes and always be liberated.

śrutim apare smṛtim itare bhāratam anye bhajantu bhava-bhītāḥ
aham iha nandaṁ vande yasyālinde paraṁ brahma

TEXT 22

तावङ्घ्रियुग्ममनुकृष्य सरीसृपन्तौ
घोषप्रघोषरुचिरं व्रजकर्दमेषु ।

तन्नादहृष्टमनसावनुसृत्य लोकं
मुग्धप्रभीतवदुपेयतुरन्ति मात्रोः ॥२२॥

tāv aṅghri-yugmam anukṛṣya sarīsṛpantau
ghoṣa-praghoṣa-ruciraṁ vraja-kardameṣu
tan-nāda-hṛṣṭa-manasāv anusṛtya lokaṁ
mugdha-prabhītavad upeyatur anti mātroḥ

tau—Kṛṣṇa and Balarāma; *aṅghri-yugmam anukṛṣya*—dragging Their legs; *sarīsṛpantau*—crawling like snakes; *ghoṣa-praghoṣa-ruciram*—producing a sound with Their ankle bells that was very, very sweet to hear; *vraja-kardameṣu*—in the mud created by cow dung and cow urine on the earth of Vrajabhūmi; *tat-nāda*—by the sound of those ankle bells; *hṛṣṭa-manasau*—being very much pleased; *anusṛtya*—following; *lokam*—other persons; *mugdha*—thus being enchanted; *prabhīta-vat*—then again being afraid of them; *upeyatuḥ*—immediately returned; *anti mātroḥ*—toward Their mothers.

TRANSLATION

When Kṛṣṇa and Balarāma, with the strength of Their legs, crawled in the muddy places created in Vraja by cow dung and cow urine, Their crawling resembled the crawling of serpents, and the sound of Their ankle bells was very charming. Very much pleased by the sound of other people's ankle bells, They used to follow these people as if going to Their mothers, but when They saw that these were other people, They became afraid and returned to Their real mothers, Yaśodā and Rohiṇī.

PURPORT

When Kṛṣṇa and Balarāma were crawling about Vrajabhūmi, They were enchanted by the sound of ankle bells. Thus They sometimes followed other people, who would enjoy the crawling of Kṛṣṇa and Balarāma and exclaim, "Oh, see how Kṛṣṇa and Balarāma are crawling!" Upon hearing this, Kṛṣṇa and Balarāma could understand that these were not Their mothers They were following, and They would return to Their actual mothers. Thus the crawling of Kṛṣṇa and Balarāma was enjoyed by the people of the neighborhood, as well as by mother Yaśodā and Rohiṇī and the two children Themselves.

TEXT 23

तन्मातरौ निजसुतौ घृणया स्नुवन्त्यौ
पङ्काङ्गरागरुचिरावुपगृह्य दोर्भ्याम् ।
दत्त्वा स्तनं प्रपिबतोः स्म मुखं निरीक्ष्य
मुग्धस्मिताल्पदशनं ययतुः प्रमोदम् ॥२३॥

tan-mātarau nija-sutau ghṛṇayā snuvantyau
paṅkāṅga-rāga-rucirāv upagṛhya dorbhyām
dattvā stanaṁ prapibatoḥ sma mukhaṁ nirīkṣya
mugdha-smitālpa-daśanaṁ yayatuḥ pramodam

tat-mātarau—Their mothers (Rohiṇī and Yaśodā); *nija-sutau*—their own respective sons; *ghṛṇayā*—with great affection; *snuvantyau*—allowed to suck the flowing milk from Their breasts very happily; *paṅka-aṅga-rāga-rucirau*—whose beautiful transcendental bodies were covered with muddy cow dung and urine; *upagṛhya*—taking care of; *dorbhyām*—by their arms; *dattvā*—delivering Them; *stanam*—the breast; *prapibatoḥ*—when the babies were sucking; *sma*—indeed; *mukham*—the mouth; *nirīkṣya*—and seeing; *mugdha-smita-alpa-daśanam*—smiling with little teeth coming out of Their mouths (they were more and more attracted); *yayatuḥ*—and enjoyed; *pramodam*—transcendental bliss.

TRANSLATION

Dressed with muddy earth mixed with cow dung and cow urine, the babies looked very beautiful, and when They went to Their mothers, both Yaśodā and Rohiṇī picked Them up with great affection, embraced Them and allowed Them to suck the milk flowing from their breasts. While sucking the breast, the babies smiled, and Their small teeth were visible. Their mothers, upon seeing those beautiful teeth, enjoyed great transcendental bliss.

PURPORT

As the mothers cared for their respective babies, by the arrangement of *yogamāyā* the babies thought, "Here is My mother," and the mothers thought, "Here is my son." Because of affection, milk naturally flowed from the mothers' breasts, and the babies drank it. When the mothers saw small teeth coming in, they would count them and be happy, and when the babies saw Their mothers allowing Them to drink their breast milk, the babies also felt transcendental pleasure. As this transcendental affection continued between Rohiṇī and Balarāma and Yaśodā and Kṛṣṇa, they all enjoyed transcendental bliss.

TEXT 24

यर्ह्यङ्गनादर्शनीयकुमारलीला-
वन्तर्व्रजे तदबलाः प्रगृहीतपुच्छैः ।
वत्सैरितस्तत उभावनुकृष्यमाणौ
प्रेक्षन्त्य उज्झितगृहा जहृषुर्हसन्त्यः॥२४॥

yarhy aṅganā-darśanīya-kumāra-līlāv
antar-vraje tad abalāḥ pragṛhīta-pucchaiḥ
vatsair itas tata ubhāv anukṛṣyamāṇau
prekṣantya ujjhita-gṛhā jahṛṣur hasantyaḥ

yarhi—when; *aṅganā-darśanīya*—visible only to the ladies within the house; *kumāra-līlau*—the pastimes Śrī Kṛṣṇa and Balarāma exhibited as children; *antaḥ-vraje*—within the inside of Vraja, in the house of Nanda Mahārāja; *tat*—at that time; *abalāḥ*—all the ladies; *pragṛhīta-pucchaiḥ*—the ends of their tails having been caught by Kṛṣṇa and Balarāma; *vatsaiḥ*—by the calves; *itaḥ tataḥ*—here and there; *ubhau*—both Kṛṣṇa and Balarāma; *anukṛṣyamāṇau*—being dragged; *prekṣantyaḥ*—seeing such things; *ujjhita*—given up; *gṛhāḥ*—their household affairs; *jahṛṣuḥ*—enjoyed very much; *hasantyaḥ*—while laughing.

TRANSLATION

Within the house of Nanda Mahārāja, the cowherd ladies would enjoy seeing the pastimes of the babies Rāma and Kṛṣṇa. The

babies would catch the ends of the calves' tails, and the calves would drag Them here and there. When the ladies saw these pastimes, they certainly stopped their household activities and laughed and enjoyed the incidents.

PURPORT

While crawling in curiosity, Kṛṣṇa and Balarāma would sometimes catch the ends of the tails of calves. The calves, feeling that someone had caught them, would begin to flee here and there, and the babies would hold on very tightly, being afraid of how the calves were moving. The calves, seeing that the babies were holding them tightly, would also become afraid. Then the ladies would come to rescue the babies and gladly laugh. This was their enjoyment.

TEXT 25

शृङ्ग्यग्निदंष्ट्र्यसिजलद्विजकण्टकेभ्यः
क्रीडापरावतिचलौ स्वसुतौ निषेद्धुम् ।
गृह्याणि कर्तुमपि यत्र न तज्जनन्यौ
शेकात आपतुरलं मनसोऽनवस्थाम् ॥२५॥

śṛṅgy-agni-daṁṣṭry-asi-jala-dvija-kaṇṭakebhyaḥ
krīḍā-parāv aticalau sva-sutau niṣeddhum
gṛhyāṇi kartum api yatra na taj-jananyau
śekāta āpatur alaṁ manaso 'navasthām

śṛṅgī—with the cows; *agni*—fire; *daṁṣṭrī*—monkeys and dogs; *asi*—swords; *jala*—water; *dvija*—birds; *kaṇṭakebhyaḥ*—and thorns; *krīḍā-parau ati-calau*—the babies, being too restless, engaged in play; *sva-sutau*—their own two sons; *niṣeddhum*—just to stop Them; *gṛhyāṇi*—household duties; *kartum api*—by executing; *yatra*—when; *na*—not; *tat-jananyau*—Their mothers (Rohiṇī and Yaśodā); *śekāte*—able; *āpatuḥ*—obtained; *alam*—indeed; *manasaḥ*—of the mind; *ana-vasthām*—equilibrium.

TRANSLATION

When mother Yaśodā and Rohiṇī were unable to protect the babies from calamities threatened by horned cows, by fire, by animals with claws and teeth such as monkeys, dogs and cats, and by thorns, swords and other weapons on the ground, they were always in anxiety, and their household engagements were disturbed. At that time, they were fully equipoised in the transcendental ecstasy known as the distress of material affection, for this was aroused within their minds.

PURPORT

All these pastimes of Kṛṣṇa, and the great enjoyment exhibited by the mothers, are transcendental; nothing about them is material. They are described in the *Brahma-saṁhitā* as *ānanda-cinmaya-rasa.* In the spiritual world there is anxiety, there is crying, and there are other feelings similar to those of the material world, but because the reality of these feelings is in the transcendental world, of which this world is only an imitation, mother Yaśodā and Rohiṇī enjoyed them transcendentally.

TEXT 26

कालेनाल्पेन राजर्षे रामः कृष्णश्च गोकुले ।
अघृष्टजानुभिः पद्भिर्विचक्रमतुरञ्जसा ॥२६॥

kālenālpena rājarṣe
rāmaḥ kṛṣṇaś ca gokule
aghṛṣṭa-jānubhiḥ padbhir
vicakramatur añjasā

kālena alpena—within a very short time; *rājarṣe*—O King (Mahārāja Parīkṣit); *rāmaḥ kṛṣṇaḥ ca*—both Rāma and Kṛṣṇa; *gokule*—in the village of Gokula; *aghṛṣṭa-jānubhiḥ*—without the help of crawling on Their knees; *padbhiḥ*—by Their legs alone; *vicakramatuḥ*—began to walk; *añjasā*—very easily.

TRANSLATION

O King Parīkṣit, within a very short time both Rāma and Kṛṣṇa began to walk very easily in Gokula on Their legs, by Their own strength, without the need to crawl.

PURPORT

Instead of crawling with Their knees, the babies could now stand up by holding on to something and walk little by little, without difficulty, by the strength of Their legs.

TEXT 27

ततस्तु भगवान् कृष्णो वयस्यैर्व्रजबालकैः ।
सहरामो व्रजस्त्रीणां चिक्रीडे जनयन् मुदम् ॥२७॥

tatas tu bhagavān kṛṣṇo
vayasyair vraja-bālakaiḥ
saha-rāmo vraja-strīṇāṁ
cikrīḍe janayan mudam

tataḥ—thereafter; *tu*—but; *bhagavān*—the Supreme Personality of Godhead; *kṛṣṇaḥ*—Lord Kṛṣṇa; *vayasyaiḥ*—with Their playmates; *vraja-bālakaiḥ*—with other small children in Vraja; *saha-rāmaḥ*—along with Balarāma; *vraja-strīṇām*—of all the ladies of Vraja; *cikrīḍe*—played very happily; *janayan*—awakening; *mudam*—transcendental bliss.

TRANSLATION

Thereafter, Lord Kṛṣṇa, along with Balarāma, began to play with the other children of the cowherd men, thus awakening the transcendental bliss of the cowherd women.

PURPORT

The word *saha-rāmaḥ*, meaning "along with Balarāma," is significant in this verse. In such transcendental pastimes, Kṛṣṇa is the chief hero, and Balarāma provides additional help.

TEXT 28

कृष्णस्य गोप्यो रुचिरं वीक्ष्य कौमारचापलम् ।
शृण्वंत्याः किल तन्मातुरिति होचुः समागताः॥२८॥

kṛṣṇasya gopyo ruciraṁ
vīkṣya kaumāra-cāpalam
śṛṇvantyāḥ kila tan-mātur
iti hocuḥ samāgatāḥ

kṛṣṇasya—of Kṛṣṇa; *gopyaḥ*—all the *gopīs; ruciram*—very attractive; *vīkṣya*—observing; *kaumāra-cāpalam*—the restlessness of the childish pastimes; *śṛṇvantyāḥ*—just to hear them again and again; *kila*—indeed; *tat-mātuḥ*—in the presence of His mother; *iti*—thus; *ha*—indeed; *ūcuḥ*—said; *samāgatāḥ*—assembled there.

TRANSLATION

Observing the very attractive childish restlessness of Kṛṣṇa, all the gopīs in the neighborhood, to hear about Kṛṣṇa's activities again and again, would approach mother Yaśodā and speak to her as follows.

PURPORT

Kṛṣṇa's activities are always very attractive to devotees. Therefore the neighbors, who were friends of mother Yaśodā, informed mother Yaśodā of whatever they saw Kṛṣṇa doing in the neighborhood. Mother Yaśodā, just to hear about the activities of her son, stopped her household duties and enjoyed the information given by the neighborhood friends.

TEXT 29

वत्सान् मुञ्चन् क्वचिदसमये क्रोशसंजातहासः
स्तेयं स्वाद्वत्त्यथ दधिपयः कल्पितैः स्तेययोगैः ।
मर्कान् भोक्ष्यन् विभजति स चेन्नात्ति भाण्डं भिनत्ति
द्रव्यालाभे सगृहकुपितो यात्युपक्रोश्य तोकान्॥२९॥

vatsān muñcan kvacid asamaye krośa-sañjāta-hāsaḥ
steyaṁ svādv atty atha dadhi-payaḥ kalpitaiḥ steya-yogaiḥ

markān bhokṣyan vibhajati sa cen nātti bhāṇḍaṁ bhinnatti
dravyālābhe sagṛha-kupito yāty upakrośya tokān

vatsān—the calves; *muñcan*—releasing; *kvacit*—sometimes; *asamaye*—at odd times; *krośa-sañjāta-hāsaḥ*—after this, when the head of the house is angry, Kṛṣṇa begins to smile; *steyam*—obtained by stealing; *svādu*—very tasteful; *atti*—eats; *atha*—thus; *dadhi-payaḥ*—pot of curd and milk; *kalpitaiḥ*—devised; *steya-yogaiḥ*—by some sort of stealing process; *markān*—to the monkeys; *bhokṣyan*—giving to eat; *vibhajati*—divides their portion; *saḥ*—the monkey; *cet*—if; *na*—not; *atti*—eats; *bhāṇḍam*—the pot; *bhinnatti*—He breaks; *dravya-alābhe*—when eatables are unavailable or He cannot find such pots; *sa-gṛha-kupitaḥ*—He becomes angry at the residents of the house; *yāti*—He goes away; *upakrośya*—irritating and pinching; *tokān*—the small children.

TRANSLATION

"Our dear friend Yaśodā, your son sometimes comes to our houses before the milking of the cows and releases the calves, and when the master of the house becomes angry, your son merely smiles. Sometimes He devises some process by which He steals palatable curd, butter and milk, which He then eats and drinks. When the monkeys assemble, He divides it with them, and when the monkeys have their bellies so full that they won't take more, He breaks the pots. Sometimes, if He gets no opportunity to steal butter or milk from a house, He will be angry at the householders, and for His revenge He will agitate the small children by pinching them. Then, when the children begin crying, Kṛṣṇa will go away.

PURPORT

The narration of Kṛṣṇa's naughty childhood activities would be presented to mother Yaśodā in the form of complaints. Sometimes Kṛṣṇa would enter the house of a neighbor, and if He found no one there, He would release the calves before the time for the cows to be milked. The calves are actually supposed to be released when their mothers are milked, but Kṛṣṇa would release them before that time, and naturally the calves would drink all the milk from their mothers. When the cowherd men saw this, they would chase Kṛṣṇa and try to catch Him, saying,

"Here is Kṛṣṇa doing mischief," but He would flee and enter another house, where He would again devise some means to steal butter and curd. Then the cowherd men would again try to capture Him, saying, "Here is the butter thief. Better capture Him!" And they would be angry. But Kṛṣṇa would simply smile, and they would forget everything. Sometimes, in their presence, He would begin eating the curd and butter. There was no need for Kṛṣṇa to eat butter, since His belly was always full, but He would try to eat it, or else He would break the pots and distribute the contents to the monkeys. In this way, Kṛṣṇa was always engaged in mischief-making. If in any house He could not find any butter or curd to steal, He would go into a room and agitate the small children sleeping there by pinching them, and when they cried He would go away.

TEXT 30

हस्ताग्राह्ये रचयति विधिं पीठकोलूखलाद्यै-
छिद्रं ह्यन्तर्निहितवयुनः शिक्यभाण्डेषु तद्वित् ।
ध्वान्तागारे धृतमणिगणं स्वाङ्गमर्थप्रदीपं
काले गोप्यो यर्हि गृहकृत्येषु सुव्यग्रचित्ताः ॥३०॥

hastāgrāhye racayati vidhiṁ pīṭhakolūkhalādyaiś
chidraṁ hy antar-nihita-vayunaḥ śikya-bhāṇḍeṣu tad-vit
dhvāntāgāre dhṛta-maṇi-gaṇaṁ svāṅgam artha-pradīpaṁ
kāle gopyo yarhi gṛha-kṛtyeṣu suvyagra-cittāḥ

hasta-agrāhye—when the destination is out of the reach of His hands; *racayati*—He arranges to make; *vidhim*—a means; *pīṭhaka*—by wooden planks piled together; *ulūkhala-ādyaiḥ*—and by overturning the stone mortar for grinding spices; *chidram*—a hole; *hi*—indeed; *antaḥ-nihita*—about the contents of the pot; *vayunaḥ*—with such knowledge; *śikya*—hanging by a swing; *bhāṇḍeṣu*—in the pots; *tat-vit*—expert in that knowledge, or in full knowledge; *dhvānta-āgāre*—in a very dark room; *dhṛta-maṇi-gaṇam*—because of being decorated with valuable jewels; *sva-aṅgam*—His own body; *artha-pradīpam*—is the light required for seeing in darkness; *kāle*—after that, in due course of time;

gopyaḥ—the elderly *gopīs; yarhi*—as soon as; *gṛha-kṛtyeṣu*—in discharging household affairs; *su-vyagra-cittāḥ*—are busily engaged.

TRANSLATION

"When the milk and curd are kept high on a swing hanging from the ceiling and Kṛṣṇa and Balarāma cannot reach it, They arrange to reach it by piling up various planks and turning upside down the mortar for grinding spices. Being quite aware of the contents of a pot, They pick holes in it. While the elderly gopīs go about their household affairs, Kṛṣṇa and Balarāma sometimes go into a dark room, brightening the place with the valuable jewels and ornaments on Their bodies and taking advantage of this light by stealing.

PURPORT

Formerly, in every household, yogurt and butter were kept for use in emergencies. But Kṛṣṇa and Balarāma would pile up planks so that They could reach the pots and would then pick holes in the pots with Their hands so that the contents would leak out and They could drink it. This was another means for stealing butter and milk. When the butter and milk were kept in a dark room, Kṛṣṇa and Balarāma would go there and make the place bright with the valuable jewels on Their bodies. On the whole, Kṛṣṇa and Balarāma engaged in stealing butter and milk from the neighborhood houses in many ways.

TEXT 31

एवं धार्ष्ट्यान्युशति कुरुते मेहनादीनि वास्तौ
स्तेयोपायैर्विरचितकृतिः सुप्रतीको यथास्ते ।
इत्थं स्त्रीभिः सभयनयनश्रीमुखालोकिनीभि-
र्व्याख्यातार्था प्रहसितमुखी न ह्युपालब्धुमैच्छत् ।३१।

evaṁ dhārṣṭyāny uśati kurute mehanādīni vāstau
steyopāyair viracita-kṛtiḥ supratīko yathāste
itthaṁ strībhiḥ sa-bhaya-nayana-śrī-mukhālokinībhir
vyākhyātārthā prahasita-mukhī na hy upālabdhum aicchat

evam—in this way; *dhārṣṭyāni*—naughty activities; *uśati*—in a neat and clean place; *kurute*—sometimes does; *mehana-ādīni*—passing stool and urine; *vāstau*—in our houses; *steya-upāyaiḥ*—and by inventing different devices to steal butter and milk; *viracita-kṛtiḥ*—is very expert; *su-pratīkaḥ*—is now sitting down here like a very good, well-behaved child; *yathā āste*—while staying here; *ittham*—all these topics of conversation; *strībhiḥ*—by the *gopīs; sa-bhaya-nayana*—just now sitting there with fearful eyes; *śrī-mukha*—such a beautiful face; *ālokinībhiḥ*—by the *gopīs*, who were enjoying the pleasure of seeing; *vyākhyāta-arthā*—and while complaining against Him before mother Yaśodā; *prahasita-mukhī*—they were smiling and enjoying; *na*—not; *hi*—indeed; *upālabdhum*—to chastise and threaten (rather, she enjoyed how Kṛṣṇa was sitting there as a very good boy); *aicchat*—she desired.

TRANSLATION

"When Kṛṣṇa is caught in His naughty activities, the master of the house will say to Him, 'Oh, You are a thief,' and artificially express anger at Kṛṣṇa. Kṛṣṇa will then reply, 'I am not a thief. You are a thief.' Sometimes, being angry, Kṛṣṇa passes urine and stool in a neat, clean place in our houses. But now, our dear friend Yaśodā, this expert thief is sitting before you like a very good boy." Sometimes all the gopīs would look at Kṛṣṇa sitting there, His eyes fearful so that His mother would not chastise Him, and when they saw Kṛṣṇa's beautiful face, instead of chastising Him they would simply look upon His face and enjoy transcendental bliss. Mother Yaśodā would mildly smile at all this fun, and she would not want to chastise her blessed transcendental child.

PURPORT

Kṛṣṇa's business in the neighborhood was not only to steal but sometimes to pass stool and urine in a neat, clean house. When caught by the master of the house, Kṛṣṇa would chastise him, saying, "You are a thief." Aside from being a thief in His childhood affairs, Kṛṣṇa acted as an expert thief when He was young by attracting young girls and enjoying them in the *rāsa* dance. This is Kṛṣṇa's business. He is also violent, as the killer of many demons. Although mundane people like nonviolence and other such brilliant qualities, God, the Absolute Truth, being always the same, is good in any activities, even so-called immoral activities like stealing, killing and violence. Kṛṣṇa is always pure, and He is always the Supreme Absolute Truth. Kṛṣṇa may do anything supposedly abominable in material life, yet still He is attractive. Therefore His name is Kṛṣṇa, meaning "all-attractive." This is the platform on which transcendental loving affairs and service are exchanged. Because of the features of Kṛṣṇa's face, the mothers were so attracted that they could not chastise Him. Instead of chastising Him, they smiled and enjoyed hearing of Kṛṣṇa's activities. Thus the *gopīs* remained satisfied, and Kṛṣṇa enjoyed their happiness. Therefore another name of Kṛṣṇa is Gopī-jana-vallabha because He invented such activities to please the *gopīs*.

TEXT 32

एकदा क्रीडमानास्ते रामाद्या गोपदारकाः ।
कृष्णो मृदं भक्षितवानिति मात्रे न्यवेदयन् ॥३२॥

ekadā krīḍamānās te
rāmādyā gopa-dārakāḥ
kṛṣṇo mṛdaṁ bhakṣitavān
iti mātre nyavedayan

ekadā—once upon a time; *krīḍamānāḥ*—now Kṛṣṇa, being still more grown up, was playing with other children of the same age; *te*—they; *rāma-ādyāḥ*—Balarāma and others; *gopa-dārakāḥ*—other boys born in the same neighborhood of the cowherd men; *kṛṣṇaḥ mṛdam bhakṣitavān*—O Mother, Kṛṣṇa has eaten earth (a complaint was lodged); *iti*—thus; *mātre*—unto mother Yaśodā; *nyavedayan*—they submitted.

TRANSLATION

One day while Kṛṣṇa was playing with His small playmates, including Balarāma and other sons of the gopas, all His friends came together and lodged a complaint to mother Yaśodā. "Mother," they submitted, "Kṛṣṇa has eaten earth."

PURPORT

Here is another of Kṛṣṇa's transcendental activities invented to please the *gopīs*. First a complaint was lodged with mother Yaśodā about Kṛṣṇa's stealing, but mother Yaśodā did not chastise Him. Now, in an attempt to awaken mother Yaśodā's anger so that she would chastise Kṛṣṇa, another complaint was invented—that Kṛṣṇa had eaten earth.

TEXT 33

सा गृहीत्वा करे कृष्णमुपालभ्य हितैषिणी ।
यशोदा भयसम्भ्रान्तप्रेक्षणाक्षमभाषत ॥३३॥

sā gṛhītvā kare kṛṣṇam
upālabhya hitaiṣiṇī
yaśodā bhaya-sambhrānta-
prekṣaṇākṣam abhāṣata

sā—mother Yaśodā; *gṛhītvā*—taking; *kare*—within the hands (being anxious about what Kṛṣṇa might have eaten); *kṛṣṇam*—Kṛṣṇa; *upālabhya*—wanted to chastise Him; *hita-eṣiṇī*—because she was anxious for the welfare of Kṛṣṇa, she became very much agitated, thinking, "How is it that Kṛṣṇa has eaten earth?"; *yaśodā*—mother Yaśodā; *bhaya-sambhrānta-prekṣaṇa-akṣam*—began to look very carefully within Kṛṣṇa's mouth in fear, to see if Kṛṣṇa had eaten something dangerous; *abhāṣata*—began to address Kṛṣṇa.

TRANSLATION

Upon hearing this from Kṛṣṇa's playmates, mother Yaśodā, who was always full of anxiety over Kṛṣṇa's welfare, picked Kṛṣṇa up with her hands to look into His mouth and chastise Him. Her eyes fearful, she spoke to her son as follows.

TEXT 34

कस्मान्मृदमदान्तात्मन् भवान् भक्षितवान् रहः ।
वदन्ति तावका ह्येते कुमारास्तेऽग्रजोऽप्ययम् ॥३४॥

kasmān mṛdam adāntātman
bhavān bhakṣitavān rahaḥ
vadanti tāvakā hy ete
kumārās te 'grajo 'py ayam

kasmāt—why; *mṛdam*—dirt; *adānta-ātman*—You restless boy; *bhavān*—You; *bhakṣitavān*—have eaten; *rahaḥ*—in a solitary place; *vadanti*—are lodging this complaint; *tāvakāḥ*—Your friends and playmates; *hi*—indeed; *ete*—all of them; *kumārāḥ*—boys; *te*—Your; *agrajaḥ*—older brother; *api*—also (confirms); *ayam*—this.

TRANSLATION

Dear Kṛṣṇa, why are You so restless that You have eaten dirt in a solitary place? This complaint has been lodged against You by all Your playmates, including Your elder brother, Balarāma. How is this?

PURPORT

Mother Yaśodā was agitated by Kṛṣṇa's restless misbehavior. Her house was full of sweetmeats. Why then should the restless boy eat dirt in a solitary place? Kṛṣṇa replied, "My dear mother, they have plotted together and lodged a complaint against Me so that you will punish Me. My elder brother, Balarāma, has joined them. Actually, I have not done this. Take My words as true. Do not be angry and chastise Me."

TEXT 35

नाहं भक्षितवानम्ब सर्वे मिथ्याभिशंसिनः ।
यदि सत्यगिरस्तर्हि समक्षं पश्य मे मुखम् ॥३५॥

nāhaṁ bhakṣitavān amba
sarve mithyābhiśaṁsinaḥ
yadi satya-giras tarhi
samakṣaṁ paśya me mukham

na—not; *aham*—I; *bhakṣitavān*—have eaten dirt; *amba*—My dear mother; *sarve*—all of them; *mithya-abhiśaṁsinaḥ*—all liars, simply complaining against Me so that you may chastise Me; *yadi*—if it is actually a fact; *satya-giraḥ*—that they have spoken the truth; *tarhi*—then; *samakṣam*—directly; *paśya*—see; *me*—My; *mukham*—mouth.

TRANSLATION

Lord Śrī Kṛṣṇa replied: My dear mother, I have never eaten dirt. All My friends complaining against Me are liars. If you think they are being truthful, you can directly look into My mouth and examine it.

PURPORT

Kṛṣṇa presented Himself as an innocent child to increase the transcendental ecstasy of maternal affection. As described in the *śāstra, tāḍana-bhayān mithyoktir vātsalya-rasa-poṣikā.* This means that sometimes a small child speaks lies. For example, he may have stolen something or eaten something and yet deny that he has done so. We ordinarily see this in the material world, but in relation to Kṛṣṇa it is different; such activities are meant to endow the devotee with transcendental ecstasy. The Supreme Personality of Godhead was playing as a liar and accusing all the other devotees of being liars. As stated in *Śrīmad-Bhāgavatam* (10.12.11), *kṛta-puṇya-puñjāḥ:* a devotee may attain such an ecstatic position after many, many births of devotional service. Persons who have amassed the results of a vast amount of pious activities can attain the stage of associating with Kṛṣṇa and playing with Him like ordinary playmates. One should not consider these transactions of transcendental service to be untruthful accusations. One should never accuse such devotees of being ordinary boys speaking lies, for they attained this stage of associating with Kṛṣṇa by great austerities (*tapasā brahmacaryeṇa śamena ca damena ca*).

TEXT 36

यद्येवं तर्हि व्यादेहीत्युक्तः स भगवान् हरिः ।
व्यादत्ताव्याहतैश्वर्यः क्रीडामनुजबालकः ॥३६॥

yady evaṁ tarhi vyādehī-
ty uktaḥ sa bhagavān hariḥ
vyādattāvyāhataiśvaryaḥ
krīḍā-manuja-bālakaḥ

yadi—if; *evam*—it is so; *tarhi*—then; *vyādehi*—open Your mouth wide (I want to see); *iti uktaḥ*—in this way ordered by mother Yaśodā; *saḥ*—He; *bhagavān*—the Supreme Personality of Godhead; *hariḥ*—the Supreme Lord; *vyādatta*—opened His mouth; *avyāhata-aiśvaryaḥ*—without minimizing any potencies of absolute opulence (*aiśvaryasya samagrasya*); *krīḍā*—pastimes; *manuja-bālakaḥ*—exactly like the child of a human being.

TRANSLATION

Mother Yaśodā challenged Kṛṣṇa, "If You have not eaten earth, then open Your mouth wide." When challenged by His mother in this way, Kṛṣṇa, the son of Nanda Mahārāja and Yaśodā, to exhibit pastimes like a human child, opened His mouth. Although the Supreme Personality of Godhead, Kṛṣṇa, who is full of all opulences, did not disturb His mother's parental affection, His opulence was automatically displayed, for Kṛṣṇa's opulence is never lost at any stage, but is manifest at the proper time.

PURPORT

Without disturbing the ecstasy of His mother's affection, Kṛṣṇa opened His mouth and displayed His own natural opulences. When a person is given varieties of food, there may be a hundred and one varieties, but if one likes ordinary *śāka*, spinach, he prefers to eat that. Similarly, although Kṛṣṇa was full of opulences, now, by the order of mother Yaśodā, He opened wide His mouth like a human child and did not neglect the transcendental humor of maternal affection.

TEXTS 37–39

सा तत्र ददृशे विश्वं जगत् स्थास्नु च खं दिशः ।
साद्रिद्वीपाब्धिभूगोलं सवाय्वग्नीन्दुतारकम् ॥३७॥

ज्योतिश्चक्रं जलं तेजो नभस्वान् वियदेव च।
वैकारिकाणीन्द्रियाणि मनो मात्रा गुणास्त्रयः॥३८॥
एतद् विचित्रं सह जीवकाल-
स्वभावकर्माशयलिङ्गभेदम् ।
सूनोस्तनौ वीक्ष्य विदारितास्ये
व्रजं सहात्मानमवाप शङ्काम् ॥३९॥

sā tatra dadṛśe viśvaṁ
jagat sthāsnu ca khaṁ diśaḥ
sādri-dvīpābdhi-bhūgolaṁ
sa-vāyv-agnīndu-tārakam

jyotiś-cakraṁ jalaṁ tejo
nabhasvān viyad eva ca
vaikārikāṇīndriyāṇi
mano mātrā guṇās trayaḥ

etad vicitraṁ saha-jīva-kāla-
svabhāva-karmāśaya-liṅga-bhedam
sūnos tanau vīkṣya vidāritāsye
vrajaṁ sahātmānam avāpa śaṅkām

sā—mother Yaśodā; *tatra*—within the wide-open mouth of Kṛṣṇa; *dadṛśe*—saw; *viśvam*—the whole universe; *jagat*—moving entities; *sthāsnu*—maintenance of nonmoving entities; *ca*—and; *kham*—the sky; *diśaḥ*—the directions; *sa-adri*—with the mountains; *dvīpa*—islands; *abdhi*—and oceans; *bhū-golam*—the surface of the earth; *sa-vāyu*—with the blowing wind; *agni*—fire; *indu*—the moon; *tārakam*—stars; *jyotiḥ-cakram*—the planetary systems; *jalam*—water; *tejaḥ*—light; *nabhasvān*—outer space; *viyat*—the sky; *eva*—also; *ca*—and; *vaikārikāṇi*—creation by transformation of *ahaṅkāra; indriyāṇi*—the senses; *manaḥ*—mind; *mātrāḥ*—sense perception; *guṇāḥ trayaḥ*—the three material qualities (*sattva, rajas* and *tamas*); *etat*—all these; *vicitram*—varieties; *saha*—along with; *jīva-kāla*—the duration of life of all living entities; *svabhāva*—natural instinct; *karma-āśaya*—resultant action and desire for material enjoyment; *liṅga-bhedam*—varieties of bodies according to desire; *sūnoḥ tanau*—in the body of her son; *vīkṣya*—seeing; *vidārita-āsye*—within the wide-open mouth; *vrajam*—Vṛndāvana-dhāma, Nanda Mahārāja's place; *saha-ātmānam*—along with herself; *avāpa*—was struck; *śaṅkām*—with all doubts and wonder.

TRANSLATION

When Kṛṣṇa opened His mouth wide by the order of mother Yaśodā, she saw within His mouth all moving and nonmoving entities, outer space, and all directions, along with mountains, islands, oceans, the surface of the earth, the blowing wind, fire, the moon and the stars. She saw the planetary systems, water, light, air, sky, and creation by transformation of ahaṅkāra. She also saw the senses, the mind, sense perception, and the three qualities goodness, passion and ignorance. She saw the time allotted for the living entities, she saw natural instinct and the reactions of karma, and she saw desires and different varieties of bodies, moving and nonmoving. Seeing all these aspects of the cosmic manifestation, along with herself and Vṛndāvana-dhāma, she became doubtful and fearful of her son's nature.

PURPORT

All the cosmic manifestations that exist on the gross and subtle elements, as well as the means of their agitation, the three *guṇas*, the living entity, creation, maintenance, annihilation and everything going on in the external energy of the Lord—all this comes from the Supreme Personality of Godhead, Govinda. Everything is within the control of the Supreme Personality of Godhead. This is also confirmed in *Bhagavad-gītā* (9.10). *Mayādhyakṣeṇa prakṛtiḥ sūyate sa-carācaram:* everything in the material nature (*prakṛti*) works under His control. Because all these manifestations come from Govinda, they could all be visible within the mouth of Govinda. Quite astonishingly, mother Yaśodā was afraid because of intense maternal affection. She could not believe that within the mouth of her son such things could appear. Yet she saw them, and therefore she was struck with fear and wonder.

TEXT 40

किं स्वप्न एतदुत देवमाया
किं वा मदीयो बत बुद्धिमोहः ।
अथो अमुष्यैव ममार्भकस्य
यः कश्चनौत्पत्तिक आत्मयोगः ॥४०॥

kiṁ svapna etad uta devamāyā
kiṁ vā madīyo bata buddhi-mohaḥ
atho amuṣyaiva mamārbhakasya
yaḥ kaścanautpattika ātma-yogaḥ

kim—whether; *svapnaḥ*—a dream; *etat*—all this; *uta*—or otherwise; *deva-māyā*—an illusory manifestation by the external energy; *kim vā*—or else; *madīyaḥ*—my personal; *bata*—indeed; *buddhi-mohaḥ*—illusion of intelligence; *atho*—otherwise; *amuṣya*—of such; *eva*—indeed; *mama arbhakasya*—of my child; *yaḥ*—which; *kaścana*—some; *autpattikaḥ*—natural; *ātma-yogaḥ*—personal mystic power.

TRANSLATION

[Mother Yaśodā began to argue within herself:] Is this a dream, or is it an illusory creation by the external energy? Has this been manifested by my own intelligence, or is it some mystic power of my child?

PURPORT

When mother Yaśodā saw this wonderful manifestation within the mouth of her child, she began to argue within herself about whether it was a dream. Then she considered, "I am not dreaming, because my eyes are open. I am actually seeing what is happening. I am not sleeping, nor am I dreaming. Then maybe this is an illusion created by *devamāyā*. But that is also not possible. What business would the demigods have showing such things to me? I am an insignificant woman with no connection with the demigods. Why should they take the trouble to put me into *devamāyā*? That also is not possible." Then mother Yaśodā considered whether the vision might be due to bewilderment: "I am fit in health; I am not diseased. Why should there be any bewilderment? It is not possible that my brain is deranged, since I am ordinarily quite fit to think. Then this vision must be due to some mystic power of my son, as predicted by Gargamuni." Thus she finally concluded that the vision was due to her son's activities, and nothing else.

TEXT 41

अथो यथावन्न वितर्कगोचरं
चेतोमनःकर्मवचोभिरञ्जसा ।
यदाश्रयं येन यतः प्रतीयते
सुदुर्विभाव्यं प्रणतास्मि तत्पदम् ॥४१॥

atho yathāvan na vitarka-gocaraṁ
ceto-manaḥ-karma-vacobhir añjasā
yad-āśrayaṁ yena yataḥ pratīyate
sudurvibhāvyaṁ praṇatāsmi tat-padam

atho—therefore she decided to surrender unto the Supreme Lord; *yathā-vat*—as perfectly as one can perceive; *na*—not; *vitarka-gocaram*—beyond all arguments, reason and sense perception; *cetaḥ*—by consciousness; *manaḥ*—by mind; *karma*—by activities; *vacobhiḥ*—or by words; *añjasā*—taking all of them together, we cannot understand them; *yat-āśrayam*—under whose control; *yena*—by whom; *yataḥ*—from whom; *pratīyate*—can be conceived only that from Him everything emanates; *su-durvibhāvyam*—beyond our sense perception or consciousness; *praṇatā asmi*—let me surrender; *tat-padam*—at His lotus feet.

TRANSLATION

Therefore let me surrender unto the Supreme Personality of Godhead and offer my obeisances unto Him, who is beyond the conception of human speculation, the mind, activities, words and arguments, who is the original cause of this cosmic manifestation, by whom the entire cosmos is maintained, and by whom we can conceive of its existence. Let me simply offer my obeisances, for

He is beyond my contemplation, speculation and meditation. He is beyond all of my material activities.

PURPORT

One simply has to realize the greatness of the Supreme Personality of Godhead. One should not try to understand Him by any material means, subtle or gross. Mother Yaśodā, being a simple woman, could not find out the real cause of the vision; therefore, out of maternal affection, she simply offered obeisances unto the Supreme Lord to protect her child. She could do nothing but offer obeisances to the Lord. It is said, *acintyāḥ khalu ye bhāvā na tāṁs tarkeṇa yojayet* (*Mahābhārata, Bhīṣma Parva* 5.22). One should not try to understand the supreme cause by argument or reasoning. When we are beset by some problem for which we can find no reason, there is no alternative than to surrender to the Supreme Lord and offer Him our respectful obeisances. Then our position will be secure. This was the means adopted in this instance also by mother Yaśodā. Whatever happens, the original cause is the Supreme Personality of Godhead (*sarva-kāraṇa-kāraṇam*). When the immediate cause cannot be ascertained, let us simply offer our obeisances at the lotus feet of the Lord. Mother Yaśodā concluded that the wonderful things she saw within the mouth of her child were due to Him, although she could not clearly ascertain the cause. Therefore when a devotee cannot ascertain the cause of suffering, he concludes:

tat te 'nukampāṁ susamīkṣamāṇo
bhuñjāna evātma-kṛtaṁ vipākam
hṛd-vāg-vapurbhir vidadhan namas te
jīveta yo mukti-pade sa dāya-bhāk
(*Bhāg.* 10.14.8)

The devotee accepts that it is due to his own past misdeeds that the Supreme Personality of Godhead has caused him some small amount of suffering. Thus he offers obeisances to the Lord again and again. Such a devotee is called *mukti-pade sa dāya-bhāk;* that is, he is guaranteed his liberation from this material world. As stated in *Bhagavad-gītā* (2.14):

mātrā-sparśās tu kaunteya
śītoṣṇa-sukha-duḥkha-dāḥ
āgamāpāyino nityās
tāṁs titikṣasva bhārata

We should know that material suffering due to the material body will come and go. Therefore we must tolerate the suffering and proceed with discharging our duty as ordained by our spiritual master.

TEXT 42

अहं ममासौ पतिरेष मे सुतो
व्रजेश्वरस्याखिलवित्तपा सती ।
गोप्यश्च गोपाः सहगोधनाश्च मे
यन्माययेत्थं कुमतिः स मे गतिः ॥४२॥

ahaṁ mamāsau patir eṣa me suto
vrajeśvarasyākhila-vittapā satī
gopyaś ca gopāḥ saha-godhanāś ca me
yan-māyayetthaṁ kumatiḥ sa me gatiḥ

aham—my existence ("I am something"); *mama*—my; *asau*—Nanda Mahārāja; *patiḥ*—husband; *eṣaḥ*—this (Kṛṣṇa); *me sutaḥ*—is my son; *vraja-īśvarasya*—of my husband, Nanda Mahārāja; *akhila-vitta-pā*—I am the possessor of unlimited opulence and wealth; *satī*—because I am his wife; *gopyaḥ ca*—and all the damsels of the cowherd men; *gopāḥ*—all the cowherd men (are my subordinates); *saha-godhanāḥ ca*—with the cows and calves; *me*—my; *yat-māyayā*—all such things addressed by me are, after all, given by the mercy of the Supreme; *ittham*—thus; *kumatiḥ*—I am wrongly thinking they are my possessions; *saḥ me gatiḥ*—He is therefore my only shelter (I am simply instrumental).

TRANSLATION

It is by the influence of the Supreme Lord's māyā that I am wrongly thinking that Nanda Mahārāja is my husband, that Kṛṣṇa

is my son, and that because I am the queen of Nanda Mahārāja, all the wealth of cows and calves are my possessions and all the cowherd men and their wives are my subjects. Actually, I also am eternally subordinate to the Supreme Lord. He is my ultimate shelter.

PURPORT

Following in the footsteps of mother Yaśodā, everyone should follow this mentality of renunciation. Whatever wealth, opulence or whatever else we may possess belongs not to us but to the Supreme Personality of Godhead, who is the ultimate shelter of everyone and the ultimate owner of everything. As stated by the Lord Himself in *Bhagavad-gītā* (5.29):

bhoktāraṁ yajña-tapasāṁ
sarva-loka-maheśvaram
suhṛdaṁ sarva-bhūtānāṁ
jñātvā māṁ śāntim ṛcchati

"The sages, knowing Me as the ultimate purpose of all sacrifices and austerities, the Supreme Lord of all planets and demigods and the benefactor and well-wisher of all living entities, attain peace from the pangs of material miseries."

We should not be proud of our possessions. As expressed by mother Yaśodā herein, "I am not the owner of possessions, the opulent wife of Nanda Mahārāja. The estate, the possessions, the cows and calves and the subjects like the *gopīs* and cowherd men are all given to me." One should give up thinking of "my possessions, my son and my husband" (*janasya moho 'yam ahaṁ mameti*). Nothing belongs to anyone but the Supreme Lord. Only because of illusion do we wrongly think, "I am existing" or "Everything belongs to me." Thus mother Yaśodā completely surrendered unto the Supreme Lord. For the moment, she was rather disappointed, thinking, "My endeavors to protect my son by charity and other auspicious activities are useless. The Supreme Lord has given me many things, but unless He takes charge of everything, there is no assurance of protection. I must therefore ultimately seek shelter of the Supreme Personality of Godhead." As stated by Prahlāda Mahārāja (*Bhāg.* 7.9.19), *bālasya neha śaraṇaṁ pitarau nṛsiṁha:* a father and mother cannot ultimately take care of their children. *Ato gṛha-kṣetra-sutāpta-vittair janasya moho 'yam ahaṁ mameti* (*Bhāg.* 5.5.8). One's land, home, wealth and all of one's possessions belong to the Supreme Personality of Godhead, although we wrongly think, "I am this" and "These things are mine."

TEXT 43

इत्थं विदिततत्त्वायां गोपिकायां स ईश्वरः ।
वैष्णवीं व्यतनोन्मायां पुत्रस्नेहमयीं विभुः ॥४३॥

itthaṁ vidita-tattvāyāṁ
gopikāyāṁ sa īśvaraḥ
vaiṣṇavīṁ vyatanon māyāṁ
putra-snehamayīṁ vibhuḥ

ittham—in this way; *vidita-tattvāyām*—when she understood the truth of everything philosophically; *gopikāyām*—unto mother Yaśodā; *saḥ*—the Supreme Lord; *īśvaraḥ*—the supreme controller; *vaiṣṇavīm*—*viṣṇumāyā*, or *yogamāyā; vyatanot*—expanded; *māyām*—*yogamāyā; putra-sneha-mayīm*—very much attached because of maternal affection for her son; *vibhuḥ*—the Supreme Lord.

TRANSLATION

Mother Yaśodā, by the grace of the Lord, could understand the real truth. But then again, the supreme master, by the influence of the internal potency, yogamāyā, inspired her to become absorbed in intense maternal affection for her son.

PURPORT

Although mother Yaśodā understood the whole philosophy of life, at the next moment she was overwhelmed by affection for her son by the influence of *yogamāyā.* Unless she took care of her son Kṛṣṇa, she thought, how could He be protected? She could not think otherwise, and thus she forgot all her philosophical speculations. This forgetfulness is described by Śrīla Viśvanātha Cakravartī Ṭhākura as being inspired by the influence of *yogamāyā* (*mohana-sādharmyān māyām*). Materialistic persons are captivated by *mahāmāyā*, whereas devotees, by the arrangement of the spiritual energy, are captivated by *yogamāyā*.

TEXT 44

सद्योनष्टस्मृतिर्गोपी सारोप्यारोहमात्मजम् ।
प्रवृद्धस्नेहकलिलहृदयासीद् यथा पुरा ॥४४॥

sadyo naṣṭa-smṛtir gopī
sāropyāroham ātmajam
pravṛddha-sneha-kalila-
hṛdayāsīd yathā purā

sadyaḥ—after all these philosophical speculations, mother Yaśodā fully surrendered to the Supreme Personality of Godhead; *naṣṭa-smṛtiḥ*—having gotten rid of the memory of seeing the universal form within Kṛṣṇa's mouth; *gopī*—mother Yaśodā; *sā*—she; *āropya*—seating; *āroham*—on the lap; *ātmajam*—her son; *pravṛddha*—increased; *sneha*—by affection; *kalila*—affected; *hṛdayā*—the core of her heart; *āsīt*—became situated; *yathā purā*—as she was formerly.

TRANSLATION

Immediately forgetting yogamāyā's illusion that Kṛṣṇa had shown the universal form within His mouth, mother Yaśodā took her son on her lap as before, feeling increased affection in her heart for her transcendental child.

PURPORT

Mother Yaśodā regarded the vision of the universal form within Kṛṣṇa's mouth as an arrangement of *yogamāyā*, like a dream. As one forgets everything after a dream, mother Yaśodā immediately forgot the entire incident. As her natural feeling of affection increased, she decided to herself, "Now let this incident be forgotten. I do not mind. Here is my son. Let me kiss Him."

TEXT 45

त्रय्या चोपनिषद्भिश्च सांख्ययोगैश्च सात्वतैः ।
उपगीयमानमाहात्म्यं हरिं सामन्यतात्मजम् ॥४५॥

trayyā copaniṣadbhiś ca
sāṅkhya-yogaiś ca sātvataiḥ
upagīyamāna-māhātmyaṁ
hariṁ sāmanyatātmajam

trayyā—by studying the three *Vedas* (*Sāma*, *Yajur* and *Atharva*); *ca*—also; *upaniṣadbhiḥ ca*—and by studying the Vedic knowledge of the *Upaniṣads; sāṅkhya-yogaiḥ*—by reading the literature of *sāṅkhya-yoga; ca*—and; *sātvataiḥ*—by the great sages and devotees, or by reading *Vaiṣṇava-tantra, Pancarātras; upagīyamāna-māhātmyam*—whose glories are worshiped (by all these Vedic literatures); *harim*—unto the Supreme Personality of Godhead; *sā*—she; *amanyata*—considered (ordinary); *ātmajam*—as her own son.

TRANSLATION

The glories of the Supreme Personality of Godhead are studied through the three Vedas, the Upaniṣads, the literature of sāṅkhya-yoga, and other Vaiṣṇava literature, yet mother Yaśodā considered that Supreme Person her ordinary child.

PURPORT

As stated in *Bhagavad-gītā* (15.15) by the Supreme Personality of Godhead, Kṛṣṇa, the purpose of studying the *Vedas* is to understand Him (*vedaiś ca sarvair aham eva vedyaḥ*). Śrī Caitanya Mahāprabhu explained to Sanātana Gosvāmī that there are three purposes in the *Vedas.* One is to understand our relationship with Kṛṣṇa (*sambandha*), another is to act according to that relationship (*abhidheya*), and the third is to reach the ultimate goal (*prayojana*). The word *prayojana* means "necessities," and the ultimate necessity is explained by Śrī Caitanya Mahāprabhu. *Premā pum-artho mahān:* the greatest necessity for a human being is the achievement of love for the Supreme Personality of

Godhead. Here we see that mother Yaśodā is on the highest stage of necessity, for she is completely absorbed in love for Kṛṣṇa.

In the beginning, the Vedic purpose is pursued in three ways (*trayī*)—by *karma-kāṇḍa*, *jñāna-kāṇḍa* and *upāsanā-kāṇḍa*. When one reaches the complete, perfect stage of *upāsanā-kāṇḍa*, one comes to worship Nārāyaṇa, or Lord Viṣṇu. When Pārvatī asked Lord Mahādeva, Lord Śiva, what is the best method of *upāsanā*, or worship, Lord Śiva answered, *ārādhanānāṁ sarveṣāṁ viṣṇor ārādhanaṁ param. Viṣṇūpāsanā*, or *viṣṇv-ārādhana*, worship of Lord Viṣṇu, is the highest stage of perfection, as realized by Devakī. But here mother Yaśodā performs no *upāsanā*, for she has developed transcendental ecstatic love for Kṛṣṇa. Therefore her position is better than that of Devakī. In order to show this, Śrīla Vyāsadeva enunciates this verse, *trayyā copaniṣadbhiḥ* etc.

When a human being enters into the study of the *Vedas* to obtain *vidyā*, knowledge, he begins to take part in human civilization. Then he advances further to study the *Upaniṣads* and gain *brahma-jñāna*, impersonal realization of the Absolute Truth, and then he advances still further, to *sāṅkhya-yoga*, in order to understand the supreme controller, who is indicated in *Bhagavad-gītā* (*paraṁ brahma paraṁ dhāma pavitraṁ paramaṁ bhavān/ puruṣaṁ śāśvatam*). When one understands that *puruṣa*, the supreme controller, to be Paramātmā, one is engaged in the method of *yoga* (*dhyānāvasthita-tad-gatena manasā paśyanti yaṁ yoginaḥ*). But mother Yaśodā has surpassed all these stages. She has come to the platform of loving Kṛṣṇa as her beloved child, and therefore she is accepted to be on the highest stage of spiritual realization. The Absolute Truth is realized in three features (*brahmeti paramātmeti bhagavān iti śabdyate*), but she is in such ecstasy that she does not care to understand what is Brahman, what is Paramātmā or what is Bhagavān. Bhagavān has personally descended to become her beloved child. Therefore there is no comparison to mother Yaśodā's good fortune, as declared by Śrī Caitanya Mahāprabhu (*ramyā kācid upāsanā vrajavadhū-vargeṇa yā kalpitā*). The Absolute Truth, the Supreme Personality of Godhead, may be realized in different stages. As the Lord says in *Bhagavad-gītā* (4.11):

ye yathā māṁ prapadyante
tāṁs tathaiva bhajāmy aham

mama vartmānuvartante
manuṣyāḥ pārtha sarvaśaḥ

"As men surrender unto Me, I reward them accordingly. Everyone follows My path in all respects, O son of Pṛthā." One may be a *karmī*, a *jñānī*, a *yogī* and then a *bhakta* or *prema-bhakta*. But the ultimate stage of realization is *prema-bhakti*, as actually demonstrated by mother Yaśodā.

TEXT 46

श्रीराजोवाच
नन्दः किमकरोद् ब्रह्मन् श्रेय एवं महोदयम् ।
यशोदा च महाभागा पपौ यस्याः स्तनं हरिः ॥४६॥

śrī-rājovāca
nandaḥ kim akarod brahman
śreya evaṁ mahodayam
yaśodā ca mahā-bhāgā
papau yasyāḥ stanaṁ hariḥ

śrī-rājā uvāca—Mahārāja Parīkṣit further inquired (from Śukadeva Gosvāmī); *nandaḥ*—Mahārāja Nanda; *kim*—what; *akarot*—performed; *brahman*—O learned *brāhmaṇa; śreyaḥ*—auspicious activities, like performing penances and austerities; *evam*—as exhibited by him; *mahā-udayam*—from which they achieved the greatest perfection; *yaśodā*—mother Yaśodā; *ca*—also; *mahā-bhāgā*—most fortunate; *papau*—drank; *yasyāḥ*—of whom; *stanam*—the breast milk; *hariḥ*—the Supreme Personality of Godhead.

TRANSLATION

Having heard of the great fortune of mother Yaśodā, Parīkṣit Mahārāja inquired from Śukadeva Gosvāmī: O learned brāhmaṇa, mother Yaśodā's breast milk was sucked by the Supreme Personality of Godhead. What past auspicious activities did she and Nanda Mahārāja perform to achieve such perfection in ecstatic love?

PURPORT

As stated in *Bhagavad-gītā* (7.16), *catur-vidhā bhajante māṁ janāḥ sukṛtino 'rjuna*. Without *sukṛti*, or pious activities, no one can come to the shelter of the Supreme Personality of Godhead. The Lord is approached by four kinds of pious men (*ārto jijñāsur arthārthī jñānī ca*), but here we see that Nanda Mahārāja and Yaśodā surpassed all of them. Therefore Parīkṣit Mahārāja naturally inquired, "What kind of pious activities did they perform in their past lives by which they achieved such a stage of perfection?" Of course, Nanda Mahārāja and Yaśodā are accepted as the father and mother of Kṛṣṇa, yet mother Yaśodā was more fortunate than Nanda Mahārāja, Kṛṣṇa's father, because Nanda Mahārāja was sometimes separated from Kṛṣṇa whereas Yaśodā, Kṛṣṇa's mother, was not separated from Kṛṣṇa at any moment. From Kṛṣṇa's babyhood to His childhood and from His childhood to His youth, mother Yaśodā was always in association with Kṛṣṇa. Even when Kṛṣṇa was grown up, He would go to Vṛndāvana and sit on the lap of mother Yaśodā. Therefore there is no comparison to the fortune of mother Yaśodā, and Parīkṣit Mahārāja naturally inquired, *yaśodā ca mahā-bhāgā.*

TEXT 47

पितरौ नान्वविन्देतां कृष्णोदारार्भकेहितम् ।
गायन्त्यद्यापि कवयो यल्लोकशमलापहम् ॥४७॥

pitarau nānvavindetāṁ
kṛṣṇodārārbhakehitam
gāyanty adyāpi kavayo
yal loka-śamalāpaham

pitarau—the actual father and mother of Kṛṣṇa; *na*—not; *anvavindetām*—enjoyed; *kṛṣṇa*—of Kṛṣṇa; *udāra*—magnanimous; *arbhaka-īhitam*—the childhood pastimes He performed; *gāyanti*—are glorifying; *adya api*—even today; *kavayaḥ*—great, great sages and saintly persons; *yat*—which is; *loka-śamala-apaham*—by hearing of which the contamination of the whole material world is vanquished.

TRANSLATION

Although Kṛṣṇa was so pleased with Vasudeva and Devakī that He descended as their son, they could not enjoy Kṛṣṇa's magnanimous childhood pastimes, which are so great that simply chanting about them vanquishes the contamination of the material world. Nanda Mahārāja and Yaśodā, however, enjoyed these pastimes fully, and therefore their position is always better than that of Vasudeva and Devakī.

PURPORT

Kṛṣṇa actually took birth from the womb of Devakī, but just after His birth He was transferred to the home of mother Yaśodā. Devakī could not even have Kṛṣṇa suck her breast. Therefore Parīkṣit Mahārāja was astonished. How had mother Yaśodā and Nanda Mahārāja become so fortunate that they enjoyed the complete childhood pastimes of Kṛṣṇa, which are still glorified by saintly persons? What had they done in the past by which they were elevated to such an exalted position?

TEXT 48

श्रीशुक उवाच

द्रोणो वसूनां प्रवरो धरया भार्यया सह ।
करिष्यमाण आदेशान् ब्रह्मणस्तमुवाच ह ॥४८॥

śrī-śuka uvāca
droṇo vasūnāṁ pravaro
dharayā bhāryayā saha
kariṣyamāṇa ādeśān
brahmaṇas tam uvāca ha

śrī-śukaḥ uvāca—Śrī Śukadeva Gosvāmī said; *droṇaḥ*—by the name Droṇa; *vasūnām*—of the eight Vasus (a type of demigod); *pravaraḥ*—who was the best; *dharayā*—with Dharā; *bhāryayā*—His wife; *saha*—with; *kariṣyamāṇaḥ*—just to execute; *ādeśān*—the orders; *brahmaṇaḥ*—of Lord Brahmā; *tam*—unto him; *uvāca*—said; *ha*—in the past.

TRANSLATION

Śukadeva Gosvāmī said: To follow the orders of Lord Brahmā, Droṇa, the best of the Vasus, along with his wife, Dharā, spoke to Lord Brahmā in this way.

PURPORT

As stated in the *Brahma-saṁhitā* (5.37):

ānanda-cinmaya-rasa-pratibhāvitābhis
tābhir ya eva nija-rūpatayā kalābhiḥ
goloka eva nivasaty akhilātma-bhūto
govindam ādi-puruṣaṁ tam ahaṁ bhajāmi

When Kṛṣṇa descends anywhere, He is accompanied by His own associates. These associates are not ordinary living beings. Kṛṣṇa's pastimes are eternal, and when He descends, He comes with His associates. Therefore Nanda and mother Yaśodā are the eternal father and mother of Kṛṣṇa. This means that whenever Kṛṣṇa descends, Nanda and Yaśodā, as well as Vasudeva and Devakī, also descend as the Lord's father and mother. Their personalities are expansions of Kṛṣṇa's personal body; they are not ordinary living beings. Mahārāja Parīkṣit knew this, but he was curious to know from Śukadeva Gosvāmī whether it is possible for an ordinary human being to come to this stage by *sādhana-siddhi.* There are two kinds of perfection—*nitya-siddhi* and *sādhana-siddhi.* A *nitya-siddha* is one who is eternally Kṛṣṇa's associate, an expansion of Kṛṣṇa's personal body, whereas a *sādhana-siddha* is an ordinary human being who, by executing pious activities and following regulative principles of devotional service, also comes to that stage. Thus the purpose of Mahārāja Parīkṣit's inquiry was to determine whether an ordinary human being can attain the position of mother Yaśodā and Nanda Mahārāja. Śukadeva Gosvāmī answered this question as follows.

TEXT 49

जातयोर्नौ महादेवे भुवि विश्वेश्वरे हरौ ।
भक्तिः स्यात् परमा लोके ययाञ्जो दुर्गतिं तरेत् ॥४९॥

jātayor nau mahādeve
bhuvi viśveśvare harau
bhaktiḥ syāt paramā loke
yayāñjo durgatiṁ taret

jātayoḥ—after we two have taken birth; *nau*—both husband and wife, Droṇa and Dharā; *mahādeve*—in the Supreme Person, the Supreme Personality of Godhead; *bhuvi*—on the earth; *viśva-īśvare*—in the master of all the planetary systems; *harau*—in the Supreme Lord; *bhaktiḥ*—devotional service; *syāt*—will be spread; *paramā*—the ultimate goal of life; *loke*—in the world; *yayā*—by which; *añjaḥ*—very easily; *durgatim*—miserable life; *taret*—one can avoid and be delivered.

TRANSLATION

Droṇa and Dharā said: Please permit us to be born on the planet earth so that after our appearance, the Supreme Lord, the Personality of Godhead, the supreme controller and master of all planets, will also appear and spread devotional service, the ultimate goal of life, so that those born in this material world may very easily be delivered from the miserable condition of materialistic life by accepting this devotional service.

PURPORT

This statement by Droṇa clearly indicates that Droṇa and Dharā are the eternal father and mother of Kṛṣṇa. Whenever there is a necessity of Kṛṣṇa's appearance, Droṇa and Dharā appear first, and then Kṛṣṇa appears. Kṛṣṇa says in *Bhagavad-gītā* that His birth is not ordinary (*janma karma ca me divyam*).

ajo 'pi sann avyayātmā
bhūtānām īśvaro 'pi san
prakṛtiṁ svām adhiṣṭhāya
sambhavāmy ātma-māyayā

"Although I am unborn and My transcendental body never deteriorates, and although I am the Lord of all sentient beings, I still appear in every millennium in My original transcendental form." (Bg. 4.6) Before Kṛṣṇa's appearance, Droṇa and Dharā appear in order to become His father and mother. It is they who appear as Nanda Mahārāja and his wife, Yaśodā. In other words, it is not possible for a *sādhana-siddha* living being to become the father or mother of Kṛṣṇa, for Kṛṣṇa's father and mother are already designated. But by following the principles exhibited by Nanda Mahārāja and Yaśodā and their associates, the inhabitants of Vṛndāvana, ordinary living beings may attain such affection as exhibited by Nanda and Yaśodā.

When Droṇa and Dharā were requested to beget children, they chose to come to this world to have the Supreme Personality of Godhead as their son, Kṛṣṇa. Kṛṣṇa's appearance means *paritrāṇāya sādhūnāṁ vināśāya ca duṣkṛtām*—the devotees are protected, and the miscreants are vanquished. Whenever Kṛṣṇa comes, He distributes the highest goal of life, devotional service. He appears as Caitanya Mahāprabhu for the same purpose because unless one comes to devotional service, one cannot be delivered from the miseries of the material world (*duḥkhālayam aśāśvatam*), where the living beings struggle for existence. The Lord says in *Bhagavad-gītā* (15.7):

mamaivāṁśo jīva-loke
jīva-bhūtaḥ sanātanaḥ
manaḥ ṣaṣṭhānīndriyāṇi
prakṛti-sthāni karṣati

"The living entities in this conditioned world are My eternal, fragmental parts. Because of conditioned life, they are struggling very hard with the six senses, which include the mind." The living entities are struggling to become happy, but unless they take to the *bhakti* cult, their happiness is not possible. Kṛṣṇa clearly says:

aśraddadhānāḥ puruṣā
dharmasyāsya parantapa
aprāpya māṁ nivartante
mṛtyu-saṁsāra-vartmani

"Those who are not faithful on the path of devotional service cannot attain Me, O conqueror of foes, but return to birth and death in this material world." (Bg. 9.3)

Foolish persons do not know how risky life is here if one does not follow the instructions of Kṛṣṇa. The Kṛṣṇa consciousness movement, therefore, has been started so that by practicing Kṛṣṇa consciousness one can avoid the risky life of this material existence. There is no question of accepting or not accepting Kṛṣṇa consciousness. It is not optional; it is compulsory. If we do not take to Kṛṣṇa consciousness, our life is very risky. Everything is explained in *Bhagavad-gītā*. Therefore, to learn how to become free from the miserable condition of material existence, *Bhagavad-gītā As It Is* is the preliminary study. Then, if one understands *Bhagavad-gītā*, one can proceed to *Śrīmad-Bhāgavatam*, and if one advances further, one may study *Caitanya-caritāmṛta*. We are therefore presenting these invaluable books to the whole world so that people may study them and be happy, being delivered from miserable conditional life.

TEXT 50

अस्त्वित्युक्तः स भगवान् व्रजे द्रोणो महायशाः ।
जज्ञे नन्द इति ख्यातो यशोदा सा धराभवत् ॥५०॥

astv ity uktaḥ sa bhagavān
vraje droṇo mahā-yaśāḥ
jajñe nanda iti khyāto
yaśodā sā dharābhavat

astu—when Brahmā agreed, "Yes, it is all right"; *iti uktaḥ*—thus being ordered by him; *saḥ*—he (Droṇa); *bhagavān*—eternally the father of Kṛṣṇa (Bhagavān's father is also Bhagavān); *vraje*—in Vrajabhūmi, Vṛndāvana; *droṇaḥ*—Droṇa, the most powerful Vasu; *mahā-yaśāḥ*—the very famous transcendentalist; *jajñe*—appeared; *nandaḥ*—as Nanda Mahārāja; *iti*—thus; *khyātaḥ*—is celebrated; *yaśodā*—as mother Yaśodā; *sā*—she; *dharā*—the same Dharā; *abhavat*—appeared.

TRANSLATION

When Brahmā said, "Yes, let it be so," the most fortune Droṇa, who was equal to Bhagavān, appeared in Vrajapura, Vṛndāvana, as

the most famous Nanda Mahārāja, and his wife, Dharā, appeared as mother Yaśodā.

PURPORT

Because whenever Kṛṣṇa appears on this earth He superficially needs a father and mother, Droṇa and Dharā, His eternal father and mother, appeared on earth before Kṛṣṇa as Nanda Mahārāja and Yaśodā. In contrast to Sutapā and Pṛśnigarbha, they did not undergo severe penances and austerities to become the father and mother of Kṛṣṇa. This is the difference between *nitya-siddha* and *sādhana-siddha.*

TEXT 51

ततो भक्तिर्भगवति पुत्रीभूते जनार्दने ।
दम्पत्योर्नितरामासीद् गोपगोपीषु भारत ॥५१॥

tato bhaktir bhagavati
putrī-bhūte janārdane
dampatyor nitarām āsīd
gopa-gopīṣu bhārata

tataḥ—thereafter; *bhaktiḥ bhagavati*—the cult of *bhakti,* devotional service unto the Supreme Personality of Godhead; *putrī-bhūte*—in the Lord, who had appeared as the son of mother Yaśodā; *janārdane*—in Lord Kṛṣṇa; *dam-patyoḥ*—of both husband and wife; *nitarām*—continuously; *āsīt*—there was; *gopa-gopīṣu*—all the inhabitants of Vṛndāvana, the *gopas* and the *gopīs,* associating with Nanda Mahārāja and Yaśodā and following in their footsteps; *bhārata*—O Mahārāja Parīkṣit.

TRANSLATION

Thereafter, O Mahārāja Parīkṣit, best of the Bhāratas, when the Supreme Personality of Godhead became the son of Nanda Mahārāja and Yaśodā, they maintained continuous, unswerving devotional love in parental affection. And in their association, all the other inhabitants of Vṛndāvana, the gopas and gopīs, developed the culture of kṛṣṇa-bhakti.

PURPORT

Although when the Supreme Personality of Godhead stole the butter, curd and milk of the neighboring *gopas* and *gopīs* this teasing superficially seemed troublesome, in fact it was an exchange of affection in the ecstasy of devotional service. The more the *gopas* and *gopīs* exchanged feelings with the Lord, the more their devotional service increased. Sometimes we may superficially see that a devotee is in difficulty because of being engaged in devotional service, but the fact is different. When a devotee suffers for Kṛṣṇa, that suffering is transcendental enjoyment. Unless one becomes a devotee, this cannot be understood. When Kṛṣṇa exhibited His childhood pastimes, not only did Nanda Mahārāja and Yaśodā increase their devotional affection, but those in their association also increased in devotional service. In other words, persons who follow the activities of Vṛndāvana will also develop devotional service in the highest perfection.

TEXT 52

कृष्णो ब्रह्मण आदेशं सत्यं कर्तुं व्रजे विभुः ।
सहरामो वसंश्चक्रे तेषां प्रीतिं स्वलीलया ॥५२॥

kṛṣṇo brahmaṇa ādeśaṁ
satyaṁ kartuṁ vraje vibhuḥ
saha-rāmo vasaṁś cakre
teṣāṁ prītiṁ sva-līlayā

kṛṣṇaḥ—the Supreme Personality, Kṛṣṇa; *brahmaṇaḥ*—of Lord Brahmā; *ādeśam*—the order; *satyam*—truthful; *kartum*—to make; *vraje*—in Vrajabhūmi, Vṛndāvana; *vibhuḥ*—the supreme powerful; *saha-rāmaḥ*—along with Balarāma; *vasan*—residing; *cakre*—increased; *teṣām*—of all the inhabitants of Vṛndāvana; *prītim*—the pleasure; *sva-līlayā*—by His transcendental pastimes.

TRANSLATION

Thus the Supreme Personality, Kṛṣṇa, along with Balarāma, lived in Vrajabhūmi, Vṛndāvana, just to substantiate the benediction of Brahmā. By exhibiting different pastimes in His childhood,

He increased the transcendental pleasure of Nanda and the other inhabitants of Vṛndāvana.

Thus end the Bhaktivedanta purports of the Tenth Canto, Eighth Chapter, of the Śrīmad-Bhāgavatam, *entitled, "Lord Kṛṣṇa Shows the Universal Form Within His Mouth."*

CHAPTER NINE

Mother Yaśodā Binds Lord Kṛṣṇa

While mother Yaśodā was allowing Kṛṣṇa to drink her breast milk, she was forced to stop because she saw the milk pan boiling over on the oven. The maidservants being engaged in other business, she stopped allowing Kṛṣṇa to drink from her breast and immediately attended to the overflowing milk pan. Kṛṣṇa became very angry because of His mother's behavior and devised a means of breaking the pots of yogurt. Because He created this disturbance, mother Yaśodā decided to bind Him. These incidents are described in this chapter.

One day, the maidservants being engaged in other work, mother Yaśodā was churning the yogurt into butter herself, and in the meantime Kṛṣṇa came and requested her to allow Him to suck her breast milk. Of course, mother Yaśodā immediately allowed Him to do so, but then she saw that the hot milk on the oven was boiling over, and therefore she immediately stopped allowing Kṛṣṇa to drink the milk of her breast and went to stop the milk on the oven from overflowing. Kṛṣṇa, however, having been interrupted in His business of sucking the breast, was very angry. He took a piece of stone, broke the churning pot and entered a room, where He began to eat the freshly churned butter. When mother Yaśodā, after attending to the overflowing milk, returned and saw the pot broken, she could understand that this was the work of Kṛṣṇa, and therefore she went to search for Him. When she entered the room, she saw Kṛṣṇa standing on the *ulūkhala*, a large mortar for grinding spices. Having turned the mortar upside down, He was stealing butter hanging from a swing and was distributing the butter to the monkeys. As soon as Kṛṣṇa saw that His mother had come, He immediately began to run away, and mother Yaśodā began to follow Him. After going some distance, mother Yaśodā was able to catch Kṛṣṇa, who because of His offense was crying. Mother Yaśodā, of course, threatened to punish Kṛṣṇa if He acted that way again, and she decided to bind Him with rope. Unfortunately, when the time came to knot the rope, the rope with which she wanted to bind Him was short by a distance equal to the width of two fingers. When she made the rope longer by adding another rope, she again saw that it was short by two fingers. Again and again she tried, and again and again she found the rope too short by two fingers. Thus she became very tired, and Kṛṣṇa, seeing His affectionate mother so tired, allowed Himself to be bound. Now, being compassionate, He did not show her His unlimited potency. After mother Yaśodā bound Kṛṣṇa and became engaged in other household affairs, Kṛṣṇa observed two *yamala-arjuna* trees, which were actually Nalakūvara and Maṇigrīva, two sons of Kuvera who had been condemned by Nārada Muni to become trees. Kṛṣṇa, by His mercy, now began to proceed toward the trees to fulfill the desire of Nārada Muni.

TEXTS 1–2

श्रीशुक उवाच

एकदा गृहदासीषु यशोदा नन्दगेहिनी ।
कर्मान्तरनियुक्तासु निर्ममन्थ स्वयं दधि ॥ १ ॥
यानि यानीह गीतानि तद्बालचरितानि च ।
दधिनिर्मन्थने काले स्मरन्ती तान्यगायत ॥ २ ॥

śrī-śuka uvāca
ekadā gṛha-dāsīṣu
yaśodā nanda-gehinī
karmāntara-niyuktāsu
nirmamantha svayaṁ dadhi

yāni yānīha gītāni
tad-bāla-caritāni ca
dadhi-nirmanthane kāle
smarantī tāny agāyata

śrī-śukaḥ uvāca—Śrī Śukadeva Gosvāmī said; *ekadā*—one day; *gṛha-dāsīṣu*—when all the maidservants of the household were otherwise engaged; *yaśodā*—mother Yaśodā; *nanda-gehinī*—the queen of Nanda Mahārāja; *karma-antara*—in other household affairs; *niyuktāsu*—being engaged; *nirmamantha*—churned; *svayam*—personally; *dadhi*—the yogurt; *yāni*—all such; *yāni*—such; *iha*—in this connection; *gītāni*—

songs; *tat-bāla-caritāni*—in which the activities of her own child were enacted; *ca*—and; *dadhi-nirmanthane*—while churning the yogurt; *kāle*—at that time; *smarantī*—remembering; *tāni*—all of them (in the form of songs); *agāyata*—chanted.

TRANSLATION

Śrī Śukadeva Gosvāmī continued: One day when mother Yaśodā saw that all the maidservants were engaged in other household affairs, she personally began to churn the yogurt. While churning, she remembered the childish activities of Kṛṣṇa, and in her own way she composed songs and enjoyed singing to herself about all those activities.

PURPORT

Śrīla Viśvanātha Cakravartī Ṭhākura, quoting from the *Vaiṣṇava-toṣaṇī* of Śrīla Sanātana Gosvāmī, says that the incident of Kṛṣṇa's breaking the pot of yogurt and being bound by mother Yaśodā took place on the Dipavali Day, or Dīpa-mālikā. Even today in India, this festival is generally celebrated very gorgeously in the month of Kārtika by fireworks and lights, especially in Bombay. It is to be understood that among all the cows of Nanda Mahārāja, several of mother Yaśodā's cows ate only grasses so flavorful that the grasses would automatically flavor the milk. Mother Yaśodā wanted to collect the milk from these cows, make it into yogurt and churn it into butter personally, since she thought that this child Kṛṣṇa was going to the houses of neighborhood *gopas* and *gopīs* to steal butter because He did not like the milk and yogurt ordinarily prepared.

While churning the butter, mother Yaśodā was singing about the childhood activities of Kṛṣṇa. It was formerly a custom that if one wanted to remember something constantly, he would transform it into poetry or have this done by a professional poet. It appears that mother Yaśodā did not want to forget Kṛṣṇa's activities at any time. Therefore she poeticized all of Kṛṣṇa's childhood activities, such as the killing of Pūtanā, Aghāsura, Śakaṭāsura and Tṛṇāvarta, and while churning the butter, she sang about these activities in poetical form. This should be the practice of persons eager to remain Kṛṣṇa conscious twenty-four hours a day. This incident shows how Kṛṣṇa conscious mother Yaśodā was. To stay in Kṛṣṇa consciousness, we should follow such persons.

TEXT 3

क्षौमं वासः पृथुकटितटे बिभ्रती सूत्रनद्धं
पुत्रस्नेहस्नुतकुचयुगं जातकम्पं च सुभ्रूः ।
रज्ज्वाकर्षश्रमभुजचलत्कङ्कणौ कुण्डले च
स्विन्नं वक्त्रं कबरविगलन्मालती निर्ममन्थ ॥ ३ ॥

kṣaumaṁ vāsaḥ pṛthu-kaṭi-taṭe bibhratī sūtra-naddhaṁ
putra-sneha-snuta-kuca-yugaṁ jāta-kampaṁ ca subhrūḥ
rajjv-ākarṣa-śrama-bhuja-calat-kaṅkaṇau kuṇḍale ca
svinnaṁ vaktraṁ kabara-vigalan-mālatī nirmamantha

kṣaumam—saffron and yellow mixed; *vāsaḥ*—mother Yaśodā was wearing such a sari; *pṛthu-kaṭi-taṭe*—surrounding her large hips; *bibhratī*—shaking; *sūtra-naddham*—bound with a belt; *putra-sneha-snuta*—because of intense love for her child, became wet with milk; *kuca-yugam*—the nipples of her breasts; *jāta-kampam ca*—as they were very nicely moving and quivering; *su-bhrūḥ*—who had very beautiful eyebrows; *rajju-ākarṣa*—by pulling on the rope of the churning rod; *śrama*—because of the labor; *bhuja*—on whose hands; *calat-kaṅkaṇau*—the two bangles were moving; *kuṇḍale*—the two earrings; *ca*—also; *svinnam*—her hair was black like a cloud, so perspiration was dropping like rain; *vaktram*—throughout her face; *kabara-vigalat-mālatī*—and *mālatī* flowers were dropping from her hair; *nir-mamantha*—thus mother Yaśodā was churning the butter.

TRANSLATION

Dressed in a saffron-yellow sari, with a belt tied about her full hips, mother Yaśodā pulled on the churning rope, laboring considerably, her bangles and earrings moving and vibrating and her whole body shaking. Because of her intense love for her child, her breasts were wet with milk. Her face, with its very beautiful

eyebrows, was wet with perspiration, and mālatī flowers were falling from her hair.

PURPORT

Anyone who desires to be Kṛṣṇa conscious in motherly affection or parental affection should contemplate the bodily features of mother Yaśodā. It is not that one should desire to become like Yaśodā, for this is Māyāvāda. Either in parental affection or conjugal love, friendship or servitorship—in any way—we must follow in the footsteps of the inhabitants of Vṛndāvana, not try to become like them. Therefore this description is provided here. Advanced devotees must cherish this description, always thinking of mother Yaśodā's features—how she was dressed, how she was working and perspiring, how beautifully the flowers were arranged in her hair, and so on. One should take advantage of the full description provided here by thinking of mother Yaśodā in maternal affection for Kṛṣṇa.

TEXT 4

तां स्तन्यकाम आसाद्य मथ्नन्तीं जननीं हरिः ।
गृहीत्वा दधिमन्थानं न्यषेधत् प्रीतिमावहन् ॥ ४ ॥

tāṁ stanya-kāma āsādya
mathnantīṁ jananīṁ hariḥ
gṛhītvā dadhi-manthānaṁ
nyaṣedhat prītim āvahan

tām—unto mother Yaśodā; *stanya-kāmaḥ*—Kṛṣṇa, who was desiring to drink her breast milk; *āsādya*—appearing before her; *mathnantīm*—while she was churning butter; *jananīm*—to the mother; *hariḥ*—Kṛṣṇa; *gṛhītvā*—catching; *dadhi-manthānam*—the churning rod; *nyaṣedhat*—forbade; *prītim āvahan*—creating a situation of love and affection.

TRANSLATION

While mother Yaśodā was churning butter, Lord Kṛṣṇa, desiring to drink the milk of her breast, appeared before her, and in order

to increase her transcendental pleasure, He caught hold of the churning rod and began to prevent her from churning.

PURPORT

Kṛṣṇa was sleeping within the room, and as soon as He got up, He became hungry and went to His mother. Wanting to stop her from churning and drink the milk of her breasts, He stopped her from moving the churning rod.

TEXT 5

तमङ्कमारूढमपाययत् स्तनं
स्नेहस्नुतं सस्मितमीक्षती मुखम् ।
अतृप्तमुत्सृज्य जवेन सा यया-
वुत्सिच्यमाने पयसि त्वधिश्रिते ॥ ५ ॥

tam aṅkam ārūḍham apāyayat stanaṁ
sneha-snutaṁ sa-smitam īkṣatī mukham
atṛptam utsṛjya javena sā yayāv
utsicyamāne payasi tv adhiśrite

tam—unto Kṛṣṇa; *aṅkam ārūḍham*—very affectionately allowing Him to sit down on her lap; *apāyayat*—allowed to drink; *stanam*—her breast; *sneha-snutam*—which was flowing with milk because of intense affection; *sa-smitam īkṣatī mukham*—mother Yaśodā was smiling and observing the smiling face of Kṛṣṇa; *atṛptam*—Kṛṣṇa, who was still not fully satisfied by drinking the milk; *utsṛjya*—putting Him aside; *javena*—very hastily; *sā*—mother Yaśodā; *yayau*—left that place; *utsicyamāne payasi*—because of seeing that the milk was overflowing; *tu*—but; *adhiśrite*—in the milk pan on the oven.

TRANSLATION

Mother Yaśodā then embraced Kṛṣṇa, allowed Him to sit down on her lap, and began to look upon the face of the Lord with great love and affection. Because of her intense affection, milk was flowing from her breast. But when she saw that the milk pan on the

oven was boiling over, she immediately left her son to take care of the overflowing milk, although the child was not yet fully satisfied with drinking the milk of His mother's breast.

PURPORT

Everything in the household affairs of mother Yaśodā was meant for Kṛṣṇa. Although Kṛṣṇa was drinking the breast milk of mother Yaśodā, when she saw that the milk pan in the kitchen was overflowing, she had to take care of it immediately, and thus she left her son, who then became very angry, not having been fully satisfied with drinking the milk of her breast. Sometimes one must take care of more than one item of important business for the same purpose. Therefore mother Yaśodā was not unjust when she left her son to take care of the overflowing milk. On the platform of love and affection, it is the duty of the devotee to do one thing first and other things later. The proper intuition by which to do this is given by Kṛṣṇa.

teṣāṁ satata-yuktānāṁ
bhajatāṁ prīti-pūrvakam
dadāmi buddhi-yogaṁ taṁ
yena mām upayānti te
(Bg. 10.10)

In Kṛṣṇa consciousness, everything is dynamic. Kṛṣṇa guides the devotee in what to do first and what to do next on the platform of absolute truth.

TEXT 6

सञ्जातकोपः स्फुरितारुणाधरं
संदश्य दद्भिर्दधिमन्थभाजनम् ।
भित्त्वा मृषाश्रुर्दृषदश्मना रहो
जघास हैयङ्गवमन्तरं गतः ॥ ६ ॥

sañjāta-kopaḥ sphuritāruṇādharaṁ
sandaśya dadbhir dadhi-mantha-bhājanam
bhittvā mṛṣāśrur dṛṣad-aśmanā raho
jaghāsa haiyaṅgavam antaraṁ gataḥ

sañjāta-kopaḥ—in this way, Kṛṣṇa being very angry; *sphurita-aruṇa-adharam*—swollen reddish lips; *sandaśya*—capturing; *dadbhiḥ*—by His teeth; *dadhi-mantha-bhājanam*—the pot in which yogurt was being churned; *bhittvā*—breaking; *mṛṣā-aśruḥ*—with false tears in the eyes; *dṛṣat-aśmanā*—with a piece of stone; *rahaḥ*—in a solitary place; *jaghāsa*—began to eat; *haiyaṅgavam*—the freshly churned butter; *antaram*—within the room; *gataḥ*—having gone.

TRANSLATION

Being very angry and biting His reddish lips with His teeth, Kṛṣṇa, with false tears in His eyes, broke the container of yogurt with a piece of stone. Then He entered a room and began to eat the freshly churned butter in a solitary place.

PURPORT

It is natural that when a child becomes angry he can begin crying with false tears in his eyes. So Kṛṣṇa did this, and biting His reddish lips with His teeth, He broke the pot with a stone, entered a room and began to eat the freshly churned butter.

TEXT 7

उत्तार्य गोपी सुशृतं पयः पुनः
प्रविश्य संदृश्य च दध्यमत्रकम् ।
भग्नं विलोक्य स्वसुतस्य कर्म त-
ज्जहास तं चापि न तत्र पश्यती ॥ ७ ॥

uttārya gopī suśṛtaṁ payaḥ punaḥ
praviśya sandṛśya ca dadhy-amatrakam
bhagnaṁ vilokya sva-sutasya karma taj
jahāsa taṁ cāpi na tatra paśyatī

uttārya—putting down from the oven; *gopī*—mother Yaśodā; *su-śṛtam*—very hot; *payaḥ*—the milk; *punaḥ*—again; *praviśya*—entered the churning spot; *sandṛśya*—by observing; *ca*—also; *dadhi-amatrakam*—the container of yogurt; *bhagnam*—broken; *vilokya*—

seeing this; *sva-sutasya*—of her own child; *karma*—work; *tat*—that; *jahāsa*—smiled; *tam ca*—Kṛṣṇa also; *api*—at the same time; *na*—not; *tatra*—there; *paśyatī*—finding.

TRANSLATION

Mother Yaśodā, after taking down the hot milk from the oven, returned to the churning spot, and when she saw that the container of yogurt was broken and that Kṛṣṇa was not present, she concluded that the breaking of the pot was the work of Kṛṣṇa.

PURPORT

Seeing the pot broken and Kṛṣṇa not present, Yaśodā definitely concluded that the breaking of the pot was the work of Kṛṣṇa. There was no doubt about it.

TEXT 8

उलूखलाङ्घ्रेरुपरि व्यवस्थितं
मर्काय कामं ददतं शिचि स्थितम् ।
हैयङ्गवं चौर्यविशङ्कितेक्षणं
निरीक्ष्य पश्चात् सुतमागमच्छनैः ॥ ८ ॥

ulūkhalāṅghrer upari vyavasthitaṁ
markāya kāmaṁ dadataṁ śici sthitam
haiyaṅgavaṁ caurya-viśaṅkitekṣaṇaṁ
nirīkṣya paścāt sutam āgamac chanaiḥ

ulūkhala-aṅghreḥ—of the mortar in which spices were ground and which was being kept upside down; *upari*—on top; *vyavasthitam*—Kṛṣṇa was sitting; *markāya*—unto a monkey; *kāmam*—according to His satisfaction; *dadatam*—delivering shares; *śici sthitam*—situated in the butter pot hanging on the swing; *haiyaṅgavam*—butter and other milk preparations; *caurya-viśaṅkita*—because of stealing, were anxiously looking hither and thither; *īkṣaṇam*—whose eyes; *nirīkṣya*—by seeing these activities; *paścāt*—from behind; *sutam*—her son; *āgamat*—she reached; *śanaiḥ*—very slowly, cautiously.

TRANSLATION

Kṛṣṇa, at that time, was sitting on an upside-down wooden mortar for grinding spices and was distributing milk preparations such as yogurt and butter to the monkeys as He liked. Because of having stolen, He was looking all around with great anxiety, suspecting that He might be chastised by His mother. Mother Yaśodā, upon seeing Him, very cautiously approached Him from behind.

PURPORT

Mother Yaśodā was able to trace Kṛṣṇa by following His butter-smeared footprints. She saw that Kṛṣṇa was stealing butter, and thus she smiled. Meanwhile, the crows also entered the room and came out in fear. Thus mother Yaśodā found Kṛṣṇa stealing butter and very anxiously looking here and there.

TEXT 9

तामात्तयष्टिं प्रसमीक्ष्य सत्वर-
स्ततोऽवरुह्यापससार भीतवत् ।
गोप्यन्वधावन्न यमाप योगिनां
क्षमं प्रवेष्टुं तपसेरितं मनः ॥ ९ ॥

tām ātta-yaṣṭiṁ prasamīkṣya satvaras
tato 'varuhyāpasasāra bhītavat
gopy anvadhāvan na yam āpa yogināṁ
kṣamaṁ praveṣṭuṁ tapaseritaṁ manaḥ

tām—unto mother Yaśodā; *ātta-yaṣṭim*—carrying in her hand a stick; *prasamīkṣya*—Kṛṣṇa, seeing her in that attitude; *satvaraḥ*—very quickly; *tataḥ*—from there; *avaruhya*—getting down; *apasasāra*—began to flee; *bhīta-vat*—as if very much afraid; *gopī*—mother Yaśodā; *anvadhāvat*—began to follow Him; *na*—not; *yam*—unto whom; *āpa*—failed to reach; *yoginām*—of great *yogīs*, mystics; *kṣamam*—who could reach Him; *praveṣṭum*—trying to enter into the Brahman effulgence or Paramātmā; *tapasā*—with great austerities and penances; *īritam*—trying for that purpose; *manaḥ*—by meditation.

TRANSLATION

When Lord Śrī Kṛṣṇa saw His mother, stick in hand, He very quickly got down from the top of the mortar and began to flee as if very much afraid. Although yogīs try to capture Him as Paramātmā by meditation, desiring to enter into the effulgence of the Lord with great austerities and penances, they fail to reach Him. But mother Yaśodā, thinking that same Personality of Godhead, Kṛṣṇa, to be her son, began following Kṛṣṇa to catch Him.

PURPORT

Yogīs, mystics, want to catch Kṛṣṇa as Paramātmā, and with great austerities and penances they try to approach Him, yet they cannot. Here we see, however, that Kṛṣṇa is going to be caught by Yaśodā and is running away in fear. This illustrates the difference between the *bhakta* and the *yogī*. *Yogīs* cannot reach Kṛṣṇa, but for pure devotees like mother Yaśodā, Kṛṣṇa is already caught. Kṛṣṇa was even afraid of mother Yaśodā's stick. This was mentioned by Queen Kuntī in her prayers: *bhaya-bhāvanayā sthitasya* (*Bhāg.* 1.8.31). Kṛṣṇa is afraid of mother Yaśodā, and *yogīs* are afraid of Kṛṣṇa. *Yogīs* try to reach Kṛṣṇa by *jñāna-yoga* and other *yogas*, but fail. Yet although mother Yaśodā was a woman, Kṛṣṇa was afraid of her, as clearly described in this verse.

TEXT 10

अन्वञ्चमाना जननी बृहच्चल-
च्छ्रोणीभराक्रान्तगतिः सुमध्यमा ।
जवेन विस्रंसितकेशबन्धन-
च्युतप्रसूनानुगतिः परामृशत् ॥१०॥

anvañcamānā jananī bṛhac-calac-
chroṇī-bharākrānta-gatiḥ sumadhyamā
javena visraṁsita-keśa-bandhana-
cyuta-prasūnānugatiḥ parāmṛśat

anvañcamānā—following Kṛṣṇa very swiftly; *jananī*—mother Yaśodā; *bṛhat-calat-śroṇī-bhara-ākrānta-gatiḥ*—being overburdened by the weight of her large breasts, she became tired and had to reduce her speed; *su-madhyamā*—because of her thin waist; *javena*—because of going very fast; *visraṁsita-keśa-bandhana*—from her arrangement of hair, which had become loosened; *cyuta-prasūna-anugatiḥ*—she was followed by the flowers falling after her; *parāmṛśat*—finally captured Kṛṣṇa without fail.

TRANSLATION

While following Kṛṣṇa, mother Yaśodā, her thin waist overburdened by her heavy breasts, naturally had to reduce her speed. Because of following Kṛṣṇa very swiftly, her hair became loose, and the flowers in her hair were falling after her. Yet she did not fail to capture her son Kṛṣṇa.

PURPORT

Yogīs cannot capture Kṛṣṇa by severe penances and austerities, but mother Yaśodā, despite all obstacles, was finally able to catch Kṛṣṇa without difficulty. This is the difference between a *yogī* and a *bhakta. Yogīs* cannot enter even the effulgence of Kṛṣṇa. *Yasya prabhā prabhavato jagad-aṇḍa-koṭi-koṭiṣu* (*Brahma-saṁhitā* 5.40). In that effulgence there are millions of universes, but *yogīs* and *jñānīs* cannot enter that effulgence even after many, many years of austerities, whereas *bhaktas* can capture Kṛṣṇa simply by love and affection. This is the example shown here by mother Yaśodā. Kṛṣṇa therefore confirms that if one wants to capture Him, one must undertake devotional service.

bhaktyā mām abhijānāti
yāvān yaś cāsmi tattvataḥ
tato māṁ tattvato jñātvā
viśate tad-anantaram
(Bg. 18.55)

Bhaktas enter even the planet of Kṛṣṇa very easily, but the less intelligent *yogīs* and *jñānīs*, by their meditation, remain running after Kṛṣṇa. Even if they enter Kṛṣṇa's effulgence, they fall down.

TEXT 11

कृतागसं तं प्ररुदन्तमक्षिणी
कषन्तमञ्जन्मषिणी स्वपाणिना ।
उद्वीक्षमाणं भयविह्वलेक्षणं
हस्ते गृहीत्वा भिषयन्त्यवागुरत् ॥११॥

kṛtāgasaṁ taṁ prarudantam akṣiṇī
kaṣantam añjan-maṣiṇī sva-pāṇinā
udvīkṣamāṇaṁ bhaya-vihvalekṣaṇaṁ
haste gṛhītvā bhiṣayanty avāgurat

kṛta-āgasam—who was an offender; *tam*—unto Kṛṣṇa; *pra-rudantam*—with a crying attitude; *akṣiṇī*—His two eyes; *kaṣantam*—rubbing; *añjat-maṣiṇī*—from whose eyes the blackish ointment was distributed all over His face with tears; *sva-pāṇinā*—with His own hand; *udvīkṣamāṇam*—who was seen in that attitude by mother Yaśodā; *bhaya-vihvala-īkṣaṇam*—whose eyes appeared distressed because of such fear of His mother; *haste*—by the hand; *gṛhītvā*—catching; *bhi-ṣayantī*—mother Yaśodā was threatening Him; *avāgurat*—and thus she very mildly chastised Him.

TRANSLATION

When caught by mother Yaśodā, Kṛṣṇa became more and more afraid and admitted to being an offender. As she looked upon Him, she saw that He was crying, His tears mixing with the black ointment around His eyes, and as He rubbed His eyes with His hands, He smeared the ointment all over His face. Mother Yaśodā, catching her beautiful son by the hand, mildly began to chastise Him.

PURPORT

From these dealings between mother Yaśodā and Kṛṣṇa, we can understand the exalted position of a pure devotee in loving service to the Lord. *Yogīs*, *jñānīs*, *karmīs* and Vedāntists cannot even approach Kṛṣṇa; they must remain very, very far away from Him and try to enter His bodily effulgence, although this also they are unable to do. Great demigods like Lord Brahmā and Lord Śiva always worship the Lord by meditation and by service. Even the most powerful Yamarāja fears Kṛṣṇa. Therefore, as we find in the history of Ajāmila, Yamarāja instructed his followers not even to approach the devotees, what to speak of capturing them. In other words, Yamarāja also fears Kṛṣṇa and Kṛṣṇa's devotees. Yet this Kṛṣṇa became so dependent on mother Yaśodā that when she simply showed Kṛṣṇa the stick in her hand, Kṛṣṇa admitted to being an offender and began to cry like an ordinary child. Mother Yaśodā, of course, did not want to chastise her beloved child very much, and therefore she immediately threw her stick away and simply rebuked Kṛṣṇa, saying, "Now I shall bind You so that You cannot commit any further offensive activities. Nor for the time being can You play with Your playmates." This shows the position of a pure devotee, in contrast with others, like *jñānīs*, *yogīs* and the followers of Vedic ritualistic ceremonies, in regarding the transcendental nature of the Absolute Truth.

TEXT 12

त्यक्त्वा यष्टिं सुतं भीतं विज्ञायार्भकवत्सला ।
इयेष किल तं बद्धुं दाम्नातद्वीर्यकोविदा ॥१२॥

tyaktvā yaṣṭiṁ sutaṁ bhītaṁ
vijñāyārbhaka-vatsalā
iyeṣa kila taṁ baddhuṁ
dāmnātad-vīrya-kovidā

tyaktvā—throwing away; *yaṣṭim*—the stick in her hand; *sutam*—her son; *bhītam*—considering her son's great fear; *vijñāya*—understanding; *arbhaka-vatsalā*—the most affectionate mother of Kṛṣṇa; *iyeṣa*—desired; *kila*—indeed; *tam*—Kṛṣṇa; *baddhum*—to bind; *dāmnā*—with a rope; *a-tat-vīrya-kovidā*—without knowledge of the supremely powerful Personality of Godhead (because of intense love for Kṛṣṇa).

TRANSLATION

Mother Yaśodā was always overwhelmed by intense love for Kṛṣṇa, not knowing who Kṛṣṇa was or how powerful He was. Be-

cause of maternal affection for Kṛṣṇa, she never even cared to know who He was. Therefore, when she saw that her son had become excessively afraid, she threw the stick away and desired to bind Him so that He would not commit any further naughty activities.

PURPORT

Mother Yaśodā wanted to bind Kṛṣṇa not in order to chastise Him but because she thought that the child was so restless that He might leave the house in fear. That would be another disturbance. Therefore, because of full affection, to stop Kṛṣṇa from leaving the house, she wanted to bind Him with rope. Mother Yaśodā wanted to impress upon Kṛṣṇa that since He was afraid merely to see her stick, He should not perform such disturbing activities as breaking the container of yogurt and butter and distributing its contents to the monkeys. Mother Yaśodā did not care to understand who Kṛṣṇa was and how His power spreads everywhere. This is an example of pure love for Kṛṣṇa.

TEXTS 13–14

न चान्तर्न बहिर्यस्य न पूर्वं नापि चापरम् ।
पूर्वापरं बहिश्चान्तर्जगतो यो जगच्च यः ॥१३॥
तं मत्वात्मजमव्यक्तं मर्त्यलिङ्गमधोक्षजम् ।
गोपिकोलूखले दाम्ना बबन्ध प्राकृतं यथा ॥१४॥

na cāntar na bahir yasya
na pūrvaṁ nāpi cāparam
pūrvāparaṁ bahiś cāntar
jagato yo jagac ca yaḥ

taṁ matvātmajam avyaktaṁ
martya-liṅgam adhokṣajam
gopikolūkhale dāmnā
babandha prākṛtaṁ yathā

na—not; *ca*—also; *antaḥ*—interior; *na*—nor; *bahiḥ*—exterior; *yasya*—whose; *na*—neither; *pūrvam*—beginning; *na*—nor; *api*—

indeed; *ca*—also; *aparam*—end; *pūrva-aparam*—the beginning and the end; *bahiḥ ca antaḥ*—the external and the internal; *jagataḥ*—of the whole cosmic manifestation; *yaḥ*—one who is; *jagat ca yaḥ*—and who is everything in creation in total; *tam*—Him; *matvā*—considering; *ātma-jam*—her own son; *avyaktam*—the unmanifested; *martya-liṅgam*—appearing as a human being; *adhokṣajam*—beyond sense perception; *gopikā*—mother Yaśodā; *ulūkhale*—to the grinding mortar; *dāmnā*—by a rope; *babandha*—bound; *prākṛtam yathā*—as done to a common human child.

TRANSLATION

The Supreme Personality of Godhead has no beginning and no end, no exterior and no interior, no front and no rear. In other words, He is all-pervading. Because He is not under the influence of the element of time, for Him there is no difference between past, present and future; He exists in His own transcendental form at all times. Being absolute, beyond relativity, He is free from distinctions between cause and effect, although He is the cause and effect of everything. That unmanifested person, who is beyond the perception of the senses, had now appeared as a human child, and mother Yaśodā, considering Him her own ordinary child, bound Him to the wooden mortar with a rope.

PURPORT

In *Bhagavad-gītā* (10.12), Kṛṣṇa is described as the Supreme Brahman (*paraṁ brahma paraṁ dhāma*). The word *brahma* means "the greatest." Kṛṣṇa is greater than the greatest, being unlimited and all-pervading. How can it be possible for the all-pervading to be measured or bound? Then again, Kṛṣṇa is the time factor. Therefore, He is all-pervading not only in space but also in time. We have measurements of time, but although we are limited by past, present and future, for Kṛṣṇa these do not exist. Every individual person can be measured, but Kṛṣṇa has already shown that although He also is an individual, the entire cosmic manifestation is within His mouth. All these points considered, Kṛṣṇa cannot be measured. How then did Yaśodā want to measure Him and bind Him? We must conclude that this took place simply on the platform of pure transcendental love. This was the only cause.

advaitam acyutam anādim ananta-rūpam
ādyaṁ purāṇa-puruṣaṁ nava-yauvanaṁ ca
vedeṣu durlabham adurlabham ātma-bhaktau
govindam ādi-puruṣaṁ tam ahaṁ bhajāmi
(*Brahma-saṁhitā* 5.33)

Everything is one because Kṛṣṇa is the supreme cause of everything. Kṛṣṇa cannot be measured or calculated by Vedic knowledge (*vedeṣu durlabham*). He is available only to devotees (*adurlabham ātma-bhaktau*). Devotees can handle Him because they act on the basis of loving service (*bhaktyā mām abhijānāti yāvān yaś cāsmi tattvataḥ*). Thus mother Yaśodā wanted to bind Him.

TEXT 15

तद् दाम बध्यमानस्य स्वार्भकस्य कृतागसः ।
द्व्यङ्गुलोनमभूत्तेन सन्दधेऽन्यच्च गोपिका ॥१५॥

tad dāma badhyamānasya
svārbhakasya kṛtāgasaḥ
dvy-aṅgulonam abhūt tena
sandadhe 'nyac ca gopikā

tat dāma—that binding rope; *badhyamānasya*—who was being bound by mother Yaśodā; *sva-arbhakasya*—of her own son; *kṛta-āgasaḥ*—who was an offender; *dvi-aṅgula*—by a measurement of two fingers; *ūnam*—short; *abhūt*—became; *tena*—with that rope; *sandadhe*—joined; *anyat ca*—another rope; *gopikā*—mother Yaśodā.

TRANSLATION

When mother Yaśodā was trying to bind the offending child, she saw that the binding rope was short by a distance the width of two fingers. Thus she brought another rope to join to it.

PURPORT

Here is the first chapter in Kṛṣṇa's exhibition of unlimited potency to mother Yaśodā when she tried to bind Him: the rope was too short. The

Lord had already shown His unlimited potency by killing Pūtanā, Śakaṭāsura and Tṛṇāvarta. Now Kṛṣṇa exhibited another *vibhūti*, or display of potency, to mother Yaśodā. "Unless I agree," Kṛṣṇa desired to show, "you cannot bind Me." Thus although mother Yaśodā, in her attempt to bind Kṛṣṇa, added one rope after another, ultimately she was a failure. When Kṛṣṇa agreed, however, she was successful. In other words, one must be in transcendental love with Kṛṣṇa, but that does not mean that one can control Kṛṣṇa. When Kṛṣṇa is satisfied with one's devotional service, He does everything Himself. *Sevonmukhe hi jihvādau svayam eva sphuraty adaḥ.* He reveals more and more to the devotee as the devotee advances in service. *Jihvādau:* this service begins with the tongue, with chanting and with taking the *prasāda* of Kṛṣṇa.

ataḥ śrī-kṛṣṇa-nāmādi
na bhaved grāhyam indriyaiḥ
sevonmukhe hi jihvādau
svayam eva sphuraty adaḥ
(*Bhakti-rasāmṛta-sindhu* 1.2.234)

TEXT 16

यदासीत्तदपि न्यूनं तेनान्यदपि सन्दधे ।
तदपि द्व्यङ्गुलं न्यूनं यद् यदादत्त बन्धनम् ॥१६॥

yadāsīt tad api nyūnaṁ
tenānyad api sandadhe
tad api dvy-aṅgulaṁ nyūnaṁ
yad yad ādatta bandhanam

yadā—when; *āsīt*—became; *tat api*—even the new rope that had been joined; *nyūnam*—still short; *tena*—then, with the second rope; *anyat api*—another rope also; *sandadhe*—she joined; *tat api*—that also; *dvi-aṅgulam*—by a measurement of two fingers; *nyūnam*—remained short; *yat yat ādatta*—in this way, one after another, whatever ropes she joined; *bandhanam*—for binding Kṛṣṇa.

TRANSLATION

This new rope also was short by a measurement of two fingers, and when another rope was joined to it, it was still two fingers too short. As many ropes as she joined, all of them failed; their shortness could not be overcome.

TEXT 17

एवं स्वगेहदामानि यशोदा सन्दधत्यपि ।
गोपीनां सुस्मयन्तीनां स्मयन्ती विस्मिताभवत् ॥१७॥

evaṁ sva-geha-dāmāni
yaśodā sandadhaty api
gopīnāṁ susmayantīnāṁ
smayantī vismitābhavat

evam—in this manner; *sva-geha-dāmāni*—all the ropes available in the household; *yaśodā*—mother Yaśodā; *sandadhati api*—although she was joining one after another; *gopīnām*—when all the other elderly *gopī* friends of mother Yaśodā; *su-smayantīnām*—were all taking pleasure in this funny affair; *smayantī*—mother Yaśodā was also smiling; *vismitā abhavat*—all of them were struck with wonder.

TRANSLATION

Thus mother Yaśodā joined whatever ropes were available in the household, but still she failed in her attempt to bind Kṛṣṇa. Mother Yaśodā's friends, the elderly gopīs in the neighborhood, were smiling and enjoying the fun. Similarly, mother Yaśodā, although laboring in that way, was also smiling. All of them were struck with wonder.

PURPORT

Actually this incident was wonderful because Kṛṣṇa was only a child with small hands. To bind Him should have required only a rope not more than two feet long. All the ropes in the house combined together might have been hundreds of feet long, but still He was impossible to bind, for all the ropes together were still too short. Naturally mother Yaśodā and her *gopī* friends thought, "How is this possible?" Seeing this funny affair, all of them were smiling. The first rope was short by a measurement the width of two fingers, and after the second rope was added, it was still two fingers too short. If the shortness of all the ropes were added together, it must have amounted to the width of hundreds of fingers. Certainly this was astonishing. This was another exhibition of Kṛṣṇa's inconceivable potency to His mother and His mother's friends.

TEXT 18

स्वमातुः स्विन्नगात्राया विस्रस्तकबरस्रजः ।
दृष्ट्वा परिश्रमं कृष्णः कृपयासीत् स्वबन्धने ॥१८॥

sva-mātuḥ svinna-gātrāyā
visrasta-kabara-srajaḥ
dṛṣṭvā pariśramaṁ kṛṣṇaḥ
kṛpayāsīt sva-bandhane

sva-mātuḥ—of His own mother (Kṛṣṇa's mother, Yaśodādevī); *svinna-gātrāyāḥ*—when Kṛṣṇa saw His mother perspiring all over because of unnecessary labor; *visrasta*—were falling down; *kabara*—from her hair; *srajaḥ*—of whom the flowers; *dṛṣṭvā*—by seeing the condition of His mother; *pariśramam*—He could understand that she was now overworked and feeling fatigued; *kṛṣṇaḥ*—the Supreme Personality of Godhead; *kṛpayā*—by His causeless mercy upon His devotee and mother; *āsīt*—agreed; *sva-bandhane*—in binding Him.

TRANSLATION

Because of mother Yaśodā's hard labor, her whole body became covered with perspiration, and the flowers and comb were falling from her hair. When child Kṛṣṇa saw His mother thus fatigued, He became merciful to her and agreed to be bound.

PURPORT

When mother Yaśodā and the other ladies finally saw that Kṛṣṇa, although decorated with many bangles and other jeweled ornaments, could not be bound with all the ropes available in the house, they decided that Kṛṣṇa was so fortunate that He could not be bound by any material condition. Thus they gave up the idea of binding Him. But in competition between Kṛṣṇa and His devotee, Kṛṣṇa sometimes agrees to be defeated. Thus Kṛṣṇa's internal energy, *yogamāyā*, was brought to work, and Kṛṣṇa agreed to be bound by mother Yaśodā.

TEXT 19

एवं संदर्शिता ह्यङ्ग हरिणा भृत्यवश्यता ।
स्ववशेनापि कृष्णेन यस्येदं सेश्वरं वशे ॥१९॥

evaṁ sandarśitā hy aṅga
hariṇā bhṛtya-vaśyatā
sva-vaśenāpi kṛṣṇena
yasyedaṁ seśvaraṁ vaśe

evam—in this manner; *sandarśitā*—was exhibited; *hi*—indeed; *aṅga*—O Mahārāja Parīkṣit; *hariṇā*—by the Supreme Personality of Godhead; *bhṛtya-vaśyatā*—His transcendental quality of becoming subordinate to His servitor or devotee; *sva-vaśena*—who is within the control only of His own self; *api*—indeed; *kṛṣṇena*—by Kṛṣṇa; *yasya*—of whom; *idam*—the whole universe; *sa-īśvaram*—with the powerful demigods like Lord Śiva and Lord Brahmā; *vaśe*—under the control.

TRANSLATION

O Mahārāja Parīkṣit, this entire universe, with its great, exalted demigods like Lord Śiva, Lord Brahmā and Lord Indra, is under the control of the Supreme Personality of Godhead. Yet the Supreme Lord has one transcendental attribute: He comes under the control of His devotees. This was now exhibited by Kṛṣṇa in this pastime.

PURPORT

This pastime of Kṛṣṇa's is very difficult to understand, but devotees can understand it. It is therefore said, *darśayaṁs tad-vidāṁ loka ātmano bhakta-vaśyatām* (*Bhāg.* 10.11.9): the Lord displays the transcendental attribute of coming under the control of His devotees. As stated in the *Brahma-saṁhitā* (5.35):

eko 'py asau racayituṁ jagad-aṇḍa-koṭiṁ
yac-chaktir asti jagad-aṇḍa-cayā yad antaḥ
aṇḍāntara-stha-paramāṇu-cayāntara-sthaṁ
govindam ādi-puruṣaṁ tam ahaṁ bhajāmi

By His one plenary portion as Paramātmā, the Lord controls innumerable universes, with all their demigods; yet He agrees to be controlled by a devotee. In the *Upaniṣads* it is said that the Supreme Personality of Godhead can run with more speed than the mind, but here we see that although Kṛṣṇa wanted to avoid being arrested by His mother, He was finally defeated, and mother Yaśodā captured Him. *Lakṣmī-sahasra-śata-sambhrama-sevyamānam:* Kṛṣṇa is served by hundreds and thousands of goddesses of fortune. Nonetheless, He steals butter like one who is poverty-stricken. Yamarāja, the controller of all living entities, fears the order of Kṛṣṇa, yet Kṛṣṇa is afraid of His mother's stick. These contradictions cannot be understood by one who is not a devotee, but a devotee can understand how powerful is unalloyed devotional service to Kṛṣṇa; it is so powerful that Kṛṣṇa can be controlled by an unalloyed devotee. This *bhṛtya-vaśyatā* does not mean that He is under the control of the servant; rather, He is under the control of the servant's pure love. In *Bhagavad-gītā* (1.21) it is said that Kṛṣṇa became the chariot driver of Arjuna. Arjuna ordered Him, *senayor ubhayor madhye rathaṁ sthāpaya me 'cyuta:* "My dear Kṛṣṇa, You have agreed to be my charioteer and to execute my orders. Place my chariot between the two armies of soldiers." Kṛṣṇa immediately executed this order, and therefore one may argue that Kṛṣṇa also is not independent. But this is one's *ajñāna*, ignorance. Kṛṣṇa is always fully independent; when He becomes subordinate to His devotees, this is a display of *ānanda-cinmaya-rasa*, the humor of transcendental qualities that increases His transcendental pleasure. Everyone worships Kṛṣṇa as the Supreme Personality of Godhead, and therefore He sometimes desires to be controlled by someone else. Such a controller can be no one else but a pure devotee.

TEXT 20

नेमं विरिञ्चो न भवो न श्रीरप्यङ्गसंश्रया ।
प्रसादं लेभिरे गोपी यत्तत् प्राप विमुक्तिदात् ॥२०॥

nemaṁ viriñco na bhavo
na śrīr apy aṅga-saṁśrayā
prasādaṁ lebhire gopī
yat tat prāpa vimuktidāt

na—not; *imam*—this exalted position; *viriñcaḥ*—Lord Brahmā; *na*—nor; *bhavaḥ*—Lord Śiva; *na*—nor; *śrīḥ*—the goddess of fortune; *api*—indeed; *aṅga-saṁśrayā*—although she is always the better half of the Supreme Personality of Godhead; *prasādam*—mercy; *lebhire*—obtained; *gopī*—mother Yaśodā; *yat tat*—as that which; *prāpa*—obtained; *vimukti-dāt*—from Kṛṣṇa, who gives deliverance from this material world.

TRANSLATION

Neither Lord Brahmā, nor Lord Śiva, nor even the goddess of fortune, who is always the better half of the Supreme Lord, can obtain from the Supreme Personality of Godhead, the deliverer from this material world, such mercy as received by mother Yaśodā.

PURPORT

This is a comparative study between mother Yaśodā and other devotees of the Lord. As stated in *Caitanya-caritāmṛta* (*Ādi* 5.142), *ekale īśvara kṛṣṇa, āra saba bhṛtya:* the only supreme master is Kṛṣṇa, and all others are His servants. Kṛṣṇa has the transcendental quality of *bhṛtya-vaśyatā,* becoming subordinate to His *bhṛtya,* or servant. Now, although everyone is *bhṛtya* and although Kṛṣṇa has the quality of becoming subordinate to His *bhṛtya,* the position of mother Yaśodā is the greatest. Lord Brahmā is *bhṛtya,* a servant of Kṛṣṇa, and he is *ādi-kavi,* the original creator of this universe (*tene brahma hṛdā ya ādi-kavaye*). Nonetheless, even he could not obtain such mercy as mother Yaśodā. As for Lord Śiva, he is the topmost Vaiṣṇava (*vaiṣṇavānāṁ yathā śambhuḥ*). What to speak of Lord

Brahmā and Lord Śiva, the goddess of fortune, Lakṣmī, is the Lord's constant companion in service, since she always associates with His body. But even she could not get such mercy. Therefore Mahārāja Parīkṣit was surprised, thinking, "What did mother Yaśodā and Nanda Mahārāja do in their previous lives by which they got such a great opportunity, the opportunity to be the affectionate father and mother of Kṛṣṇa?"

In this verse there are three negative pronouncements—*na, na, na.* When anything is uttered three times—"do it, do it, do it"—one should understand that this is meant to indicate great stress on a fact. In this verse, we find *na lebhire, na lebhire, na lebhire.* Yet mother Yaśodā is in the supermost exalted position, and thus Kṛṣṇa has become completely subordinate to her.

The word *vimuktidāt* is also significant. There are different types of liberation, such as *sāyujya, sālokya, sārūpya, sārṣṭi* and *sāmīpya,* but *vimukti* means "special *mukti.*" When after liberation one is situated on the platform of *prema-bhakti,* one is said to have achieved *vimukti,* "special *mukti.*" Therefore the word *na* is mentioned. That exalted platform of *premā* is described by Śrī Caitanya Mahāprabhu as *premā pum-artho mahān,* and mother Yaśodā naturally acts in such an exalted position in loving affairs. She is therefore a *nitya-siddha* devotee, an expansion of Kṛṣṇa's *hlādinī* potency, His potency to enjoy transcendental bliss through expansions who are special devotees (*ānanda-cinmaya-rasa-pratibhāvitābhiḥ*). Such devotees are not *sādhana-siddha.*

TEXT 21

नायं सुखापो भगवान् देहिनां गोपिकासुतः ।
ज्ञानिनां चात्मभूतानां यथा भक्तिमतामिह ॥२१॥

nāyaṁ sukhāpo bhagavān
dehināṁ gopikā-sutaḥ
jñānināṁ cātma-bhūtānāṁ
yathā bhaktimatām iha

na—not; *ayam*—this; *sukha-āpaḥ*—very easily obtainable, or an object of happiness; *bhagavān*—the Supreme Personality of Godhead; *dehinām*—of persons in the bodily concept of life, especially the *karmīs;*

gopikā-sutaḥ—Kṛṣṇa, the son of mother Yaśodā (Kṛṣṇa as the son of Vasudeva is called Vāsudeva, and as the son of mother Yaśodā He is known as Kṛṣṇa); *jñāninām ca*—and of the *jñānīs*, who try to be free from material contamination; *ātma-bhūtānām*—of self-sufficient *yogīs; yathā*—as; *bhakti-matām*—of the devotees; *iha*—in this world.

TRANSLATION

The Supreme Personality of Godhead, Kṛṣṇa, the son of mother Yaśodā, is accessible to devotees engaged in spontaneous loving service, but He is not as easily accessible to mental speculators, to those striving for self-realization by severe austerities and penances, or to those who consider the body the same as the self.

PURPORT

Kṛṣṇa, the Supreme Personality of Godhead as the son of mother Yaśodā, is very easily available to devotees, but not to *tapasvīs*, *yogīs*, *jñānīs* and others who have a bodily concept of life. Although they may sometimes be called *śānta-bhaktas*, real *bhakti* begins with *dāsya-rasa.* Kṛṣṇa says in *Bhagavad-gītā* (4.11):

ye yathā māṁ prapadyante
tāṁs tathaiva bhajāmy aham
mama vartmānuvartante
manuṣyāḥ pārtha sarvaśaḥ

"As living entities surrender unto Me, I reward them accordingly. Everyone follows My path in all respects, O son of Pṛthā." Everyone is seeking Kṛṣṇa, for He is the Supersoul of all individual souls. Everyone loves his body and wants to protect it because he is within the body as the soul, and everyone loves the soul because the soul is part and parcel of the Supersoul. Therefore, everyone is actually seeking to achieve happiness by reviving his relationship with the Supersoul. As the Lord says in *Bhagavad-gītā* (15.15), *vedaiś ca sarvair aham eva vedyaḥ:* "By all the *Vedas,* it is I who am to be known." Therefore, the *karmīs*, *jñānīs*, *yogīs* and saintly persons are all seeking Kṛṣṇa. But by following in the footsteps of devotees who are in a direct relationship with Kṛṣṇa, especially the inhabitants of Vṛndāvana, one can reach the supreme position of associating with Kṛṣṇa. As it is said, *vṛndāvanaṁ parityajya padam ekaṁ na gacchati:* Kṛṣṇa does not leave Vṛndāvana even for a moment. The *vṛndāvana-vāsīs*—mother Yaśodā, Kṛṣṇa's friends and Kṛṣṇa's conjugal lovers, the younger *gopīs* with whom He dances—have very intimate relationships with Kṛṣṇa, and if one follows in the footsteps of these devotees, Kṛṣṇa is available. Although the *nitya-siddha* expansions of Kṛṣṇa always remain with Kṛṣṇa, if those engaged in *sādhana-siddhi* follow in the footsteps of Kṛṣṇa's *nitya-siddha* associates, such *sādhana-siddhas* also can easily attain Kṛṣṇa without difficulty. But there are those who are attached to bodily concepts of life. Lord Brahmā and Lord Śiva, for example, have very prestigious positions, and thus they have the sense of being very exalted *īśvaras.* In other words, because Lord Brahmā and Lord Śiva are *guṇa-avatāras* and have exalted positions, they have some small sense of being like Kṛṣṇa. But the pure devotees who inhabit Vṛndāvana do not possess any bodily conception. They are fully dedicated to the service of the Lord in sublime affection, *premā.* Śrī Caitanya Mahāprabhu has therefore recommended, *premā pum-artho mahān:* the highest perfection of life is *premā,* pure love in relationship with Kṛṣṇa. And mother Yaśodā appears to be the topmost of devotees who have attained this perfection.

TEXT 22

कृष्णस्तु गृहकृत्येषु व्यग्रायां मातरि प्रभुः ।
अद्राक्षीदर्जुनौ पूर्वं गुह्यकौ धनदात्मजौ ॥२२॥

kṛṣṇas tu gṛha-kṛtyeṣu
vyagrāyāṁ mātari prabhuḥ
adrākṣīd arjunau pūrvaṁ
guhyakau dhanadātmajau

kṛṣṇaḥ tu—in the meantime; *gṛha-kṛtyeṣu*—in engagement in household affairs; *vyagrāyām*—very busy; *mātari*—when His mother; *prabhuḥ*—the Lord; *adrākṣīt*—observed; *arjunau*—the twin *arjuna* trees; *pūrvam*—before Him; *guhyakau*—which in a former millennium had been demigods; *dhanada-ātmajau*—the sons of Kuvera, the treasurer of the demigods.

TRANSLATION

While mother Yaśodā was very busy with household affairs, the Supreme Lord, Kṛṣṇa, observed twin trees known as yamala-arjuna, which in a former millennium had been the demigod sons of Kuvera.

TEXT 23

पुरा नारदशापेन वृक्षतां प्रापितौ मदात् ।
नलकूवरमणिग्रीवाविति ख्यातौ श्रियान्वितौ ॥२३॥

purā nārada-śāpena
vṛkṣatāṁ prāpitau madāt
nalakūvara-maṇigrīvāv
iti khyātau śriyānvitau

purā—formerly; *nārada-śāpena*—being cursed by Nārada Muni; *vṛkṣatām*—the forms of trees; *prāpitau*—obtained; *madāt*—because of madness; *nalakūvara*—one of them was Nalakūvara; *maṇigrīvau*—the other was Maṇigrīva; *iti*—thus; *khyātau*—well known; *śriyā anvitau*—very opulent.

TRANSLATION

In their former birth, these two sons, known as Nalakūvara and Maṇigrīva, were extremely opulent and fortunate. But because of pride and false prestige, they did not care about anyone, and thus Nārada Muni cursed them to become trees.

Thus end the Bhaktivedanta purports of the Tenth Canto, Ninth Chapter, of the Śrīmad-Bhāgavatam, *entitled "Mother Yaśodā Binds Lord Kṛṣṇa."*

CHAPTER TEN

Deliverance of the Yamala-arjuna Trees

This chapter describes how Kṛṣṇa broke the twin *arjuna* trees, from which Nalakūvara and Maṇigrīva, the sons of Kuvera, then came out.

Nalakūvara and Maṇigrīva were great devotees of Lord Śiva, but because of material opulence they became so extravagant and senseless that one day they were enjoying with naked girls in a lake and shamelessly walking here and there. Suddenly Nārada Muni passed by, but they were so maddened by their wealth and false prestige that even though they saw Nārada Muni present, they remained naked and were not even ashamed. In other words, because of opulence and false prestige, they lost their sense of common decency. Of course, it is the nature of the material qualities that when one becomes very much opulent in terms of wealth and a prestigious position, one loses one's sense of etiquette and does not care about anyone, even a sage like Nārada Muni. For such bewildered persons (*ahaṅkāra-vimūḍhātmā*), who especially deride devotees, the proper punishment is to be again stricken with poverty. The Vedic rules and regulations prescribe how to control the false sense of prestige by the practice of *yama, niyama* and so on (*tapasā brahmacaryeṇa śamena ca damena ca*). A poor man can be convinced very easily that the prestige of an opulent position in this material world is temporary, but a rich man cannot. Therefore Nārada Muni set an example by cursing these two persons, Nalakūvara and Maṇigrīva, to become dull and unconscious like trees. This was a fit punishment. But because Kṛṣṇa is always merciful, even though they were punished they were fortunate enough to see the Supreme Personality of Godhead face to face. Therefore the punishment given by Vaiṣṇavas is not at all punishment; rather, it is another kind of mercy. By the curse of the *devarṣi*, Nalakūvara and Maṇigrīva became twin *arjuna* trees and remained in the courtyard of mother Yaśodā and Nanda Mahārāja, waiting for the opportunity to see Kṛṣṇa directly. Lord Kṛṣṇa, by the desire of His devotee, uprooted these *yamala-arjuna* trees, and when Nalakūvara and Maṇigrīva were thus delivered by Kṛṣṇa after one hundred years of the *devas*, their old consciousness revived, and they offered Kṛṣṇa prayers suitable to be offered by demigods. Having thus gotten the opportunity to see Kṛṣṇa face to face, they understood how merciful Nārada Muni was, and therefore they expressed their indebtedness to him and thanked him. Then, after circumambulating the Supreme Personality of Godhead, Kṛṣṇa, they departed for their respective abodes.

TEXT 1

श्रीराजोवाच
कथ्यतां भगवन्नेतत्तयोः शापस्य कारणम् ।
यत्तद् विगर्हितं कर्म येन वा देवर्षेस्तमः ॥ १ ॥

śrī-rājovāca
kathyatāṁ bhagavann etat
tayoḥ śāpasya kāraṇam
yat tad vigarhitaṁ karma
yena vā devarṣes tamaḥ

śrī-rājā uvāca—the King further inquired; *kathyatām*—please describe; *bhagavan*—O supremely powerful one; *etat*—this; *tayoḥ*—of both of them; *śāpasya*—of cursing; *kāraṇam*—the cause; *yat*—which; *tat*—that; *vigarhitam*—abominable; *karma*—act; *yena*—by which; *vā*—either; *devarṣeḥ tamaḥ*—the great sage Nārada became so angry.

TRANSLATION

King Parīkṣit inquired from Śukadeva Gosvāmī: O great and powerful saint, what was the cause of Nalakūvara's and Maṇigrīva's having been cursed by Nārada Muni? What did they do that was so abominable that even Nārada, the great sage, became angry at them? Kindly describe this to me.

TEXTS 2–3

श्रीशुक उवाच
रुद्रस्यानुचरौ भूत्वा सुदृप्तौ धनदात्मजौ ।
कैलासोपवने रम्ये मन्दाकिन्यां मदोत्कटौ ॥ २ ॥

वारुणीं मदिरां पीत्वा मदाघूर्णितलोचनौ ।
स्त्रीजनैरनुगायद्भिश्चेरतुः पुष्पिते वने ॥ ३ ॥

śrī-śuka uvāca
rudrasyānucarau bhūtvā
sudṛptau dhanadātmajau
kailāsopavane ramye
mandākinyāṁ madotkaṭau

vāruṇīṁ madirāṁ pītvā
madāghūrṇita-locanau
strī-janair anugāyadbhiś
ceratuḥ puṣpite vane

śrī-śukaḥ uvāca—Śrī Śukadeva Gosvāmī replied; *rudrasya*—of Lord Śiva; *anucarau*—two great devotees or associates; *bhūtvā*—being elevated to that post; *su-dṛptau*—being proud of that position and their beautiful bodily features; *dhanada-ātmajau*—the two sons of Kuvera, treasurer of the demigods; *kailāsa-upavane*—in a small garden attached to Kailāsa Parvata, the residence of Lord Śiva; *ramye*—in a very beautiful place; *mandākinyām*—on the River Mandākinī; *mada-utkaṭau*—terribly proud and mad; *vāruṇīm*—a kind of liquor named Vāruṇī; *madirām*—intoxication; *pītvā*—drinking; *mada-āghūrṇita-locanau*—their eyes rolling with intoxication; *strī-janaiḥ*—with women; *anugāyadbhiḥ*—vibrating songs sung by them; *ceratuḥ*—wandered; *puṣpite vane*—in a nice flower garden.

TRANSLATION

Śukadeva Gosvāmī said: O King Parīkṣit, because the two sons of Kuvera had been elevated to the association of Lord Śiva, of which they were very much proud, they were allowed to wander in a garden attached to Kailāsa Hill, on the bank of the Mandākinī River. Taking advantage of this, they used to drink a kind of liquor called Vāruṇī. Accompanied by women singing after them, they would wander in that garden of flowers, their eyes always rolling in intoxication.

PURPORT

This verse mentions some of the material advantages afforded to persons associated with or devoted to Lord Śiva. Apart from Lord Śiva, if one is a devotee of any other demigod, one receives some material advantages. Foolish people, therefore, become devotees of demigods. This has been pointed out and criticized by Lord Kṛṣṇa in *Bhagavad-gītā* (7.20): *kāmais tais tair hṛta-jñānāḥ prapadyante 'nya-devatāḥ.* Those who are not devotees of Kṛṣṇa have a taste for women, wine and so forth, and therefore they have been described as *hṛta-jñāna*, bereft of sense. The Kṛṣṇa consciousness movement can very easily point out such foolish persons, for they have been indicated in *Bhagavad-gītā* (7.15), where Lord Kṛṣṇa says:

na māṁ duṣkṛtino mūḍhāḥ
prapadyante narādhamāḥ
māyayāpahṛta-jñānā
āsuraṁ bhāvam āśritāḥ

"Those miscreants who are grossly foolish, lowest among mankind, whose knowledge is stolen by illusion, and who partake of the atheistic nature of demons, do not surrender unto Me." Anyone who is not a devotee of Kṛṣṇa and does not surrender to Kṛṣṇa must be considered *narādhama*, the lowest of men, and *duṣkṛtī*, one who always commits sinful activities. Thus there is no difficulty in finding out who is a third-class or fourth-class man, for one's position can be understood simply by this crucial test: is he or is he not a devotee of Kṛṣṇa?

Why are devotees of the demigods greater in number than the Vaiṣṇavas? The answer is given herein. Vaiṣṇavas are not interested in such fourth-class pleasures as wine and women, nor does Kṛṣṇa allow them such facilities.

TEXT 4

अन्तः प्रविश्य गङ्गायामम्भोजवनराजिनि ।
चिक्रीडतुर्युवतिभिर्गजाविव करेणुभिः ॥ ४ ॥

antaḥ praviśya gaṅgāyām
ambhoja-vana-rājini

cikrīḍatur yuvatibhir
gajāv iva kareṇubhiḥ

antaḥ—within; *praviśya*—entering; *gaṅgāyām*—the Ganges, known as Mandākinī; *ambhoja*—of lotus flowers; *vana-rājini*—where there was a congested forest; *cikrīḍatuḥ*—the two of them used to enjoy; *yuvatibhiḥ*—in the company of young girls; *gajau*—two elephants; *iva*—just like; *kareṇubhiḥ*—with female elephants.

TRANSLATION

Within the waters of the Mandākinī Ganges, which were crowded with gardens of lotus flowers, the two sons of Kuvera would enjoy young girls, just like two male elephants enjoying in the water with female elephants.

PURPORT

People generally go to the Ganges to be purified of the effects of sinful life, but here is an example of how foolish persons enter the Ganges to become involved in sinful life. It is not that everyone becomes purified by entering the Ganges. Everything, spiritual and material, depends on one's mental condition.

TEXT 5

यदृच्छया च देवर्षिर्भगवांस्तत्र कौरव ।
अपश्यन्नारदो देवौ क्षीबाणौ समबुध्यत ॥ ५ ॥

yadṛcchayā ca devarṣir
bhagavāṁs tatra kaurava
apaśyan nārado devau
kṣībāṇau samabudhyata

yadṛcchayā—by chance, while wandering all over the universe; *ca*—and; *deva-ṛṣiḥ*—the supreme saintly person among the demigods; *bhagavān*—the most powerful; *tatra*—there (where the two sons of Kuvera were enjoying life); *kaurava*—O Mahārāja Parīkṣit; *apaśyat*—when he saw; *nāradaḥ*—the great saint; *devau*—the two boys of the demigods; *kṣībāṇau*—with eyes maddened by intoxication; *samabudhyata*—he could understand (their position).

TRANSLATION

O Mahārāja Parīkṣit, by some auspicious opportunity for the two boys, the great saint Devarṣi Nārada once appeared there by chance. Seeing them intoxicated, with rolling eyes, he could understand their situation.

PURPORT

It is said:

'sādhu-saṅga,' 'sādhu-saṅga'——sarva-śāstre kaya
lava-mātra sādhu-saṅge sarva-siddhi haya
(Cc. *Madhya* 22.54)

Wherever Nārada Muni goes, any moment at which he appears is understood to be extremely auspicious. It is also said:

brahmāṇḍa bhramite kona bhāgyavān jīva
guru-kṛṣṇa-prasāde pāya bhakti-latā-bīja

"According to their *karma*, all living entities are wandering throughout the entire universe. Some of them are being elevated to the upper planetary systems, and some are going down into the lower planetary systems. Out of many millions of wandering living entities, one who is very fortunate gets an opportunity to associate with a bona fide spiritual master by the grace of Kṛṣṇa. By the mercy of both Kṛṣṇa and the spiritual master, such a person receives the seed of the creeper of devotional service." (Cc. *Madhya* 19.151) Nārada appeared in the garden to give the two sons of Kuvera the seed of devotional service, even though they were intoxicated. Saintly persons know how to bestow mercy upon the fallen souls.

TEXT 6

तं दृष्ट्वा व्रीडिता देव्यो विवस्त्राः शापशङ्किताः ।
वासांसि पर्यधुः शीघ्रं विवस्त्रौ नैव गुह्यकौ ॥ ६ ॥

taṁ dṛṣṭvā vrīḍitā devyo
vivastrāḥ śāpa-śaṅkitāḥ
vāsāṁsi paryadhuḥ śīghraṁ
vivastrau naiva guhyakau

tam—Nārada Muni; *dṛṣṭvā*—seeing; *vrīḍitāḥ*—being ashamed; *devyaḥ*—the young girls of the demigods; *vivastrāḥ*—although they were naked; *śāpa-śaṅkitāḥ*—being afraid of being cursed; *vāsāṁsi*—garments; *paryadhuḥ*—covered the body; *śīghram*—very swiftly; *vivastrau*—who were also naked; *na*—not; *eva*—indeed; *guhyakau*—the two sons of Kuvera.

TRANSLATION

Upon seeing Nārada, the naked young girls of the demigods were very much ashamed. Afraid of being cursed, they covered their bodies with their garments. But the two sons of Kuvera did not do so; instead, not caring about Nārada, they remained naked.

TEXT 7

तौ दृष्ट्वा मदिरामत्तौ श्रीमदान्धौ सुरात्मजौ ।
तयोरनुग्रहार्थाय शापं दास्यन्निदं जगौ ॥ ७ ॥

tau dṛṣṭvā madirā-mattau
śrī-madāndhau surātmajau
tayor anugrahārthāya
śāpaṁ dāsyann idaṁ jagau

tau—the two boys of the demigods; *dṛṣṭvā*—seeing; *madirā-mattau*—very intoxicated because of drinking liquor; *śrī-mada-andhau*—being blind with false prestige and opulence; *sura-ātmajau*—the two sons of the demigods; *tayoḥ*—unto them; *anugraha-arthāya*—for the purpose of giving special mercy; *śāpam*—a curse; *dāsyan*—desiring to offer them; *idam*—this; *jagau*—uttered.

TRANSLATION

Seeing the two sons of the demigods naked and intoxicated by opulence and false prestige, Devarṣi Nārada, in order to show them

special mercy, desired to give them a special curse. Thus he spoke as follows.

PURPORT

Although in the beginning Nārada Muni appeared very angry and cursed them, at the end the two demigods Nalakūvara and Maṇigrīva were able to see the Supreme Personality of Godhead, Kṛṣṇa, face to face. Thus the curse was ultimately auspicious and brilliant. One has to judge what kind of curse Nārada placed upon them. Śrīla Viśvanātha Cakravartī Ṭhākura gives herein a good example. When a father finds his child deeply asleep but the child has to take some medicine to cure some disease, the father pinches the child so that the child will get up and take the medicine. In a similar way, Nārada Muni cursed Nalakūvara and Maṇigrīva in order to cure their disease of material blindness.

TEXT 8

श्रीनारद उवाच

न ह्यन्यो जुषतो जोष्यान् बुद्धिभ्रंशो रजोगुणः ।
श्रीमदादाभिजात्यादिर्यत्र स्त्री द्यूतमासवः ॥ ८ ॥

śrī-nārada uvāca
na hy anyo juṣato joṣyān
buddhi-bhraṁśo rajo-guṇaḥ
śrī-madād ābhijātyādir
yatra strī dyūtam āsavaḥ

śrī-nāradaḥ uvāca—Nārada Muni said; *na*—there is not; *hi*—indeed; *anyaḥ*—another material enjoyment; *juṣataḥ*—of one who is enjoying; *joṣyān*—things very attractive in the material world (different varieties of eating, sleeping, mating and defense); *buddhi-bhraṁśaḥ*—such enjoyments attract the intelligence; *rajaḥ-guṇaḥ*—being controlled by the mode of passion; *śrī-madāt*—than riches; *ābhijātya-ādiḥ*—among the four material principles (attractive personal bodily features, birth in an aristocratic family, being very learned, and being very rich); *yatra*—wherein; *strī*—women; *dyūtam*—gambling; *āsavaḥ*—wine (wine, women and gambling are very prominent).

TRANSLATION

Nārada Muni said: Among all the attractions of material enjoyment, the attraction of riches bewilders one's intelligence more than having beautiful bodily features, taking birth in an aristocratic family, and being learned. When one is uneducated but falsely puffed up by wealth, the result is that one engages his wealth in enjoying wine, women and gambling.

PURPORT

Among the three modes of material nature—goodness, passion and ignorance—people are certainly conducted by the lower qualities, namely passion and ignorance, and especially by passion. Conducted by the mode of passion, one becomes more and more involved in material existence. Therefore human life is meant for subduing the modes of passion and ignorance and advancing in the mode of goodness.

tadā rajas-tamo-bhāvāḥ
kāma-lobhādayaś ca ye
ceta etair anāviddhaṁ
sthitaṁ sattve prasīdati
(*Bhāg.* 1.2.19)

This is culture: one must subdue the modes of passion and ignorance. In the mode of passion, when one is falsely proud of wealth, one engages his wealth only for three things, namely wine, women and gambling. We can actually see, especially in this age, that those who have unnecessary riches simply try to enjoy these three things. In Western civilization, these three things are very prominent because of an unnecessary increase of wealth. Nārada Muni considered all this in the case of Maṇigrīva and Nalakūvara because he found in them so much pride in the wealth of their father, Kuvera.

TEXT 9

हन्यन्ते पशवो यत्र निर्दयैरजितात्मभिः ।
मन्यमानैरिमं देहमजरामृत्यु नश्वरम् ॥ ९ ॥

hanyante paśavo yatra
nirdayair ajitātmabhiḥ
manyamānair imaṁ deham
ajarāmṛtyu naśvaram

hanyante—are killed in many ways (especially by slaughterhouses); *paśavaḥ*—four-legged animals (horses, sheep, cows, hogs, etc.); *yatra*—wherein; *nirdayaiḥ*—by those merciless persons who are conducted by the mode of passion; *ajita-ātmabhiḥ*—rascals who are unable to control the senses; *manyamānaiḥ*—are thinking; *imam*—this; *deham*—body; *ajara*—will never become old or diseased; *amṛtyu*—death will never come; *naśvaram*—although the body is destined to be annihilated.

TRANSLATION

Unable to control their senses, rascals who are falsely proud of their riches or their birth in aristocratic families are so cruel that to maintain their perishable bodies, which they think will never grow old or die, they kill poor animals without mercy. Sometimes they kill animals merely to enjoy an excursion.

PURPORT

When the modes of passion and ignorance increase in human society, giving rise to unnecessary economic development, the result is that people become involved with wine, women and gambling. Then, being mad, they maintain big slaughterhouses or occasionally go on pleasure excursions to kill animals. Forgetting that however one may try to maintain the body, the body is subject to birth, death, old age and disease, such foolish rascals engage in sinful activities, one after another. Being *duṣkṛtīs*, they completely forget the existence of the supreme controller, who is sitting within the core of everyone's heart (*īśvaraḥ sarva-bhūtānāṁ hṛd-deśe 'rjuna tiṣṭhati*). That supreme controller is observing every bit of one's activity, and He rewards or punishes everyone by giving one a suitable body made by material nature (*bhrāmayan sarva-bhūtāni yantrārūḍhāni māyayā*). In this way, sinful persons automatically receive punishment in different types of bodies. The root cause of this punishment is that when one unnecessarily accumulates wealth, one becomes more and more degraded, not knowing that his wealth will be finished with his next birth.

na sādhu manye yata ātmano 'yam
asann api kleśada āsa dehaḥ
(*Bhāg.* 5.5.4)

Animal killing is prohibited. Every living being, of course, has to eat something (*jīvo jīvasya jīvanam*). But one should be taught what kind of food one should take. Therefore the *Īśopaniṣad* instructs, *tena tyaktena bhuñjīthāḥ:* one should eat whatever is allotted for human beings. Kṛṣṇa says in *Bhagavad-gītā* (9.26):

patraṁ puṣpaṁ phalaṁ toyaṁ
yo me bhaktyā prayacchati
tad ahaṁ bhakty-upahṛtam
aśnāmi prayatātmanaḥ

"If one offers Me with love and devotion a leaf, a flower, fruit or water, I will accept it." A devotee, therefore, does not eat anything that would require slaughterhouses for poor animals. Rather, devotees take *prasāda* of Kṛṣṇa (*tena tyaktena bhuñjīthāḥ*). Kṛṣṇa recommends that one give Him *patraṁ puṣpaṁ phalaṁ toyam*—a leaf, a flower, fruit or water. Animal food is never recommended for human beings; instead, a human being is recommended to take *prasāda*, remnants of food left by Kṛṣṇa. *Yajña-śiṣṭāśinaḥ santo mucyante sarva-kilbiṣaiḥ* (Bg. 3.13). If one practices eating *prasāda*, even if there is some little sinful activity involved, one becomes free from the results of sinful acts.

TEXT 10

देवसंज्ञितमप्यन्ते कृमिविड्भस्मसंज्ञितम् ।
भूतध्रुक् तत्कृते स्वार्थं किं वेद निरयो यतः ॥१०॥

deva-saṁjñitam apy ante
kṛmi-viḍ-bhasma-saṁjñitam

bhūta-dhruk tat-kṛte svārthaṁ
kiṁ veda nirayo yataḥ

deva-saṁjñitam—the body now known as a very exalted person, like president, minister or even demigod; *api*—even if the body is so exalted; *ante*—after death; *kṛmi*—turns into worms; *viṭ*—or into stool; *bhasma-saṁjñitam*—or into ashes; *bhūta-dhruk*—a person who does not accept the śāstric injunctions and is unnecessarily envious of other living entities; *tat-kṛte*—by acting in that way; *sva-artham*—self-interest; *kim*—who is there; *veda*—who knows; *nirayaḥ yataḥ*—because from such sinful activities one must suffer hellish conditions.

TRANSLATION

While living one may be proud of one's body, thinking oneself a very big man, minister, president or even demigod, but whatever one may be, after death this body will turn either into worms, into stool or into ashes. If one kills poor animals to satisfy the temporary whims of this body, one does not know that he will suffer in his next birth, for such a sinful miscreant must go to hell and suffer the results of his actions.

PURPORT

In this verse the three words *kṛmi-viḍ-bhasma* are significant. After death, the body may become *kṛmi*, which means "worms," for if the body is disposed of without cremation, it may be eaten by worms; or else it may be eaten by animals like hogs and vultures and be turned into stool. Those who are more civilized burn the dead body, and thus it becomes ashes (*bhasma-saṁjñitam*). Yet although the body will be turned into worms, stool or ashes, foolish persons, just to maintain it, commit many sinful activities. This is certainly regrettable. The human form of body is actually meant for *jīvasya tattva-jijñāsā*, enlightenment in knowledge of spiritual values. Therefore, one must seek shelter of a bona fide spiritual master. *Tasmād guruṁ prapadyeta:* one must approach a *guru.* Who is a *guru*? *Śābde pare ca niṣṇātam* (*Bhāg.* 11.3.21): a *guru* is one who has full transcendental knowledge. Unless one approaches a spiritual master, one remains in ignorance. *Ācāryavān puruṣo veda*

(*Chāndogya Upaniṣad* 6.14.2): one has full knowledge about life when one is *ācāryavān*, controlled by the *ācārya*. But when one is conducted by *rajo-guṇa* and *tamo-guṇa*, one does not care about anything; instead, one acts like an ordinary foolish animal, risking his life (*mṛtyu-saṁsāra-vartmani*) and therefore continuing to go through suffering after suffering. *Na te viduḥ svārtha-gatiṁ hi viṣṇum* (*Bhāg.* 7.5.31). Such a foolish person does not know how to elevate himself in this body. Instead, he indulges in sinful activities and goes deeper and deeper into hellish life.

TEXT 11

देहः किमन्नदातुः स्वं निषेक्तुर्मातुरेव च ।
मातुः पितुर्वा बलिनः क्रेतुरग्नेः शुनोऽपि वा ॥११॥

dehaḥ kim anna-dātuḥ svaṁ
niṣektur mātur eva ca
mātuḥ pitur vā balinaḥ
kretur agneḥ śuno 'pi vā

dehaḥ—this body; *kim anna-dātuḥ*—does it belong to the employer who gives me the money to maintain it; *svam*—or does it belong to me personally; *niṣektuḥ*—(or does it belong) to the person who discharged the semen; *mātuḥ eva*—(or does it belong) to the mother who maintained this body within her womb; *ca*—and; *mātuḥ pituḥ vā*—or (does it belong) to the father of the mother (because sometimes the father of the mother takes a grandson as an adopted son); *balinaḥ*—(or does it belong) to the person who takes this body away by force; *kretuḥ*—or to the person who purchases the body as a slave; *agneḥ*—or to the fire (because ultimately the body is burned); *śunaḥ*—or to the dogs and vultures that ultimately eat it; *api*—even; *vā*—or.

TRANSLATION

While alive, does this body belong to its employer, to the self, to the father, the mother, or the mother's father? Does it belong to the person who takes it away by force, to the slave master who purchases it, or to the sons who burn it in the fire? Or, if the body is not burned, does it belong to the dogs that eat it? Among the

many possible claimants, who is the rightful claimant? Not to ascertain this but instead to maintain the body by sinful activities is not good.

TEXT 12

एवं साधारणं देहमव्यक्तप्रभवाप्ययम् ।
को विद्वानात्मसात् कृत्वा हन्ति जन्तूनृतेऽसतः ॥१२॥

evaṁ sādhāraṇaṁ deham
avyakta-prabhavāpyayam
ko vidvān ātmasāt kṛtvā
hanti jantūn ṛte 'sataḥ

evam—in this way; *sādhāraṇam*—common property; *deham*—the body; *avyakta*—from unmanifested nature; *prabhava*—manifested in that way; *apyayam*—and again merged with the unmanifested ("for dust thou art, and unto dust shalt thou return"); *kaḥ*—who is that person; *vidvān*—one who is actually in knowledge; *ātmasāt kṛtvā*—claiming as his own; *hanti*—kills; *jantūn*—poor animals; *ṛte*—except; *asataḥ*—rascals who have no knowledge, no clear understanding.

TRANSLATION

This body, after all, is produced by the unmanifested nature and again annihilated and merged in the natural elements. Therefore, it is the common property of everyone. Under the circumstances, who but a rascal claims this property as his own and while maintaining it commits such sinful activities as killing animals just to satisfy his whims? Unless one is a rascal, one cannot commit such sinful activities.

PURPORT

Atheists do not believe in the existence of the soul. Nonetheless, unless one is very cruel, why should one kill animals unnecessarily? The body is a manifestation of a combination of matter. In the beginning it was nothing, but by a combination of matter it has come into existence. Then again, when the combination is dismantled, the body will no longer exist.

In the beginning it was nothing, and in the end it will be nothing. Why then should one commit sinful activities when it is manifested? It is not possible for anyone to do this unless he is rascal number one.

TEXT 13

असतः श्रीमदान्धस्य दारिद्र्यं परमञ्जनम् ।
आत्मौपम्येन भूतानि दरिद्रः परमीक्षते ॥१३॥

asataḥ śrī-madāndhasya
dāridryaṁ param añjanam
ātmaupamyena bhūtāni
daridraḥ param īkṣate

asataḥ—of such a foolish rascal; *śrī-mada-andhasya*—who is blinded by temporarily possessing riches and opulence; *dāridryam*—poverty; *param añjanam*—the best ointment for the eyes, by which to see things as they are; *ātma-aupamyena*—with comparison to himself; *bhūtāni*—living beings; *daridraḥ*—a poverty-stricken man; *param*—perfectly; *īkṣate*—can see things as they are.

TRANSLATION

Atheistic fools and rascals who are very much proud of wealth fail to see things as they are. Therefore, returning them to poverty is the proper ointment for their eyes so they may see things as they are. At least a poverty-stricken man can realize how painful poverty is, and therefore he will not want others to be in a painful condition like his own.

PURPORT

Even today, if a man who was formerly poverty-stricken gets money, he is inclined to utilize his money to perform many philanthropic activities, like opening schools for uneducated men and hospitals for the diseased. In this connection there is an instructive story called *punar mūṣiko bhava*, "Again Become a Mouse." A mouse was very much harassed by a cat, and therefore the mouse approached a saintly person to request to become a cat. When the mouse became a cat, he was harassed by a dog, and then when he became a dog, he was harassed by a tiger. But when he became a tiger, he stared at the saintly person, and when the saintly person asked him, "What do you want?" the tiger said, "I want to eat you." Then the saintly person cursed him, saying, "May you again become a mouse." A similar thing is going on all over the universe. One is going up and down, sometimes becoming a mouse, sometimes a tiger, and so on. Śrī Caitanya Mahāprabhu said:

brahmāṇḍa bhramite kona bhāgyavān jīva
guru-kṛṣṇa-prasāde pāya bhakti-latā-bīja
(Cc. *Madhya* 19.151)

The living entities are promoted and degraded by the laws of nature, but if one is very, very fortunate, by association with saintly persons he gets the seed of devotional service, and his life becomes successful. Nārada Muni wanted to bring Nalakūvara and Maṇigrīva to the platform of devotional service through poverty, and thus he cursed them. Such is the mercy of a Vaiṣṇava. Unless one is brought to the Vaiṣṇava platform, one cannot be a good man. *Harāv abhaktasya kuto mahad-guṇāḥ* (*Bhāg.* 5.18.12). An *avaiṣṇava* never becomes a good man, however severely he is punished.

TEXT 14

यथा कण्टकविद्धाङ्गो जन्तोर्नेच्छति तां व्यथाम् ।
जीवसाम्यं गतो लिङ्गैर्न तथाविद्धकण्टकः ॥१४॥

yathā kaṇṭaka-viddhāṅgo
jantor necchati tāṁ vyathām
jīva-sāmyaṁ gato liṅgair
na tathāviddha-kaṇṭakaḥ

yathā—just as; *kaṇṭaka-viddha-aṅgaḥ*—a person whose body has been pinpricked; *jantoḥ*—of such an animal; *na*—not; *icchati*—desires; *tām*—a particular; *vyathām*—pain; *jīva-sāmyam gataḥ*—when he understands that the position is the same for everyone; *liṅgaiḥ*—by possessing a particular type of body; *na*—not; *tathā*—so; *aviddha-kaṇṭakaḥ*—a person who has not been pinpricked.

TRANSLATION

By seeing their faces, one whose body has been pricked by pins can understand the pain of others who are pinpricked. Realizing that this pain is the same for everyone, he does not want others to suffer in this way. But one who has never been pricked by pins cannot understand this pain.

PURPORT

There is a saying, "The happiness of wealth is enjoyable by a person who has tasted the distress of poverty." There is also another common saying, *vandhyā ki bujhibe prasava-vedanā:* "A woman who has not given birth to a child cannot understand the pain of childbirth." Unless one comes to the platform of actual experience, one cannot realize what is pain and what is happiness in this material world. The laws of nature act accordingly. If one has killed an animal, one must himself be killed by that same animal. This is called *māṁsa. Mām* means "me," and *sa* means "he." As I am eating an animal, that animal will have the opportunity to eat me. In every state, therefore, it is ordinarily the custom that if a person commits murder he is hanged.

TEXT 15

दरिद्रो निरहंस्तम्भो मुक्तः सर्वमदैरिह ।
कृच्छ्रं यदृच्छयाप्नोति तद्धि तस्य परं तपः ॥१५॥

daridro nirahaṁ-stambho
muktaḥ sarva-madair iha
kṛcchraṁ yadṛcchayāpnoti
tad dhi tasya paraṁ tapaḥ

daridraḥ—a poverty-stricken person; *nir-aham-stambhaḥ*—is automatically freed from all false prestige; *muktaḥ*—liberated; *sarva*—all;

madaiḥ—from false ego; *iha*—in this world; *kṛcchram*—with great difficulty; *yadṛcchayā āpnoti*—what he gains by chance from providence; *tat*—that; *hi*—indeed; *tasya*—his; *param*—perfect; *tapaḥ*—austerity.

TRANSLATION

A poverty-stricken man must automatically undergo austerities and penances because he does not have the wealth to possess anything. Thus his false prestige is vanquished. Always in need of food, shelter and clothing, he must be satisfied with what is obtained by the mercy of providence. Undergoing such compulsory austerities is good for him because this purifies him and completely frees him from false ego.

PURPORT

A saintly person voluntarily accepts a state of poverty just to become free from material false prestige. Many great kings left their princely standard of living and went to the forest to practice austerity according to Vedic culture, just to become purified. But if one who cannot voluntarily accept such austerity is put into a situation of poverty, he automatically must practice austerity. Austerity is good for everyone because it frees one from material conditions. Therefore, if one is very much proud of his material position, putting him into poverty is the best way to rectify his foolishness. *Dāridrya-doṣo guṇa-rāśi-nāśi:* when a person is poverty-stricken, naturally his false pride in aristocracy, wealth, education and beauty is smashed. Thus corrected, he is in the right position for liberation.

TEXT 16

नित्यं क्षुत्क्षामदेहस्य दरिद्रस्यान्नकाङ्क्षिणः ।
इन्द्रियाण्यनुशुष्यन्ति हिंसापि विनिवर्तते ॥१६॥

nityaṁ kṣut-kṣāma-dehasya
daridrasyānna-kāṅkṣiṇaḥ
indriyāṇy anuśuṣyanti
hiṁsāpi vinivartate

nityam—always; *kṣut*—with hunger; *kṣāma*—weak, without necessary strength; *dehasya*—of the body of a poor man; *daridrasya*—poverty-stricken; *anna-kāṅkṣiṇaḥ*—always desiring to get sufficient food; *indriyāṇi*—the senses, which are compared to snakes; *anuśuṣyanti*—gradually become weaker and weaker, with less potency; *hiṁsā api*—the tendency to be envious of others; *vinivartate*—reduces.

TRANSLATION

Always hungry, longing for sufficient food, a poverty-stricken man gradually becomes weaker and weaker. Having no extra potency, his senses are automatically pacified. A poverty-stricken man, therefore, is unable to perform harmful, envious activities. In other words, such a man automatically gains the results of the austerities and penances adopted voluntarily by saintly persons.

PURPORT

According to the opinion of experienced medical practitioners, diabetes is a result of voracious eating, and tuberculosis is a disease of undereating. We should desire neither to be diabetic nor to be tubercular. *Yāvad artha-prayojanam.* We should eat frugally and keep the body fit for advancing in Kṛṣṇa consciousness. As recommended elsewhere in *Śrīmad-Bhāgavatam* (1.2.10):

kāmasya nendriya-prītir
lābho jīveta yāvatā
jīvasya tattva-jijñāsā
nārtho yaś ceha karmabhiḥ

The real business of human life is to keep oneself fit for advancement in spiritual realization. Human life is not meant for making the senses unnecessarily strong so that one suffers from disease and one increases in an envious, fighting spirit. In this age of Kali, however, human civilization is so misled that people are unnecessarily increasing in economic development, and as a result they are opening more and more slaughterhouses, liquor shops and brothels. In this way, the whole civilization is being spoiled.

TEXT 17

दरिद्रस्यैव युज्यन्ते साधवः समदर्शिनः ।
सद्भिः क्षिणोति तं तर्षं तत आराद् विशुद्ध्यति ॥१७॥

daridrasyaiva yujyante
sādhavaḥ sama-darśinaḥ
sadbhiḥ kṣiṇoti taṁ tarṣaṁ
tata ārād viśuddhyati

daridrasya—of a person who is poverty-stricken; *eva*—indeed; *yujyante*—may easily associate; *sādhavaḥ*—saintly persons; *sama-darśinaḥ*—although *sādhus* are equal to everyone, to the poor and the rich, the poor man can take advantage of their association; *sadbhiḥ*—by the association of such saintly persons; *kṣiṇoti*—reduces; *tam*—the original cause of material suffering; *tarṣam*—the desire for material enjoyment; *tataḥ*—thereafter; *ārāt*—very soon; *viśuddhyati*—his material contamination is cleansed off.

TRANSLATION

Saintly persons may freely associate with those who are poverty-stricken, but not with those who are rich. A poverty-stricken man, by association with saintly persons, very soon becomes uninterested in material desires, and the dirty things within the core of his heart are cleansed away.

PURPORT

It is said, *mahad-vicalanaṁ nṝṇāṁ gṛhiṇāṁ dīna-cetasām* (*Bhāg.* 10.8.4). The only business of a saintly person or *sannyāsī*, a person in the renounced order, is to preach Kṛṣṇa consciousness. *Sādhus*, saintly persons, want to preach to both the poor and the rich, but the poor take more advantage of the *sādhus'* preaching than the rich do. A poor man receives *sādhus* very quickly, offers them obeisances, and tries to take advantage of their presence, whereas a rich man keeps a big greyhound dog at his door so that no one can enter his house. He posts a sign saying "Beware of Dog" and avoids the association of saintly persons, whereas a poor man keeps his door open for them and thus benefits by their association more than a rich man does. Because Nārada Muni, in his previous life, was the poverty-stricken son of a maidservant, he got the association of saintly persons and later became the exalted Nārada Muni. This was his actual experience. Therefore, he is now comparing the position of a poor man with that of a rich man.

satāṁ prasaṅgān mama vīrya-saṁvido
bhavanti hṛt-karṇa-rasāyanāḥ kathāḥ
taj-joṣaṇād āśv apavarga-vartmani
śraddhā ratir bhaktir anukramiṣyati
(*Bhāg.* 3.25.25)

If one gets the advantage of association with saintly persons, by their instructions one becomes more and more purified of material desires.

kṛṣṇa-bahirmukha haiyā bhoga-vāñchā kare
nikaṭa-stha māyā tāre jāpaṭiyā dhare
(*Prema-vivarta*)

Material life means that one forgets Kṛṣṇa and that one increases in one's desires for sense gratification. But if one receives the advantage of instructions from saintly persons and forgets the importance of material desires, one is automatically purified. *Ceto-darpaṇa-mārjanaṁ bhava-mahādāvāgni-nirvāpaṇam* (*Śikṣāṣṭaka* 1). Unless the core of a materialistic person's heart is purified, he cannot get rid of the pangs of *bhava-mahādāvāgni*, the blazing fire of material existence.

TEXT 18

साधूनां समचित्तानां मुकुन्दचरणैषिणाम् ।
उपेक्ष्यैः किं धनस्तम्भैरसद्भिरसदाश्रयैः ॥१८॥

sādhūnāṁ sama-cittānāṁ
mukunda-caraṇaiṣiṇām
upekṣyaiḥ kiṁ dhana-stambhair
asadbhir asad-āśrayaiḥ

sādhūnām—of saintly persons; *sama-cittānām*—of those who are equal to everyone; *mukunda-caraṇa-eṣiṇām*—whose only business is to serve Mukunda, the Supreme Personality of Godhead, and who always aspire for that service; *upekṣyaiḥ*—neglecting the association; *kim*—what; *dhana-stambhaiḥ*—rich and proud; *asadbhiḥ*—with the association of undesirable persons; *asat-āśrayaiḥ*—taking shelter of those who are *asat*, or nondevotees.

TRANSLATION

Saintly persons [sādhus] think of Kṛṣṇa twenty-four hours a day. They have no other interest. Why should people neglect the association of such exalted spiritual personalities and try to associate with materialists, taking shelter of nondevotees, most of whom are proud and rich?

PURPORT

A *sādhu* is one who is engaged in devotional service to the Lord without deviation (*bhajate mām ananya-bhāk*).

titikṣavaḥ kāruṇikāḥ
suhṛdaḥ sarva-dehinām
ajāta-śatravaḥ śāntāḥ
sādhavaḥ sādhu-bhūṣaṇāḥ

"The symptoms of a *sādhu* are that he is tolerant, merciful and friendly to all living entities. He has no enemies, he is peaceful, he abides by the scriptures, and all his characteristics are sublime." (*Bhāg.* 3.25.21) A *sādhu* is *suhṛdaḥ sarva-dehinām*, the friend of everyone. Why then should the rich, instead of associating with *sādhus*, waste their valuable time in association with other rich men who are averse to spiritual life? Both the poor man and the rich man can take advantage of the Kṛṣṇa consciousness movement, and here it is advised that everyone do so. There is no profit in avoiding the association of the members of the Kṛṣṇa consciousness movement. Narottama dāsa Ṭhākura has said:

sat-saṅga chāḍi' kainu asate vilāsa
te-kāraṇe lāgila ye karma-bandha-phāṅsa

If we give up the association of *sādhus*, saintly persons engaged in Kṛṣṇa consciousness, and associate with persons seeking sense gratification and accumulating wealth for this purpose, our life is spoiled. The word *asat* refers to an *avaiṣṇava*, one who is not a devotee of Kṛṣṇa, and *sat* refers to a Vaiṣṇava, Kṛṣṇa's devotee. One should always seek the association of Vaiṣṇavas and not spoil one's life by mixing with *avaiṣṇavas*. In *Bhagavad-gītā* (7.15), the distinction between Vaiṣṇava and *avaiṣṇava* is enunciated:

na māṁ duṣkṛtino mūḍhāḥ
prapadyante narādhamāḥ
māyayāpahṛta-jñānā
āsuraṁ bhāvam āśritāḥ

Anyone who is not surrendered to Kṛṣṇa is a most sinful person (*duṣkṛtī*), a rascal (*mūḍha*), and the lowest of men (*narādhama*). Therefore one should not avoid the association of Vaiṣṇavas, which is now available all over the world in the form of the Kṛṣṇa consciousness movement.

TEXT 19

तदहं मत्तयोर्माध्व्या वारुण्या श्रीमदान्धयोः ।
तमोमदं हरिष्यामि स्त्रैणयोरजितात्मनोः ॥१९॥

tad ahaṁ mattayor mādhvyā
vāruṇyā śrī-madāndhayoḥ
tamo-madaṁ hariṣyāmi
straiṇayor ajitātmanoḥ

tat—therefore; *aham*—I; *mattayoḥ*—of these two drunken persons; *mādhvyā*—by drinking liquor; *vāruṇyā*—named Vāruṇī; *śrī-mada-andhayoḥ*—who are blinded by celestial opulence; *tamaḥ-madam*—this false prestige due to the mode of ignorance; *hariṣyāmi*—I shall take away; *straiṇayoḥ*—because they have become so attached to women; *ajita-ātmanoḥ*—being unable to control the senses.

TRANSLATION

Therefore, since these two persons, drunk with the liquor named Vāruṇī, or Mādhvī, and unable to control their senses, have

been blinded by the pride of celestial opulence and have become attached to women, I shall relieve them of their false prestige.

PURPORT

When a *sādhu* chastises or punishes someone, he does not do so for revenge. Mahārāja Parīkṣit had inquired why Nārada Muni was subject to such a spirit of revenge (*tamaḥ*). But this was not *tamaḥ*, for Nārada Muni, in full knowledge of what was for the good of the two brothers, wisely thought of how to cure them. Vaiṣṇavas are good physicians. They know how to protect a person from material disease. Thus they are never in *tamo-guṇa. Sa guṇān samatītyaitān brahma-bhūyāya kalpate* (Bg. 14.26). Vaiṣṇavas are always situated on the transcendental platform, the Brahman platform. They cannot be subject to mistakes or the influence of the modes of material nature. Whatever they do, after full consideration, is meant just to lead everyone back home, back to Godhead.

TEXTS 20–22

यदिमौ लोकपालस्य पुत्रौ भूत्वा तमःप्लुतौ ।
न विवाससमात्मानं विजानीतः सुदुर्मदौ ॥२०॥
अतोऽर्हतः स्थावरतां स्यातां नैवं यथा पुनः ।
स्मृतिः स्यान्मत्प्रसादेन तत्रापि मदनुग्रहात् ॥२१॥
वासुदेवस्य सान्निध्यं लब्ध्वा दिव्यशरच्छते ।
वृत्ते स्वर्लोकतां भूयो लब्धभक्ती भविष्यतः ॥२२॥

yad imau loka-pālasya
putrau bhūtvā tamaḥ-plutau
na vivāsasam ātmānaṁ
vijānītaḥ sudurmadau

ato 'rhataḥ sthāvaratāṁ
syātāṁ naivaṁ yathā punaḥ
smṛtiḥ syān mat-prasādena
tatrāpi mad-anugrahāt

vāsudevasya sānnidhyaṁ
labdhvā divya-śarac-chate
vṛtte svarlokatāṁ bhūyo
labdha-bhaktī bhaviṣyataḥ

yat—because; *imau*—these two young demigods; *loka-pālasya*—of the great demigod Kuvera; *putrau*—born as sons; *bhūtvā*—being so (they should not have become like that); *tamaḥ-plutau*—so absorbed in the mode of darkness; *na*—not; *vivāsasam*—without any dress, completely naked; *ātmānam*—their personal bodies; *vijānītaḥ*—could understand that they were naked; *su-durmadau*—because they were very much fallen due to false pride; *ataḥ*—therefore; *arhataḥ*—they deserve; *sthāvaratām*—immobility like that of a tree; *syātām*—they may become; *na*—not; *evam*—in this way; *yathā*—as; *punaḥ*—again; *smṛtiḥ*—remembrance; *syāt*—may continue; *mat-prasādena*—by my mercy; *tatra api*—over and above that; *mat-anugrahāt*—by my special favor; *vāsudevasya*—of the Supreme Personality of Godhead; *sānnidhyam*—the personal association, face to face; *labdhvā*—obtaining; *divya-śarat-śate vṛtte*—after the expiry of one hundred years by the measurement of the demigods; *svarlokatām*—the desire to live in the celestial world; *bhūyaḥ*—again; *labdha-bhaktī*—having revived their natural condition of devotional service; *bhaviṣyataḥ*—will become.

TRANSLATION

These two young men, Nalakūvara and Maṇigrīva, are by fortune the sons of the great demigod Kuvera, but because of false prestige and madness after drinking liquor, they are so fallen that they are naked but cannot understand that they are. Therefore, because they are living like trees (for trees are naked but are not conscious), these two young men should receive the bodies of trees. This will be proper punishment. Nonetheless, after they become trees and until they are released, by my mercy they will have remembrance of their past sinful activities. Moreover, by my special favor, after the expiry of one hundred years by the measurement of the demigods, they will be able to see the Supreme Personality of Godhead, Vāsudeva, face to face, and thus revive their real position as devotees.

PURPORT

A tree has no consciousness: when cut, it feels no pain. But Nārada Muni wanted the consciousness of Nalakūvara and Maṇigrīva to continue, so that even after being released from the life of trees, they would not forget the circumstances under which they had been punished. Therefore, to bestow upon them special favor, Nārada Muni arranged things in such a way that after being released, they would be able to see Kṛṣṇa in Vṛndāvana and thus revive their dormant *bhakti.*

Each day of the demigods in the upper planetary system equals six months of our measurement. Although the demigods in the upper planetary system are attached to material enjoyment, they are all devotees, and therefore they are called demigods. There are two kinds of persons, namely the *devas* and the *asuras. Asuras* forget their relationship with Kṛṣṇa (*āsuraṁ bhāvam āśritāḥ*), whereas the *devas* do not forget.

dvau bhūta-sargau loke 'smin
daiva āsura eva ca
viṣṇu-bhaktaḥ smṛto daiva
āsuras tad-viparyayaḥ
(*Padma Purāṇa*)

The distinction between a pure devotee and a *karma-miśra* devotee is this: a pure devotee does not desire anything for material enjoyment, whereas a mixed devotee becomes a devotee to become a first-class enjoyer of this material world. One who is in direct touch with the Supreme Personality of Godhead in devotional service remains pure, uncontaminated by material desires (*anyābhilāṣitā-śūnyaṁ jñāna-karmādy-anāvṛtam*).

By *karma-miśra-bhakti* one is elevated to the celestial kingdom, by *jñāna-miśra-bhakti* one is able to merge in the Brahman effulgence, and by *yoga-miśra-bhakti* one is able to realize the omnipotency of the Supreme Personality of Godhead. But pure *bhakti* does not depend on *karma, jñāna* or *yoga,* for it simply consists of loving affairs. The liberation of the *bhakta,* therefore, which is called not just *mukti* but *vimukti,* surpasses the five other kinds of liberation—*sāyujya, sārūpya, sālokya, sārṣṭi* and *sāmīpya.* A pure devotee always engages in pure service (*ānukūlyena kṛṣṇānuśīlanaṁ bhaktir uttamā*). Taking birth in the upper planetary system as a demigod is a chance to become a further purified devotee and go back home, back to Godhead. Nārada Muni indirectly gave Maṇigrīva and Nalakūvara the greatest opportunity by his so-called curse.

TEXT 23

श्रीशुक उवाच
एवमुक्त्वा स देवर्षिर्गतो नारायणाश्रमम् ।
नलकूवरमणिग्रीवावासतुर्यमलार्जुनौ ॥२३॥

śrī-śuka uvāca
evam uktvā sa devarṣir
gato nārāyaṇāśramam
nalakūvara-maṇigrīvāv
āsatur yamalārjunau

śrī-śukaḥ uvāca—Śrī Śukadeva Gosvāmī continued to speak; *evam uktvā*—thus uttering; *saḥ*—he; *devarṣiḥ*—the greatest saintly person, Nārada; *gataḥ*—left that place; *nārāyaṇa-āśramam*—for his own *āśrama*, known as Nārāyaṇa-āśrama; *nalakūvara*—Nalakūvara; *maṇi-grīvau*—and Maṇigrīva; *āsatuḥ*—remained there to become; *yamala-arjunau*—twin *arjuna* trees.

TRANSLATION

Śukadeva Gosvāmī continued: Having thus spoken, the great saint Devarṣi Nārada returned to his āśrama, known as Nārāyaṇa-āśrama, and Nalakūvara and Maṇigrīva became twin arjuna trees.

PURPORT

Arjuna trees are still found in many forests, and their skin is used by cardiologists to prepare medicine for heart trouble. This means that even though they are trees, they are disturbed when skinned for medical science.

TEXT 24

ऋषेर्भागवतमुख्यस्य सत्यं कर्तुं वचो हरिः ।
जगाम शनकैस्तत्र यत्रास्तां यमलार्जुनौ ॥२४॥

ṛṣer bhāgavata-mukhyasya
satyaṁ kartuṁ vaco hariḥ
jagāma śanakais tatra
yatrāstāṁ yamalārjunau

ṛṣeḥ—of the great sage and saintly person Nārada; *bhāgavata-mukhyasya*—of the topmost of all devotees; *satyam*—truthful; *kartum*—to prove; *vacaḥ*—his words; *hariḥ*—the Supreme Personality of Godhead, Kṛṣṇa; *jagāma*—went there; *śanakaiḥ*—very slowly; *tatra*—there; *yatra*—to the spot where; *āstām*—there were; *yamala-arjunau*—the twin *arjuna* trees.

TRANSLATION

The Supreme Personality of Godhead, Śrī Kṛṣṇa, to fulfill the truthfulness of the words of the greatest devotee, Nārada, slowly went to that spot where the twin arjuna trees were standing.

TEXT 25

देवर्षिर्मे प्रियतमो यदिमौ धनदात्मजौ ।
तत्तथा साधयिष्यामि यद् गीतं तन्महात्मना ॥२५॥

devarṣir me priyatamo
yad imau dhanadātmajau
tat tathā sādhayiṣyāmi
yad gītaṁ tan mahātmanā

devarṣiḥ—the great saint Devarṣi Nārada; *me*—My; *priya-tamaḥ*—most beloved devotee; *yat*—although; *imau*—these two persons (Nalakūvara and Maṇigrīva); *dhanada-ātmajau*—born of a rich father and being nondevotees; *tat*—the words of Devarṣi; *tathā*—just so; *sādhayiṣyāmi*—I shall execute (because he wanted Me to come face to face with the *yamala-arjuna*, I shall do so); *yat gītam*—as already stated; *tat*—that; *mahātmanā*—by Nārada Muni.

TRANSLATION

"Although these two young men are the sons of the very rich Kuvera and I have nothing to do with them, Devarṣi Nārada is My very dear and affectionate devotee, and therefore because he wanted Me to come face to face with them, I must do so for their deliverance."

PURPORT

Nalakūvara and Maṇigrīva actually had nothing to do with devotional service or seeing the Supreme Personality of Godhead face to face, for this is not an ordinary opportunity. It is not that because one is very rich or learned or was born in an aristocratic family one will be able to see the Supreme Personality of Godhead face to face. This is impossible. But in this case, because Nārada Muni desired that Nalakūvara and Maṇigrīva see Vāsudeva face to face, the Supreme Personality of Godhead wanted to fulfill the words of His very dear devotee Nārada Muni. If one seeks the favor of a devotee instead of directly asking favors from the Supreme Personality of Godhead, one is very easily successful. Śrīla Bhaktivinoda Ṭhākura has therefore recommended: *vaiṣṇava ṭhākura tomāra kukkura bhuliyā jānaha more, kṛṣṇa se tomāra kṛṣṇa dite pāra.* One should desire to become like a dog in strictly following a devotee. Kṛṣṇa is in the hand of a devotee. *Adurlabham ātma-bhaktau.* Thus without the favor of a devotee, one cannot directly approach Kṛṣṇa, what to speak of engaging in His service. Narottama dāsa Ṭhākura therefore sings, *chāḍiyā vaiṣṇava-sevā nistāra pāyeche kebā:* unless one becomes a servant of a pure devotee, one cannot be delivered from the material condition of life. In our Gauḍīya Vaiṣṇava society, following in the footsteps of Rūpa Gosvāmī, our first business is to seek shelter of a bona fide spiritual master (*ādau gurv-āśrayaḥ*).

TEXT 26

इत्यन्तरेणार्जुनयोः कृष्णस्तु यमयोर्ययौ ।
आत्मनिर्वेशमात्रेण तिर्यग्गतमुलूखलम् ॥२६॥

ity antareṇārjunayoḥ
kṛṣṇas tu yamayor yayau
ātma-nirveśa-mātreṇa
tiryag-gatam ulūkhalam

iti—thus deciding; *antareṇa*—between; *arjunayoḥ*—the two *arjuna* trees; *kṛṣṇaḥ tu*—Lord Kṛṣṇa; *yamayoḥ yayau*—entered between the two trees; *ātma-nirveśa-mātreṇa*—as soon as He entered (between the two trees); *tiryak*—crossways; *gatam*—so became; *ulūkhalam*—the big mortar for grinding spices.

TRANSLATION

Having thus spoken, Kṛṣṇa soon entered between the two arjuna trees, and thus the big mortar to which He was bound turned crosswise and stuck between them.

TEXT 27

बालेन निष्कर्षयतान्वगुलूखलं तद्
दामोदरेण तरसोत्कलिताङ्घ्रिबन्धौ ।
निष्पेततुः परमविक्रमितातिवेप-
स्कन्धप्रवालविटपौ कृतचण्डशब्दौ ॥२७॥

bālena niṣkarṣayatānvag ulūkhalaṁ tad
dāmodareṇa tarasotkalitāṅghri-bandhau
niṣpetatuḥ parama-vikramitātivepa-
skandha-pravāla-viṭapau kṛta-caṇḍa-śabdau

bālena—by the boy Kṛṣṇa; *niṣkarṣayatā*—who was dragging; *anvak*—following the dragging of Kṛṣṇa; *ulūkhalam*—the wooden mortar; *tat*—that; *dāma-udareṇa*—by Kṛṣṇa, who was tied by the belly; *tarasā*—with great force; *utkalita*—uprooted; *aṅghri-bandhau*—the roots of the two trees; *niṣpetatuḥ*—fell down; *parama-vikramita*—by the supreme power; *ati-vepa*—trembling severely; *skandha*—trunk; *pravāla*—bunches of leaves; *viṭapau*—those two trees, along with their branches; *kṛta*—having made; *caṇḍa-śabdau*—a fierce sound.

TRANSLATION

By dragging behind Him with great force the wooden mortar tied to His belly, the boy Kṛṣṇa uprooted the two trees. By the great strength of the Supreme Person, the two trees, with their trunks, leaves and branches, trembled severely and fell to the ground with a great crash.

PURPORT

This is the pastime of Kṛṣṇa known as *dāmodara-līlā.* Therefore another of Kṛṣṇa's names is Dāmodara. As stated in the *Hari-vaṁśa:*

sa ca tenaiva nāmnā tu
kṛṣṇo vai dāma-bandhanāt
goṣṭhe dāmodara iti
gopībhiḥ parigīyate

TEXT 28

तत्र श्रिया परमया ककुभः स्फुरन्तौ
सिद्धावुपेत्य कुजयोरिव जातवेदाः ।
कृष्णं प्रणम्य शिरसाखिललोकनाथं
बद्धाञ्जली विरजसाविदमूचतुः स्म ॥२८॥

tatra śriyā paramayā kakubhaḥ sphurantau
siddhāv upetya kujayor iva jāta-vedāḥ
kṛṣṇaṁ praṇamya śirasākhila-loka-nāthaṁ
baddhāñjalī virajasāv idam ūcatuḥ sma

tatra—there, on the very spot where the two *arjunas* fell; *śriyā*—with beautification; *paramayā*—superexcellent; *kakubhaḥ*—all directions; *sphurantau*—illuminating by effulgence; *siddhau*—two perfect persons; *upetya*—then coming out; *kujayoḥ*—from between the two trees; *iva*—like; *jāta-vedāḥ*—fire personified; *kṛṣṇam*—unto Lord Kṛṣṇa; *praṇamya*—offering obeisances; *śirasā*—with the head; *akhila-loka-nātham*—to the Supreme Person, the controller of everything;

baddha-añjalī—with folded hands; *virajasau*—fully cleansed of the mode of ignorance; *idam*—the following words; *ūcatuḥ sma*—uttered.

TRANSLATION

Thereafter, in that very place where the two arjuna trees had fallen, two great, perfect personalities, who appeared like fire personified, came out of the two trees. The effulgence of their beauty illuminating all directions, with bowed heads they offered obeisances to Kṛṣṇa, and with hands folded they spoke the following words.

TEXT 29

कृष्ण कृष्ण महायोगिंस्त्वमाद्यः पुरुषः परः ।
व्यक्ताव्यक्तमिदं विश्वं रूपं ते ब्राह्मणा विदुः ॥२९॥

kṛṣṇa kṛṣṇa mahā-yogiṁs
tvam ādyaḥ puruṣaḥ paraḥ
vyaktāvyaktam idaṁ viśvaṁ
rūpaṁ te brāhmaṇā viduḥ

kṛṣṇa kṛṣṇa—O Lord Kṛṣṇa, O Lord Kṛṣṇa; *mahā-yogin*—O master of mysticism; *tvam*—You, the exalted personality; *ādyaḥ*—the root cause of everything; *puruṣaḥ*—the Supreme Person; *paraḥ*—beyond this material creation; *vyakta-avyaktam*—this material cosmic manifestation, consisting of cause and effect, or gross and subtle forms; *idam*—this; *viśvam*—whole world; *rūpam*—form; *te*—Your; *brāhmaṇāḥ*—learned *brāhmaṇas; viduḥ*—know.

TRANSLATION

O Lord Kṛṣṇa, Lord Kṛṣṇa, Your opulent mysticism is inconceivable. You are the supreme, original person, the cause of all causes, immediate and remote, and You are beyond this material creation. Learned brāhmaṇas know [on the basis of the Vedic statement sarvaṁ khalv idaṁ brahma] that You are everything and that this cosmic manifestation, in its gross and subtle aspects, is Your form.

PURPORT

The two demigods Nalakūvara and Maṇigrīva, because of their continuing memory, could understand the supremacy of Kṛṣṇa by the grace of Nārada. Now they admitted, "That we should be delivered by the blessings of Nārada Muni was all Your plan. Therefore You are the supreme mystic. Everything—past, present and future—is known to You. Your plan was made so nicely that although we stayed here as twin *arjuna* trees, You have appeared as a small boy to deliver us. This was all Your inconceivable arrangement. Because You are the Supreme Person, You can do everything."

TEXTS 30–31

त्वमेकः सर्वभूतानां देहास्वात्मेन्द्रियेश्वरः ।
त्वमेव कालो भगवान् विष्णुरव्यय ईश्वरः ॥३०॥
त्वं महान् प्रकृतिः सूक्ष्मा रजःसत्त्वतमोमयी ।
त्वमेव पुरुषोऽध्यक्षः सर्वक्षेत्रविकारवित् ॥३१॥

tvam ekaḥ sarva-bhūtānāṁ
dehāsv-ātmendriyeśvaraḥ
tvam eva kālo bhagavān
viṣṇur avyaya īśvaraḥ

tvaṁ mahān prakṛtiḥ sūkṣmā
rajaḥ-sattva-tamomayī
tvam eva puruṣo 'dhyakṣaḥ
sarva-kṣetra-vikāra-vit

tvam—Your Lordship; *ekaḥ*—one; *sarva-bhūtānām*—of all living entities; *deha*—of the body; *asu*—of the life force; *ātma*—of the soul; *indriya*—of the senses; *īśvaraḥ*—the Supersoul, the controller; *tvam*—Your Lordship; *eva*—indeed; *kālaḥ*—the time factor; *bhagavān*—the Supreme Personality of Godhead; *viṣṇuḥ*—all-pervading; *avyayaḥ*—imperishable; *īśvaraḥ*—controller; *tvam*—Your Lordship; *mahān*—the greatest; *prakṛtiḥ*—the cosmic manifestation; *sūkṣmā*—subtle; *rajaḥ-sattva-tamaḥ-mayī*—consisting of three modes of nature (passion, goodness and ignorance); *tvam eva*—Your Lordship is indeed; *puruṣaḥ*—the

Supreme Person; *adhyakṣaḥ*—the proprietor; *sarva-kṣetra*—in all living entities; *vikāra-vit*—knowing the restless mind.

TRANSLATION

You are the Supreme Personality of Godhead, the controller of everything. The body, life, ego and senses of every living entity are Your own self. You are the Supreme Person, Viṣṇu, the imperishable controller. You are the time factor, the immediate cause, and You are material nature, consisting of the three modes passion, goodness and ignorance. You are the original cause of this material manifestation. You are the Supersoul, and therefore You know everything within the core of the heart of every living entity.

PURPORT

Śrīpāda Madhvācārya has quoted from the *Vāmana Purāṇa* as follows:

rūpyatvāt tu jagad rūpaṁ
viṣṇoḥ sākṣāt sukhātmakam
nitya-pūrṇaṁ samuddiṣṭaṁ
svarūpaṁ paramātmanaḥ

TEXT 32

गृह्यमाणैस्त्वमग्राह्यो विकारैः प्राकृतैर्गुणैः ।
को न्विहार्हति विज्ञातुं प्राक्सिद्धं गुणसंवृतः ॥३२॥

gṛhyamāṇais tvam agrāhyo
vikāraiḥ prākṛtair guṇaiḥ
ko nv ihārhati vijñātuṁ
prāk siddhaṁ guṇa-saṁvṛtaḥ

gṛhyamāṇaiḥ—accepting the body made of material nature as existing at the present moment because of being visible; *tvam*—You; *agrāhyaḥ*—not confined in a body made of material nature; *vikāraiḥ*—

agitated by the mind; *prākṛtaiḥ guṇaiḥ*—by the material modes of nature (*sattva-guṇa, rajo-guṇa* and *tamo-guṇa*); *kaḥ*—who is there; *nu*—after that; *iha*—in this material world; *arhati*—who deserves; *vijñātum*—to know; *prāk siddham*—that which existed before the creation; *guṇa-saṁvṛtaḥ*—because of being covered by the material qualities.

TRANSLATION

O Lord, You exist before the creation. Therefore, who, trapped by a body of material qualities in this material world, can understand You?

PURPORT

As it is said:

ataḥ śrī-kṛṣṇa-nāmādi
na bhaved grāhyam indriyaiḥ
sevonmukhe hi jihvādau
svayam eva sphuraty adaḥ
(*Bhakti-rasāmṛta-sindhu* 1.2.234)

Kṛṣṇa's name, attributes and form are Absolute Truth, existing before the creation. Therefore, how can those who are created—that is, those entrapped in bodies created of material elements—understand Kṛṣṇa perfectly? This is not possible. But, *sevonmukhe hi jihvādau svayam eva sphuraty adaḥ:* Kṛṣṇa reveals Himself to those engaged in devotional service. This is also confirmed in *Bhagavad-gītā* (18.15) by the Lord Himself: *bhaktyā mām abhijānāti.* Even the descriptions of Kṛṣṇa in *Śrīmad-Bhāgavatam* are sometimes misunderstood by less intelligent men with a poor fund of knowledge. Therefore, the best course by which to know Him is to engage oneself in pure devotional activities. The more one advances in devotional activities, the more one can understand Him as He is. If from the material platform one could understand Kṛṣṇa, then, since Kṛṣṇa is everything (*sarvaṁ khalv idaṁ brahma*), one could understand Kṛṣṇa by seeing anything within this material world. But that is not possible.

mayā tatam idaṁ sarvaṁ
jagad avyakta-mūrtinā
mat-sthāni sarva-bhūtāni
na cāhaṁ teṣv avasthitaḥ
(Bg. 9.4)

Everything is resting on Kṛṣṇa, and everything is Kṛṣṇa, but this is not to be realized by persons on the material platform.

TEXT 33

तस्मै तुभ्यं भगवते वासुदेवाय वेधसे ।
आत्मद्योतगुणैश्छन्नमहिम्ने ब्रह्मणे नमः ॥३३॥

tasmai tubhyaṁ bhagavate
vāsudevāya vedhase
ātma-dyota-guṇaiś channa-
mahimne brahmaṇe namaḥ

tasmai—(because You are not to be understood from the material platform, we simply offer obeisances) unto Him; *tubhyam*—unto You; *bhagavate*—unto the Supreme Personality of Godhead; *vāsudevāya*—unto Vāsudeva, the origin of Saṅkarṣaṇa, Pradyumna and Aniruddha; *vedhase*—unto the origin of creation; *ātma-dyota-guṇaiḥ channa-mahimne*—unto You whose glories are covered by Your personal energy; *brahmaṇe*—unto the Supreme Brahman; *namaḥ*—our respectful obeisances.

TRANSLATION

O Lord, whose glories are covered by Your own energy, You are the Supreme Personality of Godhead. You are Saṅkarṣaṇa, the origin of creation, and You are Vāsudeva, the origin of the catur-vyūha. Because You are everything and are therefore the Supreme Brahman, we simply offer our respectful obeisances unto You.

PURPORT

Instead of trying to understand Kṛṣṇa in detail, it is better to offer our respectful obeisances unto Him, for He is the origin of everything and

He is everything. Because we are covered by the material modes of nature, He is very difficult for us to understand unless He reveals Himself to us. Therefore it is better for us to acknowledge that He is everything and offer obeisances unto His lotus feet.

TEXTS 34–35

यस्यावतारा ज्ञायन्ते शरीरेष्वशरीरिणः ।
तैस्तैरतुल्यातिशयैर्वीर्यैर्देहिष्वसंगतैः ॥३४॥
स भवान् सर्वलोकस्य भवाय विभवाय च ।
अवतीर्णोऽंशभागेन साम्प्रतं पतिराशिषाम् ॥३५॥

yasyāvatārā jñāyante
śarīreṣv aśarīriṇaḥ
tais tair atulyātiśayair
vīryair dehiṣv asaṅgataiḥ

sa bhavān sarva-lokasya
bhavāya vibhavāya ca
avatīrṇo 'ṁśa-bhāgena
sāmpratam patir āśiṣām

yasya—of whom; *avatārāḥ*—the different incarnations, like Matsya, Kūrma and Varāha; *jñāyante*—are speculated; *śarīreṣu*—in different bodies, differently visible; *aśarīriṇaḥ*—they are not ordinary material bodies, but are all transcendental; *taiḥ taiḥ*—by such bodily activities; *atulya*—incomparable; *ati-śayaiḥ*—unlimited; *vīryaiḥ*—by strength and power; *dehiṣu*—by those who actually have material bodies; *asaṅgataiḥ*—which activities, enacted in different incarnations, are impossible to be performed; *saḥ*—the same Supreme; *bhavān*—Your Lordship; *sarva-lokasya*—of everyone; *bhavāya*—for the elevation; *vibhavāya*—for the liberation; *ca*—and; *avatīrṇaḥ*—have now appeared; *aṁśa-bhāgena*—in full potency, with different parts and parcels; *sāmpratam*—at the present moment; *patiḥ āśiṣām*—You are the Supreme Personality of Godhead, the master of all auspiciousness.

TRANSLATION

Appearing in bodies like those of an ordinary fish, tortoise and hog, You exhibit activities impossible for such creatures to perform—extraordinary, incomparable, transcendental activities of unlimited power and strength. These bodies of Yours, therefore, are not made of material elements, but are incarnations of Your Supreme Personality. You are the same Supreme Personality of Godhead, who have now appeared, with full potency, for the benefit of all living entities within this material world.

PURPORT

As stated in *Bhagavad-gītā* (4.7–8):

yadā yadā hi dharmasya
glānir bhavati bhārata
abhyutthānam adharmasya
tadātmānaṁ sṛjāmy aham

paritrāṇāya sādhūnāṁ
vināśāya ca duṣkṛtām
dharma-saṁsthāpanārthāya
sambhavāmi yuge yuge

Kṛṣṇa appears as an incarnation when real spiritual life declines and when rogues and thieves increase to disturb the situation of the world. Unfortunate, less intelligent persons, bereft of devotional service, cannot understand the Lord's activities, and therefore such persons describe these activities as *kalpanā*—mythology or imagination—because they are rascals and the lowest of men (*na māṁ duṣkṛtino mūḍhāḥ prapadyante narādhamāḥ*). Such men cannot understand that the events described by Vyāsadeva in the *Purāṇas* and other *śāstras* are not fictitious or imaginary, but factual.

Kṛṣṇa, in His full, unlimited potency, here shows that He is the Supreme Personality of Godhead, for although the two trees were so large and sturdy that even many elephants could not move them, Kṛṣṇa, as a child, exhibited such extraordinary strength that they fell down with a great sound. From the very beginning, by killing Pūtanā, Śakaṭāsura and Tṛṇāvartāsura, by causing the trees to fall, and by showing the entire universe within His mouth, Kṛṣṇa proved that He is the Supreme Personality of Godhead. The lowest of men (*mūḍhas*), because of sinful activities, cannot understand this, but devotees can accept it without a doubt. Thus the position of a devotee is different from that of a nondevotee.

TEXT 36

नमः परमकल्याण नमः परममङ्गल ।
वासुदेवाय शान्ताय यदूनां पतये नमः ॥३६॥

namaḥ parama-kalyāṇa
namaḥ parama-maṅgala
vāsudevāya śāntāya
yadūnāṁ pataye namaḥ

namaḥ—we therefore offer our respectful obeisances; *parama-kalyāṇa*—You are the supreme auspiciousness; *namaḥ*—our respectful obeisances unto You; *parama-maṅgala*—whatever You do is good; *vāsudevāya*—unto the original Personality of Godhead, Vāsudeva; *śāntāya*—unto the most peaceful; *yadūnām*—of the Yadu dynasty; *pataye*—unto the controller; *namaḥ*—our respectful obeisances unto You.

TRANSLATION

O supremely auspicious, we offer our respectful obeisances unto You, who are the supreme good. O most famous descendant and controller of the Yadu dynasty, O son of Vasudeva, O most peaceful, let us offer our obeisances unto Your lotus feet.

PURPORT

The word *parama-kalyāṇa* is significant because Kṛṣṇa, in any of His incarnations, appears in order to protect the *sādhus* (*paritrāṇāya sādhūnām*). The *sādhus*, saintly persons or devotees, are always harassed by nondevotees, and Kṛṣṇa appears in His incarnations to give them relief. This is His first concern. If we study the history of Kṛṣṇa's life, we shall find that for most of His life He predominantly engaged in killing demons one after another.

TEXT 37

अनुजानीहि नौ भूमंस्तवानुचरकिङ्करौ ।
दर्शनं नौ भगवत ऋषेरासीदनुग्रहात् ॥३७॥

anujānīhi nau bhūmaṁs
tavānucara-kiṅkarau
darśanaṁ nau bhagavata
ṛṣer āsīd anugrahāt

anujānīhi—may we have permission; *nau*—we; *bhūman*—O greatest universal form; *tava anucara-kiṅkarau*—because of being servants of Your most confidential devotee Nārada Muni; *darśanam*—to see personally; *nau*—of us; *bhagavataḥ*—of You, the Supreme Personality of Godhead; *ṛṣeḥ*—of the great saint Nārada; *āsīt*—there was (in the form of a curse); *anugrahāt*—from the mercy.

TRANSLATION

O supreme form, we are always servants of Your servants, especially of Nārada Muni. Now give us permission to leave for our home. It is by the grace and mercy of Nārada Muni that we have been able to see You face to face.

PURPORT

Unless delivered or blessed by a devotee, one cannot realize that Kṛṣṇa is the Supreme Personality of Godhead. *Manuṣyāṇāṁ sahasreṣu kaścid yatati siddhaye.* According to this verse of *Bhagavad-gītā* (7.3), there are so many *siddhas* or *yogīs* who cannot understand Kṛṣṇa; instead, they misunderstand Him. But if one takes shelter of a devotee descending from the *paramparā* system of Nārada (*svayambhūr nāradaḥ śambhuḥ*), one can then understand who is an incarnation of the Supreme Personality of Godhead. In this age, many pseudo incarnations are advertised simply for having exhibited some magical performances, but except for persons who are servants of Nārada and other servants of Kṛṣṇa, no one can understand who is God and who is not. This is confirmed by Narottama dāsa Ṭhākura. *Chāḍiyā vaiṣṇava-sevā nistāra pāyeche kebā:* no one is delivered from the material conception of life unless favored by a Vaiṣṇava. Others can never understand, neither by speculation nor by any other bodily or mental gymnastics.

TEXT 38

वाणी गुणानुकथने श्रवणौ कथायां
हस्तौ च कर्मसु मनस्तव पादयोर्नः ।
स्मृत्यां शिरस्तव निवासजगत्प्रणामे
दृष्टिः सतां दर्शनेऽस्तु भवत्तनूनाम् ॥३८॥

vāṇī guṇānukathane śravaṇau kathāyāṁ
hastau ca karmasu manas tava pādayor naḥ
smṛtyāṁ śiras tava nivāsa-jagat-praṇāme
dṛṣṭiḥ satāṁ darśane 'stu bhavat-tanūnām

vāṇī—words, the power of speech; *guṇa-anukathane*—always engaged in talking about Your pastimes; *śravaṇau*—the ear, or aural reception; *kathāyām*—in talks about You and Your pastimes; *hastau*—hands and legs and other senses; *ca*—also; *karmasu*—engaging them in executing Your mission; *manaḥ*—the mind; *tava*—Your; *pādayoḥ*—of Your lotus feet; *naḥ*—our; *smṛtyām*—in remembrance always engaged in meditation; *śiraḥ*—the head; *tava*—Your; *nivāsa-jagat-praṇāme*—because You are all-pervading, You are everything, and our heads should bow down, not looking for enjoyment; *dṛṣṭiḥ*—the power of sight; *satām*—of the Vaiṣṇavas; *darśane*—in seeing; *astu*—let all of them be engaged in this way; *bhavat-tanūnām*—who are nondifferent from You.

TRANSLATION

Henceforward, may all our words describe Your pastimes, may our ears engage in aural reception of Your glories, may our hands, legs and other senses engage in actions pleasing to You, and may

our minds always think of Your lotus feet. May our heads offer our obeisances to everything within this world, because all things are also Your different forms, and may our eyes see the forms of Vaiṣṇavas, who are nondifferent from You.

PURPORT

Here the process of understanding the Supreme Personality of Godhead is given. This process is *bhakti.*

śravaṇaṁ kīrtanaṁ viṣṇoḥ
smaraṇaṁ pāda-sevanam
arcanaṁ vandanaṁ dāsyaṁ
sakhyam ātma-nivedanam
(*Bhāg.* 7.5.23)

Everything should be engaged in the service of the Lord. *Hṛṣīkeṇa hṛṣīkeśa-sevanaṁ bhaktir ucyate* (*Nārada-pañcarātra*). Everything—the mind, the body and all the sense organs—should be engaged in Kṛṣṇa's service. This is to be learned from expert devotees like Nārada, Svayambhū and Śambhu. This is the process. We cannot manufacture our own way of understanding the Supreme Personality of Godhead, for it is not that everything one manufactures or concocts will lead to understanding God. Such a proposition—*yata mata, tata patha*—is foolish. Kṛṣṇa says, *bhaktyāham ekayā grāhyaḥ:* "Only by executing the activities of *bhakti* can one understand Me." (*Bhāg.* 11.14.21) This is called *ānukūlyena kṛṣṇānuśīlanam*, remaining engaged favorably in the service of the Lord.

TEXT 39

श्रीशुक उवाच
इत्थं संकीर्तितस्ताभ्यां भगवान् गोकुलेश्वरः ।
दाम्ना चोलूखले बद्धः प्रहसन्नाह गुह्यकौ ॥३९॥

śrī-śuka uvāca
itthaṁ saṅkīrtitas tābhyāṁ
bhagavān gokuleśvaraḥ

dāmnā colūkhale baddhaḥ
prahasann āha guhyakau

śrī-śukaḥ uvāca—Śrī Śukadeva Gosvāmī continued to speak; *ittham*—in this way, as aforesaid; *saṅkīrtitaḥ*—being glorified and praised; *tābhyām*—by the two young demigods; *bhagavān*—the Supreme Personality of Godhead; *gokula-īśvaraḥ*—the master of Gokula (because He is *sarva-loka-maheśvara*); *dāmnā*—by the rope; *ca*—also; *ulūkhale*—on the wooden mortar; *baddhaḥ*—bound; *prahasan*—smiling; *āha*—said; *guhyakau*—unto the two young demigods.

TRANSLATION

Śukadeva Gosvāmī continued: The two young demigods thus offered prayers to the Supreme Personality of Godhead. Although Śrī Kṛṣṇa, the Supreme Godhead, is the master of all and was certainly Gokuleśvara, the master of Gokula, He was bound to the wooden mortar by the ropes of the gopīs, and therefore, smiling widely, He spoke to the sons of Kuvera the following words.

PURPORT

Kṛṣṇa was smiling because He was thinking to Himself, "These two young demigods fell from the higher planetary system to this planet, and I have delivered them from the bondage of standing for a long time as trees, but as for Me, I am bound by the ropes of the *gopīs* and am subject to their chastisements." In other words, Kṛṣṇa submits to being chastised and bound by the *gopīs* because of pure love and affection worthy of being praised by a devotee in so many ways.

TEXT 40

श्रीभगवानुवाच
ज्ञातं मम पुरैवैतदृषिणा करुणात्मना ।
यच्छ्रीमदान्धयोर्वाग्भिर्विभ्रंशोऽनुग्रहः कृतः ॥४०॥

śrī-bhagavān uvāca
jñātaṁ mama puraivaitad
ṛṣiṇā karuṇātmanā

yac chrī-madāndhayor vāgbhir
vibhraṁśo 'nugrahaḥ kṛtaḥ

śrī-bhagavān uvāca—the Supreme Personality of Godhead said; *jñātam*—everything is known; *mama*—to Me; *purā*—in the past; *eva*—indeed; *etat*—this incident; *ṛṣiṇā*—by the great sage Nārada; *karuṇā-ātmanā*—because he was very, very kind to you; *yat*—which; *śrī-mada-andhayoḥ*—who had become mad after material opulence and had thus become blind; *vāgbhiḥ*—by words or by cursing; *vibhraṁśaḥ*—falling down from the heavenly planet to become *arjuna* trees here; *anugrahaḥ kṛtaḥ*—this was a great favor done by him to you.

TRANSLATION

The Supreme Personality of Godhead said: The great saint Nārada Muni is very merciful. By his curse, he showed the greatest favor to both of you, who were mad after material opulence and who had thus become blind. Although you fell from the higher planet Svargaloka and became trees, you were most favored by him. I knew of all these incidents from the very beginning.

PURPORT

It is now confirmed by the Supreme Personality of Godhead that the curse of a devotee is also to be regarded as mercy. As Kṛṣṇa, God, is all-good, a Vaiṣṇava is also all-good. Whatever he does is good for everyone. This is explained in the following verse.

TEXT 41

साधूनां समचित्तानां सुतरां मत्कृतात्मनाम् ।
दर्शनान्नो भवेद् बन्धः पुंसोऽक्ष्णोः सवितुर्यथा ॥४१॥

sādhūnāṁ sama-cittānāṁ
sutarāṁ mat-kṛtātmanām
darśanān no bhaved bandhaḥ
puṁso 'kṣṇoḥ savitur yathā

sādhūnām—of devotees; *sama-cittānām*—who are equally disposed toward everyone; *sutarām*—excessively, completely; *mat-kṛta-ātmanām*—of persons who are fully surrendered, determined to render service unto Me; *darśanāt*—simply by the audience; *no bhavet bandhaḥ*—freedom from all material bondage; *puṁsaḥ*—of a person; *akṣṇoḥ*—of the eyes; *savituḥ yathā*—as by being face to face with the sun.

TRANSLATION

When one is face to face with the sun, there is no longer darkness for one's eyes. Similarly, when one is face to face with a sādhu, a devotee, who is fully determined and surrendered to the Supreme Personality of Godhead, one will no longer be subject to material bondage.

PURPORT

As stated by Caitanya Mahāprabhu (Cc. *Madhya* 22.54):

'sādhu-saṅga,' 'sādhu-saṅga'——sarva-śāstre kaya
lava-mātra sādhu-saṅge sarva-siddhi haya

If by chance one meets a *sādhu*, a devotee, one's life is immediately successful, and one is freed from material bondage. It may be argued that whereas someone may receive a *sādhu* with great respect, someone else may not receive a *sādhu* with such respect. A *sādhu*, however, is always equipoised toward everyone. Because of being a pure devotee, a *sādhu* is always ready to deliver Kṛṣṇa consciousness without discrimination. As soon as one sees a *sādhu*, one naturally becomes free. Nonetheless, persons who are too much offensive, who commit *vaiṣṇava-aparādhas*, or offenses to a *sādhu*, will have to take some time before being rectified. This is also indicated herein.

TEXT 42

तद् गच्छतं मत्परमौ नलकूवर सादनम् ।
सञ्जातो मयि भावो वामीप्सितः परमोऽभवः ॥४२॥

tad gacchataṁ mat-paramau
nalakūvara sādanam
sañjāto mayi bhāvo vām
īpsitaḥ paramo 'bhavaḥ

tat gacchatam—now both of you may return; *mat-paramau*—accepting Me as the supreme destination of life; *nalakūvara*—O Nalakūvara and Maṇigrīva; *sādanam*—to your home; *sañjātaḥ*—being saturated with; *mayi*—unto Me; *bhāvaḥ*—devotional service; *vām*—by you; *īpsitaḥ*—which was desired; *paramaḥ*—supreme, highest, always engaged with all senses; *abhavaḥ*—from which there is no falldown into material existence.

TRANSLATION

O Nalakūvara and Maṇigrīva, now you may both return home. Since you desire to be always absorbed in My devotional service, your desire to develop love and affection for Me will be fulfilled, and now you will never fall from that platform.

PURPORT

The highest perfection of life is to come to the platform of devotional service and always engage in devotional activities. Understanding this, Nalakūvara and Maṇigrīva desired to attain that platform, and the Supreme Personality of Godhead blessed them with the fulfillment of their transcendental desire.

TEXT 43

श्रीशुक उवाच
इत्युक्तौ तौ परिक्रम्य प्रणम्य च पुनः पुनः ।
बद्धोलूखलमामन्त्र्य जग्मतुर्दिशमुत्तराम् ॥४३॥

śrī-śuka uvāca
ity uktau tau parikramya
praṇamya ca punaḥ punaḥ
baddholūkhalam āmantrya
jagmatur diśam uttarām

śrī-śukaḥ uvāca—Śrī Śukadeva Gosvāmī said; *iti uktau*—having been ordered by the Supreme Personality of Godhead in this way; *tau*—Nalakūvara and Maṇigrīva; *parikramya*—circumambulating; *praṇamya*—offering obeisances; *ca*—also; *punaḥ punaḥ*—again and again; *baddha-ulūkhalam āmantrya*—taking the permission of the Supreme Personality of Godhead, who was bound to the wooden mortar; *jagmatuḥ*—departed; *diśam uttarām*—to their respective destinations.

TRANSLATION

Śukadeva Gosvāmī said: The Supreme Personality of Godhead having spoken to the two demigods in this way, they circumambulated the Lord, who was bound to the wooden mortar, and offered obeisances to Him. After taking the permission of Lord Kṛṣṇa, they returned to their respective homes.

Thus end the Bhaktivedanta purports of the Tenth Canto, Tenth Chapter, of the Śrīmad-Bhāgavatam, *entitled "Deliverance of the Yamala-arjuna Trees."*

CHAPTER ELEVEN

The Childhood Pastimes of Kṛṣṇa

This chapter describes how the inhabitants of Gokula left Gokula and went to Vṛndāvana and how Kṛṣṇa killed Vatsāsura and Bakāsura.

When the *yamala-arjuna* trees fell, they made a tremendous sound, like that of falling thunderbolts. Being surprised, Kṛṣṇa's father, Nanda, and the other elderly inhabitants of Gokula went to the spot, where they saw the fallen trees and Kṛṣṇa standing between them, bound to the *ulūkhala,* the wooden mortar. They could find no cause for the trees' having fallen and Kṛṣṇa's being there. They thought this might be the work of some other *asura* who had met Kṛṣṇa on this spot, and they inquired from the playmates of Kṛṣṇa about how the whole incident had taken place. The children properly described how everything had happened, but the elderly persons could not believe the story. Some of them, however, thought that it might be true, since they had already seen many wonderful incidents in connection with Kṛṣṇa. Anyway, Nanda Mahārāja immediately released Kṛṣṇa from the ropes.

In this way, Kṛṣṇa, at every day and every moment, displayed wonderful incidents to increase the parental affection of Nanda Mahārāja and Yaśodā, who thus felt both surprise and joy. The breaking of the *yamala-arjunas* was one of these wonderful pastimes.

One day a fruit vendor approached Nanda Mahārāja's house, and Kṛṣṇa gathered some food grains with His little palms and went to the vendor to exchange the grains for fruit. On the way, almost all the grains fell from His palms, only one or two grains remaining, but the fruit vendor, out of full affection, accepted these grains in exchange for as much fruit as Kṛṣṇa could take. As soon as she did this, her basket became filled with gold and jewels.

Thereafter, all the elderly *gopas* decided to leave Gokula because they saw that in Gokula there was always some disturbance. They decided to go to Vṛndāvana, Vraja-dhāma, and the next day they all departed. In Vṛndāvana, both Kṛṣṇa and Balarāma, after finishing Their childhood pastimes, began to take charge of the calves and send them to the pasturing grounds (*go-caraṇa*). During this time, a demon named Vatsāsura entered among the calves and was killed, and another *asura*, in the shape of a big duck, was also killed. The playmates of Kṛṣṇa narrated all these stories to their mothers. The mothers could not believe their children, Kṛṣṇa's playmates, but because of full affection they enjoyed these narrations of Kṛṣṇa's activities.

TEXT 1

श्रीशुक उवाच
गोपा नन्दादयः श्रुत्वा द्रुमयोः पततोरवम् ।
तत्राजग्मुः कुरुश्रेष्ठ निर्घातभयशङ्किताः ॥ १ ॥

śrī-śuka uvāca
gopā nandādayaḥ śrutvā
drumayoḥ patato ravam
tatrājagmuḥ kuru-śreṣṭha
nirghāta-bhaya-śaṅkitāḥ

śrī-śukaḥ uvāca—Śrī Śukadeva Gosvāmī said; *gopāḥ*—all the cowherd men; *nanda-ādayaḥ*—headed by Nanda Mahārāja; *śrutvā*—hearing; *drumayoḥ*—of the two trees; *patatoḥ*—falling down; *ravam*—the high sound, as terrible as a thunderbolt; *tatra*—there, on the spot; *ājagmuḥ*—went; *kuru-śreṣṭha*—O Mahārāja Parīkṣit; *nirghāta-bhaya-śaṅkitāḥ*—who were afraid of falling thunderbolts.

TRANSLATION

Śukadeva Gosvāmī continued: O Mahārāja Parīkṣit, when the yamala-arjuna trees fell, all the cowherd men in the neighborhood, hearing the fierce sound and fearing thunderbolts, went to the spot.

TEXT 2

भूम्यां निपतितौ तत्र ददृशुर्यमलार्जुनौ ।
बभ्रमुस्तदविज्ञाय लक्ष्यं पतनकारणम् ॥ २ ॥

bhūmyāṁ nipatitau tatra
dadṛśur yamalārjunau

babhramus tad avijñāya
lakṣyaṁ patana-kāraṇam

bhūmyām—on the ground; *nipatitau*—which had fallen; *tatra*—there; *dadṛśuḥ*—all of them saw; *yamala-arjunau*—the twin *arjuna* trees; *babhramuḥ*—they became bewildered; *tat*—that; *avijñāya*—but they could not trace out; *lakṣyam*—although they could directly perceive that the trees had fallen; *patana-kāraṇam*—the cause of their falling (how could it have happened all of a sudden?).

TRANSLATION

There they saw the fallen yamala-arjuna trees on the ground, but they were bewildered because even though they could directly perceive that the trees had fallen, they could not trace out the cause for their having done so.

PURPORT

Considering all the circumstances, had this been done by Kṛṣṇa? He was standing on the spot, and His playmates described that this had been done by Him. Had Kṛṣṇa actually done this, or were these merely stories? This was a cause of bewilderment.

TEXT 3

उलूखलं विकर्षन्तं दाम्ना बद्धं च बालकम् ।
कस्येदं कुत आश्चर्यमुत्पात इति कातराः ॥ ३ ॥

ulūkhalaṁ vikarṣantaṁ
dāmnā baddhaṁ ca bālakam
kasyedaṁ kuta āścaryam
utpāta iti kātarāḥ

ulūkhalam—the wooden mortar; *vikarṣantam*—dragging; *dāmnā*—with the rope; *baddham ca*—and bound by the belly; *bālakam*—Kṛṣṇa; *kasya*—of whom; *idam*—this; *kutaḥ*—wherefrom; *āścaryam*—these wonderful happenings; *utpātaḥ*—disturbance; *iti*—thus; *kātarāḥ*—they were very much agitated.

TRANSLATION

Kṛṣṇa was bound by the rope to the ulūkhala, the mortar, which He was dragging. But how could He have pulled down the trees? Who had actually done it? Where was the source for this incident? Considering all these astounding things, the cowherd men were doubtful and bewildered.

PURPORT

The cowherd men were very much agitated because the child Kṛṣṇa, after all, had been standing between the two trees, and if by chance the trees had fallen upon Him, He would have been smashed. But He was standing as He was, and still the things had happened, so who had done all this? How could these events have happened in such a wonderful way? These considerations were some of the reasons they were agitated and bewildered. They thought, however, that by chance Kṛṣṇa had been saved by God so that nothing had happened to Him.

TEXT 4

बाला ऊचुरनेनेति तिर्यग्गतमुलूखलम् ।
विकर्षता मध्यगेन पुरुषावप्यचक्ष्महि ॥ ४ ॥

bālā ūcur aneneti
tiryag-gatam ulūkhalam
vikarṣatā madhya-gena
puruṣāv apy acakṣmahi

bālāḥ—all the other boys; *ūcuḥ*—said; *anena*—by Him (Kṛṣṇa); *iti*—thus; *tiryak*—crosswise; *gatam*—which had become; *ulūkhalam*—the wooden mortar; *vikarṣatā*—by Kṛṣṇa, who was dragging; *madhya-gena*—going between the two trees; *puruṣau*—two beautiful persons; *api*—also; *acakṣmahi*—we have seen with our own eyes.

TRANSLATION

Then all the cowherd boys said: It is Kṛṣṇa who has done this. When He was in between the two trees, the mortar fell crosswise. Kṛṣṇa dragged the mortar, and the two trees fell down. After that,

two beautiful men came out of the trees. We have seen this with our own eyes.

PURPORT

Kṛṣṇa's playmates wanted to inform Kṛṣṇa's father of the exact situation by explaining that not only did the trees break, but out of the broken trees came two beautiful men. "All these things happened," they said. "We have seen them with our own eyes."

TEXT 5

न ते तदुक्तं जगृहुर्न घटेतेति तस्य तत् ।
बालस्योत्पाटनं तर्वोः केचित् सन्दिग्धचेतसः ॥ ५ ॥

na te tad-uktaṁ jagṛhur
na ghaṭeteti tasya tat
bālasyotpāṭanaṁ tarvoḥ
kecit sandigdha-cetasaḥ

na—not; *te*—all the *gopas; tat-uktam*—being spoken by the boys; *jagṛhuḥ*—would accept; *na ghaṭeta*—it cannot be; *iti*—thus; *tasya*—of Kṛṣṇa; *tat*—the activity; *bālasya*—of a small boy like Kṛṣṇa; *utpāṭanam*—the uprooting; *tarvoḥ*—of the two trees; *kecit*—some of them; *sandigdha-cetasaḥ*—became doubtful about what could be done (because Gargamuni had predicted that this child would be equal to Nārāyaṇa).

TRANSLATION

Because of intense paternal affection, the cowherd men, headed by Nanda, could not believe that Kṛṣṇa could have uprooted the trees in such a wonderful way. Therefore they could not put their faith in the words of the boys. Some of the men, however, were in doubt. "Since Kṛṣṇa was predicted to equal Nārāyaṇa," they thought, "it might be that He could have done it."

PURPORT

One view was that it was impossible for a small boy like this to have done such a thing as pulling down the trees. But there were doubts because Kṛṣṇa had been predicted to equal Nārāyaṇa. Therefore the cowherd men were in a dilemma.

TEXT 6

उलूखलं विकर्षन्तं दाम्ना बद्धं स्वमात्मजम् ।
विलोक्य नन्दः प्रहसद्वदनो विमुमोच ह ॥ ६ ॥

ulūkhalaṁ vikarṣantaṁ
dāmnā baddhaṁ svam ātmajam
vilokya nandaḥ prahasad-
vadano vimumoca ha

ulūkhalam—the wooden mortar; *vikarṣantam*—dragging; *dāmnā*—by the rope; *baddham*—bound; *svam ātmajam*—his own son Kṛṣṇa; *vilokya*—by seeing; *nandaḥ*—Mahārāja Nanda; *prahasat-vadanaḥ*—whose face began to smile when he saw the wonderful child; *vimumoca ha*—released Him from the bonds.

TRANSLATION

When Nanda Mahārāja saw his own son bound with ropes to the wooden mortar and dragging it, he smiled and released Kṛṣṇa from His bonds.

PURPORT

Nanda Mahārāja was surprised that Yaśodā, Kṛṣṇa's mother, could have bound her beloved child in such a way. Kṛṣṇa was exchanging love with her. How then could she have been so cruel as to bind Him to the wooden mortar? Nanda Mahārāja understood this exchange of love, and therefore he smiled and released Kṛṣṇa. In other words, as Kṛṣṇa, the Supreme Personality of Godhead, binds a living entity in fruitive activities, He binds mother Yaśodā and Nanda Mahārāja in parental affection. This is His pastime.

TEXT 7

गोपीभिः स्तोभितोऽनृत्यद् भगवान् बालवत् क्वचित् ।
उद्गायति क्वचिन्मुग्धस्तद्वशो दारुयन्त्रवत् ॥ ७ ॥

gopībhiḥ stobhito 'nṛtyad
bhagavān bālavat kvacit
udgāyati kvacin mugdhas
tad-vaśo dāru-yantravat

gopībhiḥ—by the *gopīs* (by flattery and offers of prizes); *stobhitaḥ*—encouraged, induced; *anṛtyat*—the small Kṛṣṇa danced; *bhagavān*—although He was the Supreme Personality of Godhead; *bāla-vat*—exactly like a human child; *kvacit*—sometimes; *udgāyati*—He would sing very loudly; *kvacit*—sometimes; *mugdhaḥ*—being amazed; *tat-vaśaḥ*—under their control; *dāru-yantra-vat*—like a wooden doll.

TRANSLATION

The gopīs would say, "If You dance, my dear Kṛṣṇa, then I shall give You half a sweetmeat." By saying these words or by clapping their hands, all the gopīs encouraged Kṛṣṇa in different ways. At such times, although He was the supremely powerful Personality of Godhead, He would smile and dance according to their desire, as if He were a wooden doll in their hands. Sometimes He would sing very loudly, at their bidding. In this way, Kṛṣṇa came completely under the control of the gopīs.

TEXT 8

बिभर्ति क्वचिदाज्ञप्तः पीठकोन्मानपादुकम् ।
बाहुक्षेपं च कुरुते स्वानां च प्रीतिमावहन् ॥ ८ ॥

bibharti kvacid ājñaptaḥ
pīṭhakonmāna-pādukam
bāhu-kṣepaṁ ca kurute
svānāṁ ca prītim āvahan

bibharti—Kṛṣṇa would simply stand and touch articles as if unable to raise them; *kvacit*—sometimes; *ājñaptaḥ*—being ordered; *pīṭhaka-unmāna*—the wooden seat and wooden measuring pot; *pādukam*—bringing the wooden shoes; *bāhu-kṣepam ca*—striking the arms on the body; *kurute*—does; *svānām ca*—of His own relatives, the *gopīs* and other intimate friends; *prītim*—the pleasure; *āvahan*—inviting.

TRANSLATION

Sometimes mother Yaśodā and her gopī friends would tell Kṛṣṇa, "Bring this article" or "Bring that article." Sometimes they would order Him to bring a wooden plank, wooden shoes or a wooden measuring pot, and Kṛṣṇa, when thus ordered by the mothers, would try to bring them. Sometimes, however, as if unable to raise these things, He would touch them and stand there. Just to invite the pleasure of His relatives, He would strike His body with His arms to show that He had sufficient strength.

TEXT 9

दर्शयंस्तद्विदां लोक आत्मनो भृत्यवश्यताम् ।
व्रजस्योवाह वै हर्षं भगवान् बालचेष्टितैः ॥ ९ ॥

darśayaṁs tad-vidāṁ loka
ātmano bhṛtya-vaśyatām
vrajasyovāha vai harṣaṁ
bhagavān bāla-ceṣṭitaiḥ

darśayan—exhibiting; *tat-vidām*—unto persons who can understand Kṛṣṇa's activities; *loke*—throughout the whole world; *ātmanaḥ*—of Himself; *bhṛtya-vaśyatām*—how He is agreeable to carrying out the orders of His servants, His devotees; *vrajasya*—of Vrajabhūmi; *uvāha*—executed; *vai*—indeed; *harṣam*—pleasure; *bhagavān*—the Supreme Personality of Godhead; *bāla-ceṣṭitaiḥ*—by His activities like those of a child trying to do so many things.

TRANSLATION

To pure devotees throughout the world who could understand His activities, the Supreme Personality of Godhead, Kṛṣṇa, exhibited how much He can be subdued by His devotees, His servants. In this way He increased the pleasure of the Vrajavāsīs by His childhood activities.

PURPORT

That Kṛṣṇa performed childhood activities to increase the pleasure of His devotees was another transcendental humor. He exhibited these activities not only to the inhabitants of Vrajabhūmi, but also to others, who were captivated by His external potency and opulence. Both the internal devotees, who were simply absorbed in love of Kṛṣṇa, and the external devotees, who were captivated by His unlimited potency, were informed of Kṛṣṇa's desire to be submissive to His servants.

TEXT 10

क्रीणीहि भोः फलानीति श्रुत्वा सत्वरमच्युतः ।
फलार्थी धान्यमादाय ययौ सर्वफलप्रदः ॥१०॥

krīṇīhi bhoḥ phalānīti
śrutvā satvaram acyutaḥ
phalārthī dhānyam ādāya
yayau sarva-phala-pradaḥ

krīṇīhi—please come and purchase; *bhoḥ*—O neighborhood residents; *phalāni*—ripe fruits; *iti*—thus; *śrutvā*—hearing; *satvaram*—very soon; *acyutaḥ*—Kṛṣṇa; *phala-arthī*—as if He wanted some fruits; *dhānyam ādāya*—capturing some grains of paddy; *yayau*—went to the fruit vendor; *sarva-phala-pradaḥ*—the Supreme Personality of Godhead, who can give all kinds of fruit to everyone, had now become in need of fruits.

TRANSLATION

Once a woman selling fruit was calling, "O inhabitants of Vrajabhūmi, if you want to purchase some fruits, come here!" Upon hearing this, Kṛṣṇa immediately took some grains and went to barter as if He needed some fruits.

PURPORT

Aborigines generally go to the villagers to sell fruits. How much the aborigines were attached to Kṛṣṇa is here described. Kṛṣṇa, to show His favor to the aborigines, would immediately go purchase fruits, bartering with paddy in His hand as He had seen others do.

TEXT 11

फलविक्रयिणी तस्य च्युतधान्यकरद्वयम् ।
फलैरपूरयद् रत्नैः फलभाण्डमपूरि च ॥११॥

phala-vikrayiṇī tasya
cyuta-dhānya-kara-dvayam
phalair apūrayad ratnaiḥ
phala-bhāṇḍam apūri ca

phala-vikrayiṇī—the aborigine fruit vendor, who was an elderly woman; *tasya*—of Kṛṣṇa; *cyuta-dhānya*—the paddy He brought to barter having mostly fallen; *kara-dvayam*—palms of the hands; *phalaiḥ apūrayat*—the fruit vendor filled His small palms with fruits; *ratnaiḥ*—in exchange for jewels and gold; *phala-bhāṇḍam*—the basket of fruit; *apūri ca*—filled.

TRANSLATION

While Kṛṣṇa was going to the fruit vendor very hastily, most of the grains He was holding fell. Nonetheless, the fruit vendor filled Kṛṣṇa's hands with fruits, and her fruit basket was immediately filled with jewels and gold.

PURPORT

In *Bhagavad-gītā* (9.26) Kṛṣṇa says:

patraṁ puṣpaṁ phalaṁ toyaṁ
yo me bhaktyā prayacchati
tad ahaṁ bhakty-upahṛtam
aśnāmi prayatātmanaḥ

Kṛṣṇa is so kind that if anyone offers Him a leaf, a fruit, a flower or some water, He will immediately accept it. The only condition is that these things should be offered with *bhakti* (*yo me bhaktyā prayacchati*).

Otherwise, if one is puffed up with false prestige, thinking, "I have so much opulence, and I am giving something to Kṛṣṇa," one's offering will not be accepted by Kṛṣṇa. The fruit vendor, although a woman belonging to the poor aborigine class, dealt with Kṛṣṇa with great affection, saying, "Kṛṣṇa, You have come to me to take some fruit in exchange for grains. All the grains have fallen, but still You may take whatever You like." Thus she filled Kṛṣṇa's palms with whatever fruits He could carry. In exchange, Kṛṣṇa filled her whole basket with jewels and gold.

From this incident one should learn that for anything offered to Kṛṣṇa with love and affection, Kṛṣṇa can reciprocate many millions of times over, both materially and spiritually. The basic principle involved is an exchange of love. Therefore Kṛṣṇa teaches in *Bhagavad-gītā* (9.27):

yat karoṣi yad aśnāsi
yaj juhoṣi dadāsi yat
yat tapasyasi kaunteya
tat kuruṣva mad-arpaṇam

"O son of Kuntī, all that you do, all that you eat, all that you offer and give away, as well as all austerities that you may perform, should be done as an offering unto Me." With love and affection, one should try to give something to Kṛṣṇa from one's source of income. Then one's life will be successful. Kṛṣṇa is full in all opulences; He does not need anything from anyone. But if one is prepared to give something to Kṛṣṇa, that is for one's own benefit. The example given in this connection is that when one's real face is decorated, the reflection of one's face is automatically decorated. Similarly, if we try to serve Kṛṣṇa with all our opulences, we, as parts and parcels or reflections of Kṛṣṇa, will become happy in exchange. Kṛṣṇa is always happy, for He is *ātmārāma*, fully satisfied with His own opulence.

TEXT 12

सरित्तीरगतं कृष्णं भग्नार्जुनमथाह्वयत् ।
रामं च रोहिणी देवी क्रीडन्तं बालकैर्भृशम् ॥१२॥

sarit-tīra-gataṁ kṛṣṇaṁ
bhagnārjunam athāhvayat

rāmaṁ ca rohiṇī devī
krīḍantaṁ bālakair bhṛśam

sarit-tīra—to the riverside; *gatam*—who had gone; *kṛṣṇam*—unto Kṛṣṇa; *bhagna-arjunam*—after the pastime of breaking the *yamala-arjuna* trees; *atha*—then; *āhvayat*—called; *rāmam ca*—as well as Balarāma; *rohiṇī*—the mother of Balarāma; *devī*—the goddess of fortune; *krīḍantam*—who were engaged in playing; *bālakaiḥ*—with many other boys; *bhṛśam*—with deep attention.

TRANSLATION

Once, after the uprooting of the yamala-arjuna trees, Rohiṇī-devī went to call Rāma and Kṛṣṇa, who had both gone to the riverside and were playing with the other boys with deep attention.

PURPORT

Mother Yaśodā was more attached to Kṛṣṇa and Balarāma than Rohiṇīdevī was, although Rohiṇīdevī was the mother of Balarāma. Mother Yaśodā sent Rohiṇīdevī to call Rāma and Kṛṣṇa from Their play, since it was the right time for lunch. Therefore Rohiṇīdevī went to call Them, breaking Their engagement in play.

TEXT 13

नोपेयातां यदाहूतौ क्रीडासङ्गेन पुत्रकौ ।
यशोदां प्रेषयामास रोहिणी पुत्रवत्सलाम् ॥१३॥

nopeyātāṁ yadāhūtau
krīḍā-saṅgena putrakau
yaśodāṁ preṣayām āsa
rohiṇī putra-vatsalām

na upeyātām—would not return home; *yadā*—when; *āhūtau*—They were called back from playing; *krīḍā-saṅgena*—because of so much attachment to playing with other boys; *putrakau*—the two sons (Kṛṣṇa and Balarāma); *yaśodām preṣayām āsa*—sent mother Yaśodā to call Them;

rohiṇī—mother Rohiṇī; *putra-vatsalām*—because mother Yaśodā was a more affectionate mother to Kṛṣṇa and Balarāma.

TRANSLATION

Because of being too attached to playing with the other boys, Kṛṣṇa and Balarāma did not return upon being called by Rohiṇī. Therefore Rohiṇī sent mother Yaśodā to call Them back, because mother Yaśodā was more affectionate to Kṛṣṇa and Balarāma.

PURPORT

Yaśodāṁ preṣayām āsa. These very words show that since Kṛṣṇa and Balarāma did not care to return in response to the order of Rohiṇī, Rohiṇī thought that if Yaśodā called They would have to return, for Yaśodā was more affectionate to Kṛṣṇa and Balarāma.

TEXT 14

क्रीडन्तं सा सुतं बालैरतिवेलं सहाग्रजम् ।
यशोदाजोहवीत् कृष्णं पुत्रस्नेहस्नुतस्तनी ॥१४॥

krīḍantaṁ sā sutaṁ bālair
ativelaṁ sahāgrajam
yaśodājohavīt kṛṣṇaṁ
putra-sneha-snuta-stanī

krīḍantam—engaged in playing; *sā*—mother Yaśodā; *sutam*—her son; *bālaiḥ*—with the other boys; *ati-velam*—although it was too late; *saha-agrajam*—who was playing with His elder brother, Balarāma; *yaśodā*—mother Yaśodā; *ajohavīt*—called ("Kṛṣṇa and Balarāma, come here!"); *kṛṣṇam*—unto Kṛṣṇa; *putra-sneha-snuta-stanī*—while she was calling Them, milk flowed from her breast because of her ecstatic love and affection.

TRANSLATION

Kṛṣṇa and Balarāma, being attached to Their play, were playing with the other boys although it was very late. Therefore mother Yaśodā called Them back for lunch. Because of her ecstatic love

and affection for Kṛṣṇa and Balarāma, milk flowed from her breasts.

PURPORT

The word *ajohavīt* means "calling them again and again." "Kṛṣṇa and Balarāma," she called, "please come back. You are late for Your lunch. You have played sufficiently. Come back."

TEXT 15

कृष्ण कृष्णारविन्दाक्ष तात एहि स्तनं पिब ।
अलं विहारैः क्षुत्क्षान्तः क्रीडाश्रान्तोऽसि पुत्रक ॥१५॥

kṛṣṇa kṛṣṇāravindākṣa
tāta ehi stanaṁ piba
alaṁ vihāraiḥ kṣut-kṣāntaḥ
krīḍā-śrānto 'si putraka

kṛṣṇa kṛṣṇa aravinda-akṣa—O Kṛṣṇa, my son, lotus-eyed Kṛṣṇa; *tāta*—O darling; *ehi*—come here; *stanam*—the milk of my breast; *piba*—drink; *alam vihāraiḥ*—after this there is no necessity of playing; *kṣut-kṣāntaḥ*—tired because of hunger; *krīḍā-śrāntaḥ*—fatigued from playing; *asi*—You must be; *putraka*—O my son.

TRANSLATION

Mother Yaśodā said: My dear son Kṛṣṇa, lotus-eyed Kṛṣṇa, come here and drink the milk of my breast. My dear darling, You must be very tired because of hunger and the fatigue of playing so long. There is no need to play any more.

TEXT 16

हे रामागच्छ ताताशु सानुजः कुलनन्दन ।
प्रातरेव कृताहारस्तद् भवान् भोक्तुमर्हति ॥१६॥

he rāmāgaccha tātāśu
sānujaḥ kula-nandana

prātar eva kṛtāhāras
tad bhavān bhoktum arhati

he rāma—my dear son Balarāma; *āgaccha*—please come here; *tāta*—my dear darling; *āśu*—immediately; *sa-anujaḥ*—with Your younger brother; *kula-nandana*—the great hope of our family; *prātaḥ eva*—certainly in the morning; *kṛta-āhāraḥ*—have taken Your breakfast; *tat*—therefore; *bhavān*—You; *bhoktum*—to eat something more; *arhati*—deserve.

TRANSLATION

My dear Baladeva, best of our family, please come immediately with Your younger brother, Kṛṣṇa. You both ate in the morning, and now You ought to eat something more.

TEXT 17

प्रतीक्षते त्वां दाशार्ह भोक्ष्यमाणो व्रजाधिपः ।
एह्यावयोः प्रियं धेहि स्वगृहान् यात बालकाः ॥१७॥

pratīkṣate tvāṁ dāśārha
bhokṣyamāṇo vrajādhipaḥ
ehy āvayoḥ priyaṁ dhehi
sva-gṛhān yāta bālakāḥ

pratīkṣate—is waiting; *tvām*—for both of You (Kṛṣṇa and Balarāma); *dāśārha*—O Balarāma; *bhokṣyamāṇaḥ*—desiring to eat; *vraja-adhipaḥ*—the King of Vraja, Nanda Mahārāja; *ehi*—come here; *āvayoḥ*—our; *priyam*—pleasure; *dhehi*—just consider; *sva-gṛhān*—to their respective homes; *yāta*—let them go; *bālakāḥ*—the other boys.

TRANSLATION

Nanda Mahārāja, the King of Vraja, is now waiting to eat. O my dear son Balarāma, he is waiting for You. Therefore, come back to please us. All the boys playing with You and Kṛṣṇa should now go to their homes.

PURPORT

It appears that Nanda Mahārāja regularly took his food with his two sons, Kṛṣṇa and Balarāma. Yaśodā told the other boys, "Now you should go to your homes." Father and son generally sit together, so mother Yaśodā requested Kṛṣṇa and Balarāma to return, and she advised the other boys to go home so that their parents would not have to wait for them.

TEXT 18

धूलिधूसरिताङ्गस्त्वं पुत्र मज्जनमावह ।
जन्मर्क्षं तेऽद्य भवति विप्रेभ्यो देहि गाः शुचिः ॥१८॥

dhūli-dhūsaritāṅgas tvaṁ
putra majjanam āvaha
janmarkṣaṁ te 'dya bhavati
viprebhyo dehi gāḥ śuciḥ

dhūli-dhūsarita-aṅgaḥ tvam—You have become covered with dust and sand all over Your body; *putra*—my dear son; *majjanam āvaha*—now come here, take Your bath and cleanse Yourself; *janma-ṛkṣam*—the auspicious star of Your birth; *te*—of You; *adya*—today; *bhavati*—it is; *viprebhyaḥ*—unto the pure *brāhmaṇas; dehi*—give in charity; *gāḥ*—cows; *śuciḥ*—being purified.

TRANSLATION

Mother Yaśodā further told Kṛṣṇa: My dear son, because of playing all day, Your body has become covered with dust and sand. Therefore, come back, take Your bath and cleanse Yourself. Today the moon is conjoined with the auspicious star of Your birth. Therefore, be pure and give cows in charity to the brāhmaṇas.

PURPORT

It is a custom of Vedic culture that whenever there is any auspicious ceremony, one should give valuable cows in charity to the *brāhmaṇas.* Therefore mother Yaśodā requested Kṛṣṇa, "Instead of being enthusiastic in playing, now please come and be enthusiastic in charity."

Yajña-dāna-tapaḥ-karma na tyājyaṁ kāryam eva tat. As advised in *Bhagavad-gītā* (18.5), sacrifice, charity and austerity should never be given up. *Yajño dānaṁ tapaś caiva pāvanāni manīṣiṇām:* even if one is very much advanced in spiritual life, one should not give up these three duties. To observe one's birthday ceremony, one should do something in terms of one of these three items (*yajña, dāna* or *tapaḥ*), or all of them together.

TEXT 19

पश्य पश्य वयस्यांस्ते मातृमृष्टान् स्वलङ्कृतान् ।
त्वं च स्नातः कृताहारो विहरस्व स्वलङ्कृतः ॥१९॥

paśya paśya vayasyāṁs te
mātṛ-mṛṣṭān svalaṅkṛtān
tvaṁ ca snātaḥ kṛtāhāro
viharasva svalaṅkṛtaḥ

paśya paśya—just see, just see; *vayasyān*—boys of Your age; *te*—Your; *mātṛ-mṛṣṭān*—cleansed by their mothers; *su-alaṅkṛtān*—decorated with nice ornaments; *tvam ca*—You also; *snātaḥ*—after taking a bath; *kṛta-āhāraḥ*—and eating Your lunch; *viharasva*—enjoy with them; *su-alaṅkṛtaḥ*—fully decorated like them.

TRANSLATION

Just see how all Your playmates of Your own age have been cleansed and decorated with beautiful ornaments by their mothers. You should come here, and after You have taken Your bath, eaten Your lunch and been decorated with ornaments, You may play with Your friends again.

PURPORT

Generally young boys are competitive. If one friend has done something, another friend also wants to do something. Therefore mother Yaśodā pointed out how Kṛṣṇa's playmates were decorated, so that Kṛṣṇa might be induced to decorate Himself like them.

TEXT 20

इत्थं यशोदा तमशेषशेखरं
मत्वा सुतं स्नेहनिबद्धधीर्नृप ।
हस्ते गृहीत्वा सहराममच्युतं
नीत्वा स्ववाटं कृतवत्यथोदयम् ॥२०॥

ittham yaśodā tam aśeṣa-śekharaṁ
matvā sutaṁ sneha-nibaddha-dhīr nṛpa
haste gṛhītvā saha-rāmam acyutaṁ
nītvā sva-vāṭaṁ kṛtavaty athodayam

ittham—in this way; *yaśodā*—mother Yaśodā; *tam aśeṣa-śekharam*—unto Kṛṣṇa, who was on the peak of everything auspicious, with no question of dirtiness or uncleanliness; *matvā*—considering; *sutam*—as her son; *sneha-nibaddha-dhīḥ*—because of an intense spirit of love; *nṛpa*—O King (Mahārāja Parīkṣit); *haste*—in the hand; *gṛhītvā*—taking; *saha-rāmam*—with Balarāma; *acyutam*—Kṛṣṇa, the infallible; *nītvā*—bringing; *sva-vāṭam*—at home; *kṛtavatī*—performed; *atha*—now; *udayam*—brilliancy by bathing Him, dressing Him and decorating Him with ornaments.

TRANSLATION

My dear Mahārāja Parīkṣit, because of intense love and affection, mother Yaśodā, Kṛṣṇa's mother, considered Kṛṣṇa, who was at the peak of all opulences, to be her own son. Thus she took Kṛṣṇa by the hand, along with Balarāma, and brought Them home, where she performed her duties by fully bathing Them, dressing Them and feeding Them.

PURPORT

Kṛṣṇa is always neat, clean and opulent and does not need to be washed, bathed or dressed, yet mother Yaśodā, because of affection, considered Him her ordinary child and did her duties to keep her son brilliant.

TEXT 21

श्रीशुक उवाच
गोपवृद्धा महोत्पातानतुभूय बृहद्वने ।
नन्दादयः समागम्य व्रजकार्यममन्त्रयन् ॥२१॥

śrī-śuka uvāca
gopa-vṛddhā mahotpātān
anubhūya bṛhadvane
nandādayaḥ samāgamya
vraja-kāryam amantrayan

śrī-śukaḥ uvāca—Śrī Śukadeva Gosvāmī said; *gopa-vṛddhāḥ*—the elderly persons among the cowherd men; *mahā-utpātān*—very great disturbances; *anubhūya*—after experiencing; *bṛhadvane*—in the place known as Bṛhadvana; *nanda-ādayaḥ*—the cowherd men, headed by Nanda Mahārāja; *samāgamya*—assembled, came together; *vraja-kāryam*—the business of Vrajabhūmi; *amantrayan*—deliberated on how to stop the continuous disturbances in Mahāvana.

TRANSLATION

Śrī Śukadeva Gosvāmī continued: Then one time, having seen the great disturbances in Bṛhadvana, all the elderly persons among the cowherd men, headed by Nanda Mahārāja, assembled and began to consider what to do to stop the continuous disturbing situations in Vraja.

TEXT 22

तत्रोपानन्दनामाह गोपो ज्ञानवयोऽधिकः ।
देशकालार्थतत्त्वज्ञः प्रियकृद् रामकृष्णयोः ॥२२॥

tatropānanda-nāmāha
gopo jñāna-vayo-'dhikaḥ
deśa-kālārtha-tattva-jñaḥ
priya-kṛd rāma-kṛṣṇayoḥ

tatra—in the assembly; *upānanda-nāmā*—by the name Upānanda (the elder brother of Nanda Mahārāja); *āha*—said; *gopaḥ*—the cowherd man; *jñāna-vayaḥ-adhikaḥ*—who by knowledge and by age was the eldest of all; *deśa-kāla-artha-tattva-jñaḥ*—very experienced according to time, place and circumstances; *priya-kṛt*—just for the benefit; *rāma-kṛṣṇayoḥ*—of Balarāma and Kṛṣṇa, the Supreme Personalities of Godhead.

TRANSLATION

At this meeting of all the inhabitants of Gokula, a cowherd man named Upānanda, who was the most mature in age and knowledge and was very experienced according to time, circumstances and country, made this suggestion for the benefit of Rāma and Kṛṣṇa.

TEXT 23

उत्थातव्यमितोऽस्माभिर्गोकुलस्य हितैषिभिः ।
आयान्त्यत्र महोत्पाता बालानां नाशहेतवः ॥२३॥

utthātavyam ito 'smābhir
gokulasya hitaiṣibhiḥ
āyānty atra mahotpātā
bālānāṁ nāśa-hetavaḥ

utthātavyam—now this place should be left; *itaḥ*—from here, from Gokula; *asmābhiḥ*—by all of us; *gokulasya*—of this place, Gokula; *hita-eṣibhiḥ*—by persons who desire good for this place; *āyānti*—are happening; *atra*—here; *mahā-utpātāḥ*—many great disturbances; *bālānām*—for the boys like Rāma and Kṛṣṇa; *nāśa-hetavaḥ*—having the definite purpose of killing Them.

TRANSLATION

He said: My dear friends the cowherd men, in order to do good to this place, Gokula, we should leave it, because so many disturbances are always occurring here, just for the purpose of killing Rāma and Kṛṣṇa.

TEXT 24

मुक्तः कथञ्चिद् राक्षस्या बालघ्न्या बालको ह्यसौ ।
हरेरनुग्रहान्नूनमनश्चोपरि नापतत् ॥२४॥

muktaḥ kathañcid rākṣasyā
bāla-ghnyā bālako hy asau
harer anugrahān nūnam
anaś copari nāpatat

muktaḥ—was delivered; *kathañcit*—somehow or other; *rākṣasyāḥ*—from the hands of the Rākṣasī Pūtanā; *bāla-ghnyāḥ*—who was determined to kill small children; *bālakaḥ*—especially the child Kṛṣṇa; *hi*—because; *asau*—He; *hareḥ anugrahāt*—by the mercy of the Supreme Personality of Godhead; *nūnam*—indeed; *anaḥ ca*—and the handcart; *upari*—on top of the child; *na*—not; *apatat*—did fall down.

TRANSLATION

The child Kṛṣṇa, simply by the mercy of the Supreme Personality of Godhead, was somehow or other rescued from the hands of the Rākṣasī Pūtanā, who was determined to kill Him. Then, again by the mercy of the Supreme Godhead, the handcart missed falling upon the child.

TEXT 25

चक्रवातेन नीतोऽयं दैत्येन विपदं वियत् ।
शिलायां पतितस्तत्र परित्रातः सुरेश्वरैः ॥२५॥

cakra-vātena nīto 'yaṁ
daityena vipadaṁ viyat
śilāyāṁ patitas tatra
paritrātaḥ sureśvaraiḥ

cakra-vātena—by the demon in the shape of a whirlwind (Tṛṇāvarta); *nītaḥ ayam*—Kṛṣṇa was taken away; *daityena*—by the demon; *vipadam*—dangerous; *viyat*—to the sky; *śilāyām*—on a slab of stone; *patitaḥ*—fallen; *tatra*—there; *paritrātaḥ*—was saved; *sura-īśvaraiḥ*—by the mercy of Lord Viṣṇu or His associates.

TRANSLATION

Then again, the demon Tṛṇāvarta, in the form of a whirlwind, took the child away into the dangerous sky to kill Him, but the

demon fell down onto a slab of stone. In that case also, by the mercy of Lord Viṣṇu or His associates, the child was saved.

TEXT 26

यन्न म्रियेत द्रुमयोरन्तरं प्राप्य बालकः ।
असावन्यतमो वापि तदप्यच्युतरक्षणम् ॥२६॥

yan na mriyeta drumayor
antaraṁ prāpya bālakaḥ
asāv anyatamo vāpi
tad apy acyuta-rakṣaṇam

yat—then again; *na mriyeta*—did not die; *drumayoḥ antaram*—between the two trees; *prāpya*—although He was between; *bālakaḥ asau*—that child, Kṛṣṇa; *anyatamaḥ*—another child; *vā api*—or; *tat api acyuta-rakṣaṇam*—in that case also, He was saved by the Supreme Personality of Godhead.

TRANSLATION

Even the other day, neither Kṛṣṇa nor any of His playmates died from the falling of the two trees, although the children were near the trees or even between them. This also is to be considered the mercy of the Supreme Personality of Godhead.

TEXT 27

यावदौत्पातिकोऽरिष्टो व्रजं नाभिभवेदितः ।
तावद् बालानुपादाय यास्यामोऽन्यत्र सानुगाः॥२७॥

yāvad autpātiko 'riṣṭo
vrajaṁ nābhibhaved itaḥ
tāvad bālān upādāya
yāsyāmo 'nyatra sānugāḥ

yāvat—so long; *autpātikaḥ*—disturbing; *ariṣṭaḥ*—the demon; *vrajam*—this Gokula Vrajabhūmi; *na*—not; *abhibhavet itaḥ*—go away from this place; *tāvat*—so long; *bālān upādāya*—for the benefit of the boys; *yāsyāmaḥ*—we shall go; *anyatra*—somewhere else; *sa-anugāḥ*—with our followers.

TRANSLATION

All these incidents are being caused by some unknown demon. Before he comes here to create another disturbance, it is our duty to go somewhere else with the boys until there are no more disturbances.

PURPORT

Upānanda suggested, "By the mercy of Lord Viṣṇu, Kṛṣṇa has always been saved from so many dangerous incidents. Now let us leave this place and go someplace where we may worship Lord Viṣṇu undisturbed, before there is another cause of death from some demon who may attack us." A devotee desires only that he may execute devotional service undisturbed. Actually we see, however, that even during the presence of Kṛṣṇa, when Nanda Mahārāja and the other cowherd men had the Supreme Personality of Godhead in their presence, there were disturbances. Of course, in every case, Kṛṣṇa came out victorious. The instruction we may derive from this is that we should not be disturbed by so-called disturbances. There have been so many disturbances to our Kṛṣṇa consciousness movement, but we cannot give up our forward march. On the contrary, people are receiving this movement very enthusiastically all over the world, and they are purchasing literature about Kṛṣṇa consciousness with redoubled energy. Thus there are both encouragements and disturbances. This was so even in Kṛṣṇa's time.

TEXT 28

वनं वृन्दावनं नाम पशव्यं नवकाननम् ।
गोपगोपीगवां सेव्यं पुण्याद्रितृणवीरुधम् ॥२८॥

vanaṁ vṛndāvanaṁ nāma
paśavyaṁ nava-kānanam
gopa-gopī-gavāṁ sevyaṁ
puṇyādri-tṛṇa-vīrudham

vanam—another forest; *vṛndāvanam nāma*—named Vṛndāvana; *paśavyam*—a very suitable place for maintenance of the cows and other animals; *nava-kānanam*—there are many new gardenlike places; *gopa-gopī-gavām*—for all the cowherd men, the members of their families, and the cows; *sevyam*—a very happy, very suitable place; *puṇya-adri*—there are nice mountains; *tṛṇa*—plants; *vīrudham*—and creepers.

TRANSLATION

Between Nandeśvara and Mahāvana is a place named Vṛndāvana. This place is very suitable because it is lush with grass, plants and creepers for the cows and other animals. It has nice gardens and tall mountains and is full of facilities for the happiness of all the gopas and gopīs and our animals.

PURPORT

Vṛndāvana is situated between Nandeśvara and Mahāvana. Formerly the cowherd men had shifted to Mahāvana, but still there were disturbances. Therefore the cowherd men selected Vṛndāvana, which was between the two villages, and decided to go there.

TEXT 29

तत्तत्राद्यैव यास्यामः शकटान् युङ्क्त मा चिरम् ।
गोधनान्यग्रतो यान्तु भवतां यदि रोचते ॥२९॥

tat tatrādyaiva yāsyāmaḥ
śakaṭān yuṅkta mā ciram
godhanāny agrato yāntu
bhavatāṁ yadi rocate

tat—therefore; *tatra*—there; *adya eva*—just today; *yāsyāmaḥ*—let us go; *śakaṭān*—all the carts; *yuṅkta*—make ready; *mā ciram*—without delay; *go-dhanāni*—all the cows; *agrataḥ*—in front; *yāntu*—let them go; *bhavatām*—of all of you; *yadi*—if; *rocate*—it is pleasing to accept it.

TRANSLATION

Therefore, let us immediately go today. There is no need to wait any further. If you agree to my proposal, let us prepare all the bullock carts and put the cows in front of us, and let us go there.

TEXT 30

तच्छ्रुत्वैकधियो गोपाः साधु साध्विति वादिनः ।
व्रजान् स्वान् स्वान् समायुज्य ययू रूढपरिच्छदाः ॥३०॥

tac chrutvaika-dhiyo gopāḥ
sādhu sādhv iti vādinaḥ
vrajān svān svān samāyujya
yayū rūḍha-paricchadāḥ

tat śrutvā—hearing this advice of Upānanda's; *eka-dhiyaḥ*—voting unanimously; *gopāḥ*—all the cowherd men; *sādhu sādhu*—very nice, very nice; *iti*—thus; *vādinaḥ*—speaking, declaring; *vrajān*—cows; *svān svān*—own respective; *samāyujya*—assembling; *yayuḥ*—started; *rūḍha-paricchadāḥ*—all the dresses and paraphernalia having been kept on the carts.

TRANSLATION

Upon hearing this advice from Upānanda, the cowherd men unanimously agreed. "Very nice," they said. "Very nice." Thus they sorted out their household affairs, placed their clothing and other paraphernalia on the carts, and immediately started for Vṛndāvana.

TEXTS 31–32

वृद्धान् बालान् स्त्रियो राजन् सर्वोपकरणानि च ।
अनः स्वारोप्य गोपाला यत्ता आत्तशरासनाः ॥३१॥
गोधनानि पुरस्कृत्य शृङ्गाण्यापूर्य सर्वतः ।
तूर्यघोषेण महता ययुः सहपुरोहिताः ॥३२॥

vṛddhān bālān striyo rājan
sarvopakaraṇāni ca
anaḥsv āropya gopālā
yattā ātta-śarāsanāḥ

godhanāni puraskṛtya
śṛṅgāṇy āpūrya sarvataḥ

tūrya-ghoṣeṇa mahatā
yayuḥ saha-purohitāḥ

vṛddhān—first all the old men; *bālān*—children; *striyaḥ*—women; *rājan*—O King Parīkṣit; *sarva-upakaraṇāni ca*—then all sorts of necessities and whatever belongings they had; *anaḥsu*—on the bullock carts; *āropya*—keeping; *gopālāḥ*—all the cowherd men; *yattāḥ*—with great care; *ātta-śara-asanāḥ*—fully equipped with arrows and bows; *go-dhanāni*—all the cows; *puraskṛtya*—keeping in front; *śṛṅgāṇi*—bugles or horns; *āpūrya*—vibrating; *sarvataḥ*—all around; *tūrya-ghoṣeṇa*—with the resounding of the bugles; *mahatā*—loud; *yayuḥ*—started; *saha-purohitāḥ*—with the priests.

TRANSLATION

Keeping all the old men, women, children and household paraphernalia on the bullock carts and keeping all the cows in front, the cowherd men picked up their bows and arrows with great care and sounded bugles made of horn. O King Parīkṣit, in this way, with bugles vibrating all around, the cowherd men, accompanied by their priests, began their journey.

PURPORT

In this connection it is to be noted that although the inhabitants of Gokula were mostly cowherd men and cultivators, they knew how to defend themselves from danger and how to give protection to the women, the old men, the cows and the children, as well as to the brahminical *purohitas*.

TEXT 33

गोप्यो रूढरथा नूत्नकुचकुङ्कुमकान्तयः ।
कृष्णलीला जगुः प्रीत्या निष्ककण्ठ्यः सुवाससः ॥३३॥

gopyo rūḍha-rathā nūtna-
kuca-kuṅkuma-kāntayaḥ
kṛṣṇa-līlā jaguḥ prītyā
niṣka-kaṇṭhyaḥ suvāsasaḥ

gopyaḥ—all the cowherd women; *rūḍha-rathāḥ*—while riding on the bullock carts; *nūtna-kuca-kuṅkuma-kāntayaḥ*—their bodies, especially their breasts, were decorated with fresh *kuṅkuma; kṛṣṇa-līlāḥ*—the pastimes of Kṛṣṇa; *jaguḥ*—they chanted; *prītyā*—with great pleasure; *niṣka-kaṇṭhyaḥ*—decorated with lockets on their necks; *su-vāsasaḥ*—very well dressed.

TRANSLATION

The cowherd women, riding on the bullock carts, were dressed very nicely with excellent garments, and their bodies, especially their breasts, were decorated with fresh kuṅkuma powder. As they rode, they began to chant with great pleasure the pastimes of Kṛṣṇa.

TEXT 34

तथा यशोदारोहिण्यावेकं शकटमास्थिते ।
रेजतुः कृष्णरामाभ्यां तत्कथाश्रवणोत्सुके ॥३४॥

tathā yaśodā-rohiṇyāv
ekaṁ śakaṭam āsthite
rejatuḥ kṛṣṇa-rāmābhyāṁ
tat-kathā-śravaṇotsuke

tathā—as well as; *yaśodā-rohiṇyau*—both mother Yaśodā and mother Rohiṇī; *ekam śakaṭam*—on one bullock cart; *āsthite*—seated; *rejatuḥ*—very beautiful; *kṛṣṇa-rāmābhyām*—Kṛṣṇa and Balarāma, along with Their mothers; *tat-kathā*—of the pastimes of Kṛṣṇa and Balarāma; *śravaṇa-utsuke*—being situated in hearing with great transcendental pleasure.

TRANSLATION

Thus hearing about the pastimes of Kṛṣṇa and Balarāma with great pleasure, mother Yaśodā and Rohiṇīdevī, so as not to be separated from Kṛṣṇa and Balarāma for even a moment, got up with Them on one bullock cart. In this situation, they all looked very beautiful.

PURPORT

It appears that mother Yaśodā and Rohiṇī could not be separated from Kṛṣṇa and Balarāma even for a moment. They used to pass their time either by taking care of Kṛṣṇa and Balarāma or by chanting about Their pastimes. Thus mother Yaśodā and Rohiṇī looked very beautiful.

TEXT 35

वृन्दावनं संप्रविश्य सर्वकालसुखावहम् ।
तत्र चक्रुर्व्रजावासं शकटैरर्धचन्द्रवत् ॥३५॥

vṛndāvanaṁ sampraviśya
sarva-kāla-sukhāvaham
tatra cakrur vrajāvāsaṁ
śakaṭair ardha-candravat

vṛndāvanam—the sacred place by the name Vṛndāvana; *sampraviśya*—after entering; *sarva-kāla-sukha-āvaham*—where in all seasons it is pleasing to live; *tatra*—there; *cakruḥ*—they made; *vraja-āvāsam*—inhabitation of Vraja; *śakaṭaiḥ*—by the bullock carts; *ardha-candravat*—making a semicircle like a half moon.

TRANSLATION

In this way they entered Vṛndāvana, where it is always pleasing to live in all seasons. They made a temporary place to inhabit by placing their bullock carts around them in the shape of a half moon.

PURPORT

As stated in the *Viṣṇu Purāṇa:*

śakaṭī-vāṭa-paryantaś
candrārdha-kāra-saṁsthite

And as stated in the *Hari-vaṁśa:*

kaṇṭakībhiḥ pravṛddhābhis
tathā kaṇṭakībhir drumaiḥ

nikhātocchrita-śākhābhir
abhiguptaṁ samantataḥ

There was no need to make fences all around. One side was already defended by thorn trees, and thus the thorn trees, the bullock carts and the animals encircled the inhabitants in their temporary residence.

TEXT 36

वृन्दावनं गोवर्धनं यमुनापुलिनानि च ।
वीक्ष्यासीदुत्तमा प्रीती राममाधवयोर्नृप ॥३६॥

vṛndāvanaṁ govardhanaṁ
yamunā-pulināni ca
vīkṣyāsīd uttamā prītī
rāma-mādhavayor nṛpa

vṛndāvanam—the place known as Vṛndāvana; *govardhanam*—along with Govardhana Hill; *yamunā-pulināni ca*—and the banks of the River Yamunā; *vīkṣya*—seeing this situation; *āsīt*—remained or was enjoyed; *uttamā prītī*—first-class pleasure; *rāma-mādhavayoḥ*—of Kṛṣṇa and Balarāma; *nṛpa*—O King Parīkṣit.

TRANSLATION

O King Parīkṣit, when Rāma and Kṛṣṇa saw Vṛndāvana, Govardhana and the banks of the River Yamunā, They both enjoyed great pleasure.

TEXT 37

एवं व्रजौकसां प्रीतिं यच्छन्तौ बालचेष्टितैः ।
कलवाक्यैः स्वकालेन वत्सपालौ बभूवतुः ॥३७॥

evaṁ vrajaukasāṁ prītiṁ
yacchantau bāla-ceṣṭitaiḥ
kala-vākyaiḥ sva-kālena
vatsa-pālau babhūvatuḥ

evam—in this way; *vraja-okasām*—to all the inhabitants of Vraja; *prītim*—pleasure; *yacchantau*—giving; *bāla-ceṣṭitaiḥ*—by the activities and pastimes of childhood; *kala-vākyaiḥ*—and by very sweet broken language; *sva-kālena*—in due course of time; *vatsa-pālau*—to take care of the calves; *babhūvatuḥ*—were grown up.

TRANSLATION

In this way, Kṛṣṇa and Balarāma, acting like small boys and talking in half-broken language, gave transcendental pleasure to all the inhabitants of Vraja. In due course of time, They became old enough to take care of the calves.

PURPORT

As soon as Kṛṣṇa and Balarāma were a little grown up, They were meant for taking care of the calves. Although born of a very well-to-do family, They still had to take care of the calves. This was the system of education. Those who were not born in *brāhmaṇa* families were not meant for academic education. The *brāhmaṇas* were trained in a literary, academic education, the *kṣatriyas* were trained to take care of the state, and the *vaiśyas* learned how to cultivate the land and take care of the cows and calves. There was no need to waste time going to school to be falsely educated and later increase the numbers of the unemployed. Kṛṣṇa and Balarāma taught us by Their personal behavior. Kṛṣṇa took care of the cows and played His flute, and Balarāma took care of agricultural activities with a plow in His hand.

TEXT 38

अविदूरे व्रजभुवः सह गोपालदारकैः ।
चारयामासतुर्वत्सान् नानाक्रीडापरिच्छदौ ॥३८॥

avidūre vraja-bhuvaḥ
saha gopāla-dārakaiḥ
cārayām āsatur vatsān
nānā-krīḍā-paricchadau

avidūre—not very far from the residential quarters of the Vrajavāsīs; *vraja-bhuvaḥ*—from the land known as Vraja; *saha gopāla-dārakaiḥ*—

with other boys of the same profession (cowherd boys); *cārayām āsatuḥ*—tended; *vatsān*—the small calves; *nānā*—various; *krīḍā*—sporting; *paricchadau*—dressed very nicely in different ways and equipped with implements.

TRANSLATION

Not far away from Their residential quarters, both Kṛṣṇa and Balarāma, equipped with all kinds of playthings, played with other cowherd boys and began to tend the small calves.

TEXTS 39–40

क्वचिद् वादयतो वेणुं क्षेपणैः क्षिपतः क्वचित् ।
क्वचित् पादैः किङ्किणीभिः क्वचित् कृत्रिमगोवृषैः ॥३९॥
वृषायमाणौ नर्दन्तौ युयुधाते परस्परम् ।
अनुकृत्य रुतैर्जन्तूंश्चेरतुः प्राकृतौ यथा ॥४०॥

kvacid vādayato veṇuṁ
kṣepaṇaiḥ kṣipataḥ kvacit
kvacit pādaiḥ kiṅkiṇībhiḥ
kvacit kṛtrima-go-vṛṣaiḥ

vṛṣāyamāṇau nardantau
yuyudhāte parasparam
anukṛtya rutair jantūṁś
ceratuḥ prākṛtau yathā

kvacit—sometimes; *vādayataḥ*—blowing; *veṇum*—on the flute; *kṣepaṇaiḥ*—with a device of rope for throwing; *kṣipataḥ*—throwing stones to get fruit; *kvacit*—sometimes; *kvacit pādaiḥ*—sometimes with the legs; *kiṅkiṇībhiḥ*—with the sound of ankle bells; *kvacit*—sometimes; *kṛtrima-go-vṛṣaiḥ*—by becoming artificial cows and bulls; *vṛṣāyamāṇau*—imitating the animals; *nardantau*—roaring loudly; *yuyudhāte*—They both used to fight; *parasparam*—with one another; *anukṛtya*—imitating; *rutaiḥ*—by resounding; *jantūn*—all the animals; *ceratuḥ*—They used to wander; *prākṛtau*—two ordinary human children; *yathā*—like.

TRANSLATION

Sometimes Kṛṣṇa and Balarāma would play on Their flutes, sometimes They would throw ropes and stones devised for getting fruits from the trees, sometimes They would throw only stones, and sometimes, Their ankle bells tinkling, They would play football with fruits like bael and āmalakī. Sometimes They would cover Themselves with blankets and imitate cows and bulls and fight with one another, roaring loudly, and sometimes They would imitate the voices of the animals. In this way They enjoyed sporting, exactly like two ordinary human children.

PURPORT

Vṛndāvana is full of peacocks. *Kūjat-kokila-haṁsa-sārasa-gaṇākīrṇe mayūrākule.* The Vṛndāvana forest is always full of cuckoos, ducks, swans, peacocks, cranes and also monkeys, bulls and cows. So Kṛṣṇa and Balarāma used to imitate the sounds of these animals and enjoy sporting.

TEXT 41

कदाचिद् यमुनातीरे वत्सांश्चारयतोः स्वकैः ।
वयस्यैः कृष्णबलयोर्जिघांसुर्दैत्य आगमत् ॥४१॥

kadācid yamunā-tīre
vatsāṁś cārayatoḥ svakaiḥ
vayasyaiḥ kṛṣṇa-balayor
jighāṁsur daitya āgamat

kadācit—sometimes; *yamunā-tīre*—on the bank of the Yamunā; *vatsān*—the calves; *cārayatoḥ*—when They were tending; *svakaiḥ*—Their own; *vayasyaiḥ*—with other playmates; *kṛṣṇa-balayoḥ*—both Kṛṣṇa and Balarāma; *jighāṁsuḥ*—desiring to kill Them; *daityaḥ*—another demon; *āgamat*—reached there.

TRANSLATION

One day while Rāma and Kṛṣṇa, along with Their playmates, were tending the calves on the bank of the River Yamunā, another demon arrived there, desiring to kill Them.

TEXT 42

तं वत्सरूपिणं वीक्ष्य वत्सयूथगतं हरिः ।
दर्शयन् बलदेवाय शनैर्मुग्ध इवासदत् ॥४२॥

taṁ vatsa-rūpiṇaṁ vīkṣya
vatsa-yūtha-gataṁ hariḥ
darśayan baladevāya
śanair mugdha ivāsadat

tam—unto the demon; *vatsa-rūpiṇam*—assuming the form of a calf; *vīkṣya*—seeing; *vatsa-yūtha-gatam*—when the demon entered the group of all the other calves; *hariḥ*—the Supreme Personality of Godhead, Kṛṣṇa; *darśayan*—indicating; *baladevāya*—unto Baladeva; *śanaiḥ*—very slowly; *mugdhaḥ iva*—as if He did not understand anything; *āsadat*—came near the demon.

TRANSLATION

When the Supreme Personality of Godhead saw that the demon had assumed the form of a calf and entered among the groups of other calves, He pointed out to Baladeva, "Here is another demon." Then He very slowly approached the demon, as if He did not understand the demon's intentions.

PURPORT

The import of the words *mugdha iva* is that although Kṛṣṇa knows everything, here He pretended that He did not understand why the demon had entered among the calves, and He informed Baladeva by a sign.

TEXT 43

गृहीत्वापरपादाभ्यां सहलाङ्गूलमच्युतः ।
भ्रामयित्वा कपित्थाग्रे प्राहिणोद् गतजीवितम् ।
स कपित्थैर्महाकायः पात्यमानैः पपात ह ॥४३॥

gṛhītvāpara-pādābhyāṁ
saha-lāṅgūlam acyutaḥ

bhrāmayitvā kapitthāgre
prāhiṇod gata-jīvitam
sa kapitthair mahā-kāyaḥ
pātyamānaiḥ papāta ha

gṛhītvā—capturing; *apara-pādābhyām*—with the hind legs; *saha*—along with; *lāṅgūlam*—the tail; *acyutaḥ*—Kṛṣṇa, the Supreme Personality of Godhead; *bhrāmayitvā*—twirling around very severely; *kapittha-agre*—on the top of a *kapittha* tree; *prāhiṇot*—threw him; *gata-jīvitam*—lifeless body; *saḥ*—that demon; *kapitthaiḥ*—with the *kapittha* trees; *mahā-kāyaḥ*—assumed a great body; *pātyamānaiḥ*—and while the tree fell down; *papāta ha*—he fell dead on the ground.

TRANSLATION

Thereafter, Śrī Kṛṣṇa caught the demon by the hind legs and tail, twirled the demon's whole body very strongly until the demon was dead, and threw him into the top of a kapittha tree, which then fell down, along with the body of the demon, who had assumed a great form.

PURPORT

Kṛṣṇa killed the demon in such a way as to get the *kapittha* fruits to fall so that He and Balarāma and the other boys could take advantage of the opportunity to eat them. The *kapittha* is sometimes called *kṣatbel-phala.* The pulp of this fruit is very palatable. It is sweet and sour, and everyone likes it.

TEXT 44

तं वीक्ष्य विस्मिता बालाः शशंसुः साधु साध्विति ।
देवाश्च परिसन्तुष्टा बभूवुः पुष्पवर्षिणः ॥४४॥

taṁ vīkṣya vismitā bālāḥ
śaśaṁsuḥ sādhu sādhv iti
devāś ca parisantuṣṭā
babhūvuḥ puṣpa-varṣiṇaḥ

tam—this incident; *vīkṣya*—observing; *vismitāḥ*—very much astonished; *bālāḥ*—all the other boys; *śaśaṁsuḥ*—praised highly; *sādhu*

sādhu iti—exclaiming, "Very good, very good"; *devāḥ ca*—and all the demigods from the heavenly planets; *parisantuṣṭāḥ*—being very much satisfied; *babhūvuḥ*—became; *puṣpa-varṣiṇaḥ*—showered flowers on Kṛṣṇa.

TRANSLATION

Upon seeing the dead body of the demon, all the cowherd boys exclaimed, "Well done, Kṛṣṇa! Very good, very good! Thank You." In the upper planetary system, all the demigods were pleased, and therefore they showered flowers on the Supreme Personality of Godhead.

TEXT 45

तौ वत्सपालकौ भूत्वा सर्वलोकैकपालकौ ।
सप्रातराशौ गोवत्सांश्चारयन्तौ विचेरतुः ॥४५॥

tau vatsa-pālakau bhūtvā
sarva-lokaika-pālakau
saprātar-āśau go-vatsāṁś
cārayantau viceratuḥ

tau—Kṛṣṇa and Balarāma; *vatsa-pālakau*—as if taking care of the calves; *bhūtvā*—so becoming; *sarva-loka-eka-pālakau*—although They are the maintainers of all living beings throughout the whole universe; *sa-prātaḥ-āśau*—finishing breakfast in the morning; *go-vatsān*—all the calves; *cārayantau*—tending; *viceratuḥ*—wandered here and there.

TRANSLATION

After the killing of the demon, Kṛṣṇa and Balarāma finished Their breakfast in the morning, and while continuing to take care of the calves, They wandered here and there. Kṛṣṇa and Balarāma, the Supreme Personalities of Godhead, who maintain the entire creation, now took charge of the calves as if cowherd boys.

PURPORT

Paritrāṇāya sādhūnāṁ vināśāya ca duṣkṛtām. Kṛṣṇa's daily business here in this material world was to kill the *duṣkṛtīs.* This did not hamper

His daily affairs, for it was routine work. While He tended the calves on the bank of the River Yamunā, two or three incidents took place every day, and although these were serious, killing the demons one after another appeared to be His daily routine work.

TEXT 46

स्वं स्वं वत्सकुलं सर्वे पाययिष्यन्त एकदा ।
गत्वा जलाशयाभ्याशं पाययित्वा पपुर्जलम् ॥४६॥

svaṁ svaṁ vatsa-kulaṁ sarve
pāyayiṣyanta ekadā
gatvā jalāśayābhyāśaṁ
pāyayitvā papur jalam

svam svam—own respective; *vatsa-kulam*—the group of calves; *sarve*—all the boys and Kṛṣṇa and Balarāma; *pāyayiṣyantaḥ*—desiring to have them drink water; *ekadā*—one day; *gatvā*—going; *jala-āśaya-abhyāśam*—near the water tank; *pāyayitvā*—after allowing the animals to drink water; *papuḥ jalam*—they also drank water.

TRANSLATION

One day all the boys, including Kṛṣṇa and Balarāma, each boy taking his own group of calves, brought the calves to a reservoir of water, desiring to allow them to drink. After the animals drank water, the boys drank water there also.

TEXT 47

ते तत्र ददृशुर्बाला महासत्त्वमवस्थितम् ।
तत्रसुर्वज्रनिर्भिन्नं गिरेः शृङ्गमिव च्युतम् ॥४७॥

te tatra dadṛśur bālā
mahā-sattvam avasthitam
tatrasur vajra-nirbhinnaṁ
gireḥ śṛṅgam iva cyutam

te—they; *tatra*—there; *dadṛśuḥ*—observed; *bālāḥ*—all the boys; *mahā-sattvam*—a gigantic body; *avasthitam*—situated; *tatrasuḥ*—became afraid; *vajra-nirbhinnam*—broken by a thunderbolt; *gireḥ śṛṅgam*—the peak of a mountain; *iva*—like; *cyutam*—fallen there.

TRANSLATION

Right by the reservoir, the boys saw a gigantic body resembling a mountain peak broken and struck down by a thunderbolt. They were afraid even to see such a huge living being.

TEXT 48

स वै बको नाम महानसुरो बकरूपधृक् ।
आगत्य सहसा कृष्णं तीक्ष्णतुण्डोऽग्रसद् बली ॥४८॥

sa vai bako nāma mahān
asuro baka-rūpa-dhṛk
āgatya sahasā kṛṣṇaṁ
tīkṣṇa-tuṇḍo 'grasad balī

saḥ—that creature; *vai*—indeed; *bakaḥ nāma*—by the name Bakāsura; *mahān asuraḥ*—a great, gigantic demon; *baka-rūpa-dhṛk*—assumed the bodily shape of a big duck; *āgatya*—coming there; *sahasā*—all of a sudden; *kṛṣṇam*—Kṛṣṇa; *tīkṣṇa-tuṇḍaḥ*—sharp beak; *agrasat*—swallowed; *balī*—very powerful.

TRANSLATION

That great-bodied demon was named Bakāsura. He had assumed the body of a duck with a very sharp beak. Having come there, he immediately swallowed Kṛṣṇa.

TEXT 49

कृष्णं महाबकग्रस्तं दृष्ट्वा रामादयोऽर्भकाः ।
बभूवुरिन्द्रियाणीव विना प्राणं विचेतसः ॥४९॥

kṛṣṇaṁ mahā-baka-grastaṁ
dṛṣṭvā rāmādayo 'rbhakāḥ

babhūvur indriyāṇīva
vinā prāṇaṁ vicetasaḥ

kṛṣṇam—unto Kṛṣṇa; *mahā-baka-grastam*—swallowed by the great duck; *dṛṣṭvā*—seeing this incident; *rāma-ādayaḥ arbhakāḥ*—all the other boys, headed by Balarāma; *babhūvuḥ*—became overwhelmed; *indriyāṇi*—senses; *iva*—like; *vinā*—without; *prāṇam*—life; *vicetasaḥ*—very much bewildered, almost unconscious.

TRANSLATION

When Balarāma and the other boys saw that Kṛṣṇa had been devoured by the gigantic duck, they became almost unconscious, like senses without life.

PURPORT

Although Balarāma can do everything, because of intense affection for His brother He was momentarily bewildered. A similar thing is stated to have happened in connection with *rukmiṇī-haraṇa*, the kidnapping of Rukmiṇī. When Kṛṣṇa, after kidnapping Rukmiṇī, was attacked by all the kings, Rukmiṇī was momentarily bewildered, until the Lord took the proper steps.

TEXT 50

तं तालुमूलं प्रदहन्तमग्निवद्
गोपालसूनुं पितरं जगद्गुरोः ।
चच्छर्द सद्योऽतिरुषाक्षतं बक-
स्तुण्डेन हन्तुं पुनरभ्यपद्यत ॥५०॥

taṁ tālu-mūlaṁ pradahantam agnivad
gopāla-sūnuṁ pitaraṁ jagad-guroḥ
caccharda sadyo 'tiruṣākṣataṁ bakas
tuṇḍena hantuṁ punar abhyapadyata

tam—Kṛṣṇa; *tālu-mūlam*—the root of the throat; *pradahantam*—burning; *agni-vat*—like fire; *gopāla-sūnum*—Kṛṣṇa, the son of a cowherd man; *pitaram*—the father; *jagat-guroḥ*—of Lord Brahmā;

caccharda—got out of his mouth; *sadyaḥ*—immediately; *ati-ruṣā*—with great anger; *akṣatam*—without being hurt; *bakaḥ*—Bakāsura; *tuṇḍena*—with his sharp beak; *hantum*—to kill; *punaḥ*—again; *abhyapadyata*—endeavored.

TRANSLATION

Kṛṣṇa, who was the father of Lord Brahmā but who was acting as the son of a cowherd man, became like fire, burning the root of the demon's throat, and the demon Bakāsura immediately disgorged Him. When the demon saw that Kṛṣṇa, although having been swallowed, was unharmed, he immediately attacked Kṛṣṇa again with his sharp beak.

PURPORT

Although Kṛṣṇa is always as soft as a lotus, within the throat of Bakāsura He created a burning sensation of being hotter than fire. Although Kṛṣṇa's whole body is sweeter than sugar candy, Bakāsura tasted bitterness and therefore immediately vomited Kṛṣṇa up. As stated in *Bhagavad-gītā* (4.11), *ye yathā māṁ prapadyante tāṁs tathaiva bhajāmy aham.* When Kṛṣṇa is accepted as an enemy, He becomes the most intolerable object for the nondevotee, who cannot tolerate Kṛṣṇa within or without. Here this is shown by the example of Bakāsura.

TEXT 51

तमापतन्तं स निगृह्य तुण्डयो-
दोर्भ्यां बकं कंससखं सतां पतिः ।
पश्यत्सु बालेषु ददार लीलया
मुदावहो वीरणवद् दिवौकसाम् ॥५१॥

tam āpatantaṁ sa nigṛhya tuṇḍayor
dorbhyāṁ bakaṁ kaṁsa-sakhaṁ satāṁ patiḥ
paśyatsu bāleṣu dadāra līlayā
mudāvaho vīraṇavad divaukasām

tam—unto Bakāsura; *āpatantam*—again endeavoring to attack Him; *saḥ*—Lord Kṛṣṇa; *nigṛhya*—capturing; *tuṇḍayoḥ*—by the beak;

dorbhyām—with His arms; *bakam*—Bakāsura; *kaṁsa-sakham*—who was the friend and associate of Kaṁsa; *satām patiḥ*—Lord Kṛṣṇa, the master of the Vaiṣṇavas; *paśyatsu*—while observing; *bāleṣu*—all the cowherd boys; *dadāra*—bifurcated; *līlayā*—very easily; *mudā-āvahaḥ*—this action was very much pleasing; *vīraṇa-vat*—like the grass called *vīraṇa* (as it is bifurcated); *divaukasām*—to all the denizens of heaven.

TRANSLATION

When Kṛṣṇa, the leader of the Vaiṣṇavas, saw that the demon Bakāsura, the friend of Kaṁsa, was endeavoring to attack Him, with His arms He captured the demon by the two halves of the beak, and in the presence of all the cowherd boys Kṛṣṇa very easily bifurcated Him, as a child splits a blade of vīraṇa grass. By thus killing the demon, Kṛṣṇa very much pleased the denizens of heaven.

TEXT 52

तदा बकारिं सुरलोकवासिनः
समाकिरन् नन्दनमल्लिकादिभिः ।
समीडिरे चानकशङ्खसंस्तवै-
स्तद् वीक्ष्य गोपालसुता विसिस्मिरे ॥५२॥

tadā bakāriṁ sura-loka-vāsinaḥ
samākiran nandana-mallikādibhiḥ
samīḍire cānaka-śaṅkha-saṁstavais
tad vīkṣya gopāla-sutā visismire

tadā—at that time; *baka-arim*—unto the enemy of Bakāsura; *sura-loka-vāsinaḥ*—the celestial denizens of the higher planets; *samākiran*—showered flowers; *nandana-mallikā-ādibhiḥ*—with such flowers as *mallikā*, which are grown in Nandana-kānana; *samīḍire*—also congratulated Him; *ca*—and; *ānaka-śaṅkha-saṁstavaiḥ*—by celestial kettledrums and conchshells, accompanied with prayers; *tat vīkṣya*—by seeing this; *gopāla-sutāḥ*—the cowherd boys; *visismire*—were struck with wonder.

TRANSLATION

At that time, the celestial denizens of the higher planetary system showered mallikā-puṣpa, flowers grown in Nandana-kānana, upon Kṛṣṇa, the enemy of Bakāsura. They also congratulated Him by sounding celestial kettledrums and conchshells and by offering prayers. Seeing this, the cowherd boys were struck with wonder.

TEXT 53

मुक्तं बकास्यादुपलभ्य बालका
रामादयः प्राणमिवेन्द्रियो गणः ।
स्थानागतं तं परिरभ्य निर्वृताः
प्रणीय वत्सान् व्रजमेत्य तज्जगुः ॥५३॥

muktaṁ bakāsyād upalabhya bālakā
rāmādayaḥ prāṇam ivendriyo gaṇaḥ
sthānāgataṁ taṁ parirabhya nirvṛtāḥ
praṇīya vatsān vrajam etya taj jaguḥ

muktam—thus released; *baka-āsyāt*—from the mouth of Bakāsura; *upalabhya*—getting back; *bālakāḥ*—all the boys, the playmates; *rāma-ādayaḥ*—headed by Balarāma; *prāṇam*—life; *iva*—like; *indriyaḥ*—senses; *gaṇaḥ*—all of them; *sthāna-āgatam*—going to their own place; *tam*—unto Kṛṣṇa; *parirabhya*—embracing; *nirvṛtāḥ*—being freed from the danger; *praṇīya*—after collecting; *vatsān*—all the calves; *vrajam etya*—returning to Vrajabhūmi; *tat jaguḥ*—loudly declared the incident.

TRANSLATION

Just as the senses are pacified when consciousness and life return, so when Kṛṣṇa was freed from this danger, all the boys, including Balarāma, thought that their life had been restored. They embraced Kṛṣṇa in good consciousness, and then they collected their own calves and returned to Vrajabhūmi, where they declared the incident loudly.

PURPORT

It was the practice of the inhabitants of Vrajabhūmi to compose poetry about the incidents that occurred in the forest when Kṛṣṇa performed His different activities of killing the *asuras.* They would compose all the stories in poetry or have this done by professional poets, and then they would sing about these incidents. Thus it is written here that the boys sang very loudly.

TEXT 54

श्रुत्वा तद् विस्मिता गोपा गोप्यश्चातिप्रियादृताः ।
प्रेत्यागतमिवोत्सुक्यादैक्षन्त तृषितेक्षणाः ॥५४॥

śrutvā tad vismitā gopā
gopyaś cātipriyādṛtāḥ
pretyāgatam ivotsukyād
aikṣanta tṛṣitekṣaṇāḥ

śrutvā—after hearing; *tat*—these incidents; *vismitāḥ*—being struck with wonder; *gopāḥ*—the cowherd men; *gopyaḥ ca*—and their respective wives; *ati-priya-ādṛtāḥ*—received the news with great transcendental pleasure; *pretya āgatam iva*—thought that it was as if the boys had returned from death; *utsukyāt*—with great eagerness; *aikṣanta*—began to look upon the boys; *tṛṣita-īkṣaṇāḥ*—with full satisfaction, they did not want to turn their eyes from Kṛṣṇa and the boys.

TRANSLATION

When the cowherd men and women heard about the killing of Bakāsura in the forest, they were very much astonished. Upon seeing Kṛṣṇa and hearing the story, they received Kṛṣṇa very eagerly, thinking that Kṛṣṇa and the other boys had returned from the mouth of death. Thus they looked upon Kṛṣṇa and the boys with silent eyes, not wanting to turn their eyes aside now that the boys were safe.

PURPORT

Because of intense love for Kṛṣṇa, the cowherd men and women simply remained silent, thinking of how Kṛṣṇa and the boys had been saved. The cowherd men and women looked upon Kṛṣṇa and the boys and did not desire to turn their eyes aside.

TEXT 55

अहो बतास्य बालस्य बहवो मृत्यवोऽभवन् ।
अप्यासीद् विप्रियं तेषां कृतं पूर्वं यतो भयम् ।।५५।।

aho batāsya bālasya
bahavo mṛtyavo 'bhavan
apy āsīd vipriyaṁ teṣāṁ
kṛtaṁ pūrvaṁ yato bhayam

aho bata—it is very astonishing; *asya*—of this; *bālasya*—Kṛṣṇa; *bahavaḥ*—many, many; *mṛtyavaḥ*—causes of death; *abhavan*—appeared; *api*—still; *āsīt*—there was; *vipriyam*—the cause of death; *teṣām*—of them; *kṛtam*—done; *pūrvam*—formerly; *yataḥ*—from which; *bhayam*—there was fear of death.

TRANSLATION

The cowherd men, headed by Nanda Mahārāja, began to contemplate: It is very astonishing that although this boy Kṛṣṇa has many times faced many varied causes of death, by the grace of the Supreme Personality of Godhead it was these causes of fear that were killed, instead of Him.

PURPORT

The cowherd men innocently thought, "Because our Kṛṣṇa is innocent, the causes of death that appeared before Him were themselves killed instead of Kṛṣṇa. This is the greatest grace of the Supreme Personality of Godhead."

TEXT 56

अथाप्यभिभवन्त्येनं नैव ते घोरदर्शनाः ।
जिघांसयैनमासाद्य नश्यन्त्यग्नौ पतङ्गवत् ।।५६।।

athāpy abhibhavanty enaṁ
naiva te ghora-darśanāḥ

jighāṁsayainam āsādya
naśyanty agnau pataṅgavat

atha api—although they come to attack; *abhibhavanti*—they are able to kill; *enam*—this boy; *na*—not; *eva*—certainly; *te*—all of them; *ghora-darśanāḥ*—very fierce looking; *jighāṁsayā*—because of envy; *enam*—unto Kṛṣṇa; *āsādya*—approaching; *naśyanti*—are vanquished (death occurs to the aggressor); *agnau*—in fire; *pataṅga-vat*—like flies.

TRANSLATION

Although the causes of death, the daityas, were very fierce, they could not kill this boy Kṛṣṇa. Rather, because they came to kill innocent boys, as soon as they approached they themselves were killed, exactly like flies attacking a fire.

PURPORT

Nanda Mahārāja innocently thought, "Perhaps this boy Kṛṣṇa formerly killed all these demons, and therefore in this life they are envious and are attacking Him. But Kṛṣṇa is a fire, and they are flies, and in a fight between fire and flies, the fire is always victorious." Fighting is always taking place between the demons and the power of the Supreme Personality. *Paritrāṇāya sādhūnāṁ vināśāya ca duṣkṛtām* (Bg. 4.8). Anyone who is against the control of the Supreme Personality of Godhead must be killed, life after life. Ordinary living beings are subject to *karma*, but the Supreme Personality of Godhead is always victorious over the demons.

TEXT 57

अहो ब्रह्मविदां वाचो नासत्याः सन्ति कर्हिचित् ।
गर्गो यदाह भगवानन्वभावि तथैव तत् ॥५७॥

aho brahma-vidāṁ vāco
nāsatyāḥ santi karhicit
gargo yad āha bhagavān
anvabhāvi tathaiva tat

aho—how wonderful it is; *brahma-vidām*—of persons who have full knowledge of Brahman, transcendence; *vācaḥ*—the words; *na*—never;

asatyāḥ—untruth; *santi*—become; *karhicit*—at any time; *gargaḥ*—Gargamuni; *yat*—whatever; *āha*—predicted; *bhagavān*—Gargamuni, the most powerful; *anvabhāvi*—is exactly happening; *tathā eva*—as; *tat*—that.

TRANSLATION

The words of persons in full knowledge of Brahman never become untrue. It is very wonderful that whatever Gargamuni predicted we are now actually experiencing in all detail.

PURPORT

The purpose of human life is indicated in the *Brahma-sūtra: athāto brahma-jijñāsā.* To make one's life perfect—in the past, present and future—one must learn about Brahman. Because of intense affection, Nanda Mahārāja could not understand Kṛṣṇa as He is. Gargamuni was able to know everything, past, present and future, by studying the *Vedas,* but Nanda Mahārāja could not understand Kṛṣṇa directly. Because of his intense love for Kṛṣṇa, he forgot who Kṛṣṇa was and could not understand Kṛṣṇa's potency. Although Kṛṣṇa is Nārāyaṇa Himself, Gargamuni did not disclose this. Thus Nanda Mahārāja appreciated the words of Gargamuni, but because of his deep affection he could not understand who Kṛṣṇa was, although Gargamuni had said that Kṛṣṇa's qualities would be exactly like those of Nārāyaṇa.

TEXT 58

इति नन्दादयो गोपाः कृष्णरामकथां मुदा ।
कुर्वन्तो रममाणाश्च नाविन्दन् भववेदनाम् ॥५८॥

iti nandādayo gopāḥ
kṛṣṇa-rāma-kathāṁ mudā
kurvanto ramamāṇāś ca
nāvindan bhava-vedanām

iti—in this way; *nanda-ādayaḥ*—all the cowherd men, headed by Nanda Mahārāja; *gopāḥ*—cowherd men; *kṛṣṇa-rāma-katham*—narration of incidents in connection with Bhagavān Kṛṣṇa and Rāma; *mudā*—in great transcendental pleasure; *kurvantaḥ*—doing that; *ramamāṇāḥ ca*—enjoyed life and increased their affection for Kṛṣṇa; *na*—not; *avindan*—perceived; *bhava-vedanām*—the tribulations of material existence.

TRANSLATION

In this way all the cowherd men, headed by Nanda Mahārāja, enjoyed topics about the pastimes of Kṛṣṇa and Balarāma with great transcendental pleasure, and they could not even perceive material tribulations.

PURPORT

Here is an instruction about the result of studying or discussing the *kṛṣṇa-līlās* that appear in *Śrīmad-Bhāgavatam. Sadyo hṛdy avarudhyate 'tra kṛtibhiḥ śuśrūṣubhis tat-kṣaṇāt* (*Bhāg.* 1.1.2). Nanda Mahārāja and Yaśodā in Vṛndāvana appeared like ordinary persons of this material world, but they never felt the tribulations of this world, although they sometimes met many dangerous situations created by the demons. This is a practical example. If we follow in the footsteps of Nanda Mahārāja and the *gopas*, we can all be happy simply by discussing the activities of Kṛṣṇa.

anarthopaśamaṁ sākṣād
bhakti-yogam adhokṣaje
lokasyājānato vidvāṁś
cakre sātvata-saṁhitām
(*Bhāg.* 1.7.6)

Vyāsadeva has given this literature so that everyone may understand one's transcendental position simply by discussing *bhāgavata-kathā.* Even at the present moment, everyone everywhere can be happy and free from material tribulations by following *Śrīmad-Bhāgavatam.* There is no need of austerities and penances, which in this age are very difficult to perform. Śrī Caitanya Mahāprabhu has therefore declared, *sarvātma-snapanaṁ paraṁ vijayate śrī-kṛṣṇa-saṅkīrtanam.* By our Kṛṣṇa consciousness movement, we are trying to distribute *Śrīmad-Bhāgavatam* so that anyone in any part of the world can be absorbed in the Kṛṣṇa consciousness movement by chanting and hearing about the activities of Kṛṣṇa and be free from all material tribulations.

TEXT 59

एवं विहारैः कौमारैः कौमारं जहतुर्व्रजे ।
निलायनैः सेतुबन्धैर्मर्कटोत्प्लवनादिभिः ॥५९॥

evaṁ vihāraiḥ kaumāraiḥ
kaumāraṁ jahatur vraje
nilāyanaiḥ setu-bandhair
markaṭotplavanādibhiḥ

evam—in this way; *vihāraiḥ*—by different pastimes; *kaumāraiḥ*—childish; *kaumāram*—the age of childhood; *jahatuḥ*—(Kṛṣṇa and Balarāma) passed; *vraje*—in Vrajabhūmi; *nilāyanaiḥ*—by playing hide-and-seek; *setu-bandhaiḥ*—by constructing an artificial bridge on the ocean; *markaṭa*—like the monkeys; *utplavana-ādibhiḥ*—by jumping here and there, etc.

TRANSLATION

In this way Kṛṣṇa and Balarāma passed Their childhood age in Vrajabhūmi by engaging in activities of childish play, such as playing hide-and-seek, constructing a make-believe bridge on the ocean, and jumping here and there like monkeys.

Thus end the Bhaktivedanta purports of the Tenth Canto, Eleventh Chapter, of the Śrīmad-Bhāgavatam, *entitled "The Childhood Pastimes of Kṛṣṇa."*

CHAPTER TWELVE

The Killing of the Demon Aghāsura

This chapter describes in detail Kṛṣṇa's pastime of killing Aghāsura.

One day Kṛṣṇa wanted to enjoy a picnic lunch within the forest, and therefore He went out early into the forest with the other cowherd boys, accompanied by their respective groups of calves. While they were enjoying their picnic, Aghāsura, the younger brother of Pūtanā and Bakāsura, appeared there, desiring to kill Kṛṣṇa and His companions. The demon, who had been sent by Kaṁsa, assumed the form of a python, expanding himself to a length of eight miles and the height of a mountain, his mouth seeming to extend from the surface of the earth to the heavenly planets. Having assumed this feature, Aghāsura lay on the road. Kṛṣṇa's friends, the cowherd boys, thought that the demon's form was one of the beautiful spots of Vṛndāvana. Thus they wanted to enter within the mouth of this gigantic python. The gigantic figure of the python became a subject for their sporting pleasure, and they began to laugh, confident that even if this figure were dangerous, Kṛṣṇa was there to protect them. In this way, they proceeded toward the mouth of the gigantic figure.

Kṛṣṇa knew everything about Aghāsura, and therefore He wanted to forbid His friends to enter the demon's mouth, but in the meantime all the cowherd boys, along with their groups of calves, entered the mouth of that gigantic figure. Kṛṣṇa was waiting outside, and Aghāsura was waiting for Kṛṣṇa, thinking that as soon as Kṛṣṇa entered he would close his mouth so that everyone would die. While waiting for Kṛṣṇa, he refrained from swallowing the boys. In the meantime, Kṛṣṇa was thinking of how to save the boys and kill Aghāsura. Thus He entered the mouth of the gigantic *asura,* and when He was within the demon's mouth along with His friends, He expanded His body to such an extent that the *asura* suffocated and died. After this, Kṛṣṇa, by casting His nectarean glance upon His friends, brought them back to life, and with pleasure they all came out unhurt. Thus Kṛṣṇa encouraged all the demigods, and they expressed their pleasure and happiness. For a crooked, sinful person there is no scope for *sāyujya-mukti,* or becoming one with the effulgence of Kṛṣṇa, but because the Supreme Personality of Godhead entered the body of Aghāsura, by His touch this demon got the opportunity to merge into the existence of the Brahman effulgence and thus attain *sāyujya-mukti.*

When this pastime was performed, Kṛṣṇa was only five years old. One year later, when He was six years old and He stepped into the *paugaṇḍa* age, this pastime was disclosed to the inhabitants of Vraja. Parīkṣit Mahārāja inquired, "Why is it that this pastime was disclosed only after one year and yet the inhabitants of Vraja thought that it had been performed that very day?" With this question, the Twelfth Chapter ends.

TEXT 1

श्रीशुक उवाच
क्वचिद् वनाशाय मनो दधद् व्रजात्
प्रातः समुत्थाय वयस्यवत्सपान् ।
प्रबोधयञ्छृङ्गरवेण चारुणा
विनिर्गतो वत्सपुरःसरो हरिः ॥ १ ॥

śrī-śuka uvāca
kvacid vanāśāya mano dadhad vrajāt
prātaḥ samutthāya vayasya-vatsapān
prabodhayañ chṛṅga-raveṇa cāruṇā
vinirgato vatsa-puraḥsaro hariḥ

śrī-śukaḥ uvāca—Śrī Śukadeva Gosvāmī said; *kvacit*—one day; *vana-āśāya*—just to enjoy a picnic in the forest; *manaḥ*—mind; *dadhat*—gave attention; *vrajāt*—and went out of Vrajabhūmi; *prātaḥ*—early in the morning; *samutthāya*—waking up; *vayasya-vatsa-pān*—the cowherd boys and the calves; *prabodhayan*—to get everyone to rise, waking up and informing them; *śṛṅga-raveṇa*—by sounding the bugle made of horn; *cāruṇā*—very beautiful; *vinirgataḥ*—came out of Vrajabhūmi; *vatsa-puraḥsaraḥ*—keeping the respective groups of calves in front; *hariḥ*—the Supreme Personality of Godhead.

TRANSLATION

Śukadeva Gosvāmī continued: O King, one day Kṛṣṇa decided to take His breakfast as a picnic in the forest. Having risen early in

the morning, He blew His bugle made of horn and woke all the cowherd boys and calves with its beautiful sound. Then Kṛṣṇa and the boys, keeping their respective groups of calves before them, proceeded from Vrajabhūmi to the forest.

TEXT 2

तेनैव साकं पृथुकाः सहस्रशः
स्निग्धाः सुशिग्वेत्रविषाणवेणवः ।
स्वान् स्वान् सहस्रोपरिसंख्ययान्वितान्
वत्सान् पुरस्कृत्य विनिर्ययुर्मुदा ॥ २ ॥

tenaiva sākaṁ pṛthukāḥ sahasraśaḥ
snigdhāḥ suśig-vetra-viṣāṇa-veṇavaḥ
svān svān sahasropari-saṅkhyayānvitān
vatsān puraskṛtya viniryayur mudā

tena—Him; *eva*—indeed; *sākam*—accompanied by; *pṛthukāḥ*—the boys; *sahasraśaḥ*—by the thousands; *snigdhāḥ*—very attractive; *su*—beautiful; *śik*—lunch bags; *vetra*—sticks for controlling the calves; *viṣāṇa*—horn bugles; *veṇavaḥ*—flutes; *svān svān*—their own respective; *sahasra-upari-saṅkhyayā anvitān*—numbering over a thousand; *vatsān*—the calves; *puraḥ-kṛtya*—keeping in front; *viniryayuḥ*—they came out; *mudā*—with great pleasure.

TRANSLATION

At that time, hundreds and thousands of cowherd boys came out of their respective homes in Vrajabhūmi and joined Kṛṣṇa, keeping before them their hundreds and thousands of groups of calves. The boys were very beautiful, and they were equipped with lunch bags, bugles, flutes, and sticks for controlling the calves.

TEXT 3

कृष्णवत्सैरसंख्यातैर्यूथीकृत्य स्ववत्सकान् ।
चारयन्तोऽर्भलीलाभिर्विजह्रुस्तत्र तत्र ह ॥ ३ ॥

kṛṣṇa-vatsair asaṅkhyātair
yūthī-kṛtya sva-vatsakān
cārayanto 'rbha-līlābhir
vijahrus tatra tatra ha

kṛṣṇa—of Lord Kṛṣṇa; *vatsaiḥ*—along with the calves; *asaṅkhyātaiḥ*—unlimited; *yūthī-kṛtya*—assembled them; *sva-vatsakān*—personal calves; *cārayantaḥ*—executing; *arbha-līlābhiḥ*—by boyhood pastimes; *vijahruḥ*—enjoyed; *tatra tatra*—here and there; *ha*—indeed.

TRANSLATION

Along with the cowherd boys and their own groups of calves, Kṛṣṇa came out with an unlimited number of calves assembled. Then all the boys began to sport in the forest in a greatly playful spirit.

PURPORT

In this verse the words *kṛṣṇa-vatsair asaṅkhyātaiḥ* are significant. The word *asaṅkhyāta* means "unlimited." Kṛṣṇa's calves were unlimited. We may speak of hundreds, thousands, tens of thousands, hundreds of thousands, millions, billions, trillions, tens of trillions, and so on, but when we go further to speak of numbers impossible for us to count, we are speaking of unlimited numbers. Such unlimited numbers are indicated here by the word *asaṅkhyātaiḥ*. Kṛṣṇa is unlimited, His potency is unlimited, His cows and calves are unlimited, and His space is unlimited. Therefore He is described in *Bhagavad-gītā* as Parabrahman. The word *brahman* means "unlimited," and Kṛṣṇa is the Supreme Unlimited, Parabrahman. Therefore, we should not consider the statements of this verse to be mythological. They are factual, but inconceivable. Kṛṣṇa can accommodate an unlimited number of calves and an unlimited measurement of space. This is neither mythological nor false, but if we study Kṛṣṇa's potency with our limited knowledge, that potency will never be possible to understand. *Ataḥ śrī-kṛṣṇa-nāmādi na bhaved grāhyam indriyaiḥ* (*Bhakti-rasāmṛta-sindhu* 1.2.109). Our senses cannot perceive how He could keep an unlimited number of calves and cows and have unlimited space in which to do so. But this is answered in the *Bṛhad-bhāgavatāmṛta:*

evaṁ prabhoḥ priyānāṁ ca
dhāmnaś ca samayasya ca
avicintya-prabhāvatvād
atra kiñcin na durghaṭam

Śrī Sanātana Gosvāmī, in the *Bṛhad-bhāgavatāmṛta*, states that since everything about Kṛṣṇa is unlimited, nothing is impossible for Him. It is in this sense that we have to understand this verse.

TEXT 4

फलप्रबालस्तवकसुमनःपिच्छधातुभिः ।
काचगुञ्जामणिस्वर्णभूषिता अप्यभूषयन् ॥ ४ ॥

phala-prabāla-stavaka-
sumanaḥ-piccha-dhātubhiḥ
kāca-guñjā-maṇi-svarṇa-
bhūṣitā apy abhūṣayan

phala—fruits from the forest; *prabāla*—green leaves; *stavaka*—bunches; *sumanaḥ*—beautiful flowers; *piccha*—peacock feathers; *dhātubhiḥ*—very soft and colorful minerals; *kāca*—a kind of gem; *guñjā*—small conchshells; *maṇi*—pearls; *svarṇa*—gold; *bhūṣitāḥ*—although decorated; *api abhūṣayan*—in spite of being decorated by their mothers, the boys decorated themselves still more with the above-mentioned articles.

TRANSLATION

Although all these boys were already decorated by their mothers with ornaments of kāca, guñjā, pearls and gold, when they went into the forest they further decorated themselves with fruits, green leaves, bunches of flowers, peacock feathers and soft minerals.

TEXT 5

मुष्णन्तोऽन्योन्यशिक्यादीन् ज्ञातानाराच्च चिक्षिपुः ।
तत्रत्याश्च पुनर्दूराद्धसन्तश्च पुनर्ददुः ॥ ५ ॥

muṣṇanto 'nyonya-śikyādīn
jñātān ārāc ca cikṣipuḥ
tatratyāś ca punar dūrād
dhasantaś ca punar daduḥ

muṣṇantaḥ—stealing; *anyonya*—from one another; *śikya-ādīn*—lunch bags and other belongings; *jñātān*—having been understood by the proprietor of the bag; *ārāt ca*—to a distant place; *cikṣipuḥ*—threw away; *tatratyāḥ ca*—those who were in that place also; *punaḥ dūrāt*—then again threw farther away; *hasantaḥ ca punaḥ daduḥ*—when they saw the proprietor, they threw it farther away and enjoyed laughing, and when the owner sometimes cried, his bag was given to him again.

TRANSLATION

All the cowherd boys used to steal one another's lunch bags. When a boy came to understand that his bag had been taken away, the other boys would throw it farther away, to a more distant place, and those standing there would throw it still farther. When the proprietor of the bag became disappointed, the other boys would laugh, the proprietor would cry, and then the bag would be returned.

PURPORT

This kind of playing and stealing among boys still exists even in the material world because this kind of sporting pleasure is present in the spiritual world, from which this idea of enjoyment emanates. *Janmādy asya yataḥ* (*Vedānta-sūtra* 1.1.2). This same enjoyment is displayed by Kṛṣṇa and His associates in the spiritual world, but there the enjoyment is eternal, whereas here, on the material platform, it is temporary; there the enjoyment is Brahman, whereas here the enjoyment is *jaḍa*. The Kṛṣṇa consciousness movement is meant to train one how to transfer oneself from the *jaḍa* to the Brahman, because human life is meant for this purpose. *Athāto brahma-jijñāsā* (*Vedānta-sūtra* 1.1.1). Kṛṣṇa comes down to teach us how we can enjoy with Him on the spiritual platform, in the spiritual world. Not only does He come, but He personally displays His pastimes in Vṛndāvana and attracts people to spiritual enjoyment.

TEXT 6

यदि दूरं गतः कृष्णो वनशोभेक्षणाय तम् ।
अहं पूर्वमहं पूर्वमिति संस्पृश्य रेमिरे ॥ ६ ॥

yadi dūraṁ gataḥ kṛṣṇo
vana-śobhekṣaṇāya tam
ahaṁ pūrvam ahaṁ pūrvam
iti saṁspṛśya remire

yadi—if; *dūram*—to a distant place; *gataḥ*—went; *kṛṣṇaḥ*—the Supreme Personality of Godhead; *vana-śobha*—the beauty of the forest; *īkṣaṇāya*—for visiting and enjoying; *tam*—unto Kṛṣṇa; *aham*—I; *pūrvam*—first; *aham*—I; *pūrvam*—first; *iti*—in this way; *saṁspṛśya*—by touching Him; *remire*—they enjoyed life.

TRANSLATION

Sometimes Kṛṣṇa would go to a somewhat distant place to see the beauty of the forest. Then all the other boys would run to accompany Him, each one saying, "I shall be the first to run and touch Kṛṣṇa! I shall touch Kṛṣṇa first!" In this way they enjoyed life by repeatedly touching Kṛṣṇa.

TEXTS 7–11

केचिद् वेणून् वादयन्तो ध्मान्तः शृङ्गाणि केचन ।
केचिद् भृङ्गैः प्रगायन्तः कूजन्तः कोकिलैः परे ॥७॥
विच्छायाभिः प्रधावन्तो गच्छन्तः साधु हंसकैः ।
बकैरुपविशन्तश्च नृत्यन्तश्च कलापिभिः ॥ ८ ॥
विकर्षन्तः कीशबालानारोहन्तश्च तैर्द्रुमान् ।
विकुर्वन्तश्च तैः साकं प्लवन्तश्च पलाशिषु ॥ ९ ॥
साकं भेकैर्विलङ्घन्तः सरितः स्रवसम्प्लुताः ।
विहसन्तः प्रतिच्छायाः शपन्तश्च प्रतिस्वनान् ॥१०॥

इत्थं सतां ब्रह्मसुखानुभूत्या
दास्यं गतानां परदैवतेन ।
मायाश्रितानां नरदारकेण
साकं विजह्रुः कृतपुण्यपुञ्जाः ॥११॥

kecid veṇūn vādayanto
dhmāntaḥ śṛṅgāṇi kecana
kecid bhṛṅgaiḥ pragāyantaḥ
kūjantaḥ kokilaiḥ pare

vicchāyābhiḥ pradhāvanto
gacchantaḥ sādhu-haṁsakaiḥ
bakair upaviśantaś ca
nṛtyantaś ca kalāpibhiḥ

vikarṣantaḥ kīśa-bālān
ārohantaś ca tair drumān
vikurvantaś ca taiḥ sākaṁ
plavantaś ca palāśiṣu

sākaṁ bhekair vilaṅghantaḥ
saritaḥ srava-samplutāḥ
vihasantaḥ praticchāyāḥ
śapantaś ca pratisvanān

itthaṁ satāṁ brahma-sukhānubhūtyā
dāsyaṁ gatānāṁ para-daivatena
māyāśritānāṁ nara-dārakeṇa
sākaṁ vijahruḥ kṛta-puṇya-puñjāḥ

kecit—some of them; *veṇūn*—flutes; *vādayantaḥ*—blowing; *dhmāntaḥ*—bugling; *śṛṅgāṇi*—the horn bugles; *kecana*—someone else; *kecit*—someone; *bhṛṅgaiḥ*—with the bumblebees; *pragāyantaḥ*—singing along with; *kūjantaḥ*—imitating the sound of; *kokilaiḥ*—with the cuckoos; *pare*—others; *vicchāyābhiḥ*—with running shadows; *pradhāvantaḥ*—someone running on the ground after the birds; *gacchantaḥ*—going along; *sādhu*—beautiful; *haṁsakaiḥ*—with the swans; *bakaiḥ*—with the ducks sitting in one place; *upaviśantaḥ ca*—sitting silently like them; *nṛtyantaḥ ca*—and dancing with; *kalāpibhiḥ*—with the peacocks; *vikarṣantaḥ*—attracting; *kīśa-bālān*—the young monkeys; *ārohantaḥ ca*—gliding over; *taiḥ*—with the monkeys; *drumān*—the trees; *vikurvantaḥ ca*—exactly imitating them; *taiḥ*—with the monkeys; *sākam*—along with; *plavantaḥ ca*—gliding over; *palāśiṣu*—on the trees; *sākam*—along with; *bhekaiḥ*—with the frogs; *vilaṅghantaḥ*—jumping like them; *saritaḥ*—the water; *srava-samplutāḥ*—became wet in the water of the river; *vihasantaḥ*—laughing; *praticchāyāḥ*—at the shadows; *śapantaḥ ca*—condemned; *pratisvanān*—the sound of their echoes; *ittham*—in this way; *satām*—of the transcendentalists; *brahma-sukha-anubhūtyā*—with Kṛṣṇa, the source of *brahma-sukha* (Kṛṣṇa is Parabrahman, and from Him originates His personal effulgence); *dāsyam*—servitorship; *gatānām*—of the devotees who have accepted; *para-daivatena*—with the Supreme Personality of Godhead; *māyā-āśritānām*—for those in the clutches of material energy; *nara-dārakeṇa*—with Him who is like an ordinary child; *sākam*—along with; *vijahruḥ*—enjoyed; *kṛta-puṇya-puñjāḥ*—all these boys, who had accumulated the results of life after life of pious activities.

TRANSLATION

All the boys would be differently engaged. Some boys blew their flutes, and others blew bugles made of horn. Some imitated the buzzing of the bumblebees, and others imitated the voice of the cuckoo. Some boys imitated flying birds by running after the birds' shadows on the ground, some imitated the beautiful movements and attractive postures of the swans, some sat down with the ducks, sitting silently, and others imitated the dancing of the peacocks. Some boys attracted young monkeys in the trees, some jumped into the trees, imitating the monkeys, some made faces as the monkeys were accustomed to do, and others jumped from one branch to another. Some boys went to the waterfalls and crossed over the river, jumping with the frogs, and when they saw their own reflections on the water they would laugh. They would also condemn the sounds of their own echoes. In this way, all the cowherd boys used to play with Kṛṣṇa, who is the source of the Brahman effulgence for jñānīs desiring to merge into that effulgence, who is the Supreme Personality of Godhead for

devotees who have accepted eternal servitorship, and who for ordinary persons is but another ordinary child. The cowherd boys, having accumulated the results of pious activities for many lives, were able to associate in this way with the Supreme Personality of Godhead. How can one explain their great fortune?

PURPORT

As recommended by Śrīla Rūpa Gosvāmī, *tasmāt kenāpy upāyena manaḥ kṛṣṇe niveśayet* (*Bhakti-rasāmṛta-sindhu* 1.2.4). Somehow or other, whether one thinks of Kṛṣṇa as an ordinary human child, as the source of the Brahman effulgence, as the origin of Paramātmā, or as the Supreme Personality of Godhead, one should concentrate one's full attention upon the lotus feet of Kṛṣṇa. That is also the instruction of *Bhagavad-gītā* (18.66): *sarva-dharmān parityajya mām ekaṁ śaraṇaṁ vraja. Śrīmad-Bhāgavatam* is the easiest way of directly approaching Kṛṣṇa. *Īśvaraḥ sadyo hṛdy avarudhyate 'tra kṛtibhiḥ śuśrūṣubhis tatkṣaṇāt* (*Bhāg.* 1.1.2). Diverting even a little of one's attention toward Kṛṣṇa and activities in Kṛṣṇa consciousness immediately enables one to achieve the highest perfection of life. This is the purpose of the Kṛṣṇa consciousness movement. *Lokasyājānato vidvāṁś cakre sātvata-saṁhitām* (*Bhāg.* 1.7.6). The secret of success is unknown to people in general, and therefore Śrīla Vyāsadeva, being compassionate toward the poor souls in this material world, especially in this age of Kali, has given us the *Śrīmad-Bhāgavatam. Śrīmad-bhāgavataṁ purāṇam amalaṁ yad vaiṣṇavānāṁ priyam* (*Bhāg.* 12.13.18). For Vaiṣṇavas who are somewhat advanced, or who are fully aware of the glories and potencies of the Lord, *Śrīmad-Bhāgavatam* is a beloved Vedic literature. After all, we have to change this body (*tathā dehāntara-prāptiḥ*). If we do not care about *Bhagavad-gītā* and *Śrīmad-Bhāgavatam*, we do not know what the next body will be. But if one adheres to these two books—*Bhagavad-gītā* and *Śrīmad-Bhāgavatam*—one is sure to obtain the association of Kṛṣṇa in the next life (*tyaktvā dehaṁ punar janma naiti mām eti so 'rjuna*). Therefore, distribution of *Śrīmad-Bhāgavatam* all over the world is a great welfare activity for theologians, philosophers, transcendentalists and *yogīs* (*yoginām api sarveṣām*), as well as for people in general. *Janma-lābhaḥ paraḥ puṁsām ante nārāyaṇa-smṛtiḥ* (*Bhāg.* 2.1.6): if we can somehow or other remember Kṛṣṇa, Nārāyaṇa, at the end of life, our life will be successful.

TEXT 12

यत्पादपांसुर्बहुजन्मकृच्छ्रतो
धृतात्मभिर्योगिभिरप्यलभ्यः ।
स एव यद्दृग्विषयः स्वयं स्थितः
किं वर्ण्यते दिष्टमतो व्रजौकसाम् ॥१२॥

yat-pāda-pāṁsur bahu-janma-kṛcchrato
dhṛtātmabhir yogibhir apy alabhyaḥ
sa eva yad-dṛg-viṣayaḥ svayaṁ sthitaḥ
kiṁ varṇyate diṣṭam ato vrajaukasām

yat—whose; *pāda-pāṁsuḥ*—dust of the lotus feet; *bahu-janma*—in many births; *kṛcchrataḥ*—from undergoing severe austerities and penances as a way of practicing *yoga*, meditation, etc.; *dhṛta-ātmabhiḥ*—by persons able to control the mind; *yogibhiḥ*—by such *yogīs* (*jñāna-yogīs, rāja-yogīs, dhyāna-yogīs*, etc.); *api*—indeed; *alabhyaḥ*—cannot be achieved; *saḥ*—the Supreme Personality of Godhead; *eva*—indeed; *yat-dṛk-viṣayaḥ*—has become the object of direct vision, face to face; *svayam*—personally; *sthitaḥ*—present in front of them; *kim*—what; *varṇyate*—can be described; *diṣṭam*—about the fortune; *ataḥ*—therefore; *vraja-okasām*—of the inhabitants of Vrajabhūmi, Vṛndāvana.

TRANSLATION

Yogīs may undergo severe austerities and penances for many births by practicing yama, niyama, āsana and prāṇāyāma, none of which are easily performed. Yet in due course of time, when these yogīs attain the perfection of controlling the mind, they will still be unable to taste even a particle of dust from the lotus feet of the Supreme Personality of Godhead. What then can we describe about the great fortune of the inhabitants of Vrajabhūmi, Vṛndāvana, with whom the Supreme Personality of Godhead personally lived and who saw the Lord face to face?

PURPORT

We can simply imagine the great fortune of the inhabitants of Vṛndāvana. It is impossible to describe how, after many, many births of pious activities, they have become so fortunate.

TEXT 13

अथाघनामाभ्यपतन्महासुर-
स्तेषां सुखक्रीडनवीक्षणाक्षमः ।
नित्यं यदन्तर्निजजीवितेप्सुभिः
पीतामृतैरप्यमरैः प्रतीक्ष्यते ॥१३॥

athāgha-nāmābhyapatan mahāsuras
teṣāṁ sukha-krīḍana-vīkṣaṇākṣamaḥ
nityaṁ yad-antar nija-jīvitepsubhiḥ
pītāmṛtair apy amaraiḥ pratīkṣyate

atha—thereafter; *agha-nāma*—a very powerful demon by the name Agha; *abhyapatat*—appeared on the spot; *mahā-asuraḥ*—a great, extremely powerful demon; *teṣām*—of the cowherd boys; *sukha-krīḍana*—the enjoyment of their transcendental pastimes; *vīkṣaṇa-akṣamaḥ*—being unable to see, he could not tolerate the transcendental happiness of the cowherd boys; *nityam*—perpetually; *yat-antaḥ*—the end of the life of Aghāsura; *nija-jīvita-īpsubhiḥ*—just to live undisturbed by Aghāsura; *pīta-amṛtaiḥ api*—although they drank nectar every day; *amaraiḥ*—by such demigods; *pratīkṣyate*—was also being awaited (the demigods were also awaiting the death of the great demon Aghāsura).

TRANSLATION

My dear King Parīkṣit, thereafter there appeared a great demon named Aghāsura, whose death was being awaited even by the demigods. The demigods drank nectar every day, but still they feared this great demon and awaited his death. This demon could not tolerate the transcendental pleasure being enjoyed in the forest by the cowherd boys.

PURPORT

One may ask how Kṛṣṇa's pastimes could be interrupted by a demon. Śrīla Viśvanātha Cakravartī Ṭhākura answers this question by saying that although the transcendental pleasure being enjoyed by the cowherd boys could not be stopped, unless they stopped the transcendental pleasure of their various activities they could not eat their lunch. Therefore at lunchtime Aghāsura appeared by the arrangement of *yogamāyā*, so that for the time being they could stop their activities and take lunch. Changing varieties are the mother of enjoyment. The cowherd boys would continuously play, then stop, and then again enjoy in a different way. Therefore every day a demon would come and interrupt their sporting pastimes. The demon would be killed, and then the boys would engage again in their transcendental pastimes.

TEXT 14

दृष्ट्वार्भकान् कृष्णमुखानघासुरः
कंसानुशिष्टः स बकीबकानुजः ।
अयं तु मे सोदरनाशकृत्तयो-
र्द्वयोर्ममैनं सबलं हनिष्ये ॥१४॥

dṛṣṭvārbhakān kṛṣṇa-mukhān aghāsuraḥ
kaṁsānuśiṣṭaḥ sa bakī-bakānujaḥ
ayaṁ tu me sodara-nāśa-kṛt tayor
dvayor mamainaṁ sa-balaṁ haniṣye

dṛṣṭvā—after seeing; *arbhakān*—all the cowherd boys; *kṛṣṇa-mukhān*—headed by Kṛṣṇa; *aghāsuraḥ*—the demon by the name Aghāsura; *kaṁsa-anuśiṣṭaḥ*—sent by Kaṁsa; *saḥ*—he (Aghāsura); *bakī-baka-anujaḥ*—the younger brother of Pūtanā and Bakāsura; *ayam*—this Kṛṣṇa; *tu*—indeed; *me*—my; *sodara-nāśa-kṛt*—the killer of my brother and sister; *tayoḥ*—for my brother and sister; *dvayoḥ*—for those two; *mama*—my; *enam*—Kṛṣṇa; *sa-balam*—along with His assistants, the cowherd boys; *haniṣye*—I shall kill.

TRANSLATION

Aghāsura, who had been sent by Kaṁsa, was the younger brother of Pūtanā and Bakāsura. Therefore when he came and saw Kṛṣṇa at the head of all the cowherd boys, he thought, "This Kṛṣṇa has killed my sister and brother, Pūtanā and Bakāsura. Therefore, in order to please them both, I shall kill this Kṛṣṇa, along with His assistants, the other cowherd boys."

TEXT 15

एते यदा मत्सुहृदोस्तिलापः
कृतास्तदा नष्टसमा व्रजौकसः ।
प्राणे गते वर्ष्मसु का नु चिन्ता
प्रजासवः प्राणभृतो हि ये ते ॥१५॥

ete yadā mat-suhṛdos tilāpaḥ
kṛtās tadā naṣṭa-samā vrajaukasaḥ
prāṇe gate varṣmasu kā nu cintā
prajāsavaḥ prāṇa-bhṛto hi ye te

ete—this Kṛṣṇa and His associates, the cowherd boys; *yadā*—when; *mat-suhṛdoḥ*—of my brother and sister; *tila-āpaḥ kṛtāḥ*—become the last ritualistic ceremonial offering of sesame and water; *tadā*—at that time; *naṣṭa-samāḥ*—without life; *vraja-okasaḥ*—all the inhabitants of Vrajabhūmi, Vṛndāvana; *prāṇe*—when the vital force; *gate*—has been thrown out of the body; *varṣmasu*—as far as the body is concerned; *kā*—what; *nu*—indeed; *cintā*—consideration; *prajā-asavaḥ*—those whose love for their children is the same as their love for their own life; *prāṇa-bhṛtaḥ*—those living beings; *hi*—indeed; *ye te*—all the inhabitants of Vrajabhūmi.

TRANSLATION

Aghāsura thought: If somehow or other I can make Kṛṣṇa and His associates serve as the last offering of sesame and water for the departed souls of my brother and sister, then the inhabitants of Vrajabhūmi, for whom these boys are the life and soul, will automatically die. If there is no life, there is no need for the body; consequently, when their sons are dead, naturally all the inhabitants of Vraja will die.

TEXT 16

इति व्यवस्याजगरं बृहद् वपुः
स योजनायाममहाद्रिपीवरम् ।

धृत्वाद्भुतं व्यात्तगुहाननं तदा
पथि व्यशेत ग्रसनाशया खलः ॥१६॥

iti vyavasyājagaraṁ bṛhad vapuḥ
sa yojanāyāma-mahādri-pīvaram
dhṛtvādbhutaṁ vyātta-guhānanaṁ tadā
pathi vyaśeta grasanāśayā khalaḥ

iti—in this way; *vyavasya*—deciding; *ājagaram*—python; *bṛhat vapuḥ*—a very, very large body; *saḥ*—Aghāsura; *yojana-āyāma*—occupying eight miles of land; *mahā-adri-pīvaram*—as thick as a great mountain; *dhṛtvā*—assuming this form; *adbhutam*—wonderful; *vyātta*—spread; *guhā-ānanam*—having a mouth resembling a big cave in a mountain; *tadā*—at that time; *pathi*—on the road; *vyaśeta*—occupied; *grasana-āśayā*—expecting to swallow all the cowherd boys; *khalaḥ*—the most crooked.

TRANSLATION

After thus deciding, that crooked Aghāsura assumed the form of a huge python, as thick as a big mountain and as long as eight miles. Having assumed this wonderful python's body, he spread his mouth like a big cave in the mountains and lay down on the road, expecting to swallow Kṛṣṇa and His associates the cowherd boys.

TEXT 17

धराधरोष्ठो जलदोत्तरोष्ठो
दर्याननान्तो गिरिशृङ्गदंष्ट्रः ।
ध्वान्तान्तरास्यो विततध्वजिह्वः
परुषानिलश्वासदवेक्षणोष्णः ॥१७॥

dharādharoṣṭho jaladottaroṣṭho
dary-ānanānto giri-śṛṅga-daṁṣṭraḥ
dhvāntāntar-āsyo vitatādhva-jihvaḥ
paruṣānila-śvāsa-davekṣaṇoṣṇaḥ

dharā—on the surface of the globe; *adhara-oṣṭhaḥ*—whose lower lip; *jalada-uttara-oṣṭhaḥ*—whose upper lip was touching the clouds; *darī-ānana-antaḥ*—whose mouth was expanded very widely like a mountain cave; *giri-śṛṅga*—like a mountain peak; *daṁṣṭraḥ*—whose teeth; *dhvānta-antaḥ-āsyaḥ*—within whose mouth the atmosphere was as dark as possible; *vitata-adhva-jihvaḥ*—whose tongue was like a broad way; *paruṣa-anila-śvāsa*—whose breath was like a warm wind; *dava-īkṣaṇa-uṣṇaḥ*—and whose glance was like flames of fire.

TRANSLATION

His lower lip rested on the surface of the earth, and his upper lip was touching the clouds in the sky. The borders of his mouth resembled the sides of a big cave in a mountain, and the middle of his mouth was as dark as possible. His tongue resembled a broad trafficway, his breath was like a warm wind, and his eyes blazed like fire.

TEXT 18

दृष्ट्वा तं तादृशं सर्वे मत्वा वृन्दावनश्रियम् ।
व्यात्ताजगरतुण्डेन ह्युत्प्रेक्षन्ते स्म लीलया ॥१८॥

dṛṣṭvā taṁ tādṛśaṁ sarve
matvā vṛndāvana-śriyam
vyāttājagara-tuṇḍena
hy utprekṣante sma līlayā

dṛṣṭvā—seeing; *tam*—that Aghāsura; *tādṛśam*—in that posture; *sarve*—Kṛṣṇa and all the cowherd boys; *matvā*—thought it; *vṛndāvana-śriyam*—a beautiful statue of Vṛndāvana; *vyātta*—spread; *ajagara-tuṇḍena*—with the form of a python's mouth; *hi*—indeed; *utprekṣante*—as if observing; *sma*—in the past; *līlayā*—as a matter of pastimes.

TRANSLATION

Upon seeing this demon's wonderful form, which resembled a great python, the boys thought that it must be a beautiful scenic

spot of Vṛndāvana. Thereafter, they imagined it to be similar to the mouth of a great python. In other words, the boys, unafraid, thought that it was a statue made in the shape of a great python for the enjoyment of their pastimes.

PURPORT

Some of the boys, upon seeing this wonderful phenomenon, thought that it was in fact a python, and they were fleeing from the spot. But others said, "Why are you fleeing? It is not possible that a python like this is staying here. This is a spot of beauty for sporting." This is what they imagined.

TEXT 19

अहो मित्राणि गदत सत्त्वकूटं पुरः स्थितम् ।
अस्मत्संग्रसनव्यात्तव्यालतुण्डायते न वा ॥१९॥

aho mitrāṇi gadata
sattva-kūṭaṁ puraḥ sthitam
asmat-saṅgrasana-vyātta-
vyāla-tuṇḍāyate na vā

aho—oh; *mitrāṇi*—friends; *gadata*—just let us know; *sattva-kūṭam*—dead python; *puraḥ sthitam*—as it is just before us all; *asmat*—all of us; *saṅgrasana*—to devour us altogether; *vyātta-vyāla-tuṇḍāyate*—the python has spread its mouth; *na vā*—whether it is a fact or not.

TRANSLATION

The boys said: Dear friends, is this creature dead, or is it actually a living python with its mouth spread wide just to swallow us all? Kindly clear up this doubt.

PURPORT

The friends began to discuss among themselves the reality of the wonderful creature laying before them. Was it dead, or was it actually a living python trying to swallow them up?

TEXT 20

सत्यमर्ककरारक्तमुत्तराहनुवद् घनम् ।
अधराहनुवद् रोधस्तत्प्रतिच्छाययारुणम् ॥२०॥

satyam arka-karāraktam
uttarā-hanuvad ghanam
adharā-hanuvad rodhas
tat-praticchāyayāruṇam

satyam—now the boys decided that it was in fact a living python; *arka-kara-āraktam*—appearing like the sunshine; *uttarā-hanuvat ghanam*—on the cloud resembling the upper lips; *adharā-hanuvat*—resembling the lower lips; *rodhaḥ*—big bank; *tat-praticchāyayā*—by the reflection of sunshine; *aruṇam*—reddish.

TRANSLATION

Thereafter they decided: Dear friends, this is certainly an animal sitting here to swallow us all. Its upper lip resembles a cloud reddened by the sunshine, and its lower lip resembles the reddish shadows of a cloud.

TEXT 21

प्रतिस्पर्धेते सृक्कभ्यां सव्यासव्ये नगोदरे ।
तुङ्गशृङ्गालयोऽप्येतास्तद्दंष्ट्राभिश्च पश्यत ॥२१॥

pratispardhete sṛkkabhyāṁ
savyāsavye nagodare
tuṅga-śṛṅgālayo 'py etās
tad-daṁṣṭrābhiś ca paśyata

pratispardhete—just resembling; *sṛkkabhyām*—with the corners of the mouth; *savya-asavye*—left and right; *naga-udare*—caves of a mountain; *tuṅga-śṛṅga-ālayaḥ*—the high mountain peaks; *api*—although it is so; *etāḥ tat-daṁṣṭrābhiḥ*—they resemble the teeth of the animal; *ca*—and; *paśyata*—just see.

TRANSLATION

On the left and right, the two depressions resembling mountain caves are the corners of its mouth, and the high mountain peaks are its teeth.

TEXT 22

आस्तृतायाममार्गोऽयं रसनां प्रतिगर्जति ।
एषामन्तर्गतं ध्वान्तमेतदप्यन्तराननम् ॥२२॥

āstṛtāyāma-mārgo 'yaṁ
rasanāṁ pratigarjati
eṣām antar-gataṁ dhvāntam
etad apy antar-ānanam

āstṛta-āyāma—the length and breadth; *mārgaḥ ayam*—a broad way; *rasanām*—the tongue; *pratigarjati*—resembles; *eṣām antaḥ-gatam*—on the inside of the mountains; *dhvāntam*—darkness; *etat*—this; *api*—indeed; *antaḥ-ānanam*—the inside of the mouth.

TRANSLATION

In length and breadth the animal's tongue resembles a broad trafficway, and the inside of its mouth is very, very dark, like a cave in a mountain.

TEXT 23

दावोष्णखरवातोऽयं श्वासवद् भाति पश्यत ।
तद्दग्धसत्त्वदुर्गन्धोऽप्यन्तरामिषगन्धवत् ॥२३॥

dāvoṣṇa-khara-vāto 'yaṁ
śvāsavad bhāti paśyata
tad-dagdha-sattva-durgandho
'py antar-āmiṣa-gandhavat

dāva-uṣṇa-khara-vātaḥ ayam—hot breath coming out exactly like fire; *śvāsa-vat bhāti paśyata*—just see how it resembles his breath;

tat-dagdha-sattva—of burning corpses; *durgandhaḥ*—the bad smell; *api*—indeed; *antaḥ-āmiṣa-gandha-vat*—is like the fleshy smell coming out from within.

TRANSLATION

The hot fiery wind is the breath coming out of his mouth, which is giving off the bad smell of burning flesh because of all the dead bodies he has eaten.

TEXT 24

अस्मान् किमत्र ग्रसिता निविष्टा-
नयं तथा चेद् बकवद् विनङ्क्ष्यति ।
क्षणादनेनेति बकार्युशन्मुखं
वीक्ष्योद्धसन्तः करताडनैर्ययुः ॥२४॥

asmān kim atra grasitā niviṣṭān
ayaṁ tathā ced bakavad vinaṅkṣyati
kṣaṇād aneneti bakāry-uśan-mukhaṁ
vīkṣyoddhasantaḥ kara-tāḍanair yayuḥ

asmān—all of us; *kim*—whether; *atra*—here; *grasitā*—will swallow; *niviṣṭān*—who have attempted to enter; *ayam*—this animal; *tathā*—so; *cet*—if; *baka-vat*—like Bakāsura; *vinaṅkṣyati*—he will be vanquished; *kṣaṇāt*—immediately; *anena*—by this Kṛṣṇa; *iti*—in this way; *baka-ari-uśat-mukham*—the beautiful face of Kṛṣṇa, the enemy of Bakāsura; *vīkṣya*—observing, looking at; *uddhasantaḥ*—loudly laughing; *kara-tāḍanaiḥ*—with clapping of hands; *yayuḥ*—entered the mouth.

TRANSLATION

Then the boys said, "Has this living creature come to swallow us? If he does so, he will immediately be killed like Bakāsura, without delay." Thus they looked at the beautiful face of Kṛṣṇa, the enemy of Bakāsura, and, laughing loudly and clapping their hands, they entered the mouth of the python.

PURPORT

After talking about the terrible animal this way and that way, they decided to enter the demon's mouth. They had full faith in Kṛṣṇa because they had experienced how Kṛṣṇa had saved them from the mouth of Bakāsura. Now, here was another *asura,* Aghāsura. Therefore, they wanted to enjoy the sport of entering the demon's mouth and being saved by Kṛṣṇa, the enemy of Bakāsura.

TEXT 25

इत्थं मिथोऽतथ्यमतज्ज्ञभाषितं
श्रुत्वा विचिन्त्येत्यमृषा मृषायते ।
रक्षो विदित्वाखिलभूतहृत्स्थितः
स्वानां निरोद्धुं भगवान् मनो दधे ॥२५॥

itthaṁ mitho 'tathyam ataj-jña-bhāṣitaṁ
śrutvā vicintyety amṛṣā mṛṣāyate
rakṣo viditvākhila-bhūta-hṛt-sthitaḥ
svānāṁ niroddhuṁ bhagavān mano dadhe

ittham—in this way; *mithaḥ*—or another; *atathyam*—a subject matter that is not a fact; *a-tat-jña*—without knowledge; *bhāṣitam*—while they were talking; *śrutvā*—Kṛṣṇa hearing them; *vicintya*—thinking; *iti*—thus; *amṛṣā*—actually, truly; *mṛṣāyate*—who is trying to appear as a false thing (actually the animal was Aghāsura, but because of poor knowledge they were thinking him to be a dead python); *rakṣaḥ*—(Kṛṣṇa, however, could understand that) he was a demon; *viditvā*—knowing it; *akhila-bhūta-hṛt-sthitaḥ*—because He is *antaryāmī,* situated everywhere, in the core of everyone's heart; *svānām*—of His own associates; *niroddhum*—just to forbid them; *bhagavān*—the Supreme Personality of Godhead; *manaḥ dadhe*—made up His mind.

TRANSLATION

The Supreme Personality of Godhead, Śrī Kṛṣṇa, who is situated as antaryāmī, the Supersoul, in the core of everyone's heart, heard the boys talking among themselves about the artificial python.

Unknown to them, it was actually Aghāsura, a demon who had appeared as a python. Kṛṣṇa, knowing this, wanted to forbid His associates to enter the demon's mouth.

TEXT 26

तावत् प्रविष्टास्त्वसुरोदरान्तरं
परं न गीर्णाः शिशवः सवत्साः ।
प्रतीक्षमाणेन बकारिवेशनं
हतस्वकान्तस्मरणेन रक्षसा ॥२६॥

tāvat praviṣṭās tv asurodarāntaraṁ
paraṁ na gīrṇāḥ śiśavaḥ sa-vatsāḥ
pratīkṣamāṇena bakāri-veśanaṁ
hata-sva-kānta-smaraṇena rakṣasā

tāvat—in the meantime; *praviṣṭāḥ*—all entered; *tu*—indeed; *asura-udara-antaram*—within the belly of the great demon; *param*—but; *na gīrṇāḥ*—they were not swallowed; *śiśavaḥ*—all the boys; *sa-vatsāḥ*—along with their calves; *pratīkṣamāṇena*—who was just waiting for; *baka-ari*—of the enemy of Bakāsura; *veśanam*—the entering; *hata-sva-kānta-smaraṇena*—the *asura* was thinking of his own dead relatives, who would not be satisfied unless Kṛṣṇa were dead; *rakṣasā*—by the demon.

TRANSLATION

In the meantime, while Kṛṣṇa was considering how to stop them, all the cowherd boys entered the mouth of the demon. The demon, however, did not swallow them, for he was thinking of his own relatives who had been killed by Kṛṣṇa and was just waiting for Kṛṣṇa to enter his mouth.

TEXT 27

तान् वीक्ष्य कृष्णः सकलाभयप्रदो
ह्यनन्यनाथान् स्वकरादवच्युतान् ।
दीनांश्च मृत्योर्जठराग्निघासान्
घृणार्दितो दिष्टकृतेन विस्मितः ॥२७॥

tān vīkṣya kṛṣṇaḥ sakalābhaya-prado
hy ananya-nāthān sva-karād avacyutān
dīnāṁś ca mṛtyor jaṭharāgni-ghāsān
ghṛṇārdito diṣṭa-kṛtena vismitaḥ

tān—all those boys; *vīkṣya*—seeing; *kṛṣṇaḥ*—the Supreme Personality of Godhead, Kṛṣṇa; *sakala-abhaya-pradaḥ*—who is the source of fearlessness for everyone; *hi*—indeed; *ananya-nāthān*—especially for the cowherd boys, who did not know anyone except Kṛṣṇa; *sva-karāt*—from the control of His hand; *avacyutān*—now gone out; *dīnān ca*—helpless; *mṛtyoḥ jaṭhara-agni-ghāsān*—who had all entered like straws into the fire of the abdomen of Aghāsura, who was very bold and hungry, like death personified (because the *asura* had assumed a big body, he must have had a very strong appetite); *ghṛṇā-arditaḥ*—therefore, being compassionate due to causeless mercy; *diṣṭa-kṛtena*—by things arranged by His internal potency; *vismitaḥ*—He also, for the time being, was astonished.

TRANSLATION

Kṛṣṇa saw that all the cowherd boys, who did not know anyone but Him as their Lord, had now gone out of His hand and were helpless, having entered like straws into the fire of the abdomen of Aghāsura, who was death personified. It was intolerable for Kṛṣṇa to be separated from His friends the cowherd boys. Therefore, as if seeing that this had been arranged by His internal potency, Kṛṣṇa was momentarily struck with wonder and unsure of what to do.

TEXT 28

कृत्यं किमत्रास्य खलस्य जीवनं
न वा अमीषां च सतां विहिंसनम् ।
द्वयं कथं स्यादिति संविचिन्त्य
ज्ञात्वाविशत्तुण्डमशेषदृग्घरिः ॥२८॥

kṛtyaṁ kim atrāsya khalasya jīvanaṁ
na vā amīṣāṁ ca satāṁ vihiṁsanam

dvayaṁ kathaṁ syād iti saṁvicintya
jñātvāviśat tuṇḍam aśeṣa-dṛg ghariḥ

kṛtyam kim—what to do; *atra*—in this situation; *asya khalasya*—of this envious demon; *jīvanam*—the existence of life; *na*—there should not be; *vā*—either; *amīṣām ca*—and of those who are innocent; *satām*—of the devotees; *vihiṁsanam*—the death; *dvayam*—both actions (killing the demon and saving the boys); *katham*—how; *syāt*—can be possible; *iti saṁvicintya*—very perfectly thinking about the subject matter; *jñātvā*—and deciding what to do; *aviśat*—entered; *tuṇḍam*—within the mouth of the demon; *aśeṣa-dṛk hariḥ*—Kṛṣṇa, who has unlimited potency, could understand past, future and present.

TRANSLATION

Now, what was to be done? How could both the killing of this demon and the saving of the devotees be performed simultaneously? Kṛṣṇa, being unlimitedly potent, decided to wait for an intelligent means by which He could simultaneously save the boys and kill the demon. Then He entered the mouth of Aghāsura.

PURPORT

Kṛṣṇa is known as *ananta-vīrya-sarvajña* because everything is known to Him. Because He knows everything perfectly well, it was not difficult for Him to find a means by which He could save the boys and at the same time kill the demon. Thus He also decided to enter the demon's mouth.

TEXT 29

तदा घनच्छदा देवा भयाद्धाहेति चुक्रुशुः ।
जहृषुर्ये च कंसाद्याः कौणपास्त्वघबान्धवाः ॥२९॥

tadā ghana-cchadā devā
bhayād dhā-heti cukruśuḥ
jahṛṣur ye ca kaṁsādyāḥ
kauṇapās tv agha-bāndhavāḥ

tadā—at that time; *ghana-chadāḥ*—behind the clouds; *devāḥ*—all the demigods; *bhayāt*—on account of feeling danger because Kṛṣṇa had entered the mouth of the demon; *hā-hā*—alas, alas; *iti*—in this way; *cukruśuḥ*—they exclaimed; *jahṛṣuḥ*—became jubilant; *ye*—those; *ca*—also; *kaṁsa-ādyāḥ*—Kaṁsa and others; *kauṇapāḥ*—the demons; *tu*—indeed; *agha-bāndhavāḥ*—the friends of Aghāsura.

TRANSLATION

When Kṛṣṇa entered the mouth of Aghāsura, the demigods hidden behind the clouds exclaimed, "Alas! Alas!" But the friends of Aghāsura, like Kaṁsa and other demons, were jubilant.

TEXT 30

तच्छ्रुत्वा भगवान् कृष्णस्त्वव्ययः सार्भवत्सकम् ।
चूर्णीचिकीर्षोरात्मानं तरसा ववृधे गले ॥३०॥

tac chrutvā bhagavān kṛṣṇas
tv avyayaḥ sārbha-vatsakam
cūrṇī-cikīrṣor ātmānaṁ
tarasā vavṛdhe gale

tat—that exclamation of *hā-hā; śrutvā*—hearing; *bhagavān*—the Supreme Personality of Godhead; *kṛṣṇaḥ*—Lord Kṛṣṇa; *tu*—indeed; *avyayaḥ*—never vanquishable; *sa-arbha-vatsakam*—along with the cowherd boys and the calves; *cūrṇī-cikīrṣoḥ*—of that demon, who desired to smash within the abdomen; *ātmānam*—personally, Himself; *tarasā*—very soon; *vavṛdhe*—enlarged; *gale*—within the throat.

TRANSLATION

When the invincible Supreme Personality of Godhead, Kṛṣṇa, heard the demigods crying "Alas! Alas!" from behind the clouds, He immediately enlarged Himself within the demon's throat, just to save Himself and the cowherd boys, His own associates, from the demon who wished to smash them.

PURPORT

Such are the acts of Kṛṣṇa. *Paritrāṇāya sādhūnāṁ vināśāya ca duṣkṛtām* (Bg. 4.8). By enlarging Himself within the throat of the demon, Kṛṣṇa suffocated and killed him and at the same time saved Himself and His associates from imminent death and also saved the demigods from lamentation.

TEXT 31

ततोऽतिकायस्य निरुद्धमार्गिणो
ह्युद्गीर्णदृष्टेर्भ्रमतस्त्वितस्ततः ।
पूर्णोऽन्तरङ्गे पवनो निरुद्धो
मूर्धन् विनिर्भिद्य विनिर्गतो बहिः ॥३१॥

tato 'tikāyasya niruddha-mārgiṇo
hy udgīrṇa-dṛṣṭer bhramatas tv itas tataḥ
pūrṇo 'ntar-aṅge pavano niruddho
mūrdhan vinirbhidya vinirgato bahiḥ

tataḥ—after Kṛṣṇa took action to kill the demon's body from within the mouth; *ati-kāyasya*—of that great demon, who had expanded his body to a very large size; *niruddha-mārgiṇaḥ*—because of suffocating, all outlets being stopped up; *hi udgīrṇa-dṛṣṭeḥ*—whose eyes had popped out; *bhramataḥ tu itaḥ tataḥ*—the eyeballs, or the life air, moving here and there; *pūrṇaḥ*—completely filled; *antaḥ-aṅge*—within the body; *pavanaḥ*—the life air; *niruddhaḥ*—being stopped; *mūrdhan*—the hole in the top of the head; *vinirbhidya*—breaking; *vinirgataḥ*—went out; *bahiḥ*—externally.

TRANSLATION

Then, because Kṛṣṇa had increased the size of His body, the demon extended his own body to a very large size. Nonetheless, his breathing stopped, he suffocated, and his eyes rolled here and there and popped out. The demon's life air, however, could not pass through any outlet, and therefore it finally burst out through a hole in the top of the demon's head.

TEXT 32

तेनैव सर्वेषु बहिर्गतेषु
प्राणेषु वत्सान् सुहृदः परेतान् ।
दृष्ट्या स्वयोत्थाप्य तदन्वितः पुन-
र्वक्त्रान्मुकुन्दो भगवान् विनिर्ययौ ॥३२॥

tenaiva sarveṣu bahir gateṣu
prāṇeṣu vatsān suhṛdaḥ paretān
dṛṣṭyā svayotthāpya tad-anvitaḥ punar
vaktrān mukundo bhagavān viniryayau

tena eva—through that *brahma-randhra*, or the hole in the top of the head; *sarveṣu*—all the air within the body; *bahiḥ gateṣu*—having gone out; *prāṇeṣu*—the life airs, along with the vital force; *vatsān*—the calves; *suhṛdaḥ*—the cowherd boy friends; *paretān*—who were all dead within; *dṛṣṭyā svayā*—by Kṛṣṇa's glancing over; *utthāpya*—brought them back to life; *tat-anvitaḥ*—thus accompanied by them; *punaḥ*—again; *vaktrāt*—from the mouth; *mukundaḥ*—the Supreme Personality of Godhead; *bhagavān*—Kṛṣṇa; *viniryayau*—came out.

TRANSLATION

When all the demon's life air had passed away through that hole in the top of his head, Kṛṣṇa glanced over the dead calves and cowherd boys and brought them back to life. Then Mukunda, who can give one liberation, came out from the demon's mouth with His friends and the calves.

TEXT 33

पीनाहिभोगोत्थितमद्भुतं मह-
ज्ज्योतिः स्वधाम्ना ज्वलयद् दिशो दश ।
प्रतीक्ष्य खेऽवस्थितमीशनिर्गमं
विवेश तस्मिन् मिषतां दिवौकसाम् ॥३३॥

pīnāhi-bhogotthitam adbhutaṁ mahaj
jyotiḥ sva-dhāmnā jvalayad diśo daśa
pratīkṣya khe 'vasthitam īśa-nirgamaṁ
viveśa tasmin miṣatāṁ divaukasām

pīna—very great; *ahi-bhoga-utthitam*—issuing from the serpent's body, which was meant for material enjoyment; *adbhutam*—very wonderful; *mahat*—great; *jyotiḥ*—effulgence; *sva-dhāmnā*—by his own illumination; *jvalayat*—making glaring; *diśaḥ daśa*—all the ten directions; *pratīkṣya*—waiting; *khe*—in the sky; *avasthitam*—individually staying; *īśa-nirgamam*—until the Supreme Personality of Godhead, Kṛṣṇa, came out; *viveśa*—entered; *tasmin*—in the body of Kṛṣṇa; *miṣatām*—while observing; *divaukasām*—all the demigods.

TRANSLATION

From the body of the gigantic python, a glaring effulgence came out, illuminating all directions, and stayed individually in the sky until Kṛṣṇa came out from the corpse's mouth. Then, as all the demigods looked on, this effulgence entered into Kṛṣṇa's body.

PURPORT

Apparently the serpent named Aghāsura, because of having received association with Kṛṣṇa, attained *mukti* by entering Kṛṣṇa's body. Entering the body of Kṛṣṇa is called *sāyujya-mukti*, but later verses prove that Aghāsura, like Dantavakra and others, received *sārūpya-mukti*. This has been broadly described by Śrīla Viśvanātha Cakravartī Ṭhākura with references from the *Vaiṣṇava-toṣaṇī* of Śrīla Jīva Gosvāmī. Aghāsura attained *sārūpya-mukti*, being promoted to the Vaikuṇṭha planets to live with the same four-armed bodily features as Viṣṇu. The explanation of how this is so may be summarized as follows.

The effulgence came out from the python's body and became purified, attaining spiritual *śuddha-sattva*, freedom from material contamination, because Kṛṣṇa had stayed within the serpent's body, even after the serpent's death. One may doubt that such a demon, full of mischievous activities, could attain the liberation of *sārūpya* or *sāyujya*, and one may be astonished about this. But Kṛṣṇa is so kind that in order to drive away such doubts, He had the effulgence, the individual life of the python, wait for some time in its individuality, in the presence of all the demigods.

Kṛṣṇa is the full effulgence, and every living being is part and parcel of that effulgence. As proved here, the effulgence in every living being is individual. For some time, the effulgence remained outside the demon's body, individually, and did not mix with the whole effulgence, the *brahmajyoti.* The Brahman effulgence is not visible to material eyes, but to prove that every living being is individual, Kṛṣṇa had this individual effulgence stay outside the demon's body for some time, for everyone to see. Then Kṛṣṇa proved that anyone killed by Him attains liberation, whether *sāyujya, sārūpya, sāmīpya* or whatever.

But the liberation of those who are on the transcendental platform of love and affection is *vimukti,* special liberation. Thus the serpent first entered the body of Kṛṣṇa personally and mixed with the Brahman effulgence. This merging is called *sāyujya-mukti.* But from later verses we find that Aghāsura attained *sārūpya-mukti.* Text 38 explains that Aghāsura attained a body exactly like that of Viṣṇu, and the verse after that also clearly states that he attained a completely spiritual body like that of Nārāyaṇa. Therefore in two or three places the *Bhāgavatam* has confirmed that Aghāsura attained *sārūpya-mukti.* One may then argue, How is it that he mixed with the Brahman effulgence? The answer is that as Jaya and Vijaya, after three births, again attained *sārūpya-mukti* and association with the Lord, Aghāsura received a similar liberation.

TEXT 34

ततोऽतिहृष्टाः स्वकृतोऽकृतार्हणं
पुष्पैः सुगा अप्सरसश्च नर्तनैः ।
गीतैः सुरा वाद्यधराश्च वाद्यकैः
स्तवैश्च विप्रा जयनिःस्वनैर्गणाः ॥३४॥

tato 'tihṛṣṭāḥ sva-kṛto 'kṛtārhaṇaṁ
puṣpaiḥ sugā apsarasaś ca nartanaiḥ
gītaiḥ surā vādya-dharāś ca vādyakaiḥ
stavaiś ca viprā jaya-niḥsvanair gaṇāḥ

tataḥ—thereafter; *ati-hṛṣṭāḥ*—everyone becoming very much pleased; *sva-kṛtaḥ*—own respective duty; *akṛta*—executed; *arhaṇam*—

in the shape of worshiping the Supreme Personality of Godhead; *puṣpaiḥ*—by showering flowers grown in Nandana-kānana from the heavens; *su-gāḥ*—the celestial singers; *apsarasaḥ ca*—and the celestial dancing girls; *nartanaiḥ*—by dancing; *gītaiḥ*—by singing celestial songs; *surāḥ*—all the demigods; *vādya-dharāḥ ca*—those who played on musical drums; *vādyakaiḥ*—by playing respectively; *stavaiḥ ca*—and by offering prayers; *viprāḥ*—the *brāhmaṇas; jaya-niḥsvanaiḥ*—simply by glorifying the Supreme Personality of Godhead; *gaṇāḥ*—everyone.

TRANSLATION

Thereafter, everyone being pleased, the demigods began to shower flowers from Nandana-kānana, the celestial dancing girls began to dance, and the Gandharvas, who are famous for singing, offered songs of prayer. The drummers began to beat their kettledrums, and the brāhmaṇas offered Vedic hymns. In this way, both in the heavens and on earth, everyone began to perform his own duties, glorifying the Lord.

PURPORT

Everyone has some particular duty. The *śāstra* has concluded (*nirūpitaḥ*) that everyone should glorify the Supreme Personality of Godhead by his own qualifications. If you are a singer, always glorify the Supreme Lord by singing very nicely. If you are a musician, glorify the Supreme Lord by playing musical instruments. *Svanuṣṭhitasya dharmasya saṁsiddhir hari-toṣaṇam* (*Bhāg*. 1.2.13). The perfection of life is to satisfy the Personality of Godhead. Therefore, beginning from this earth up to the celestial kingdom, everyone engaged in glorifying the Supreme Personality of Godhead. The decision of all great saintly persons is that whatever qualifications one has acquired should be utilized to glorify the Supreme Lord.

idaṁ hi puṁsas tapasaḥ śrutasya vā
sviṣṭasya sūktasya ca buddhi-dattayoḥ
avicyuto 'rthaḥ kavibhir nirūpito
yad uttamaśloka-guṇānuvarṇanam

"Learned sages have definitely concluded that the infallible purpose of the advancement of knowledge, austerity, Vedic study, sacrifice, the chanting of hymns, and charity is found in the transcendental descriptions of the qualities of the Lord, who is defined in choice poetry." (*Bhāg*. 1.5.22) This is the perfection of life. One should be trained how to glorify the Supreme Personality of Godhead by one's respective qualities. Education, austerity, penance or, in the modern world, business, industry, education and so on—all should be engaged in glorifying the Lord. Then everyone in the world will be happy.

Kṛṣṇa comes, therefore, to exhibit His transcendental activities so that people may have the chance to glorify Him in every respect. To understand how to glorify the Lord is actual research work. It is not that everything should be understood without God. That is condemned.

bhagavad-bhakti-hīnasya
jātiḥ śāstraṁ japas tapaḥ
aprāṇasyaiva dehasya
maṇḍanaṁ loka-rañjanam
(*Hari-bhakti-sudhodaya* 3.11)

Without *bhagavad-bhakti*, without glorification of the Supreme Lord, whatever we have is simply a decoration of the dead body.

TEXT 35

तदद्भुतस्तोत्रसुवाद्यगीतिका-
जयादिनैकोत्सवमङ्गलस्वनान् ।
श्रुत्वा स्वधाम्नोऽन्त्यज आगतोऽचिराद्
दृष्ट्वा महीशस्य जगाम विस्मयम् ॥३५॥

tad-adbhuta-stotra-suvādya-gītikā-
jayādi-naikotsava-maṅgala-svanān
śrutvā sva-dhāmno 'nty aja āgato 'cirād
dṛṣṭvā mahīśasya jagāma vismayam

tat—that celebration performed by the demigods in the upper planetary system; *adbhuta*—wonderful; *stotra*—prayers; *su-vādya*—glorious musical sounds of drums and other instruments; *gītikā*—celestial songs; *jaya-ādi*—sounds of *jaya*, etc.; *na-eka-utsava*—

celebrations simply for glorifying the Supreme Personality of Godhead; *maṅgala-svanān*—transcendental sounds auspicious for everyone; *śrutvā*—hearing such sounds; *sva-dhāmnaḥ*—from his abode; *anti*—nearby; *ajaḥ*—Lord Brahmā; *āgataḥ*—coming there; *acirāt*—very soon; *dṛṣṭvā*—seeing; *mahi*—the glorification; *īśasya*—of Lord Kṛṣṇa; *jagāma vismayam*—became astonished.

TRANSLATION

When Lord Brahmā heard the wonderful ceremony going on near his planet, accompanied by music and songs and sounds of "Jaya! Jaya!" he immediately came down to see the function. Upon seeing so much glorification of Lord Kṛṣṇa, he was completely astonished.

PURPORT

Here the word *anti* means "near," indicating that even in the higher planetary systems near Brahmaloka, like Maharloka, Janaloka and Tapoloka, the festival of glorification of Lord Kṛṣṇa was going on.

TEXT 36

राजन्नाजगरं चर्म शुष्कं वृन्दावनेऽद्भुतम् ।
व्रजौकसां बहुतिथं बभूवाक्रीडगह्वरम् ।।३६।।

rājann ājagaraṁ carma
śuṣkaṁ vṛndāvane 'dbhutam
vrajaukasāṁ bahu-tithaṁ
babhūvākrīḍa-gahvaram

rājan—O Mahārāja Parīkṣit; *ājagaram carma*—the dry body of Aghāsura, which remained only a big skin; *śuṣkam*—when it completely dried up; *vṛndāvane adbhutam*—like a wonderful museum piece in Vṛndāvana; *vraja-okasām*—for the inhabitants of Vrajabhūmi, Vṛndāvana; *bahu-titham*—for many days, or for a long time; *babhūva*—became; *ākrīḍa*—sporting place; *gahvaram*—a cave.

TRANSLATION

O King Parīkṣit, when the python-shaped body of Aghāsura dried up into merely a big skin, it became a wonderful place for

the inhabitants of Vṛndāvana to visit, and it remained so for a long, long time.

TEXT 37

एतत् कौमारजं कर्म हरेरात्माहिमोक्षणम् ।
मृत्योः पौगण्डके बाला दृष्ट्वोचुर्विस्मिता व्रजे ॥३७॥

etat kaumārajaṁ karma
harer ātmāhi-mokṣaṇam
mṛtyoḥ paugaṇḍake bālā
dṛṣṭvocur vismitā vraje

etat—this incident of delivering both Aghāsura and Kṛṣṇa's associates from death; *kaumāra-jam karma*—performed during their *kaumāra* age (the age of five years); *hareḥ*—of the Supreme Personality of Godhead; *ātma*—the devotees are the Lord's heart and soul; *ahi-mokṣaṇam*—their deliverance and the deliverance of the python; *mṛtyoḥ*—from the path of repeated birth and death; *paugaṇḍake*—at the age of *paugaṇḍa*, beginning with the sixth year (one year later); *bālāḥ*—all the boys; *dṛṣṭvā ūcuḥ*—disclosed the fact after one year; *vismitāḥ*—as if it had happened on that very day; *vraje*—in Vṛndāvana.

TRANSLATION

This incident of Kṛṣṇa's saving Himself and His associates from death and of giving deliverance to Aghāsura, who had assumed the form of a python, took place when Kṛṣṇa was five years old. It was disclosed in Vrajabhūmi after one year, as if it had taken place on that very day.

PURPORT

The word *mokṣaṇam* means "liberation." For the associates of Kṛṣṇa and for Kṛṣṇa Himself, there is no question about liberation; they are already liberated, being in the spiritual world. In the material world there are birth, death, old age and disease, but in the spiritual world there are no such things because everything is eternal. As for the python, however, by the association of Kṛṣṇa and His devotees, Aghāsura also achieved the same facility of eternal life. Therefore, as indicated here by the word *ātmāhi-mokṣaṇam*, if the python Aghāsura could receive eternal association with the Supreme Personality of Godhead, what is to be said of those who are already associates of the Lord? *Sākaṁ vijahruḥ kṛta-puṇya-puñjāḥ* (*Bhāg.* 10.12.11). Here is proof that God is good for everyone. Even when He kills someone, the one who is killed attains liberation. What then is to be said of those who are already in the association of the Lord?

TEXT 38

नैतद् विचित्रं मनुजार्भमायिनः
परावराणां परमस्य वेधसः ।
अघोऽपि यत्स्पर्शनधौतपातकः
प्रापात्मसाम्यं त्वसतां सुदुर्लभम् ॥३८॥

naitad vicitraṁ manujārbha-māyinaḥ
parāvarāṇāṁ paramasya vedhasaḥ
agho 'pi yat-sparśana-dhauta-pātakaḥ
prāpātma-sāmyaṁ tv asatāṁ sudurlabham

na—not; *etat*—this; *vicitram*—is wonderful; *manuja-arbha-māyinaḥ*—of Kṛṣṇa, who appeared as the son of Nanda Mahārāja and Yaśodā, being compassionate upon them; *para-avarāṇām*—of all causes and effects; *paramasya vedhasaḥ*—of the supreme creator; *aghaḥ api*—Aghāsura also; *yat-sparśana*—simply by the slight association of whom; *dhauta-pātakaḥ*—became freed from all contamination of material existence; *prāpa*—became elevated; *ātma-sāmyam*—to a body exactly resembling that of Nārāyaṇa; *tu*—but; *asatām sudurlabham*—which is not at all possible to be obtained by contaminated souls (but everything can be possible by the mercy of the Supreme Lord).

TRANSLATION

Kṛṣṇa is the cause of all causes. The causes and effects of the material world, both higher and lower, are all created by the Supreme Lord, the original controller. When Kṛṣṇa appeared as the son of Nanda Mahārāja and Yaśodā, He did so by His causeless mercy. Consequently, for Him to exhibit His unlimited opulence was not

at all wonderful. Indeed, He showed such great mercy that even Aghāsura, the most sinful miscreant, was elevated to being one of His associates and achieving sārūpya-mukti, which is actually impossible for materially contaminated persons to attain.

PURPORT

The word *māyā* is also used in connection with love. Out of *māyā*, love, a father has affection for his child. Therefore the word *māyinaḥ* indicates that Kṛṣṇa, out of love, appeared as the son of Nanda Mahārāja and assumed the form of a human child (*manujārbha*). Kṛṣṇa is the cause of all causes. He is the creator of cause and effect, and He is the supreme controller. Nothing is impossible for Him. Therefore, that He enabled even a living being like Aghāsura to attain the salvation of *sārūpya-mukti* was not at all wonderful for Kṛṣṇa. Kṛṣṇa took pleasure in entering the mouth of Aghāsura in a sporting spirit along with His associates. Therefore, when Aghāsura, by that sporting association, as maintained in the spiritual world, was purified of all contamination, he attained *sārūpya-mukti* and *vimukti* by the grace of Kṛṣṇa. For Kṛṣṇa this was not at all wonderful.

TEXT 39

सकृद् यदङ्गप्रतिमान्तराहिता
मनोमयी भागवतीं ददौ गतिम् ।
स एव नित्यात्मसुखानुभूत्यभि-
व्युदस्तमायोऽन्तर्गतो हि किं पुनः ॥३९॥

sakṛd yad-aṅga-pratimāntar-āhitā
manomayī bhāgavatīṁ dadau gatim
sa eva nityātma-sukhānubhūty-abhi-
vyudasta-māyo 'ntar-gato hi kiṁ punaḥ

sakṛt—once only; *yat*—whose; *aṅga-pratimā*—the form of the Supreme Lord (there are many forms, but Kṛṣṇa is the original form); *antaḥ-āhitā*—placing within the core of the heart, somehow or other; *manaḥ-mayī*—thinking of Him even by force; *bhāgavatīm*—which is competent to offer devotional service to the Lord; *dadau*—Kṛṣṇa gave; *gatim*—the best destination; *saḥ*—He (the Supreme Personality of Godhead); *eva*—indeed; *nitya*—always; *ātma*—of all living entities; *sukha-anubhūti*—anyone thinking of Him immediately enjoys transcendental pleasure; *abhivyudasta-māyaḥ*—because all illusion is completely removed by Him; *antaḥ-gataḥ*—He is always present within the core of the heart; *hi*—indeed; *kim punaḥ*—what to speak.

TRANSLATION

If even only once or even by force one brings the form of the Supreme Personality of Godhead into one's mind, one can attain the supreme salvation by the mercy of Kṛṣṇa, as did Aghāsura. What then is to be said of those whose hearts the Supreme Personality of Godhead enters when He appears as an incarnation, or those who always think of the lotus feet of the Lord, who is the source of transcendental bliss for all living entities and by whom all illusion is completely removed?

PURPORT

The process for receiving the favor of the Supreme Personality of Godhead is described here. *Yat-pāda-paṅkaja-palāśa-vilāsa-bhaktyā* (*Bhāg.* 4.22.39). Simply by thinking of Kṛṣṇa, one can attain Him very easily. Kṛṣṇa is also described as having His lotus feet always within the hearts of His devotees (*bhagavān bhakta-hṛdi sthitaḥ*). In the case of Aghāsura, one may argue that he was not a devotee. The answer to this is that he thought of Kṛṣṇa for a moment with devotion. *Bhaktyāham ekayā grāhyaḥ.* Without devotion, one cannot think of Kṛṣṇa; and, conversely, whenever one thinks of Kṛṣṇa, one undoubtedly has devotion. Although Aghāsura's purpose was to kill Kṛṣṇa, for a moment Aghāsura thought of Kṛṣṇa with devotion, and Kṛṣṇa and His associates wanted to sport within Aghāsura's mouth. Similarly, Pūtanā wanted to kill Kṛṣṇa by poisoning Him, but Kṛṣṇa took her as His mother because He had accepted the milk of her breast. *Svalpam apy asya dharmasya trāyate mahato bhayāt* (Bg. 2.40). Especially when Kṛṣṇa appears as an *avatāra*, anyone who thinks of Kṛṣṇa in His different incarnations (*rāmādi-mūrtiṣu kalā-niyamena tiṣṭhan*), and especially in His original form as

Kṛṣṇa, attains salvation. There are many instances of this, and among them is Aghāsura, who attained the salvation of *sārūpya-mukti.* Therefore the process is *satataṁ kīrtayanto māṁ yatantaś ca dṛḍha-vratāḥ* (Bg. 9.14). Those who are devotees always engage in glorifying Kṛṣṇa. *Advaitam acyutam anādim ananta-rūpam:* when we speak of Kṛṣṇa, we refer to all His *avatāras,* such as Kṛṣṇa, Govinda, Nārāyaṇa, Viṣṇu, Lord Caitanya, Kṛṣṇa-Balarāma and Śyāmasundara. One who always thinks of Kṛṣṇa must attain *vimukti,* special salvation as the Lord's personal associate, not necessarily in Vṛndāvana, but at least in Vaikuṇṭha. This is called *sārūpya-mukti.*

TEXT 40

श्रीसूत उवाच
इत्थं द्विजा यादवदेवदत्तः
श्रुत्वा स्वरातुश्चरितं विचित्रम् ।
पप्रच्छ भूयोऽपि तदेव पुण्यं
वैयासकिं यन्निगृहीतचेताः ॥४०॥

śrī-sūta uvāca
itthaṁ dvijā yādavadeva-dattaḥ
śrutvā sva-rātuś caritaṁ vicitram
papraccha bhūyo 'pi tad eva puṇyaṁ
vaiyāsakiṁ yan nigṛhīta-cetāḥ

śrī-sūtaḥ uvāca—Śrī Sūta Gosvāmī spoke to the assembled saints at Naimiṣāraṇya; *ittham*—in this way; *dvijāḥ*—O learned *brāhmaṇas; yādava-deva-dattaḥ*—Mahārāja Parīkṣit (or Mahārāja Yudhiṣṭhira), who was protected by Yādavadeva, Kṛṣṇa; *śrutvā*—hearing; *sva-rātuḥ*—of Kṛṣṇa, who was his savior within the womb of his mother, Uttarā; *caritam*—the activities; *vicitram*—all wonderful; *papraccha*—inquired; *bhūyaḥ api*—even again; *tat eva*—such activities; *puṇyam*—which are always full of pious activities (*śṛṇvatāṁ sva-kathāḥ kṛṣṇaḥ puṇya-śravaṇa-kīrtanaḥ:* to hear about Kṛṣṇa is always pious); *vaiyāsakim*—unto Śukadeva Gosvāmī; *yat*—because; *nigṛhīta-cetāḥ*—Parīkṣit Mahārāja had already become steady in hearing about Kṛṣṇa.

TRANSLATION

Śrī Sūta Gosvāmī said: O learned saints, the childhood pastimes of Śrī Kṛṣṇa are very wonderful. Mahārāja Parīkṣit, after hearing about those pastimes of Kṛṣṇa, who had saved him in the womb of his mother, became steady in his mind and again inquired from Śukadeva Gosvāmī to hear about those pious activities.

TEXT 41

श्रीराजोवाच
ब्रह्मन् कालान्तरकृतं तत्कालीनं कथं भवेत् ।
यत् कौमारे हरिकृतं जगुः पौगण्डकेऽर्भकाः ॥४१॥

śrī-rājovāca
brahman kālāntara-kṛtaṁ
tat-kālīnaṁ kathaṁ bhavet
yat kaumāre hari-kṛtaṁ
jaguḥ paugaṇḍake 'rbhakāḥ

śrī-rājā uvāca—Mahārāja Parīkṣit inquired; *brahman*—O learned *brāhmaṇa* (Śukadeva Gosvāmī); *kāla-antara-kṛtam*—things done in the past, at a different time (in the *kaumāra* age); *tat-kālīnam*—described as happening now (in the *paugaṇḍa* age); *katham bhavet*—how could it be so; *yat*—which pastime; *kaumāre*—in the *kaumāra* age; *hari-kṛtam*—was done by Kṛṣṇa; *jaguḥ*—they described; *paugaṇḍake*—in the *paugaṇḍa* age (after one year); *arbhakāḥ*—all the boys.

TRANSLATION

Mahārāja Parīkṣit inquired: O great sage, how could things done in the past have been described as being done at the present? Lord Śrī Kṛṣṇa performed this pastime of killing Aghāsura during His kaumāra age. How then, during His paugaṇḍa age, could the boys have described this incident as having happened recently?

TEXT 42

तद् ब्रूहि मे महायोगिन् परं कौतूहलं गुरो ।
नूनमेतद्धरेरेव माया भवति नान्यथा ॥४२॥

tad brūhi me mahā-yogin
paraṁ kautūhalaṁ guro
nūnam etad dharer eva
māyā bhavati nānyathā

tat brūhi—therefore please explain that; *me*—unto me; *mahā-yogin*—O great *yogī; param*—very much; *kautūhalam*—curiosity; *guro*—O my lord, my spiritual master; *nūnam*—otherwise; *etat*—this incident; *hareḥ*—of the Supreme Personality of Godhead; *eva*—indeed; *māyā*—the illusion; *bhavati*—becomes; *na anyathā*—nothing more.

TRANSLATION

O greatest yogī, my spiritual master, kindly describe why this happened. I am very much curious to know about it. I think that it was nothing but another illusion due to Kṛṣṇa.

PURPORT

Kṛṣṇa has many potencies: *parāsya śaktir vividhaiva śrūyate* (*Śvetāśvatara Upaniṣad* 6.8). The description of Aghāsura was disclosed after one year. Some act of Kṛṣṇa's potency must have been involved. Therefore Mahārāja Parīkṣit was very curious to know about this, and he requested Śukadeva Gosvāmī to explain it.

TEXT 43

वयं धन्यतमा लोके गुरोऽपि क्षत्रबन्धवः ।
यत् पिबामो मुहुस्त्वत्तः पुण्यं कृष्णकथामृतम् ॥४३॥

vayaṁ dhanyatamā loke
guro 'pi kṣatra-bandhavaḥ
vayaṁ pibāmo muhus tvattaḥ
puṇyaṁ kṛṣṇa-kathāmṛtam

vayam—we are; *dhanya-tamāḥ*—most glorified; *loke*—in this world; *guro*—O my lord, my spiritual master; *api*—although; *kṣatra-bandhavaḥ*—the lowest of the *kṣatriyas* (because we did not act like *kṣatriyas*); *vayam*—we are; *pibāmaḥ*—drinking; *muhuḥ*—always; *tvattaḥ*—from you; *puṇyam*—pious; *kṛṣṇa-kathā-amṛtam*—the nectar of *kṛṣṇa-kathā.*

TRANSLATION

O my lord, my spiritual master, although we are the lowest of kṣatriyas, we are glorified and benefited because we have the opportunity of always hearing from you the nectar of the pious activities of the Supreme Personality of Godhead.

PURPORT

The pious activities of the Supreme Personality of Godhead are very confidential. It is not ordinarily possible to hear such activities unless one is very, very fortunate. Parīkṣit Mahārāja placed himself as *kṣatra-bandhavaḥ*, which means "the lowest of the *kṣatriyas.*" The qualities of the *kṣatriya* are described in *Bhagavad-gītā*, and although the general quality of the *kṣatriya* is *īśvara-bhāva*, the tendency to rule, a *kṣatriya* is not supposed to rule over a *brāhmaṇa*. Thus Mahārāja Parīkṣit regretted that he had wanted to rule over the *brāhmaṇas* and had therefore been cursed. He considered himself the lowest of the *kṣatriyas. Dānam īśvara-bhāvaś ca kṣātraṁ karma svabhāvajam* (Bg. 18.43). There was no doubt that Mahārāja Parīkṣit had the good qualities of a *kṣatriya*, but as a devotee he presented himself, with submissiveness and humility, as the lowest of the *kṣatriyas*, remembering his act of wrapping a dead serpent around the neck of a *brāhmaṇa*. A student and disciple has the right to ask the *guru* about any confidential service, and it is the duty of the *guru* to explain these confidential matters to his disciple.

TEXT 44

श्रीसूत उवाच
इत्थं स्म पृष्टः स तु बादरायणि-
स्तत्स्मारितानन्तहृताखिलेन्द्रियः ।
कृच्छ्रात् पुनर्लब्धबहिर्दृशिः शनैः
प्रत्याह तं भागवतोत्तमोत्तम ॥४४॥

śrī-sūta uvāca
itthaṁ sma pṛṣṭaḥ sa tu bādarāyaṇis
tat-smāritānanta-hṛtākhilendriyaḥ
kṛcchrāt punar labdha-bahir-dṛśiḥ śanaiḥ
pratyāha taṁ bhāgavatottamottama

śrī-sūtaḥ uvāca—Śrī Sūta Gosvāmī said; *ittham*—in this way; *sma*—in the past; *pṛṣṭaḥ*—being inquired from; *saḥ*—he; *tu*—indeed; *bādarāyaṇiḥ*—Śukadeva Gosvāmī; *tat*—by him (Śukadeva Gosvāmī); *smārita-ananta*—as soon as Lord Kṛṣṇa was remembered; *hṛta*—lost in ecstasy; *akhila-indriyaḥ*—all actions of the external senses; *kṛcchrāt*—with great difficulty; *punaḥ*—again; *labdha-bahiḥ-dṛśiḥ*—having revived his external sensory perception; *śanaiḥ*—slowly; *pratyāha*—replied; *tam*—unto Mahārāja Parīkṣit; *bhāgavata-uttama-uttama*—O great saintly person, greatest of all devotees (Śaunaka).

TRANSLATION

Sūta Gosvāmī said: O Śaunaka, greatest of saints and devotees, when Mahārāja Parīkṣit inquired from Śukadeva Gosvāmī in this way, Śukadeva Gosvāmī, immediately remembering subject matters about Kṛṣṇa within the core of his heart, externally lost contact with the actions of his senses. Thereafter, with great difficulty, he revived his external sensory perception and began to speak to Mahārāja Parīkṣit about kṛṣṇa-kathā.

Thus end the Bhaktivedanta purports of the Tenth Canto, Twelfth Chapter, of the Śrīmad-Bhāgavatam, *entitled, "The Killing of the Demon Aghāsura."*

Appendixes

The Author

His Divine Grace A. C. Bhaktivedanta Swami Prabhupāda appeared in this world in 1896 in Calcutta, India. He first met his spiritual master, Śrīla Bhaktisiddhānta Sarasvatī Gosvāmī, in Calcutta in 1922. Bhaktisiddhānta Sarasvatī, a prominent devotional scholar and the founder of sixty-four Gauḍīya Maṭhas (Vedic institutes), liked this educated young man and convinced him to dedicate his life to teaching Vedic knowledge. Śrīla Prabhupāda became his student, and eleven years later (1933) at Allahabad he became his formally initiated disciple.

At their first meeting, in 1922, Śrīla Bhaktisiddhānta Sarasvatī Ṭhākura requested Śrīla Prabhupāda to broadcast Vedic knowledge through the English language. In the years that followed, Śrīla Prabhupāda wrote a commentary on the *Bhagavad-gītā*, assisted the Gauḍīya Maṭha in its work and, in 1944, without assistance, started an English fortnightly magazine, edited it, typed the manuscripts and checked the galley proofs. He even distributed the individual copies freely and struggled to maintain the publication. Once begun, the magazine never stopped; it is now being continued by his disciples in the West.

Recognizing Śrīla Prabhupāda's philosophical learning and devotion, the Gauḍīya Vaiṣṇava Society honored him in 1947 with the title "Bhaktivedanta." In 1950, at the age of fifty-four, Śrīla Prabhupāda retired from married life, and four years later he adopted the *vānaprastha* (retired) order to devote more time to his studies and writing. Śrīla Prabhupāda traveled to the holy city of Vṛndāvana, where he lived in very humble circumstances in the historic medieval temple of Rādhā-Dāmodara. There he engaged for several years in deep study and writing. He accepted the renounced order of life (*sannyāsa*) in 1959. At Rādhā-Dāmodara, Śrīla Prabhupāda began work on his life's masterpiece: a multivolume translation and commentary on the eighteen thousand verse *Śrīmad-Bhāgavatam* (*Bhāgavata Purāṇa*). He also wrote *Easy Journey to Other Planets.*

After publishing three volumes of *Bhāgavatam*, Śrīla Prabhupāda came to the United States, in 1965, to fulfill the mission of his spiritual master. Since that time, His Divine Grace has written over forty volumes of authoritative translations, commentaries and summary studies of the philosophical and religious classics of India.

In 1965, when he first arrived by freighter in New York City, Śrīla Prabhupāda was practically penniless. It was after almost a year of great difficulty that he established the International Society for Krishna Consciousness in July of 1966. Under his careful guidance, the Society has grown within a decade to a worldwide confederation of almost one hundred *āśramas*, schools, temples, institutes and farm communities.

In 1968, Śrīla Prabhupāda created New Vṛndāvana, an experimental Vedic community in the hills of West Virginia. Inspired by the success of New Vṛndāvana, now a thriving farm community of more than one thousand acres, his students have since founded several similar communities in the United States and abroad.

In 1972, His Divine Grace introduced the Vedic system of primary and secondary education in the West by founding the Gurukula school in Dallas, Texas. The school began with 3 children in 1972, and by the beginning of 1975 the enrollment had grown to 150.

Śrīla Prabhupāda has also inspired the construction of a large international center at Śrīdhāma Māyāpur in West Bengal, India, which is also the site for a planned Institute of Vedic Studies. A similar project is the magnificent Kṛṣṇa-Balarāma Temple and International Guest House in Vṛndāvana, India. These are centers where Westerners can live to gain firsthand experience of Vedic culture.

Śrīla Prabhupāda's most significant contribution, however, is his books. Highly respected by the academic community for their authoritativeness, depth and clarity, they are used as standard textbooks in numerous college courses. His writings have been translated into eleven languages. The Bhaktivedanta Book Trust, established in 1972 exclusively to publish the works of His Divine Grace, has thus become the world's largest publisher of books in the field of Indian religion and philosophy. Its latest project is the publishing of Śrīla Prabhupāda's most recent work: a seventeen-volume translation and commentary—completed by Śrīla Prabhupāda in only eighteen months—on the Bengali religious classic *Śrī Caitanya-caritāmṛta.*

In the past ten years, in spite of his advanced age, Śrīla Prabhupāda has circled the globe twelve times on lecture tours that have taken him to six continents. In spite of such a vigorous schedule, Śrīla Prabhupāda continues to write prolifically. His writings constitute a veritable library of Vedic philosophy, religion, literature and culture.

References

The purports of *Śrīmad-Bhāgavatam* are all confirmed by standard Vedic authorities. The following authentic scriptures are specifically cited in this volume:

Āyurveda-śāstra, 25

Bhagavad-gītā, 3, 10, 18, 34, 51–52, 56, 57, 62, 72–73, 85, 86–87, 88, 92–93, 123, 126–127, 128, 131, 132–133, 134, 137–138, 149, 154, 158, 164, 167, 174, 181, 193, 194, 205, 206, 208, 210, 228, 229, 235, 257, 262, 276, 292, 302, 303, 306

Bhakti-rasāmṛta-sindhu, 42, 160, 205, 270, 276

Brahma-saṁhitā, 24–25, 51, 99, 103, 136, 154, 159, 164

Brahma-sūtra. See: Vedānta-sūtra

Bṛhad-bhāgavatāmṛta, 270–271

Caitanya-caritāmṛta, 85, 165, 176, 186, 215

Chāndogya Upaniṣad, 182–183

Hari-bhakti-sudhodaya, 297

Hari-bhakti-vilāsa, 73

Hari-vaṁśa, 95, 201, 246–247

Kaṭha Upaniṣad, 97

Mahābhārata, 126

Muṇḍaka Upaniṣad, 88n

Glossary of Personal Names

A

Ādi-puruṣa—a name of the Supreme Personality of Godhead, the original person.

Aghāsura—the python-shaped demon sent by Kaṁsa to kill Kṛṣṇa.

Aja—a name of the Supreme Personality of Godhead, who is unborn.

Ajāmila—a fallen *brāhmaṇa* who was saved by calling the name Nārāyaṇa at the time of death.

Ānakadundubhi—another name of Vasudeva, the father of Kṛṣṇa.

Arjuna—one of the five Paṇḍava brothers; Kṛṣṇa became his chariot driver and spoke to him the *Bhagavad-gītā.*

B

Bakāsura—a demon who was shaped like a huge duck and who tried to kill Kṛṣṇa.

Balarāma (Baladeva)—a plenary expansion of the Personality of Godhead appearing as the son of Rohiṇī and elder brother of Lord Kṛṣṇa.

Bhakta-vatsala—a name of the Supreme Personality of Godhead, who favors His devotees.

Bhaktisiddhānta Sarasvatī Ṭhākura—the spiritual master of His Divine Grace A. C. Bhaktivedanta Swami Prabhupāda.

Bhaktivinoda Ṭhākura—a great spiritual master in the line of disciplic succession from Śrī Caitanya Mahāprabhu.

Brahmā—the first created living being and secondary creator of the material universe.

C

Caitanya Mahāprabhu—the incarnation of Lord Kṛṣṇa who descended to teach love of God through the *saṅkīrtana* movement.

Cakrī—a name of the Supreme Personality of Godhead, the carrier of the disc.

D

Dāmodara—Kṛṣṇa in His pastime of being bound by mother Yaśodā.

Devakī—wife of Vasudeva and mother of Lord Kṛṣṇa.

Devarṣi Nārada—*See:* Nārada Muni

Dharā—the name of mother Yaśodā in a previous birth.

Dhruva Mahārāja—a great devotee who as a child was denied his father's kingdom but who was later given an entire planet and the opportunity to associate personally with the Supreme Lord.

Droṇa—the name of Mahārāja Nanda in a previous birth.

G

Gadādharī—a name of the Supreme Personality of Godhead, the carrier of the club.

Gargamuni—family priest of the Yadu dynasty.

Garuḍa—the great eagle who acts as the eternal carrier of Lord Viṣṇu.

Gaurasundara—a name of Lord Śrī Caitanya Mahāprabhu, indicating His beauty and His golden complexion.

Giridhārī—a name of the Supreme Personality of Godhead, the lifter of Govardhana Hill.

Gokuleśvara—Kṛṣṇa, the master of Gokula.

Gopāla—a name of the Supreme Personality of Godhead, who protects the cows.

Gopī-jana-vallabha—a name of the Supreme Personality of Godhead, who maintains and gives pleasure to the *gopīs.*

Govinda—a name of the Supreme Personality of Godhead, who gives pleasure to the land, the cows and the senses.

H

Haladhara—a name of the Supreme Personality of Godhead, who, in the form of Balarāma, bears a plow in His hands.

Hari—a name of the Supreme Personality of Godhead, who removes all obstacles to spiritual progress.

Hiraṇyakaśipu—a demoniac king killed by the Lord's incarnation as Nṛsiṁhadeva.

I

Indra—chief of the administrative demigods and king of the heavenly planets.

Īśa—a name of the Supreme Personality of Godhead, the supreme controller.

Īśvara—a name of the Supreme Personality of Godhead, the supreme controller.

J

Jaya—a doorkeeper of Vaikuṇṭha who attained *sārūpya-mukti* after three births in the material world.

Jīva Gosvāmī—one of the six Vaiṣṇava spiritual masters who directly followed Śrī Caitanya Mahāprabhu and systematically presented His teachings.

K

Kaṁsa—a demoniac king of the Bhoja dynasty and maternal uncle of Kṛṣṇa.

Keśava—a name of the Supreme Personality of Godhead, who has fine black hair.

Kṛṣṇa—the Supreme Personality of Godhead, appearing in His original, two-armed form.

Kuntī—the mother of the Pāṇḍavas; a pure devotee and aunt of Lord Kṛṣṇa's.

Kūrma—the tortoise incarnation of the Supreme Personality of Godhead.

Kuvera—treasurer of the demigods; father of Nalakūvara and Maṇigrīva.

L

Lakṣmī—the goddess of fortune and eternal consort of the Supreme Personality of Godhead Nārāyaṇa.

M

Madhusūdana—a name of the Supreme Personality of Godhead, the killer of the demon Madhu.

Madhvācārya—a thirteenth-century Vaiṣṇava spiritual master who preached the theistic philosophy of pure dualism.

Mahādeva—a name of Lord Śiva.

Maṇigrīva—a son of Kuvera cursed by Nārada Muni to take birth as an *arjuna* tree; ultimately liberated by Lord Kṛṣṇa.

Maṇimān—a name of the Supreme Personality of Godhead, who is always ornamented with brilliant jewels.

Matsya—the fish incarnation of the Supreme Personality of Godhead.

Mukunda—a name of the Supreme Personality of Godhead, the giver of liberation.

N

Nalakūvara—a son of Kuvera cursed by Nārada Muni to take birth as an *arjuna* tree; ultimately liberated by Lord Kṛṣṇa.

Nanda Mahārāja—the King of Vraja and foster-father of Lord Kṛṣṇa.

Nārada Muni—a pure devotee of the Lord who travels throughout the universes in his eternal body, glorifying devotional service.

Nārāyaṇa—a name of the Supreme Personality of Godhead, who is the source and the goal of all living beings.

Narottama dāsa Ṭhākura—a Vaiṣṇava spiritual master in the disciplic succession from Śrī Caitanya Mahāprabhu; disciple of Kṛṣṇadāsa Kavirāja Gosvāmī and spiritual master of Viśvanātha Cakravartī Ṭhākura.

Nṛsiṁhadeva—Lord Kṛṣṇa in His incarnation as half-man and half-lion, who descended to kill the demon Hiraṇyakaśipu.

P

Parīkṣit Mahārāja—the emperor of the world who heard *Śrīmad-Bhāgavatam* from Śukadeva Gosvāmī and thus attained perfection.

Pārvatī—wife of Lord Śiva.

Prahlāda Mahārāja—a devotee persecuted by his demoniac father but protected and saved by the Lord.

Pṛśnigarbha—the name of Devakī in a previous birth.

Pṛthā—the mother of the five Pāṇḍava brothers.

Pūtanā—a witch who was sent by Kaṁsa to appear in the form of a beautiful woman to kill baby Kṛṣṇa but who was killed by Lord Kṛṣṇa and granted liberation.

R

Rāma—another name of Balarāma given by Gargamuni.

Rāmacandra—an incarnation of Lord Kṛṣṇa as a perfect king.

Rohiṇī—one of Vasudeva's wives, residing under the care of Nanda Mahārāja. Rohiṇī is the mother of Balarāma.

Ṛṣabhadeva—an incarnation of the Personality of Godhead as a devotee and king who gave important spiritual instructions to His sons and then renounced His kingdom for a life of severe austerity.

Rukmiṇī—Lord Kṛṣṇa's principal queen in Dvārakā.

Rūpa Gosvāmī—the chief of the six Vaiṣṇava spiritual masters who directly followed Śrī Caitanya Mahāprabhu and systematically presented His teachings.

S

Śakaṭāsura—a ghost who took shelter of a bullock cart with the intention to kill Lord Kṛṣṇa but who instead was killed by the Lord.

Śambhu—a name of Lord Śiva.

Sanātana Gosvāmī—one of the six Vaiṣṇava spiritual masters who directly followed Śrī Caitanya Mahāprabhu and systematically presented His teachings.

Saṅkarṣaṇa—another name of Balarāma given by Gargamuni.

Śaunaka—the chief of the sages assembled at Naimiṣāraṇya forest who heard *Śrīmad-Bhāgavatam* from Sūta Gosvāmī.

Śiva—the demigod in charge of the mode of ignorance and the destruction of the material manifestation.

Śukadeva Gosvāmī—the sage who originally spoke *Śrīmad-Bhāgavatam* to King Parīkṣit prior to the King's death.

Sūrya—the demigod of the sun.

Sūta Gosvāmī—the sage who recounted the discourses between Parīkṣit and Śukadeva to the sages assembled in the forest of Naimiṣāraṇya.

Sutapā—the name of Vasudeva in a previous birth.

Svayambhū—a name of Lord Brahmā.

Śyāmasundara—a name of the Supreme Personality of Godhead, who is blackish and very beautiful.

T

Tṛṇāvarta—a demon, in the shape of a whirlwind, sent by Kaṁsa to kill Kṛṣṇa.

U

Uddhava—a confidential friend of Śrī Kṛṣṇa's in Vṛndāvana.

Upānanda—the brother of Nanda Mahārāja and oldest and most knowledgeable of the cowherd men of Gokula.

Upendra—a name of the Supreme Personality of Godhead, who sometimes appears as the younger brother of Indra.

Urugāya—a name of the Supreme Personality of Godhead, who is worshiped by sublime prayers.

Urukrama—a name of the Supreme Personality of Godhead, who takes wonderful steps (especially as the dwarf-incarnation, Vāmanadeva).

V

Varāha—the incarnation of the Supreme Personality of Godhead as a boar.

Vasudeva—the father of Kṛṣṇa and half-brother of Nanda Mahārāja.

Vāsudeva—Kṛṣṇa, son of Vasudeva.

Vatsāsura—a calf-shaped demon who came to Vṛndāvana to kill Kṛṣṇa.

Vijaya—a doorkeeper of Vaikuṇṭha who attained *sārūpya-mukti* after three births in the material world.

Vijayadhvaja Tīrtha—a Vaiṣṇava spiritual master and commentator on *Śrīmad-Bhāgavatam* in the disciplic succession from Madhvācārya.

Viṣṇu—a name of the Supreme Personality of Godhead.

Viśvanātha Cakravartī Ṭhākura—a Vaiṣṇava spiritual master and commentator on *Śrīmad-Bhāgavatam* in the disciplic succession from Śrī Caitanya Mahāprabhu.

Vṛtrāsura—a demon killed by Indra.

Vyāsadeva—the original compiler of the *Vedas* and *Purāṇas*, and author of the *Vedānta-sūtra* and *Mahābhārata.*

Y

Yajña—a name of the Supreme Personality of Godhead, the goal and enjoyer of all sacrifices.

Yamarāja—the god of death who punishes the sinful.

Yaśodā—the foster-mother of Kṛṣṇa; the Queen of Vraja and wife of Mahārāja Nanda.

Yogamāyā—Lord Kṛṣṇa's spiritual deluding energy, who appears as the Lord's younger sister in His pastimes.

General Glossary

A

Ācārya—a spiritual master who teaches by example.
Ādhibhautika kleśa—misery caused by other living beings.
Ādhidaivika kleśa—misery caused by natural disturbances.
Adhokṣaja—the Supreme Lord, who is beyond material sense perception.
Ādhyātmika kleśa—misery caused by the body and mind.
Ādi-puruṣa—the Supreme Lord, the original person.
Ahaṅkāra—false ego.
Ānanda-cinmaya-rasa-vigraha—the personal, spiritual form of bliss and knowledge.
Aṇimā—the mystic perfection of becoming very small.
Ārati—a ceremony for greeting the Lord with offerings of food, lamps, fans, flowers and incense.
Arcanā—the devotional process of Deity worship.
Āsana—a sitting posture in *yoga* practice.
Āśrama—the four spiritual orders of life: celibate student, householder, retired life and renounced life.
Asuras—atheistic demons.
Ātmārāma—one who is self-satisfied, free from external, material desires.
Avaiṣṇavas—nondevotees.
Avatāra—a descent of the Supreme Lord.

B

Bābās—ascetics.
Bhagavad-gītā—the basic directions for spiritual life spoken by the Lord Himself.
Bhakta—a devotee.
Bhakti—devotional service to Lord Kṛṣṇa.
Bhakti-yoga—linking with the Supreme Lord by devotional service.
Brahmacarya—celibate student life; the first order of Vedic spiritual life.

Brahman—the Absolute Truth; especially the impersonal aspect of the Absolute.

Brāhmaṇa—one wise in the *Vedas* who can guide society; the first Vedic social order.

C

Catur-vyūha—the Lord's plenary expansions Vāsudeva, Saṅkarṣaṇa, Pradyumna and Aniruddha.

D

Daityas—demons.

Daśa-avatāras—the ten pastime-incarnations of Viṣṇu.

Devamāyā—the illusory potency of the demigods.

Dhāma—abode; usually referring to the Lord's abodes.

Dharma—eternal occupational duty; religious principles.

Duṣkṛtīs—miscreants.

E

Ekādaśī—a special fast day for increased remembrance of Kṛṣṇa, which comes on the eleventh day of both the waxing and waning moon.

G

Goloka (Kṛṣṇaloka)—the highest spiritual planet, containing Kṛṣṇa's personal abodes, Dvārakā, Mathurā and Vṛndāvana.

Gopa-jāti—*See: Vaiśyas*

Gopīs—Kṛṣṇa's cowherd girl friends, His most confidential servitors.

Gṛhastha—regulated householder life; the second order of Vedic spiritual life.

Guṇa-avatāras—Viṣṇu, Brahmā and Śiva, the presiding deities of the three modes of nature.

Guṇas—the modes or qualities of material nature.

Guru—a spiritual master.

H

Hare Kṛṣṇa mantra—*See: Mahā-mantra*

Haṭha-yoga—the system of practicing sitting postures for sense control.

I

Īśitva—the mystic ability to become a great controller.

J

Jaḍa—dull or material.
Jīva-tattva—the living entities, atomic parts of the Lord.
Jñāna-kāṇḍa—the *Upaniṣad* portion of the *Vedas* containing knowledge of Brahman, spirit.
Jñāna-yoga—the process of approaching the Supreme by the cultivation of knowledge.
Jñānī—one who cultivates knowledge by empirical speculation.

K

Kali-yuga (Age of Kali)—the present age, characterized by quarrel; it is last in the cycle of four and began five thousand years ago.
Kāmāvasāyitā—the mystic ability to suppress one's desires.
Karatālas—hand cymbals used in *kīrtana.*
Karma—fruitive action, for which there is always reaction, good or bad.
Karma-kāṇḍa—sections of the *Vedas* prescribing rituals for material benefits.
Karmī—a person satisfied with working hard for flickering sense gratification.
Kaumāra—the period of childhood before five years.
Kīrtana—chanting the glories of the Supreme Lord.
Kṛṣṇa-kathā—words spoken by Kṛṣṇa or about Kṛṣṇa.
Kṛṣṇa-līlā—the transcendental pastimes of Lord Kṛṣṇa.
Kṛṣṇaloka—*See:* Goloka
Kṣatriya—a warrior or administrator; the second Vedic social order.
Kuśa—auspicious grass used in Vedic rituals.

L

Laghimā—the mystic perfection of becoming very light.
Līlā-avatāras—innumerable incarnations who descend to display the spiritual pastimes of the Lord.

M

Mahā-mantra—the great chanting for deliverance:
Hare Kṛṣṇa, Hare Kṛṣṇa, Kṛṣṇa Kṛṣṇa, Hare Hare
Hare Rāma, Hare Rāma, Rāma Rāma, Hare Hare.

Mahimā—the mystic ability to become unlimitedly large.

Mantra—a sound vibration that can deliver the mind from illusion.

Manvantara-avatāra—an *avatāra* who appears in each reign of Manu.

Mathurā—Lord Kṛṣṇa's abode, surrounding Vṛndāvana, where He took birth and later returned to after performing His Vṛndāvana pastimes.

Māyā—illusion; forgetfulness of one's relationship with Kṛṣṇa.

Māyāvāda—the false theory that every living being is ultimately equal to God.

Māyāvādīs—impersonal philosophers who say that the Lord cannot have a transcendental body.

Mṛdaṅga—a clay drum used for congregational chanting.

Mukti—liberation from birth and death.

N

Nāma-karaṇa ceremony—name-giving ceremony.

Nandana-kānana—a celestial garden.

Niyama—restraint of the senses.

P

Pañca-gavya—five milk products, used in bathing a worshipable personality.

Pañca-ratna—five gems.

Pañca-śasya—five grains.

Paramparā—the chain of spiritual masters in disciplic succession.

Paugaṇḍa—the period of childhood after five years.

Prākāmya—the mystic ability to fulfill any of one's desires.

Prāṇāyāma—control of the breathing process; performed in *aṣṭāṅga-yoga.*

Prāpti—the mystic ability to immediately obtain any material object.

Prasāda—food spiritualized by being offered to the Lord.

Prema-bhakta—a devotee absorbed in pure love of God.

R

Rajo-guṇa—the material mode of passion.

Rākṣasī—a demoness.

S

Sac-cid-ānanda-vigraha—the Lord's transcendental form, which is eternal, full of knowledge and bliss.

Ṣaḍ-aiśvarya-pūrṇa—the Lord, who is full in all six opulences: wealth, knowledge, fame, renunciation, beauty, and strength.

Sālokya—the liberation of residing on the same planet as the Lord.

Sāmīpya—the liberation of becoming a personal associate of the Lord.

Saṁskāra—Vedic process for purifying a human being from the time of conception until death.

Saṅkīrtana—public chanting of the names of God, the approved *yoga* process for this age.

Sannyāsa—renounced life; the fourth order of Vedic spiritual life.

Sārṣṭi—the liberation of having the same opulences as the Lord.

Sārūpya—the liberation of having a form similar to the Lord's.

Śāstras—revealed scriptures.

Sāyujya—the liberation of merging into the spiritual effulgence of the Lord.

Śravaṇaṁ kīrtanaṁ viṣṇoḥ—the devotional processes of hearing and chanting about Lord Viṣṇu.

Śūdra—a laborer; the fourth of the Vedic social orders.

Svāmī—one who controls his mind and senses; title of one in the renounced order of life.

Svargaloka—the heavenly planets.

T

Tamo-guṇa—the material mode of ignorance.

Tapasvīs—one who performs severe penances and austerities.

Tapasya—austerity; accepting some voluntary inconvenience for a higher purpose.

Tilaka—auspicious clay marks that sanctify a devotee's body as a temple of the Lord.

U

Upāsanā-kāṇḍa—a section of the *Vedas* prescribing worship of demigods for fruitive results.

V

Vaikuṇṭha—the spiritual world.

Vaiṣṇava—a devotee of Lord Viṣṇu, Kṛṣṇa.

Vaiṣṇava-aparādhas—offenses to a devotee of the Lord.

Vaiśyas—farmers and merchants; the third Vedic social order.

Vānaprastha—one who has retired from family life; the third order of Vedic spiritual life.

Varṇa—the four occupational divisions of society: the intellectual class, the administrative class, the mercantile class, and the laborer class.

Varṇāśrama—the Vedic social system of four social and four spiritual orders.

Vaśitva—the mystic ability to control others' minds.

Vedas—the original revealed scriptures, first spoken by the Lord Himṣelf.

Vṛndāvana—Kṛṣṇa's personal abode, where He fully manifests His quality of sweetness.

Y

Yajña—an activity performed to satisfy either Lord Viṣṇu or the demigods.

Yama—regulative principles.

Yogī—a transcendentalist who, in one way or another, is striving for union with the Supreme.

Yoginī—a female *yogī.*

Yugas—ages in the life of a universe, occurring in a repeated cycle of four.

Sanskrit Pronunciation Guide

Vowels

अ a आ ā इ i ई ī उ u ऊ ū ऋ ṛ ॠ ṝ
ऌ ḷ ए e ऐ ai ओ o औ au
ं ṁ *(anusvāra)* ः ḥ *(visarga)*

Consonants

Gutturals:	क ka	ख kha	ग ga	घ gha	ङ ṅa
Palatals:	च ca	छ cha	ज ja	झ jha	ञ ña
Cerebrals:	ट ṭa	ठ ṭha	ड ḍa	ढ ḍha	ण ṇa
Dentals:	त ta	थ tha	द da	ध dha	न na
Labials:	प pa	फ pha	ब ba	भ bha	म ma
Semivowels:	य ya	र ra	ल la	व va	
Sibilants:	श śa	ष ṣa	स sa		
Aspirate:	ह ha	ऽ ' *(avagraha)* – the apostrophe			

The numerals are: ० -0 १ -1 २ -2 ३ -3 ४ -4 ५ -5 ६ -6 ७ -7 ८ -8 ९ -9

The vowels above should be pronounced as follows:

a – like the *a* in org*a*n or the *u* in b*u*t
ā – like the *a* in f*a*r but held twice as long as short *a*
i – like the *i* in p*i*n
ī – like the *i* in p*i*que but held twice as long as short *i*

u – like the *u* in p*u*sh
ū – like the *u* in r*u*le but held twice as long as short *u*
ṛ – like the *ri* in *ri*m
ṝ – like *ree* in *ree*d
ḷ – like *l* followed by *ṛ* (*lṛ*)
e – like the *e* in th*ey*
ai – like the *ai* in *ai*sle
o – like the *o* in g*o*
au – like the *ow* in h*ow*
ṁ (*anusvāra*) – a resonant nasal like the *n* in the French word *bon*
ḥ (*visarga*) – a final *h*-sound: *aḥ* is pronounced like *aha; iḥ* like *ihi*

The vowels are written as follows after a consonant:

ा ā ि i ी ī ु u ू ū ृ ṛ ॄ ṝ े e ै ai ो o ौ au

For example: क ka का kā कि ki की kī कु ku कू kū
कृ kṛ कॄ kṝ के ke कै kai को ko कौ kau

The vowel "a" is implied after a consonant with no vowel symbol.

The symbol virāma (्) indicates that there is no final vowel: क्

The consonants are pronounced as follows:

k – as in *k*ite
kh – as in Ec*kh*art
g – as in *g*ive
gh – as in di*g-h*ard
ṅ – as in si*ng*
c – as in *ch*air
ch – as in staun*ch-h*eart
j – as in *j*oy
jh – as in he*dgeh*og
ñ – as in ca*ny*on
ṭ – as in *t*ub
ṭh – as in ligh*t-h*eart
ḍ – as in *d*ove
ḍha- as in re*d-h*ot
ṇ – as r*na* (prepare to say the *r* and say *na*)

Cerebrals are pronounced with tongue to roof of mouth, but the following dentals are pronounced with tongue against teeth:

t – as in *t*ub but with tongue against teeth
th – as in ligh*t-h*eart but with tongue against teeth

d – as in *d*ove but with tongue against teeth
dh – as in re*d-h*ot but with tongue against teeth
n – as in *n*ut but with tongue between teeth
p – as in *p*ine
ph – as in u*ph*ill (not *f*)
b – as in *b*ird
bh – as in ru*b-h*ard
m – as in *m*other
y – as in *y*es
r – as in *r*un

l – as in *l*ight
v – as in *v*ine
ś (palatal) – as in the *s* in the German word *sprechen*
ṣ (cerebral) – as the *sh* in *sh*ine
s – as in *s*un
h – as in *h*ome

Generally two or more consonants in conjunction are written together in a special form, as for example: क्ष kṣa त्र tra

There is no strong accentuation of syllables in Sanskrit, or pausing between words in a line, only a flowing of short and long (twice as long as the short) syllables. A long syllable is one whose vowel is long (ā, ī, ū, e, ai, o, au), or whose short vowel is followed by more than one consonant (including anusvāra and visarga). Aspirated consonants (such as kha and gha) count as only single consonants.

Index of Sanskrit Verses

This index constitutes a complete listing of the first and third lines of each of the Sanskrit poetry verses of this volume of *Śrīmad-Bhāgavatam*, arranged in English alphabetical order. The first column gives the Sanskrit transliteration, and the second and third columns, respectively, list the chapter-verse reference and page number for each verse.

C

D

E

General Index

Numerals in boldface type indicate references to translations of the verses of *Śrīmad-Bhāgavatam.*

A

Abhidheya defined, 131
Abhyutthānam adharmasya
  verse quoted, 208
Aborigines selling fruits, Kṛṣṇa's favor to, 227–229
Absolute Truth
  Kṛṣṇa as, 117, 205
  realization of, 132–133
  See also: Cause, ultimate; Kṛṣṇa, Lord
Ācamana purification, 19
Ācārya (saintly authority), knowledge via, 183
  See also: Spiritual master
Ācāryavān puruṣo veda
  quoted, 182–183
Acintyāḥ khalu ye bhāvā
  quoted, 126
Activities. *See: Karma;* Kṛṣṇa, pastimes of; Philanthropic activities; Pious activities; Sinful activities; Welfare work
Ādau śraddhā tataḥ sādhu-
  quoted, 42
Ādi-kavi defined, 165
Administrators. *See:* Kings; *Kṣatriyas*
Advaitam acyutam anādim ananta-rūpam
  quoted, 99, 303
  verse quoted, 24–25, 159
Advancement, spiritual, fitness for, 189
  See also: Life, goal of; Perfection; Success
Āgamāpāyino nityās
  verse quoted, 127
Age of quarrel. *See:* Kali-yuga
Aghāsura (python demon)
  advent of, arrangement of, 279
  compared to Jaya & Vijaya, 295
Aghāsura (python demon)
  compared to mountain, **281, 282, 285**
  cowherd boys entered mouth of, **286**–287, **288**
  cowherd boys quoted on, **283–286**
  demigods feared, **278**
  Kṛṣṇa liberated, **294**–295, 299–300, **301, 302**–303
  Kṛṣṇa vs., **279–281, 286–294**
  in python form, **281–286, 288, 294,** 295, **298, 299**
  quoted on killing Kṛṣṇa & His associates, **279, 280**
  relatives of, **279**
Agriculture. *See:* Cows, protection of; *Vaiśyas*
Aguru scent, **29,** 30
Ahaṅkāra-vimūḍhātmā
  quoted, 171
Āhāra-nidrā-bhaya-maithunaṁ ca
  quoted, 73
Ajāmila history, Yamarāja & Kṛṣṇa's devotees in, 156
Ajāta-śatravaḥ śāntāḥ
  verse quoted, 192
Ajñāna defined, 164
Ajo 'pi sann avyayātmā
  verse quoted, 137–138
Aṁ namo 'jas tavāṅghrī avyāt
  quoted, 19
Aṁśa defined, 97
Analogies
  decorating face & serving Kṛṣṇa, 229
  father's cure & Nārada's curse, 178
  fire & Kṛṣṇa, **7, 257,** 262
  flies & demons, **262**
  snake & Kṛṣṇa, **8,** 9
  sunshine & *kṛṣṇa-avatāra,* 97

C

Cowherd men (*gopas*)
beyond material distress, 264
cart collapsing around Kṛṣṇa perplexed, **50,** 51, **52**
devotional ecstasy of, 141
happy after Kṛṣṇa survived whirlwind demon, **71**
Kṛṣṇa as friend of, **100**
Kṛṣṇa chased by, 113–114
moved to Vṛndāvana, **243–246**
Putanā's corpse and, **27, 28,** 29
quoted on Kṛṣṇa defying death, **261, 262**
received Kṛṣṇa silently after Bakāsura pastime, **260**–261
yamala-arjuna trees' fall bewildered, **220–223,** 224
Cowherd women. *See: Gopīs*
Cows
as ceremonial charity, 234
Kṛṣṇa as protected via, **17, 18**
Kṛṣṇa favors, 100–101
Nanda gave, to *brāhmaṇas* for Kṛṣṇa's welfare, **58–59**
protection of, 18, 57, 58
suckled Kṛṣṇa, **32**
value of, 18
of Yaśodā, 145
See also: Calves
Creation, the. *See:* Heavenly planets; Material world; Nature, material; Planets; Spiritual world; Universe
Culture. *See:* Civilization; Society, human; *Varṇāśrama-dharma;* Vedic culture
Curse of Nārada on Kuvera's sons (Nalakūvara & Maṇigrīva), **169, 177–178, 193–195,** 197, **214**

D

Dadāmi buddhi-yogaṁ taṁ
verse quoted, 149
Dānam īśvara-bhāvaś ca
quoted, 306
Danger
of beautiful woman, 10
mantras counteract, 21
in material world, 3, 4, 25
See also: Disturbances
Dāntaḥ defined, 56
Dantavakra, 294
Dāridrya-doṣo guṇa-rāśi-nāśi
quoted, 188
Darśayaṁs tad-vidāṁ loka
quoted, 163–164
Death
Kṛṣṇa defied, **261, 262**
remembering Kṛṣṇa at, 276
Decorating face & serving Kṛṣṇa, analogy of, 229
Dehino 'smin yathā dehe
verse quoted, 86–87
Deity of the Supreme Lord, *prasāda* offered to, 58
See also: Worship
Demigods (*devas*)
Aghāsura feared by, **278**
birth among, 197
demons (*asuras*) contrasted to, 196
devotees of, 174
humans luckier than, 43
Kṛṣṇa entering Aghāsura dismayed, **291**
Lord above, 97, 156, **163**
as materialistic devotees, 196
planets of. *See:* Heavenly planets
showered flowers on Kṛṣṇa, **253, 259, 296**
See also: names of specific demigods
Demon(s) (*asuras*)
in calf form, **250–252**
compared to flies, **262**
demigods (*devas*) contrasted to, 196
devotees contrasted to, 67–68
in duck form, **255–258**
interrupted Kṛṣṇa & cowherd boys, 278–279
Kṛṣṇa killing, 7–8, 78, **101,** 210, 253–254, 262
Upānanda suspected, in attacks on Kṛṣṇa, **241**

Devotional service
senses in, 29, 30
success by, 33
surrender in, 73
by Vṛndāvana's residents, **140–141**
See also: Kṛṣṇa, love for; Kṛṣṇa consciousness; Offerings for Kṛṣṇa
Dharā, 137, 138, 140
Dharma-saṁsthāpanārthāya
verse quoted, 208
Dhīra defined, 87
Dhīras tatra na muhyati
quoted, 86
Dhruva Mahārāja, 73
Dhyānāvasthita-tad-gatena manasā paśyanti yaṁ yoginaḥ
quoted, 132
Diabetes, case of, 189
Dipavali Day festival, 145
Dirt-eating, Kṛṣṇa accused of, **117–121**
Disciple, *guru*'s duty to, 306
See also: Brahmacārī; Devotees
Disease(s)
from eating wrong, 189
material, Vaiṣṇavas cure, 194
See also: Health; Medicine
Disturbances
devotee undisturbed by, 241
in Gokula, **237–241**
See also: Danger; Suffering
Dog, rich man keeps, 190
Drinking. *See:* Intoxication; Wine
Droṇa, 137, 138, 140
Duck demon (Bakāsura)
Kṛṣṇa vs., **255–258**
relatives of, **279**
Duḥkhālayam aśāśvatam
quoted, 138
Duṣkṛtī defined, 174
Dust storm from whirlwind demon, **63–65**
Duty
of devotee, 4, 85, 149
of everyone, 85, 88n
of father, 87
glorifying the Lord as, 296–297
Duty
of *guru* to disciple, 306
at ritualistic ceremony, 234–235
of society, 93
See also: Society, human, social orders in
Dvāpara-yuga, Kṛṣṇa's incarnation in, **96**
Dvāpare bhagavān śyāmaḥ
quoted, 97
Dvau bhūta-sargau loke 'smin
verse quoted, 196
Dvija defined, 89

E

Earth (element), Kṛṣṇa accused of eating, **117–121**
Earth planet, planetary systems below, 13
See also: Material world
Eating. *See:* Food
Economic development
by cow protection, 18
unnecessary, 180, 189
See also: Vaiśya(s)
Ecstasy. *See:* Bliss, transcendental; Enjoyment; Happiness; Kṛṣṇa, love for
Education
birthright less important than, 89
of *brāhmaṇas, kṣatriyas & vaiśyas,* 248
See also: Absolute Truth; Knowledge
Ego, false, poor man freed of, **188**
See also: Bodily concept; Illusion; Pride
Ekale īśvara kṛṣṇa, āra saba bhṛtya
quoted, 165
Eko 'py asau racayituṁ jagad-aṇḍa-koṭiṁ
verse quoted, 164
Elements, material. *See:* Earth (element); Energy, external; Fire; Nature, material
Elevation. *See:* Advancement, spiritual; Liberation; Perfection; Purification; Success
Emotions in spiritual world, 110
See also: Kṛṣṇa, love for; Kṛṣṇa, relationships with

F

G

H

I

N

Q

R

T

W

Y